DISRUPTIVE GRACE

DISRUPTIVE GRACE

Studies in the Theology of Karl Barth

GEORGE HUNSINGER

TO JIM,
WITH WARM REGARDS,

George Hunsinger

WILLIAM B. EERDMANS PUBLISHING COMPANY
GRAND RAPIDS, MICHIGAN / CAMBRIDGE, U.K.

© 2000 Wm. B. Eerdmans Publishing Co.
255 Jefferson Ave. S.E., Grand Rapids, Michigan 49503 /
P.O. Box 163, Cambridge CB3 9PU U.K.
All rights reserved

Printed in the United States of America

05 04 03 02 01 00   7 6 5 4 3 2 1

Library of Congress Cataloging-in-Publication Data

Hunsinger, George.
Disruptive grace: studies in the theology of Karl Barth / George Hunsinger.
p.   cm.
Includes bibliographical references and index.
ISBN 0-8028-4644-0 (cloth: alk. paper)
1. Barth, Karl, 1886-1968.   I. Title.

BX4827.B3 H86 2000
230′.044′092 — dc21
99-057313

Unless otherwise noted, the Scripture quotations in this publication are from the Revised Standard Version of the Bible, copyrighted 1946, 1952 © 1971, 1973 by the Division of Christian Education of the National Council of Churches of Christ in the U.S.A., and used by permission.

To Deborah van Deusen Hunsinger,
my counselor in perplexity
and companion in every joy

Contents

Acknowledgments

A difficult selection needs to be made from the long list of friends, colleagues, and institutions to whom and to which I am indebted. Of my friends from the Yale-Washington Theology group, Jim Buckley, Bill Placher, Mike Root, and Bill Werpehowski especially stand out for their generous support, encouragement, and insight over the years. Many of these essays underwent their gestation during the period I spent at the Center of Theological Inquiry. I would like to extend my heartfelt thanks to Drs. Daniel Hardy, William Lazareth, and Wallace Alston, each of whom served as director during my time there. Among my new and valued colleagues at Princeton Seminary, Daniel Migliore, Bruce McCormack, and Ivica Novakovic have been a constant source of stimulation and wisdom. Without Thomas W. Gillespie, President of Princeton Seminary, and Stephen Crocco, the seminary's Head Librarian, who were jointly responsible for establishing the seminary's new Center for Barth Studies, I would surely not have had the privilege of being installed as its first director. My debt to them is great. Last but not least, no one could be blessed with a more wonderful life-companion than I am by the woman who has stood beside me now for twenty-five precious years through every trial, perplexity, and joy. This book is dedicated to her.

GEORGE HUNSINGER
Advent 1999

Introduction

Two photographs hang side by side in my office. Identical in size and shape, they are framed in gold with dark blue matting. One is of Martin Luther King, Jr. Taken not long before his death, it shows him in a pensive mood. His profile gazes forward, his lips resting lightly against one hand. He is at the Riverside Church in New York City. It is the occasion when he will denounce the Vietnam War publicly for the first time. Well aware that he will be rebuked by other civil rights leaders for mixing the race question with opposition to the war, his conscience has left him no choice. How can he avoid the government's growing cover-up and deceit? How can he overlook the harsh reality that the young men being sent to die in this deplorable and unjust war are disproportionately African American? How, above all, can he protest social injustice at home while ignoring the noncombatants so indiscriminately terrorized and slaughtered abroad? King's decision to oppose the American war in Vietnam is perhaps his finest hour since the 1963 March on Washington, when he captured the entire nation's highest aspirations with his stirring speech, "I Have a Dream."

The other photograph is of Karl Barth. He is sitting at his desk in Basel, an old man at the time of his retirement, smoking his pipe and reading a book. His great achievements are behind him. Never having studied for a doctorate, he has done more than anyone to revitalize theology in the twentieth century, leaving a legacy that generations will continue to respect. His massive and most important work, the *Church Dogmatics,* will remain unfinished — like the cathedral in Strasbourg, he would quip, with its missing tower. Thoroughly modern, he has rejected modernism in theology. Deeply traditional, he has left no stone of tradition unturned upon another. Without deterring easy classifications from critics, he has defied easy classification. Not since Luther and Calvin

1

has there been a theologian so prodigious in written output yet so active in worldly affairs, both ecclesiastical and political. From early years when he was known as the "red pastor" for his socialist involvement with organizing workers, to his theological leadership of the confessing church that resisted Hitler, to his protest against Western prosecution of the "cold war" and his increasingly antimilitarist, antinuclear stance, he has been a public intellectual embroiled in ceaseless controversy. The photo catches him in a quiet moment. He is reputed for sharp polemic, yet his infectious childlike joy, his self-deprecating humor, his love for Mozart, and his profound understanding of Scripture have endeared him to many whose lives he has immeasurably enriched.

Martin Luther King and Karl Barth both died in the same year, 1968. On the day King was assassinated, I watched the Bedford-Stuyvesant riots from my apartment window not far from Fulton and Nostrand, the center of town. I will never forget an angry young man hurling a heavy city trash receptacle into the street and in desperation setting it ablaze. The next morning I walked through the avenues of shattered glass and burnt-out buildings with my students from the storefront Street Academy where I taught high school dropouts. Although King had been seen by many ghetto dwellers as insufficiently militant, my students shared a sense, amidst cynicism, resignation, and rage, that another ray of hope had died. By the time Karl Barth passed away later that year, I had enrolled as a ministerial student at Harvard Divinity School. One gray December morning as we were gathering up our books after an introductory theology lecture, a student shouted out to the room that, according to the front page of the *New York Times,* Karl Barth had died the night before. That was the beginning and the end of the observance of Barth's death at that institution. The chilly reception of Barth in those precincts left a lasting impression on my mind.

The twentieth century has witnessed a number of initiatives to encourage political responsibility in the church. Each achieved a measure of success before hitting on diminishing returns. The religious socialism of the '10s and '20s in Switzerland and Germany, the American social gospel of about the same era, the worker-priest movement in postwar France, the Latin American liberation theologies in the '60s and '70s with their base communities, the black theologies of the same decades in the United States and Africa, and the slightly later feminist and womanist theologies in industrialized nations — these and other efforts were progressive campaigns that made a mark but did not prevail. The recurring pattern of early promise broken by arrest and eventual decline surely had causes that were various and complex. Yet all these campaigns had at least one thing in common. Each in its own way forced the church to choose between progressive politics and traditional faith. Each made it seem as though the two were mutually exclusive. Each therefore forged an unwitting alliance with its opposition, which shared the same diagnosis, only from the opposite point of view. Each failed to see that, confronted with a forced option, the church will inevitably choose not to abandon traditional faith. Equally tragically, each failed to see that the forced option between progressive politics and traditional faith is false.[1]

The falsity of the option might have been plain from the existence of any number of prominent figures. Dorothy Day, William Stringfellow, Fanny Lou Hamer, Oscar Romero, André Trocmé, Marietta Jaeger, Helmut Gollwitzer, Lech Walesa, Kim Dae-jung, Ita Ford, Desmond Tutu, and not least, Karl Barth are among the many twentieth-century Christians known for their progressive politics. They saw no reason to choose between their love for Jesus Christ as confessed by faith and their love for the poor and the oppressed. They had learned from initiatives for political responsibility while refusing the fatal choice. Traditional faith was for them not a hindrance but an incentive for progressive political change. It sustained them in struggle through their darkest hours. It was not for them something disreputable to be hidden from those in need. Nor was it something to be rejected because it was dishonored by injustice and failure in the church. It was rather the hard-won and priceless deposit of truth that withstood every effort to discredit its relevance.

Recently another photograph has come into my possession. Though smaller in size, it too will be framed in gold with dark blue matting and posted on the wall of my office. It depicts Martin Luther King standing together with Karl Barth. King's head tilts back in laughter while Barth joins in with evident delight. Their meeting is a chance encounter. King has just preached in the Princeton University chapel where Barth had come to hear him. The year is 1962, during Barth's only visit to the United States. The photograph which shows them together symbolizes another dream, however modest and improbable — my own. In that dream the legacy of King merges with the legacy of Barth — a merger that did not occur in their lifetimes, nor one that has ever occurred since.

King's roots were in the historic black Baptist tradition, yet his theological education had led him in a different direction. Academic liberal theology, one might say, with its real and apparent sophistications, never extinguished the deeper sources of his spiritual life. In *Strength to Love* and other writings, his theology seems broadly Kantian with biblical overtones. God, freedom, and im-

---

1. I do not mean to suggest that combining progressive politics with traditional faith will guarantee success, only that forcing the church to choose between them virtually guarantees failure. Although traditional faith in harmony with progressive politics is, as it seems to me, the winning combination, it still faces many losing battles. That there will be no easy victories does not make it any the less worth striving for.

mortality constitute the explicit articles of faith, with Jesus as little more than a moral example, and the cross a moral symbol. King's belief that "unarmed truth and unconditional love will have the final word in reality"[2] was rarely placed on a sound christological basis. His teaching that undeserved nonviolent suffering would prove "redemptive" was too often supported by an instrumentalist logic that tended to overpromise and inevitably to disappoint. It did not represent a fully adequate understanding of what it means to bear the cross. Yet King's grasp of enemy-love as central to the gospel was profound, unsurpassed, and articulated with unforgettable power. Nor was the proper rationale always lacking: "Calvary is a telescope," he wrote, "through which we look into the long vista of eternity and see the love of God breaking into time. Out of the hugeness of his generosity God allowed his only-begotten Son to die that we may live."[3] King believed more, we may assume, than he often brought to speech.

Part I: Political Theology

The first five chapters of this book may be read as a modest attempt to fill out that unspoken christological basis. They expound Barth's theology of the cross as it applies to contemporary questions of justice, war, and peace. They move down paths that without King's life and work I might never have glimpsed. Because some of them were written years ago, the figures I discuss in illustration are now sometimes dated. Ever the acerbic champion of civility, for example, Richard Neuhaus has gone on to become a distinguished journalist and ecumenist. After many long years in the federal penitentiary system, Helen Woodson, tragically broken, now lives at the edge of madness. Gordon Kaufman has continued to drift ever further from the Christian faith. Greatly missed, John Howard Yoder has entered his eternal reward. With a turn toward Buddhist philosophy, Joanna Rogers Macy still helps people deal with despair. Much has undeniably changed since the essays were first written. Yet the perennial issues remain the same, I believe, as does the need to forge a stronger theological alliance between progressive politics and traditional faith.

Chapter 1, about Karl Barth and René Girard, is not only the most recent essay in the section but also the capstone that holds the next four pieces to-

2. Martin Luther King, "Nobel Peace Prize Acceptance Speech," in *A Testament of Hope: The Essential Writings of Martin Luther King*, ed. James M. Washington (New York: Harper & Row, 1986), p. 224.

3. King, *Strength to Love* (New York: Harper & Row, 1963), p. 134.

gether. Girard shows, perhaps, what King's pacifism might look like when stripped of its biblical roots. The secularized context of cultural anthropology within which Girard develops his thought seems, despite its appeal to many contemporaries, rather thin when placed beside King's relatively comparable modernism. By contrast, the more richly biblical context that King and Barth both share is here developed with reference to a high understanding of the atonement. Von Balthasar and Torrance supply an account of the saving significance of Christ's death that then becomes the basis for exploring Barth's advocacy of "practical pacifism."

The focus in chapter 2, "Karl Barth and Liberation Theology," shifts more or less from peace to justice. Barth is distinguished from neoconservatives like Neuhaus, with their apology for the satisfactions of capitalism, and aligned in social intent with Latin American liberation theologians like Gutiérrez and Segundo. Since it is always nice when one can talk left by moving right, and right by moving left, the first role is assigned to Ronald J. Sider and the second to José Míguez Bonino. The realignment of progressive politics with traditional faith again controls the agenda. Since the unexpected collapse of Soviet communism, which no democratic socialist could fail to watch without elation, the self-confidence of capitalism, it seems, has reached unprecedented heights. That this self-confidence might prove to be overweening is not a favored thought among our ruling elites. The growing wealth gap, the persisting underclass, the debt trap, and other disturbing indicators of social misery, discounted as usual, might nonetheless suggest a system swaying on shaky premises.[4] Whether hope will again be revived for a nonauthoritarian, market socialism that is politically achievable and economically viable remains to be seen. No one can doubt, as John Gray has written, that Marx's "political prescriptions were a recipe for tragedy." "But," he continues, "in illuminating, a century and a half ago, a widening gap between the imperatives of capitalism and the prerequisites of a stable liberal society, Marx identified a problem to which a solution has yet to be found."[5] Barth's voice, which, in alignment with the Latin American liberationists, raises doubts about the social consequences of capitalism, still deserves to be heard.

No essay of mine has ever received a more intensive response than chapter 3, "Barth, Barmen, and the Confessing Church Today." Eighteen supporters and critics (including, among others, Paul Lehmann, Daniel Berrigan, Monika

---

4. See, for example, Chuck Collins, Betsy Leondar-Wright, and Holly Sklar, *Shifting Fortunes: The Perils of the Growing American Wage Gap* (Boston: United for a Fair Economy, 1999).

5. John Gray, "Hollow Triumph," *Times Literary Supplement*, May 8, 1998. See also Gray, *False Dawn: The Delusions of Global Capitalism* (New York: New Press, 1999).

Hellwig, Jacques Ellul, Katherine Temple, David Little, Stanley Hauerwas, and Max Stackhouse) issued rejoinders, to which I was then permitted to reply.[6] Written in 1984 on the occasion of the fiftieth anniversary of the Barmen Declaration, the essay proposed some lessons from the German confessing church for contemporary America. Since historical analogies, as I soon learned, can be precarious, let me state for the record what I take to be obvious, that there is no small difference between the crimes of Nazi Germany and those of my own country in the second half of the twentieth century. But if the just-war theory still means anything, as I believe it does; if there is still such a thing as the criminality of the means; if noncombatant immunity is still morally indispensable; if modern weaponry from cluster bombs to napalm to nuclear weapons is still inherently indiscriminate and therefore deplorable, unjustifiable, and horrific (not to mention perilous, in the case of atomic, biological, and chemical weapons, for the fate of the earth); if governments that wage war on their own people, torture by administrative policy, and otherwise systematically violate human rights are still detestable; if sanctions that kill the weak and defenseless, including children, by the tens of thousands are still repugnant to any conscience that is in some measure alive; if billions of dollars can still instantaneously be found for reckless and ill-conceived bombing campaigns where before there had been only a pittance for peace, then my country has much to answer for — and more now than it did fifteen years ago. The silence of the church, the painful disparity between the few who speak out and the rest who do not, the distractions from distraction by distraction, the studied ability to look the other way, the refusal of noncompliance as an avoidance of the cross — to our shame these still make us, as far as I can see, into America's willing accomplices (and, I might add, from this judgment I do not exclude myself).

The question of a confessing church continues into chapter 4, "Where the Battle Rages: Confessing Christ in America Today." It is an important sequel for at least three reasons. First, war has been the defining experience of the twentieth century. A few statistics help tell the story. In this century more than 100 million people have died in major wars — out of an estimated 149 million total since the first century. In most wars fought in the 1990s, the vast majority of deaths were civilian. In 1995 world military expenditures amounted to more than $1.4 million per minute. An estimated $8 trillion dollars have been spent since 1945 on nuclear weapons. The world stockpile of nuclear weapons, de-

---

6. See *Barth, Barmen, and the Confessing Church Today*, ed. James Y. Holloway (Lewiston, N.Y.: Edwin Mellen Press, 1995). This collection includes my original essay (now chap. 3 of the volume in hand); eighteen rejoinders; and my reply to each, "The Note in the Bottle." The materials first appeared in *Katallagete* 9 (1985): 14-27 and *Katallagete* 10 (1987): 1-108.

spite recent reductions, still represents over seven hundred times the explosive power in the twentieth century's three major wars, which killed 44 million people.[7] A truly confessing church would be more faithful to the gospel of peace in this unprecedented world-historical crisis. Second, in academic circles Christian beliefs are increasingly voted up or down on the basis of their supposed social utility. As William Placher has observed, the instrumentalist approach is so widespread that "in some quarters it grows hard to explain that there might be an alternative to it."[8] A confessing church would not retreat from the gospel's life-giving, hope-sustaining truth claims. Finally, the scene is still largely dominated by churches whose profile is either conversionist or activist. A confessing church remains the neglected alternative.

The last essay in this section, chapter 5, "Karl Barth and the Politics of Sectarian Protestantism: A Dialogue with John Howard Yoder," was actually the first written of those gathered in this book. It responds to an unpublished study by John Howard Yoder on church and politics in Barth's thought. Dissenting from interpreters who emphasized Barth's democratic socialism, Yoder argued instead that Barth's radicalism was that of a "sectarian Protestant." The term "sectarian" was meant descriptively, not pejoratively. In effect Yoder was placing Barth closer to the Anabaptists than the Reformed in his attitude toward culture. Yoder's rationale was that in his later years Barth had moved increasingly in an antimilitarist and pacifist direction. Yoder was correct about the antimilitarist direction taken by Barth's later thought.[9] He was not correct, however, to recast Barth as a "sectarian" Protestant.[10]

7. See William Eckhardt, "War-Related Deaths Since 3000 B.C.," *Bulletin of Peace Proposals* (December 1991); Ruth Leger Sivard, *World Military and Social Expenditures, 1996* (Washington, D.C.: World Priorities, 1996); Mary Kaldor, *New and Old Wars: Organized Violence in a Global Era* (Stanford: Stanford University Press, 1999).

8. William C. Placher, *The Domestication of Transcendence* (Louisville: Westminster, 1996), p. 15.

9. Besides the material cited throughout the essays in Part I, it might be noted that by 1959 Barth had become so concerned about nuclear weapons that he raised the question of "active resistance" and of issuing an "open appeal" that would call upon people "to refuse to serve in military units employing such weapons." Barth did not restrict this appeal to the church. See George Casalis, *Portrait of Karl Barth* (New York: Doubleday, 1963), p. 74.

10. Again, the word is used descriptively. The fear of "sectarianism" in liberal theology, one might add, often betrays a deep-seated culture Protestantism. The use of "sectarian" as a scare word in contemporary discussion may well tell us more about a resort to rhetoric than about positions ostensibly described. Massive accommodationism — to the prevailing winds of both the academy and the larger culture (thus variously on both the right and the left) — is what most obviously characterizes contemporary theology and church. Although "sectarianism" can certainly pose its own dangers, it would take a satirist of Kierkegaard's stature to lampoon the absurdity of today's usual alarm.

The stance Barth assumed was always closer to H. Richard Niebuhr's "Christ transforming culture" than to his "Christ against culture."[11] Niebuhr recognized that a countercultural element is indispensable to the church's vitality.[12] "Where this is lacking," he wrote, "Christian faith quickly degenerates into a utilitarian device for the attainment of personal prosperity or public peace; and some imagined idol called by his name takes the place of Jesus Christ the Lord" (p. 68). Nevertheless, cultural transformers need to contend on two fronts, not just one: "against the anti-culturalism of exclusive Christianity, and against the accommodationism of culture-Christians" (p. 206). Transformers do not deny that all cultural work, being pervaded by sin, lies under divine judgment. "Yet they believe also that such culture is under God's sovereign rule, and that the Christian must carry on cultural work in obedience to the Lord" (p. 191). My essay shows that even with his later pacifism, Barth represents the transformationist type.

Part II: Doctrinal Theology

The erosion of tradition in the modern world has created the anomaly of the solitary theologian. Academic theology has largely ceased to be a communal activity whose validity can be tested by agreed-upon norms. It has become an increasingly rootless and fad-driven exercise whose orientation is uncertain and whose validity is questionable even to those who pursue it. When puzzling over why I have spent the better part of a career studying Barth, I realize that I have not found it easy to become a theologian. Teachers from whom one can fruitfully learn the tradition are hard to come by. If tradition, in Alasdair MacIntyre's phrase, is one long conversation about what constitutes the tradition itself, not many know traditional Christian theology well enough to induct one into the conversation. Barth is not only the best of teachers, but one of the most innovative within the tradition itself. The essays in this section display some of his most creative work. Although Barth was not oblivious to the ethical and political implications of Christian doctrine, he was not interested in Christian doctrine primarily for the sake of its real or imagined social utility.

11. H. Richard Niebuhr, *Christ and Culture* (New York: Harper & Row, 1951). (Hereafter page numbers cited in the text.) Yoder's incisive appreciation and critique of this influential work can be found in Glen Harold Stassen, Diane M. Yeager, and John Howard Yoder, *Authentic Transformation: A New Vision of Christ and Culture* (Nashville: Abingdon, 1996).

12. "The movement of withdrawal and renunciation is a necessary element in every Christian life, even though it be followed by an equally necessary movement of responsible engagement in cultural tasks" (p. 68).

Doctrine and ethics, he believed, belonged inseparably together; therefore, at regular intervals he included ethics within his long elaborations of church theology. Yet ethics was always the flower of which doctrine was the nourishing root. Against modern academic theology Barth thus refused to see Christology as a mere cipher for anthropology; and not forgetting Feuerbach's smile, he would have recoiled from the currently fashionable if demeaning practice of describing the Holy Trinity as our social agenda. Theology was necessarily a form of catechesis, of instructing the faithful in the substance of their faith. Most especially, theology existed in the service of a more faithful proclamation of the gospel. Well before indicating what we must do, the gospel unveiled what the Lord God had done for us. It concerned what we must properly suffer and may gladly enjoy no less than what we rightly undertake. Even the most technical questions had to be pursued, Barth believed, because doctrinal errors were not only serious in themselves, but also carried ecclesial and social consequences. God was to be worshipped, among other things, with the mind, and every thought made captive to the Lord Jesus Christ. While saying that truth is in order to goodness was not wrong, the opposite was also true, and one might add, both were also in order to beauty (and vice versa). Interrelations between the good, the beautiful, and the true, in other words, were not unidirectional, but subtle, dialectical, and complex. All the more reason, then, for doing justice to doctrine in its own right.

It will be a great day when Barth is at least rejected for positions that he actually held instead of for positions that he didn't take. Chapter 6, on Barth's Chalcedonian Christology, is an effort in this direction. Two diametrically opposite assessments of his Christology — one decrying it as "Alexandrian," the other as "Nestorian" — are examined and found wanting. Both assessments miss Barth's dialectical strategy for describing the mystery of the Word made flesh. Both fail to see that Barth rejected every attempt to describe this mystery systematically by means of a unified conceptual scheme. Here, as elsewhere in Christian doctrine, Barth's strategy is closer to narratology than to metaphysics. Although he believes that a local narrative — of God's covenant with Israel as fulfilled in Jesus Christ — bears universal significance, this local narrative is still a narrative. It is full of reversals, upsets, conundrums, and surprises. The christological surprise is the biggest of all, disrupting all efforts at metaphysical closure. Narrative depiction, from widely different and seemingly incompatible angles of vision, each of which proposes in its own way to set forth the whole, is all that is left. Doctrines are for Barth, as Hans Frei pointed out, simply conceptual redescriptions of the narratives. Rather than conforming to the one-sided, if mutually corrective, procedures of Alexandria or Antioch, Barth conceptually redescribes the identity of Jesus Christ in a dialectical way that "actualizes" the great ecumenical Definition of Chalcedon.

Internal critiques can be easier to sustain than external critiques, for internal critiques attempt to render a position untenable on the basis of its own given premises and commitments. External critiques, on the other hand, which operate with alien commitments, can sometimes masquerade as internal critiques. The difficulties begin when the critique proceeds as if crucial premises were shared when in fact they are not. An illusion is created of an agreed-upon requirement that has to be met where in fact no such agreement exists, because whether that requirement is genuine or not is actually a disputed point. The supposed failing to meet a necessary condition, often produced by mere rhetoric, not only relieves the critique of more careful analysis, but also finally obscures the magnitude of the decisions at stake.

Unfortunately, from several different quarters in recent years, Barth's view of the Holy Spirit has been subjected to this sort of treatment. By giving Barth a quiet hearing, chapter 7, "The Mediator of Communion: Karl Barth's Doctrine of the Holy Spirit," attempts to remedy the situation. At least two points, however, need to be kept in mind. First, on the Creator/creature relationship, Barth takes a stringent view of the ontological divide; second, in understanding the New Testament, he takes the perfect tense quite seriously regarding salvation in and by Jesus Christ. That is, God's being and the creature's are distinguished from one another categorically by an ontological divide so that in no sense are they implicated in one another by nature. Moreover, Jesus Christ is seen as having perfectly accomplished our salvation through his obedience as fulfilled on the cross so that this salvation needs nothing to complete it. Subsequent events can only receive it, attest it, share in it, praise it, and eagerly await its consummation (or fail to do so) — and these events of human reception, attestation, participation, adoration, and expectation are precisely the work of the Holy Spirit as the mediator of communion. Consistent with his basic commitments, Barth's view of the Holy Spirit is context-dependent. Recent critiques of his pneumatology tend to presuppose, without adequate acknowledgment, vastly different theological, christological, and soteriological schemes.

A deceptively modest aspect of Barth's project is to think Christian convictions through from an explicitly trinitarian and incarnational viewpoint. The revisions of received tradition that sometimes result, as seen for example in his doctrine of election, can be astonishing. Equally astonishing, though less well known, is Barth's effort to Christianize the standard conception of eternity. "Eternity," wrote Boethius, "is the total, simultaneous and perfect possession of interminable life." As Brian Leftow has pointed out, this definition was actually taken over unchanged from pagan philosophy. By relocating it within an explicit doctrine of the Trinity, Barth effectively shows how eternity can be interpreted as the thoroughgoing transposition of high trinitarian doctrine into a temporal key. Chapter 8, "*Mysterium Trinitatis:* Karl Barth's Conception of Eternity," unpacks the glory and complexity of this move.

After these christological, pneumatological, and trinitarian discussions, chapter 9 turns to scriptural interpretation. "Beyond Literalism and Expressivism: Karl Barth's Hermeneutical Realism" offers a new analytical typology. This new approach is, in effect, an appreciative revision of George Lindbeck's influential proposal in *The Nature of Doctrine.* Where Lindbeck suggested a scheme of cognitive propositionalism, experiential expressivism, and his own cultural-linguistic model,[13] the new typology recasts the options as literalism, expressivism, and realism. Note that Lindbeck's threefold scheme roughly corresponds to the head, the heart, and the hand, or in other words, to the cognitive, the affective, and the practical. The cultural-linguistic pragmatism of his preferred type, however, raises a question of whether finally his proposal is not so much "postliberal" as "neoliberal," since pragmatism has always been a routine liberal option.[14] In any case, the new typology adopted here does not restrict all strongly cognitive possibilities to "propositionalism"; it enlarges "expressivism" to allow for determinants that are social and political as well as affective; and it displaces cultural-linguistic pragmatism as a separate type in favor of "hermeneutical realism," by which is meant analogical discourse that is cognitively significant in its own right. Whereas Lindbeck's typology cannot really account for Barth's approach to theological language and scriptural interpretation, the proposed alternative not only can but also may prove illuminating for a wide range of other cases.[15]

13. See Lindbeck, *The Nature of Doctrine: Religion and Theology in a Postliberal Age* (Philadelphia: Westminster, 1984), pp. 16-41.

14. Indeed, in some ways Lindbeck's position bears striking similarities with the theology of Albrecht Ritschl. Besides a normative emphasis on pragmatism or ethics with respect to determining truth claims, one thinks of the antimetaphysical theme, the regulative understanding of doctrines, the formal use of philosophy in theological construction, the attempted reconciliation of tradition with historicism, the distinctive categorial adequacy of Christianity as a "religion," the cultural-linguistic priority of the church over the individual believer, and more. Vast differences, of course, also exist, not least Lindbeck's preference for Wittgenstein over Kant, and the priority he would assign to justification over moralism. What these differences really add up to, however — whether vis-à-vis academic liberal theology they are finally differences in emphasis or in kind — is a more important question than its relative neglect would suggest.

15. One might ask how my typology would account for Lindbeck's approach. The answer is that Lindbeck's cultural-linguistic pragmatism would have to be seen as a "mixed type." Insofar as his approach to truth is strongly pragmatist, it could be incorporated into standard views of expressivism. Insofar as his approach is Thomistic and cognitivist, however, it has definite affinities with "realism." Most of Lindbeck's essays since *The Nature of Doctrine* seem to show the realist aspect most conspicuously, giving his work a more nearly "postliberal" complexion.

A venerable rule of scriptural interpretation states that the obscure passages should be interpreted by the clear passages. The rule presupposes, however, that one knows just which passages are the clear ones. The traditional Augustinian understanding of eternal damnation presupposes that Matthew 25 and similar texts comprise those distinctly clear passages relative to which all others must be brought into alignment. One resulting oddity is that biblical literalists following Augustine cannot take passages literally when they include the word "all." Beginning with Augustine himself, it has been said that "all" in passages like I Timothy 2:4 ("God . . . desires all human beings to be saved") does not mean literally *all*, but only *all* under some sort of heavy qualification, such as all manner and classes of human being. The Christian tradition has always included interpreters, however, who have argued that when the New Testament says "all" it means *all*, regardless of any further hermeneutical difficulties that may ensue. Chapter 10, "Hellfire and Damnation: Four Ancient and Modern Views," discusses the major options that have existed in the historic discussion. Closer to Athanasius than to Augustine, Barth's position is described not as "universalism" — unfortunately still a common misperception — but as "reverent agnosticism." Consistent with his more nearly narratological than systematic or metaphysical outlook, Barth leaves the question of universal salvation open, yet keeping it as an object of the church's continual prayer and hope. Basing his view on the universal significance of Christ's saving death, as attested in the New Testament, and especially in Paul, Barth leaves us with strong (and in some ways even Augustinian) grounds for hope.[16]

Part III: Ecumenical Theology

"We have in Barth," wrote Hans Urs von Balthasar, "two crucial features: the most thorough and penetrating display of the Protestant view and the closest

16. One common reason for resisting something like Barth's "universalistic tendency" is the supposed impact it would have on weakening the church's mission of evangelism. This reason, it seems to me, needs to be taken seriously. Rahner's view of "anonymous Christianity," for example, has arguably had such an impact on some sectors of the Roman Catholic Church. At least two points need to be considered. First, a long and historic tradition exists of motivating evangelism out of concern for those who are in danger of being eternally lost. If this motivation is undermined, it can seem as if evangelism has forfeited its rationale. Second, on the other hand, evangelism can be motivated by better reasons than anxiety about the eternal destiny of others who, supposedly unlike oneself, are lost. Barth (whose views on those outside the church are rather different from Rahner's) takes it for granted that faithful obedience to Christ's commandment, love's desire to share something exceedingly positive, and the uplifting prospect of imparting hope itself are sufficient reasons for the church to engage in evangelism.

rapprochement with the Catholic. . . . In him Protestantism has found for the first time its most consistent representative."[17] Von Balthasar embraced Barth as an ecumenical dialogue partner, because in Barth he saw an interlocutor who was theologically serious. He admired him for knowing the crucial difference between genuine dialogue and false irenicism. He recognized that Barth feared overhasty compromises just as much as he himself did. He valued Barth's disavowal of vague ecumenical tolerance and flaccid latitudinarianism. Along with Barth he wished to strive instead for a deeper, more lasting form of reconciliation and reunion. Barth wrote:

> In the sixteenth and seventeenth centuries, Catholics and Protestants stared at each other grimly, but at least eyeball to eyeball. Then they talked to each other, sharply, harshly, but they really did speak. Whereas today we have grown weary of the old quarrelling but perhaps also of the importance of the issues. Now all we see across the board are people who talk around the issues, looking past rather than at each other, standing around without ever really confronting worthily the great high mystery that is the final point of all this hustle and bustle.[18]

Chapter 11, "Baptized into Christ's Death: Karl Barth and the Future of Roman Catholic Theology," may be read as a renewed effort to go ecumenically eyeball to eyeball. It presupposes that on decisive questions like justification by faith, writers like Küng and Pesch have not had the last word. Despite Barth's measured approval of his work, Küng never quite grasped what the Reformation meant by "imputation" and by the centrality it assigned to passages like I Corinthians 1:30 and Colossians 3:3.[19] Likewise, in attempting to explain the differences between Catholicism and the Reformation as unfortunate misunderstandings, Pesch, despite his enormously significant contribution, has not, at decisive points, convinced important scholarly authorities.[20] As my essay

17. Hans Urs von Balthasar, *The Theology of Karl Barth* (San Francisco: Ignatius, 1992), pp. 23, 22.

18. Quoted by von Balthasar, p. 6. For a different translation, see Barth, "The Concept of the Church," in *Theology and Church: Shorter Writings, 1920-1928* (London: SCM, 1962), pp. 272-73.

19. See Hans Küng, *Justification: The Doctrine of Karl Barth and a Catholic Reflection* (Philadelphia: Westminster, 1964, 1981), pp. 214-21 and 260-71. Küng still sees "salvation" as a gradual process that is essentially existential, teleological, and uncertain rather than as a completed and perfect gift which faith alone receives and in which it participates. The seeds of Küng's later departure from Barth in favor of modern liberalism are present in his earlier work, at least to that extent.

20. The eminent work at stake is Otto Hermann Pesch, *Die Theologie der Rechtfertigung bei Martin Luther und Thomas von Aquin* (Mainz: Grünewald, 1967). Despite Pesch's argument

shows, on what has taken place in Christ for our salvation *extra nos,* a Roman Catholic theologian like von Balthasar can agree with Barth fully while still disagreeing significantly on how to understand what takes place *in nobis.* Reformation (as opposed to modernist) Protestants will continue to recoil against seeing "salvation" itself as an unfinished existential process that proceeds by degrees and may be effected partially (though by grace) through human cooperation. They will continue to insist instead on salvation as a finished and perfect work, effected by Christ alone and identical with Christ himself, which is received solely by faith and in which faith participates as a gift. Overcoming this historic soteriological impasse, despite recent promising efforts, remains an ecumenical task of the highest order. To that end, Barth's critique of von Balthasar will need to be taken seriously, as will von Balthasar's critique of Barth.

In chapter 12, "What Karl Barth Learned from Martin Luther," the ecumenical axis shifts, but soteriology remains to the fore. Barth's profound retrieval of Luther gives the lie to unfortunate perceptions in some quarters that Barth was nothing if not Luther's antagonist. While Barth of course had significant disagreements with Luther, my essay shows that his debt to the Reformer was enormous. By discussing Barth and Luther in relation to Calvin, moreover, a range of unsettled questions in Reformation soteriology is explored that bears also on historic Protestant/Catholic disagreements. Faith's reception of salvation, it is suggested, involves three moments — "once for all," "again and again," and "more and more" — that are variously emphasized by Luther, Calvin, and Barth. Although Barth recovers what is most momentous and neglected in Luther, he devalues other matters of concern especially to Calvin. By allowing for all three moments in descending order of significance, Luther's breadth may offer the greatest ecumenical promise not only for advancing Reformation soteriology after Barth, but also for renewed dialogue with Catholicism.

Issues about the nature and function of theological language, as raised in chapter 9, are revisited in chapter 13, "Truth as Self-Involving: Barth and

---

of over one thousand pages, demurrals of varying intensity, both Protestant and Catholic, have been registered. Among the Protestants with substantial reservations are Heiko A. Oberman, Oswald Beyer, and Leif Grane; among the Catholics, Peter Manns and James McCue. It seems doubtful that Luther's *simul iustus et peccator* rests on a misunderstanding of Catholic views such as one finds in Aquinas, or that Aquinas as he stands can accommodate the essence of Luther's Reformation breakthrough. Luther's *simul iustus et peccator* — a thoroughly eschatological and christocentric conception — is not (contrary to Pesch) merely an expression of "existential theology" in a "confessional" (as opposed to "descriptive") mode. The best hopes for ecumenical rapprochement, it seems to me, lie not in minimizing intractable differences, nor in one side capitulating to the other, but rather in pushing forward to more complex and multidimensional soteriologies (and ecclesiologies) that can critically appropriate what is valid in opposing views.

Lindbeck." Dialogue between Barth and Lindbeck is now made explicit and pursued. It was in response to ecumenical conundrums, Lindbeck tells us, that he developed his regulative understanding of doctrines and his cultural-linguistic pragmatism. Although Lindbeck's strong reduction of doctrine to its regulative function seems unlikely to prevail, his cultural-linguistic proposal remains fruitful and suggestive, especially as a general model for understanding religion and theology. Relocated in light of my suggested typology, all three types — literalism, expressivism, and realism — could be explicated along cultural-linguistic lines. Each type, in other words, would give a distinctively different answer on how to relate the main aspects of theological language (cognitive, affective, and pragmatic), just as each would embody its own peculiar culture of linguistic induction and transmission. If Lindbeck's strong pragmatism with respect to theological truth claims were displaced by something like Barth's weaker pragmatism, as my essay suggests would be preferable, then (contrary to Lindbeck) the very notion of "doctrinal reconciliation without doctrinal change" would to that extent still seem self-contradictory.[21] Cognitive issues in ecumenical dialogue are unlikely to be removed by tour de force.

Perhaps no deeper divisions exist ecumenically than those between traditional faith, as guided by historic councils and confessions, and modern theology, as guided by rationalistic and humanistic modes of thought. These antagonistic paradigms, which cut across all denominational or confessional separations, classically confronted one another in 1923 when Adolf von Harnack challenged Karl Barth to debate. Liberals from Harnack to the present day have been perplexed by the postliberal tendency that Barth represented and pioneered. They often seem to prefer a hermeneutical universe in which the options are restricted to modern liberalism versus premodern conservatism. Barth refuses to make this choice. In chapter 14, "The Harnack/Barth Correspondence: A Paraphrase with Comments," he can be seen persistently trying to subvert the narrow alternatives that Harnack puts to him. Postliberal theology as Barth conceived it is an innovative possibility that overlaps both modernism and conservatism, learning deeply from both while transcending each.

Until recently Barth's brand of postliberalism has experienced as icy a reception from conservative evangelicals as it has from modern liberals. However, as evangelical Protestantism increasingly finds itself buffeted by conflicting tendencies, some toward maturation, others toward dissolution, Barth, who might be regarded as a liberal evangelical, is receiving a fresh and appreciative look. "What Can Evangelicals and Postliberals Learn from Each Other? The Carl Henry/Hans Frei Exchange Reconsidered," chapter 15, intervenes to clear some

---

21. Cf. Lindbeck, pp. 15-18.

new space for dialogue. As mediated, among others, by the so-called Yale school (which is less a school in any meaningful sense than a loose configuration of shifting alliances), the postliberalism of Barth and von Balthasar continues to make ecumenical inroads, especially among younger scholars. (This chapter was first presented at Wheaton College, just as that on Barth and Catholicism was first offered at Boston College; in both schools the impetus came from younger scholars.) The postliberalism of Barth and von Balthasar offers an opportunity for convergence within the Protestant and Catholic communions as well as between them. As Paul J. Griffiths has suggested, von Balthasar was "probably the most prolific Catholic theologian of this century . . . , and to my taste and judgment the greatest, not excepting Karl Rahner and Bernard Lonergan. He bears to contemporary Catholic theology something of the relation that Barth bears to Protestant: not yet fully understood, but still dominant. His contribution is more significant than any other by several orders of magnitude."[22] The ecumenical contribution of both great theologians, separately and together, and through a variety of mediations like the Yale school, would seem to hold untold promise for the twenty-first century.

The book concludes with a meditation on "the blood of Christ." Though not directly an explication of Barth's views, it displays his influence even as it captures a thread that runs through the volume as a whole, from political to doctrinal to ecumenical theology. If Jesus Christ is, as Barth urged, the center of Christian theology, Christ's cross is the center of the center. The Trinity, the incarnation, and the cross are linked, as it were, by a golden chain. Whenever the linkages among them are somehow severed or weakened, as unfortunately regularly happens, abstraction, misconception, and thinness can only be the result. The Trinity deteriorates, for example, to a social agenda, the incarnation to an experiential symbol, the cross to a supposed warrant for abuse. In the end the cross is a scandal because Israel is a scandal, with its ineffaceable particularity of election, expiation, purity, and difference for the sake of the world. The blood of Christ is repugnant to the Gentile mind, whether ancient or modern. This mind would prevail were it not continually disrupted by grace.

Grace that is not disruptive is not grace — a point that Flannery O'Connor well grasped alongside Karl Barth. Grace, strictly speaking, does not mean continuity but radical discontinuity, not reform but revolution, not violence but nonviolence, not the perfecting of virtues but the forgiveness of sins, not improvement but resurrection from the dead. It means repentance, judgment, and death as the portal to life. It means negation and the negation of the negation. The grace of God really comes to lost sinners, but in coming it dis-

---

22. Paul J. Griffiths, "One Jesus, Many Christs?" *Pro Ecclesia* 7 (1998): 153-71, on p. 166.

rupts them to the core. It slays to make alive and sets the captive free. Grace may of course work silently and secretly like a germinating seed as well as like a bolt from the blue. It is always wholly as incalculable as it is reliable, unmerited, and full of blessing. Yet it is necessarily as unsettling as it is comforting. It does not finally teach of its own sufficiency without appointing a thorn in the flesh. Grace is disruptive because God does not compromise with sin, nor ignore it, nor call it good. On the contrary, God removes it by submitting to the cross to show that love is stronger than death. Those whom God loves may be drawn to God through their suffering and be privileged to share in his sufferings in the world, because grace in its radical disruption surpasses all that we imagine or think.

PART I

POLITICAL THEOLOGY

The Politics of the Nonviolent God: Reflections on René Girard and Karl Barth

(1998)

Doctrines of the atonement in Christian theology, as Marlin E. Miller has pointed out, "usually limit their concern to reconciliation with God and, at most, consider reconciliation with others a secondary consequence of reconciliation with God."[1] Too often, in other words, the vertical aspect of reconciliation is allowed to overshadow its horizontal aspect. The vertical aspect of the atonement as it pertains directly to God is often treated in isolation as if its ethical implications were of no great importance. The reverse defect, however, would also appear to be widespread. Christian ethics as we know it today often seems to proceed as if the atoning work of Christ were of little or no relevance to its deliberations on human affairs. The social or horizontal aspect of reconciliation thereby eclipses its vertical aspect. Yet, if the cross of Christ is indeed the very center of the center of the Christian gospel, as the church has historically believed, then how can it fail to determine the substance of Christian ethics as well as that of Christian theology? Moreover, how can the centrality of the cross fail to orient them both in any attempt to specify their inner unity, order, and differentiation?

The work of René Girard emerges here, it seems to me, as rich, intriguing, and suggestive. For Girard, who teaches cultural anthropology and literary criticism at Stanford University, issues a powerful challenge to contemporary Christians at just this vital point. He challenges us to think about theology and ethics not only in their essential unity, but also as centered on the cross of

1. Marlin E. Miller, "Girardian Perspectives and Christian Atonement" (unpublished manuscript), p. 19.

Christ. More pointedly and urgently, he challenges us to see both theology and ethics as determined by the primacy of nonviolent love. Because the God revealed to us in the cross is supremely a nonviolent God, Girard argues, we ourselves are called and enabled to be a distinctively nonviolent people.

My discussion in this essay will unfold as follows. First, I will survey some major themes in Girard's work, concentrating on matters of cultural anthropology, biblical interpretation, and theological affirmation. Then, because I think Girard's understanding of Christianity, despite many strengths, is also marred by basic flaws, I will sketch the doctrine of the atonement as set forth by Hans Urs von Balthasar and Thomas F. Torrance. Finally, I will draw upon the theology of Karl Barth in order to suggest a way in which Girard's theological inadequacies can be avoided while still upholding his fundamental insights regarding the primacy of the nonviolent God.

I. Basic Themes in Girard's Work

In his work as a cultural anthropologist, Girard offers what might be called a sacrificial theory of social cohesion. The theory falls into two main parts, one explaining how human societies break apart, the other explaining how they put themselves back together. They break apart through violent social conflict that is engendered by what Girard calls "mimetic desire," and they put themselves back together again by uniting around the collective murder of innocent victims. These victims are selected because they are suitable to receive the blame for society's ills, regardless of their actual innocence.

The theory of societal cohesion as based on collective murder eventually expands into a theory of myth, ritual, and religion. All known myths, rituals, and religions throughout the world originate, Girard argues, in order to sustain the cohesion that was first obtained through collective violence. By means of myth, ritual, and religion, the founding murder is transfigured into the symbolic realm. The violence thereby forfeits its literal character but retains its initial function. Symbolically relocated, the original murder no longer appears as murder, for it has been reinscribed as a sacred act of sacrifice, just as the original victim no longer appears as the monstrous source of evil but is now enshrined in the symbolic form of a god. Through the myths and rituals of religion, as well as through the periodic ostracism, scapegoating, and murder of suitable social groups (such as Jews, communists, or homosexuals), social and cultural elites maintain the existing social system which grants them status, wealth, and power. The foundation of violence on which their position actually rests is not only legitimated by religion but obscured.

Girard's theory of social cohesion through sacrificial violence, whether actual or symbolic, has been vividly captured by Robert Hamerton-Kelly in the form of a "likely story." The first part of the story goes like this:

> Once upon a time there was a group of hominids that found itself unable to do anything in concert because of rivalry among them. Each one found himself inwardly compelled to imitate some other. As the imitation became more successful he found himself a rival of his model, and the more like the model he became the more violent became the rivalry. Cooperation was impossible until one day, the greatest day in the history of human culture, the two of them discovered that it was possible to agree on one thing, to agree to kill someone else. This was such a compelling possibility that the whole group imitated them, and so the first moment of human solidarity happened as the fellowship of the lynch mob.[2]

Two elements of Girard's theory stand out from the "likely story" as told thus far. The first is the relationship between desire and imitation, or what Girard calls "mimetic desire." Desire as Girard sees it is fundamentally acquisitive. It seeks to possess some gratifying object, some gratifying social status, or some other comparable good. Regardless of form, it is finally self-seeking. Desire, however, is also socially constructed. This is where the imitative or "mimetic" element comes in. One desires an object not because it is intrinsically valuable so much as because it is already desired or possessed by someone else. What the other person has or desires serves as a model for determining whatever is worth acquiring, and yet that person also serves as a rival for the object one has learned to desire. The rivalry inherent in mimetic desire eventually breaks out into social conflict, even as the conflict intensifies into violence. The concept of mimetic desire thus serves as Girard's basis for explaining how human society disintegrates through bloodshed.

The second element that stands out from this portion of the "likely story" concerns the process by which human society puts itself back together. Girard calls this process the "victimage mechanism." A scapegoat is selected and killed. Human society reunites itself in the process. The scapegoat is blamed for whatever seems to be threatening or disrupting society at the time. Any person, party, or group will suffice for the role of scapegoat so long as it is sufficiently alien or deviant from the mores of the prevailing culture, while also being sufficiently vulnerable to be seized, accused, and killed. Conflict in society is thus re-

---

2. Robert Hamerton-Kelly, "Sacred Violence and the Messiah: A Hermeneutical Meditation on the Marcan Passion Narrative" (unpublished paper), pp. 6-7. Quoted by James G. Williams, *The Bible, Violence, and the Sacred* (San Francisco: Harper Collins, 1991), p. 7.

solved through the victimization of a despised though innocent party. At least this is how it was in the beginning.

The "likely story" continues as follows:

> The victim, as the source of the sudden unity and order, was regarded as a savior; and he was blamed for causing the previous disorder. Thus he acquired the double valency of the sacred: attraction and revulsion. From the victim came the building blocks of the social order: prohibition to control the source of rivalry; ritual sacrifice to reenact and so represent to the group the unifying energy of the founding moment; myth to explain and obscure the violence by covering it up with transformations. The victim became the god, at the stage of the emergence of the gods. Thus society formed in the crucible of religion. Religious feeling is the individual's awareness of the group in its propensity to mimetic violence; therefore religion is essentially sacrifice, essentially threat and promise for the individual.[3]

What emerges from this part of the story is Girard's understanding of the origin and function of religion. The point of special interest to which I wish to call attention is Girard's thesis that religion is essentially sacrifice. Religious sacrifice, as Girard understands it, always carries strong connotations of lies, violence, and victimization of the innocent. The sacrificial aspects of religious myth and ritual serve to maintain social cohesion only as they also obscure, sacralize, and legitimate the murderous foundations and practices on which society actually rests. The word "sacrifice" in Girard's discourse is thus the very opposite of the word "nonviolence." For Girard nonviolence represents every positive moral trait that religious sacrifice simply negates: truth telling, peaceableness, and the defense of victimized innocents.

When Girard transposes this theory from cultural anthropology into the field of biblical interpretation, the results are astonishing. Far from further indicating what is otherwise universally the case, he claims, the Bible actually breaks decisively with the usual patterns of religion, ritual, and myth. The Bible is radically singular, says Girard, "*vis-à-vis* the mythological systems of the entire planet."[4] It offers something "absolutely distinctive."[5] Biblical religion is so unique because it does not reiterate and legitimate the "victimage mechanism,"

---

3. Hamerton-Kelly, pp. 6-7. Quoted by Williams, "Myth, Aphorism, and Christ as Sign," *Forum* 5 (1989): 73-91, on p. 81.

4. René Girard, *Things Hidden Since the Foundation of the World* (Stanford: Stanford University Press, 1987), p. 154.

5. Girard, *Things Hidden*, p. 144.

nor does it obscure the murderous consequences of "mimetic desire." Instead it powerfully reveals and unmasks them so that we can see them for what they are for the first time. Biblical religion is the one religion, unlike all others known to academic study, that does not side with powerful social elites who benefit from the violence of scapegoating. It aligns itself instead with the innocent victims. It reveals that the victims are innocent and the perpetrators guilty. In particular, the Gospels culminate a process of revelation that emerges with ever increasing clarity in the biblical writings. They do so by presenting a Jesus who refuses to enter into the spiral of violence, a Jesus who finally breaks the spiral by yielding to it despite his evident guiltlessness. "The revelation of the founding murder and of its generative power in regard to myth," says Girard, "becomes increasingly apparent in these texts. . . . By submitting to violence, Christ reveals and uproots the structural matrix of all religion."[6]

Although a more detailed study would need to explore just what Girard does with particular texts, both within and outside the biblical tradition, enough has been presented to indicate some broad areas where his claims are susceptible to critique. Apart from the controversial interpretation of how human culture originated, one may certainly wonder whether all nonbiblical religions without exception rest on the murder of innocent victims. Closer to my interests in this essay, however, one may also wonder whether biblical religion is actually unique for the reasons that Girard provides.

In a much criticized remark, for example, Girard's thesis forces him to claim: "There is nothing in the Gospels to suggest that the death of Jesus is a sacrifice, whatever definition (expiation, substitution, etc.) we may give for that sacrifice. At no point is the death of Jesus defined as a sacrifice."[7] Since the whole tendency of biblical religion is alleged to be uniquely nonviolent in its development and culmination, and since "nonviolence" is defined as the polar opposite of "sacrifice," sacrificial motifs must simply be purged from the Gospels if Girard is to sustain his thesis. Resorting to statements that are as sweeping as they are untenable, he thus proceeds to purge them.

Indeed, it does not seem unfair to say that Girard too often comes across in his writings as a champion of hermeneutical excess. Even the most sympathetic reader is likely to feel at some point that words like "all," "nothing," and "absolutely" have been used at least one too many times. Girard writes like a man in the grip of an idea who settles too many conceptual problems by resorting to rhetorical solutions. He finally leaves the impression that his theories cannot be falsified. "Whatever we *can* know that *fits* the theory," writes one per-

6. Girard, *Things Hidden*, pp. 176, 178-79.
7. Girard, *Things Hidden*, p. 180.

25

ceptive critic, "is triumphantly adduced as proof of it. Whatever we can point to as *contradicting* his theory is equally acclaimed as a proof of the built-in unawareness, and thus as a justification of his system as a whole."[8] Contradictory evidence, in other words, is explained away by the idea that religions must obscure their real origins. Girard constantly uses his theories to disclose what texts "really" mean.

The hermeneutical extravagance is so pronounced as to suggest that Girard regards his theories as canonical rather than as answerable to counterevidence. In the history of culture, as Eugene Goodheart points out, certain writers become objects of veneration:

> Their achievements are measured not by their capacity to answer to a reality external to them. They themselves are the measures of truth. Michel Foucault calls them (Freud and Marx are his examples) founders of discursivity. They provide the master texts that determine truth claims. Unlike scientists, these founders of discursivity are not required to conform to the canons of science. Their own discourse constitutes the canon that determines its truth value.[9]

Despite his extensive departures from Freud, it seems as though Girard has entered into rivalry with him over who deserves the title "founder of discursivity." He too often treats his own discourse as the canon that determines truth.[10]

Nowhere does Girard seem more eager to supply the "master text" than in his theory of biblical revelation. He is far from dismayed that no one has understood the Bible before him. "You are the first person," objects an interlocutor, "to read the Gospels in the way that you do." The objection is countered phlegmatically: "We are searching for coherence in the text," explains Girard, "and I believe we are finding it."[11] The coherence of the biblical text — "the knowledge that has been waiting there for two millennia"[12] — turns out to be Girard's own theory. Biblical revelation, we are told, has nothing to do with the ontological deity, the atoning work, or the historical resurrection of Jesus Christ, all of which Girard re-

---

8. Robert J. North, S.J., "Violence and the Bible: The Girard Connection," *Catholic Biblical Quarterly* 47 (1985): 1-27, on p. 22.

9. Eugene Goodheart, "Freud on Trial," *Dissent* 42 (1994-95): 236-43, on p. 237.

10. Girard would probably do well to reconceive his theory as a "research proposal" in need of careful testing, refinement, and delimitation. Unfortunately, however, he seems predisposed to regarding it as a "maximalist" as opposed to a more nearly "minimalist" position. See James G. Williams, "The Innocent Victim: René Girard on Violence, Sacrifice, and the Sacred," *Religious Studies Review* 14 (1988): 320-26, on p. 323.

11. Girard, *Things Hidden*, p. 210.

12. Girard, *Things Hidden*, p. 219.

pudiates.[13] What makes the Bible so unique is that it reveals the binary opposition between "nonviolence" and "sacrifice," espousing the former while rejecting the latter. This aspect of Girard's work might be glossed as: "The Bible *c'est moi.*"

When Girard insists that his theory derives mainly from a reading of the Bible, we may compare his position to a similar claim made by Kant. Kant believed that the elements of moral theory were so difficult to get straight, even for a philosopher, that without the New Testament they might never have emerged. The New Testament was thus an acknowledged source for Kant's theory, and to his mind it also remained useful to morality as an important teaching device, especially for nonphilosophers. However, Kant never simply identified his moral theory with the "real" message of the New Testament, nor did he claim that his theory was actually "revealed" by it as the knowledge hidden for millennia, not to mention "since the foundation of the world." Once derived, the theory was logically independent of the New Testament and therefore stood on its own — a point Kant not only acknowledged but insisted on. Nevertheless, although the theory was supposedly superior in principle, he never used it systematically as an external framework or canon to dictate what was or was not valid in the New Testament.

However forcefully he may have been tugged in that direction, Kant resisted the reductionist temptation. He refrained from hermeneutical extravagance with a notable success that his myriad modernist successors in the field of biblical interpretation frequently failed to match — each arriving by turns with his own new and improved, logically independent and external interpretive apparatus, whether moral, metaphysical, psychological, sociological, scientific, or whatever. Despite harboring rationalist inclinations that could hardly be surpassed, Kant took the New Testament seriously enough to leave certain deep and difficult questions open. Questions about salvation; about vicarious atonement; about justification, forgiveness, and rebirth; even about predestination all made their unexpected appearance in his deliberations. As Karl Barth points out, Kant pondered these matters "like strange visitors from another world, . . . without there being any attempt to disguise the mystery that is implied in them."[14] He treated them "with a mixture of understanding and surprise, of query and a dubious shaking of the head," yet finally acknowledging them "as conceptions that are at any rate possible, as indicative of open questions, to say the least."[15]

13. Girard, *Things Hidden,* pp. 183 (atonement), 196 (resurrection), 215-16 (ontological deity).

14. Karl Barth, *Protestant Theology in the Nineteenth Century* (Valley Forge, Pa.: Judson, 1973), p. 297.

15. Barth, *Protestant Theology,* p. 297, rev.

Perhaps more than anything else, Kant was driven to this reticence by his meditation on the depth of evil in the human heart. Although his proposed solution to the problem of evil raises questions of its own, he at least saw that the heart's evil inclinations could not be counteracted without a radical transformation from within. He saw not only that the problem was radical, but that the solution must be commensurate to the problem. Again the contrast with Girard is illuminating. Recall that the collective murder of innocents is seen as the cultural universal on which all human societies are founded. Recall further that this violence arises from the disorders of a socially constructed desire. From a theological point of view, we might say that this diagnosis is broadly "Augustinian." It roots the problem of "covetousness" (the biblical name for "mimetic desire") in the perversity of the human heart. How then is this perversity to be counteracted?

What Girard offers is an essentially "Pelagian" solution to an inherently "Augustinian" problem. All that is needed if mimetic desire and its murderous consequences are to be dispelled, he claims, is for the victimage mechanism to be revealed for what it is. "Once the basic mechanism is revealed," explains Girard, "the scapegoat mechanism, that expulsion of violence by violence, is rendered useless by the revelation. It is no longer of interest. The interest of the Gospels lies in the future offered mankind by this revelation, the end of Satan's mechanism."[16] The moral imperative of the Gospels is sufficient to bring us to our senses: "The Gospels tell us," says Girard, "that to escape violence it is necessary to love one's brother completely — to abandon the violent mimesis involved in the relationship of doubles. There is no trace of it in the Father, and all that the Father asks is that we refrain from it likewise."[17] Once we see things clearly, no more is needed, apparently, than simple renunciation.

In short, thanks to Girard's ministrations in clarifying the Gospels, "it has never been easier to change people's allegiance and to alter their behavior, since the vanity and stupidity of violence have never been more obvious. . . . For the first time, people are capable of escaping from the misunderstanding and ignorance that have surrounded mankind throughout its history."[18] Illumination is thus thought to be sufficient to annul the disorders of the heart. Even if directly theological considerations are omitted, however, and even if we adopt the viewpoint of the victim, as Girard urges, it is hard not to feel that these statements are grossly inadequate. Can Girard really believe, for example, that release from

16. Girard, *The Scapegoat* (Baltimore: Johns Hopkins University Press, 1986), p. 189.
17. Girard, *Things Hidden*, p. 215.
18. Girard, *Things Hidden*, p. 201.

retributive emotions and attitudes is as simple for victims of brutal injustice as his remarks would suggest?[19]

Nevertheless, when the more grandiose and romantic flourishes in Girard are placed to one side, regardless of how pervasive they may be, along with many claims that are incautious and ill conceived, much that is worth retrieving still seems to remain. Consider, for example, this comment on the Sermon on the Mount:

> Jesus invites all men to devote themselves to the project of getting rid of violence, a project conceived with reference to the true nature of violence, taking into account the illusions it fosters, the methods by which it gains ground, and all the laws that we have verified in the course of these discussions. Violence is the enslavement of a pervasive lie; it imposes upon men a falsified vision not only of God but also of everything else.[20]

The acuity of an insight like this seems largely to transcend the inadequacies that may otherwise attend it. The question I wish to pursue is this: How might the essence of such an insight be upheld within a richer and more complex biblical framework? How can Girard's theological deficiencies be avoided while some of his deepest insights and suggestions are retained?

Much will obviously need to be left behind. The "Pelagian" understanding of sin's remedy will have to go. The "low Christology" that reduces Jesus to little more than a moral exemplar will need to be improved by a higher view in which his incarnation, atoning death, and resurrection are taken seriously. The prominence accorded to the "innocent victim" will need to be revised in light of the radicality and universality of human sin. In short, a whole series of distortions that arise, so to speak, when the "horizontal" is emphasized at the expense of the "vertical" will need to be rectified. In what follows I will attempt to reaffirm Girard's provocative thesis that the biblical writings tend finally toward nonviolence, while challenging the premise that seems so often to lead his inquiry astray, namely, the idea that "nonviolence" and "sacrifice" are mutually exclusive.

---

19. Even when Girard appeals to "divine grace" in an effort to avoid "optimistic humanism," he seems bound by essentially Pelagian assumptions. See "Violence, Difference, Sacrifice: A Conversation with René Girard," *Religion and Literature* 25, no. 2 (summer 1993): 11-33, on p. 25.

20. Girard, *Things Hidden*, p. 197.

II. The Doctrine of the Atonement
in von Balthasar and Torrance

Girard's work has been subjected to careful theological scrutiny by Hans Urs von Balthasar. Although von Balthasar finds much to appreciate in Girard, especially in the idea of the "scapegoat mechanism,"[21] he also trenchantly critiques what he sees as Girard's one-sidedness. According to this critique, the saving significance of Jesus Christ emerges only from a context that is essentially trinitarian so that it cannot be grasped in purely cultural or inner-worldly terms. "The experience of being abandoned by God," writes von Balthasar, "in which Jesus endures the condition of the sinner before God, emanates in its inscrutability, not from any sort of cultural 'mechanism' . . . but from a trinitarian transaction of consent within history between the Father and the Son in the Holy Spirit."[22] The saving significance of Jesus Christ cannot be grasped merely from the standpoint of his having endured injustice as an innocent victim at the hands of society. It can be grasped only when his death is seen as an agreement between himself and God the Father for the sake of the world — an event for which the Father expressly sent him, and which he himself deliberately embraced.

"The idea that in his suffering Jesus bore the sins of the world," notes von Balthasar, "is a motif that has been almost completely abandoned in the modern period."[23] Although Girard to his credit has helped to revive this motif in an unexpected way through his emphasis on the importance of the scapegoat, he nonetheless fails to grasp "the mystery of redemption in Christ."[24] He fails to see that only someone who is fully God as well as fully human can enter the realm of human freedom in its fallenness in order to transform it from within before God. He fails to see that God's love cannot be divorced from God's justice and therefore from God's wrath. He therefore fails to see the extent to which the world's salvation "was embodied in a unique event."[25]

In the background of this critique are five main features of atonement that von Balthasar finds in the New Testament.[26] Although the emphasis differs from one place to the next, they are closely interrelated. The first feature concerns *self-*

21. Hans Urs von Balthasar, *Theo-Drama*, vol. 4 (San Francisco: Ignatius, 1994), pp. 298-313.

22. Hans Urs von Balthasar, "Die neue Theorie von Jesus als dem 'Sündenbock,'" *Internationale katholische Zeitschrift "Communio"* 9 (1980): 184-85, on p. 185.

23. Von Balthasar, "Die neue Theorie," p. 184.

24. Von Balthasar, "Die neue Theorie," p. 185.

25. Von Balthasar, *Theo-Drama*, p. 346 (quoting Barth).

26. Von Balthasar, *Theo-Drama*, pp. 240-44 and 317-19.

giving: the self-giving of the Son through the Father for the sake of the world. The cross of Christ took place not primarily because human actions sent Jesus to his death, but because the Father and the Son in their mutual love and freedom elected to establish the world's salvation in this way. The second feature involves *exchange:* the wondrous exchange that takes place between the one who is innocent and the many who are guilty before God. Sinners receive the righteousness of Christ because he bore their sins on the cross and bore them away. "The 'indicative' of this event," writes von Balthasar, "is always expressing itself as an 'imperative': we are to let what is true in itself be true in us and for us," for this exchange is not only an accomplished fact but also a living event "in whose active fruitfulness we can actually receive a share."[27] Third comes our being saved *from* something — from the consequences of our sin, from our self-imposed bondage to sin, evil, and death, to which we are otherwise abandoned by the wrath of God. Fourth comes the corresponding fact that we are at the same time saved *for* something — for participation (which begins here and now) in the eternal life of the Trinity, for sharing in the communion of love and freedom in which God is God. Finally, there is the question of *initiative.* The whole process of reconciliation derives from the initiative of God's love. In this process God remains true to his fundamental identity as God, and therefore to his perfect righteousness, while also remaining true to the human creature, despite its fall into sin.

Throughout this discussion von Balthasar presupposes that from a biblical standpoint there can be no separation between the cross and the Trinity. He writes: "Scripture clearly says that the events of the Cross can only be interpreted against the background of the Trinity and through faith; this is the thrust of the first and fifth motifs, namely, that God (the Father) gave up his Son out of love for the world and that all the Son's suffering, up to and including his being forsaken by God, is to be attributed to this same love. All soteriology must therefore start from this point."[28] The "horizontal" or historical aspects of the cross, in other words, can finally be understood only in a context determined by the more nearly "vertical" or eternal dimension of the Trinity.

This same basic perspective on the atonement has been elegantly consolidated and supplemented by Thomas F. Torrance through a reflection on the threefold office of Christ as prophet, priest, and king. The royal aspect of Christ's atoning work, Torrance urges, concerns the power of the cross as the means by which our bondage to sin, evil, and death is dramatically broken.[29]

27. Von Balthasar, *Theo-Drama*, p. 242.

28. Von Balthasar, *Theo-Drama*, p. 319.

29. Cf. Karl Barth, who also sees the cross as "the dominating characteristic of [Christ's] royal office" (Barth, *Church Dogmatics* IV/2 [Edinburgh: T. & T. Clark, 1958], p. 292; hereafter cited as IV/2). Christ reigns from the cross (*regnantem in cruce*) (IV/2, p. 291).

The priestly aspect concerns the intercession of the cross as the means by which Christ freely assumes and removes the objective guilt that separates us from God. The prophetic aspect, finally, concerns the proclamation of the cross in terms of the basic unity of Christ's person and work as the Word made flesh — a unity that is essential to both his royal and priestly operations.

It is especially the insight into incarnational unity that provides Torrance with a unique vantage point on the dynamics of the atonement.[30] When the cross is illegitimately separated from the incarnation, as has been the tendency of Western theology, it appears to be merely an "external transaction" between a crucified human being and a wrathful God that can be systematized "in moral or legal terms."[31] When the cross is properly understood as "the atoning work of the incarnate Son,"[32] however, then at least two things follow. First, the regrettable abstraction of Christ from his work is overcome. "We are not saved by the atoning death of Christ," writes Torrance, ". . . but by Christ Himself, who in His own person made atonement for us. . . . He is, in the identity of His person and work, Priest and sacrifice in one."[33] Like von Balthasar, Torrance stresses that the atonement is essentially and fundamentally an act of divine self-giving. "It is all one indivisible act," he observes, "in one indivisible Person. . . . The atonement is identical with Christ himself. . . . It lives for ever in the person of the Mediator. He is the Atonement."[34]

Second, just as the atoning work cannot be separated from the person of the incarnate Son, neither can his deity be separated from his humanity. The atonement ultimately occurs within a framework determined by the mystery of the incarnation. It occurs within the union of the divine and human natures that God establishes in Jesus Christ. It thus occurs as a "mystery hidden in God himself."[35] The cross is "a window opened to the very heart of God."[36] It reveals that "the suffering of Christ on the cross was not just human," but "divine as

---

30. Although Torrance offers a distinctive slant on the unity between the incarnation and the atonement, it would be wrong to suppose that this "incarnational" interpretation pits him against Barth. For example, of the conflict between divine righteousness and human sin, Barth wrote: Jesus Christ "took this conflict into his own being [as fully divine and fully human]. He bore it in himself to the bitter end. He took part in it from both sides. He endured it from both sides" (Barth, *Church Dogmatics* II/1 [Edinburgh: T. & T. Clark, 1957], p. 397; hereafter cited as II/1).

31. Thomas F. Torrance, *The Mediation of Christ,* 2nd ed. (Colorado Springs: Helmer & Howard, 1992), p. 114.

32. Torrance, *The Mediation of Christ,* p. 112.

33. Torrance, "The Priesthood of Christ" (unpublished manuscript), p. 6.

34. Torrance, "The Priesthood of Christ," p. 18.

35. Torrance, *The Mediation of Christ,* p. 114.

36. Torrance, *The Mediation of Christ,* p. 112.

well as human," disclosing the suffering love of God.[37] Again as with von Balthasar, the cross must therefore be seen as inseparable from the Trinity. "The atoning work of the incarnate Son," observes Torrance, "falls within the inner life of the Trinity."[38] While it certainly took place in the historical life and activity of Jesus from his birth to his resurrection, and supremely in his death, "it also took place in God."[39]

This complex and mysterious set of intrinsic relations — between the cross and the Trinity, between Christ's deity and his humanity, and between his person and his atoning work — establishes the context in which yet another ineffable relationship can be described. For just as the inner life of God cannot be separated from the cross of Christ, neither can God's mercy be separated from God's wrath. The cross reveals that God's judgment does not occur in separation from his grace, nor in antagonism to it. It reveals that this judgment not only accords but coincides with grace itself. Torrance writes:

> God's self-giving *is* therefore God's judgment upon man, for it is the giving of a love that will *not* have what is against love, so that the very act of God's self-giving is a judgment upon man's sin, but in the very heart of that judgment is the fact that God is opposed to man's sin, and *therefore* He is opposed to man's bondage in sin, and opposed to man's sinful reversal of the love of God. The self-giving of God in love to man is a self-giving which negates the very barrier of sin which prevents fellowship between man and God, and God and man. The judgment of sin is *in order to* the removal of that sin and its barrier to fellowship with God. In other words, in pouring out His love upon man, God affirms man as His loved one, and therefore He negates man's sin only in affirming man as the object of His unconditional love.[40]

Nowhere in the Bible, as Torrance points out, "is there any suggestion that God will pardon or redeem apart from judgment. . . . God will not pardon apart

---

37. Torrance, *The Mediation of Christ*, p. 113.
38. Torrance, *The Mediation of Christ*, p. 112.
39. Torrance, *The Mediation of Christ*, p. 112.
40. Torrance, "Reconciliation" (unpublished manuscript), p. 5, italics added. The inseparability and indeed the coincidence of grace and judgment on the divine side finds its parallel on the human side, for there we find that judgment and sin are not only inseparable but coincident: "No man can evade, elude or avoid the fact that he is loved by God — therefore when he does the inconceivable thing in the act of that love, namely, refuse it, defy it, turn away from it, that unavoidable self-giving of God is his very judgment — it opposes his refusal of God, it opposes his attempt to elude God, and is therefore his judgment in the very event of refusal" (Torrance, "Range of Redemption" [unpublished manuscript], p. 8).

from judgment and sacrificial expiation." Yet "it is ultimately God Himself and God alone who atones and removes sin and saves."[41] God does so in the mystery of that event in which the cross, the incarnation, and the Trinity are inseparably intertwined. Torrance concludes:

> Thereby in the form of a relation of himself to himself, God bridges in his incarnate life in the Lord Jesus Christ the fearful chasm of alienation between man and himself, uniting himself with us under his own righteous judgment upon sin in order to bear and expiate our guilt, all in himself as the one Mediator between God and man who is himself very God and very man. That is the astonishing event which St. Paul once described as the justification of the ungodly![42]

With this reference to "the justification of the ungodly," we have reached a decisive point. For through this idea we will be able to indicate the inner unity between "sacrifice" and "nonviolence" that so consistently eluded Girard as he reflected on the politics of the nonviolent God. But in order to do so we must now move on to Karl Barth.

III. Enemy-Love and Nonviolence in the Theology of Karl Barth

Although the views of the atonement that we have just examined obviously owe something to Barth, von Balthasar and Torrance each have their own distinctive emphases and contributions to make. In particular they seem to bring out more

---

41. Torrance, "The Understanding of Redemption in the Early Church" (unpublished manuscript), p. 11.

42. Torrance, *The Mediation of Christ*, pp. 110-11. The atonement thus has much the same complex structure for Torrance as it did for von Balthasar. On the one hand, it is true in itself. "The atonement has an absolutely objective character in that it was wrought apart from our attitude to it, and while we were yet sinners" (Torrance, "Range of Redemption," p. 11). On the other hand, it must continually become true in us and for us. "The pouring out of the Spirit is not a new event, or some additional event in atonement, . . . but the one atoning event inserting itself into man's life and actualizing itself within. . . . Thus the communion of the Spirit is our incorporation or participation in Christ our substitute, who has already perfectly fulfilled in our name and in our place, our response to God the Father" (Torrance, "Range of Redemption," p. 8). It might be noted that the perceptive discussion and critique of Girard offered by John Milbank would have been even stronger if this complexity had been more truly honored. As it is, Milbank unfortunately emphasizes the second aspect of the atonement to the complete neglect of the first. See Milbank, "Violence and Atonement (The Work of René Girard)," in *Theology and Social Theory* (Oxford: Blackwell, 1990), pp. 392-98, esp. p. 397.

clearly than does Barth the trinitarian context of the cross that he surely pre-supposed but left more implicit. More than von Balthasar, however, and to some extent than Torrance, Barth stresses the atonement as the justification of the ungodly. Enemy-love in Karl Barth's theology is the heart of the gospel. It is not only a decisive category for understanding God's love as revealed in the cross of Christ, but also for Christian discipleship as grounded and called forth by that love.

In the cross of Christ, writes Barth, God makes himself vulnerable to his enemies. In the giving of his only Son, God gives "nothing more or less than himself. . . . In giving him and giving himself — he exposes him — and himself — to the greatest danger. He sets at stake his own existence as God."[43] Through his act of self-giving in Jesus Christ, God offers and endangers his life for the sake of the world (IV/1, p. 72). Barth continues:

> The Christian message is the message of this act of God, of the atonement which was made in this way, of God's pledging of himself for his creature, for his partner in the covenant, for the human being who has opposed him as an enemy. It consists in the fact that God has given himself up into the hands of this enemy. It is in this radical sense that according to the Christian message God has loved first (πρῶτος, I John 4:19), not merely before we loved him, but while we were yet sinners, while we were yet enemies (Rom. 5:8, 10). (IV/1, p. 72, rev.)

In the cross God does not meet his enemies with malice, retaliation, or crushing force. He meets them with the mystery of suffering love. He not only treats them with restraint, but offers himself up for them all. He presents himself as a living sacrifice, saving them from their self-inflicted destruction by suffering the condemnation they deserve. He does not repay evil for evil, but overcomes evil with good, even to the point of setting at stake his own existence. The politics of God thus reveals itself as the politics of nonviolent love.[44]

It was not God who needed to be reconciled to the world, but the world that needed to be reconciled to God. "Atonement takes place," writes Barth, "only where there has been strife. According to Rom. 5:6f., those who are reconciled with God are such as were formerly weak and godless, sinners and ene-

---

43. Karl Barth, *Church Dogmatics* IV/1 (Edinburgh: T. & T. Clark, 1956), pp. 71-72; hereafter cited as IV/1.

44. The idea that the cross reveals the nonviolence of God is a commonplace in the patristic literature. See, for example, Irenaeus: "God does not use violent means to obtain what he desires" (*Against Heresies* 5.1.1); or Gregory of Nyssa: God does not liberate us from our captivity "by a violent exercise of force" (*The Great Catechism* 22).

mies" (IV/1, p. 74). The New Testament does not speak of the atonement as having removed a divine hostility toward humankind. "God does not need reconciliation with human beings," observes Barth, "but they need reconciliation with him." The New Testament "tells us that God has made this reconciliation, and how he has made it" (IV/1, p. 74). It tells us that he has made it by becoming incarnate in Jesus Christ, dying in the place of his enemies that they might live.

Although human beings are unfaithful, hostile, and antagonistic to God, God is not so toward them. However, neither the depth and seriousness of God's love nor the depth and seriousness of human sin can be known for what they are apart from the cross.

> It is here that we come to know of what we are accused and guilty, what our trespass is and means. It consists in an alienation from God, a rebellion against him, which ought to be punished in a way that involves our total destruction, and which apart from our annihilation can be punished only by God himself taking our place, and in his Son taking to himself and bearing and suffering the punishment. This is what it costs God to be righteous without annihilating us. The opposition to him in which we find ourselves is so great that it can be overcome and rendered harmless to ourselves only by God, and indeed only by his entering himself into this opposition and bearing the pain of it. (II/1, p. 399)

God fulfills the judgment that we have brought on ourselves through sin by making it his own, bearing the judgment under which we stand, willing to die, and in fact dying the death that we deserved (IV/1, p. 130). He makes an end to us as his enemies by dying in our place that we might be reconstituted as his friends (IV/1, p. 253).

At least two points follow from this analysis of the atonement that will determine how Barth develops its ethical implications. First, God does not love us because we are lovable; we are lovable because God loves us. Hostile creatures who are loved by God acquire their worth entirely from the fact that God loves them. God transforms those who are enemies into friends who can love him in return.

> God loves the fallen human creature as this enemy. He does not fail to hate that which is worthy of his hatred. He does not relax his wrath. . . . But so sovereign is he in his electing love that he loves this hostile creature who is unworthy of his love. . . . He does not elect and love him because of what that fallen creature has to offer. This could only lead to the divine rejection and hatred. He elects and loves this creature for his own sake; for the sake of

what he is as God for and to this creature; for what he as God awakens in and gives to this creature; for the new humanity which is exclusively the gift of God's love. (IV/2, p. 767, rev.)

God's love always seeks and creates fellowship for its own sake. It does so regardless of the hostility of the creature toward whom this love is directed. God's love is, furthermore, an end in itself. It includes all other divine purposes within itself, for God has no higher goal than love. God's love is a value-bestowing love that miraculously creates worthiness even where there is none. It is a love that triumphs over all that contradicts it (II/1, pp. 276-81).

Second, enemy-love is the prerogative of the divine freedom. It is not grounded in any plausibility structure other than the one it provides for itself. It cannot be explained or comprehended by any principle other than its own self-disclosure. God is free to judge his enemies in such a way that he bears their punishment himself so that they might be converted to his love. Barth writes:

> Everything is against any such judgment being even conceivable: a serious judgment of God's enemies the result of which is grace, liberation, redemption proceeding out of captivity, love out of wrath, life out of death; a judgment which in the event makes the enemies of God his friends; a judgment in which this does not happen arbitrarily but in a fixed order, not in a wild divine inconsequence but with a clear purpose and according to a firm plan; and therefore a judgment beside and after and beyond which there need be no further fear of judgment; a judgment which concludes once and for all with the redemption and salvation of the human being who had been rightly accused and condemned and had fallen a helpless victim to destruction. (IV/1, pp. 221-22, rev.)

Although every external consideration would seem to deny that such a judgment is possible, God is nonetheless God. He is free to show grace, faithfulness, and mercy to fallen and faithless humanity by judging it in this way. "That is how God has actually judged in Jesus Christ" (IV/1, p. 222).

The enemy-love enacted in the cross is what gives New Testament ethics its direction, its tendency, its dynamic — what Barth calls its "pull from the heights to the depths, from riches to poverty, from victory to defeat, from triumph to suffering, from life to death" (IV/1, p. 190). New Testament ethics is thus a reflection of God. For "God does not stand in the far distance high above this ethics, but it is his divine nature to exist in the sense of this ethics, this ethics being only a reflection of his own being" (IV/1, p. 191). "God does not only love those who love him, or greet only his kin: 'He makes his sun to rise on the evil and the good, and sends rain on the just and the unjust' (Matt. 5:45). He obviously does not have to be exalted; he can also be lowly. He does not have to be alone or among friends; he can also be abroad among enemies. He does not have to judge only; he can also forgive. And in being lowly he is exalted" (IV/1, p. 191, rev.). New Testament ethics thus sets forth the cross as "the measure and norm" of the Christian way of life (IV/1, p. 190; cf. pp. 243-44).[45]

Although Christians are to oppose evil and evil persons, they are not to do so by repaying evil with evil. They are commanded to love their enemies, not because they are to conform to an abstract if noble principle, but because they know and may never forget that this is exactly how God has loved them. Barth writes:

> Jesus Christ fought his enemies, the enemies of God — as we all are (Rom. 5:10, Col. 1:21) — no, he loved his enemies, by identifying himself with them. Compared with that what is the bit of forbearance or patience or humor or readiness to help or even intercession that we are willing and ready to bring and offer in the way of loving our enemies? But obviously when we look at what Jesus Christ became and was for us, we cannot leave out some little love for our enemies as a sign of our recognition and understanding that this is how he treated his enemies. (IV/1, p. 244)

We are clearly pointed in this direction by the cross, which dealt with our own enmity toward God in order to liberate us from it.

The cross of Christ therefore "invalidates the whole friend-foe relationship" between one human being and another (IV/2, p. 550). It therefore invalidates angry denunciation, retaliation (for example, in the form of judicial proceedings), killing, and more generally, the "fixed idea of the necessity and beneficial value of force" (IV/2, p. 549). "The direction of Jesus," writes Barth, "must have embedded itself particularly deeply in the disciples in this respect. They were neither to use force nor to fear it" (IV/2, p. 549). He continues: "What the disciples are enjoined is that they should love their enemies (Matt. 5:44). This destroys the whole friend-foe relationship, for when we love our enemy he ceases to be our enemy. It thus abolishes the whole exercise of force, which presupposes this relationship, and has no meaning apart from it" (IV/2, p. 550). The renunciation of force along with retributive emotions and attitudes is not to be regarded an abstract principle or inflexible rule.[46] But

---

45. The intrinsic connection between the divine nonviolence of the cross and the nonviolence of Christian discipleship was also commonplace in the patristic literature. See, for example, Athanasius, *On the Incarnation of the Word* 52.

46. For a discussion which carefully delimits the scope of such reflections without diminishing their primacy, see Barth, *Church Dogmatics* IV/3, second half (Edinburgh: T. & T. Clark, 1962), pp. 628-29; hereafter cited as IV/3.

for those who belong to Jesus Christ by faith, "there is a concrete and incontestable direction which has to be carried out exactly as given" (IV/2, p. 550). It is in this context that Barth issues his famous plea for a "practical pacifism." "According to the sense of the New Testament," he urges, "we cannot be pacifists in principle, only in practice. But we have to consider very closely whether, if we are called to discipleship, we can avoid being practical pacifists, or fail to be so" (IV/2, p. 550).[47]

Although Barth's ethic of enemy-love includes a strong element of imitation, it is saved from degenerating into mere moralism. The imitation of Christ, in the context of Barth's ethics, is not seen as an essentially external relationship that the Christian accomplishes by his or her own power. None of us can love our enemies in the way that is required merely by relying on our own resources, nor are we expected to do so. The needed power is received only as it is continually sought by the believer and given by Christ in the ongoing history of their relationship. The idea of imitation is thus contextualized by the ideas of participation, fellowship, and witness.

Like all forms of Christian love, enemy-love in particular is seen as "participation in the eternal life of God" as it expends itself for the life of the world (IV/2, p. 836). The condition for the possibility of such participation is Christ's presence to faith as "the presence of the Crucified" (IV/3, p. 395), and therefore fellowship with Christ as "fellowship with the Crucified" (IV/1, p. 190). The fellowship of the Christian with Christ takes the form of mutual indwelling. As the Christian lives in Christ, and Christ in the Christian, the Christian comes to participate in what Christ does (IV/3, p. 598). "The Christian in whom Christ lives," writes Barth, "and who lives in Christ, participates as a subject, and indeed as an active subject, in the action of Christ and therefore in the history of salvation, doing things with Christ even if not personally effecting them" (IV/3, p. 600, rev.). The special vocation of the Christian is to share in the living self-witness of the Crucified. This sharing results in a fellowship of action and a fellowship of suffering. The act of witness will lead to suffering, and the suffering will function as an act of witness to the cross (IV/3, pp. 596, 608, 637-42). "The special fellowship of the Christian with Christ," writes Barth, "involves participation in the passion of his cross" (IV/3, p. 604).

Nevertheless, as Barth stresses, "between Christ and the Christian, his cross and ours, it is a matter of similarity in great dissimilarity" (IV/2, p. 605). There can be no question of "an interchangeability of Christ and the Christian" (such as found in "low" or merely exemplarist Christologies) (IV/2, p. 601). It is

---

47. For a discussion of Barth's views on war, see John Howard Yoder, *Karl Barth and the Problem of War* (Nashville: Abingdon, 1970).

true that a Christian's whole life is determined by his or her "fellowship with the suffering and crucified Christ." Nevertheless, the connection between what Christians suffer and the suffering of Christ "is only indirect." "Their cross," writes Barth, "corresponds to the death of Christ. It does this with supreme realism. But it does not do more. It is not a repetition, or re-presentation of the cross of Christ" (IV/2, p. 601). Barth continues:

> Their obedience will never be more than the work of the freedom which they are given. It will always be subsequent. It will always be so stained by all kinds of disobedience that if in the mercy of God it were not invested with the character of obedience it would hardly deserve to be called obedience. Nor is their suffering even the tiniest of contributions to the reconciliation of the world with God. On the contrary, it rests on the fact that this has been perfectly accomplished, not by them but by God himself in Christ, so that it does not need to be augmented by their suffering. (IV/2, p. 604)

Neither in their fellowship with Christ in his sufferings, nor in their expressions of enemy-love in this fellowship, do Christians repeat, contribute to, or augment the redemptive work of Christ on the cross.

The dignity of the Christian's cross is the dignity of a witness to Jesus Christ. Christians do not repeat the saving work of Christ.

> They arise only as its witnesses. What they suffer is not what Jesus suffered — the judgment of God on the unrighteousness of the human creature, the divine rejection without which the election of that creature cannot be accomplished. This was suffered by Jesus for the whole world and therefore for them. They exist only — and this is quite enough — in the echo of his sentence, the shadow of his judgment, the after-pains of his rejection. In their cross they have only a small subsequent taste of what the world and they themselves deserved at the hand of God, and Jesus endured in all its frightfulness as their Head and in their place. (IV/3, p. 604, rev.)

As Christians suffer with Christ, and learn to love others as he loves them, they will enter into correspondence with his cross, however remotely, and this correspondence will point in witness not to themselves but to him.[48]

---

48. In this regard the following statistics may be of interest. In mid-1994 the average number of Christian martyrs per year was 156,000, as compared with 36,000 in 1900 and a projected 200,000 by the turn of this century. See David B. Barrett, "Annual Statistical Table on Global Mission: 1994," *International Bulletin of Missionary Research* 18 (1994): 24-25, on p. 25.

IV. Conclusion

In this essay I have tried to suggest how some of the central insights in René Girard might be retrieved within the context of a Christian theology more traditional than he supports. Christians are people who know that they owe their lives to Jesus Christ, not just as their example, but as their Savior. In gratitude they give their lives wholly to him for all that he has done in their place and continues to do on their behalf. As enemies of grace who brought him to the cross for their share in the sins of the world, they have received him into their lives by faith and are learning to be transformed by his love. They know that because of who Jesus Christ is and what he has done, in all its inexhaustible wonder and mystery, they have not been condemned to the nothingness that would otherwise have been theirs. Knowing also that God has loved them while they were yet enemies, as indeed he loves the whole world, they rededicate themselves to him each day, that through their lives they might faithfully bear witness to what he has done. By the power of his grace and in the fellowship of his love, despite many grievous failures and lapses, they renounce retaliation, retribution, and the violence spawned when these are unchecked. By a power not their own, they show forgiveness to those who harm them and compassion to those in need, as God has forgiven and shown compassion to them. They refuse to condone contrary practices and to cooperate with those who do. They are ready to die if need be, and otherwise wholly to give their lives, in service to the one who so wholly gave his life for them. In these and other ways, they would attest, and hope humbly to share in, the politics of the nonviolent God.

CHAPTER 2

Karl Barth and Liberation Theology

(1983)

If the 1970s were for theology the decade of liberation, the 1980s may prove in turn to be a decade of reaction. Reaction is perhaps not the exciting new breakthrough which just now happens to be needed, but those who care about human suffering and the concerns of liberation theology had better pay heed. For theologically articulate reactionaries are clamoring to take the offensive, being heavily bankrolled along the way by right-wing think tanks and foundations.

The lines are being drawn in our culture for a new intellectual cold war, and this cold war will have a theological front. Witness, for example, the recently issued document entitled "Christianity and Democracy: A Statement of the Institute on Religion and Democracy."[1] The report begins and ends with the words "Jesus Christ is Lord," while shamelessly confessing: ". . . we believe that America has a peculiar place in God's promises and purposes. This is not a statement of national hubris. . . ."[2] Elsewhere the document wants to invest the capitalist system with a halo of democracy while at the same time implying that theologians who question capitalism fundamentally are really communist sympathizers. In this vein we are instructed that Christians have no choice but to be "unapologetically anti-Communist" and that, "to the extent that capitalism is a necessary restraint upon the monistic [totalitarian] drives of society, it warrants our critical approval."[3]

---

1. Richard J. Neuhaus, "Christianity and Democracy: A Statement of the Institute on Religion and Democracy" (Institute on Religion and Democracy, November 1981, mimeographed).

2. Neuhaus, p. 8.

3. Neuhaus, pp. 3, 5. I make no attempt at a full-blown analysis of the Neuhaus statement. I merely isolate the core ideas around which I believe the piece is structured. For a fuller

The sentiments expressed in this document could be dismissed if they were not so ominous. Evidence exists, according to investigative journalist John S. Friedman, that the foundations funding the Institute on Religion and Democracy (IRD) have links to U.S. intelligence agencies.[4] These same foundations have also endowed another new group called the Committee for the Free World, an array of four hundred intellectuals, scholars, and artists from a dozen countries which, on April 6, 1981, ran a full-page ad in the *New York Times* under the headline, "We — a group of intellectuals and religious leaders — applaud American policy in El Salvador."[5] Being convinced, according to a press release, that "the struggle for freedom may in the end be won or lost not on battlefields but in books, newspapers, broadcasts and classrooms," the Free World committee plans "to conduct a vigorous battle in the cultural arena."[6] The Neuhaus statement on "Christianity and Democracy" seems to be part of a similar, if not indeed the very same, intellectual counterinsurgency campaign. When asked by the *National Catholic Reporter* just who he had in mind when his statement condemned "apologists for oppression," Neuhaus replied by singling out, among others, the works of liberation theologians Gustavo Gutiérrez and Juan Luis Segundo.[7]

Although neoconservatives link capitalism with virtue and liberation theologians with oppression, the explosive emergence of liberation theology in

---

discussion of the piece itself, with which I am mostly in agreement, see Peter Steinfels, "Neoconservative Theology," *Democracy* 2 (April 1982): 18-27. The same article was reprinted under the title "'Christianity and Democracy': Baptizing Reaganism," *Christianity and Crisis* 42 (March 29, 1982): 80-85. See also Richard Neuhaus and Peter Steinfels, "Continuing the Discussion: 'Christianity and Democracy,'" *Christianity and Crisis* 42 (May 10, 1982): 135-36.

4. The Institute on Religion and Democracy has received substantial grants from the Scaife Foundation and the Smith Richardson Foundation, according to the *National Catholic Reporter* 18, no. 4 (November 20, 1981): 7. On possible links between these same foundations and the CIA, see John S. Friedman, "Culture War II," *Nation* 232, no. 15 (April 18, 1981): 452-53. Friedman writes: "The Smith Richardson Foundation, which has C.I.A. officials among its consultants reviewing grants, provides management training to C.I.A. and Defense Department employees through an affiliate. Richard M. Scaife, a trustee of the Scaife Family Charitable Trusts, was listed as the owner of Forum World Features, a C.I.A.-funded news service, according to a 1975 *Washington Post* article." For information on how the IRD has influenced recent attacks on the National Council of Churches in the mass media *(Reader's Digest* and CBS TV's *60 Minutes)*, see the *National Catholic Reporter* 19, no. 15 (February 4, 1983): 1, 6-7, 18-19.

5. Quoted by Friedman, p. 452.

6. Friedman, p. 453.

7. *National Catholic Reporter* 18, no. 4 (November 20, 1981): 6. Also singled out by Neuhaus in his interview with the *National Catholic Reporter* as apologizing for oppression was "most of the stuff" published by Orbis Books and "material issued from some parts of the World Council of Churches" (p. 6).

the 1970s has served to alert church people in this country that our government is directly and indirectly complicit, as far as Latin America is concerned, in a pattern of systematic oppression. Far too often the Latin American clients installed in power and maintained by the United States have regularly engaged in such things as torture, disappearances, "murder, starvation, destruction of independent unions, virtual slavery on a massive scale, poisoning plantation workers and their families to enrich still further the tiny clique of gangsters who produce crops for export while the population starves, and the other familiar concomitants of United States intervention."[8] It is for exposing conditions like these and for dramatizing their links to capitalism that certain political forces have an interest in seeing liberation theology be discredited and its influence stopped.

I mention these dreary matters at the outset of a paper on Barth and liberation theology because they set the stage for demonstrating some things which, despite all differences, Karl Barth has in common with theologians like Gutiérrez and Segundo. Against such a backdrop, the first thing which Barth can be seen to share with them is a belief that theological integrity is subject to certain practical and basic political tests. The Free World committee intellectuals who have seen fit to applaud United States support for a government at war with its own people resemble nothing so much as the ninety-three German intellectuals who in August 1914 launched Barth's theological career when they publicly endorsed the kaiser's war policy of aggression against Belgium and France. As is well known, Barth was so disillusioned to discover the signatures of his revered theology teachers among the infamous ninety-three that from thence forward his search for a completely different theological position began. The point is that for Barth, from the beginning of his career to the very end,[9]

---

8. Noam Chomsky, "Resurgent America," *Socialist Review* 58 (July-August 1981): 152. For documentation of U.S. involvement in Latin American oppression, see Penny Lernoux, *Cry of the People: United States Involvement in the Rise of Fascism, Torture and Murder, and the Persecution of the Catholic Church in Latin America* (New York: Doubleday, 1980). See also A. J. Langguth, *Hidden Terrors: The Truth about U.S. Police Operations in Latin America* (New York: Pantheon Books, 1978). It would seem hard, after reading these books, to agree with Neuhaus that "the United States of America is the primary bearer of the democratic possibility in the world today" (Neuhaus, p. 8).

9. I take Barth's use of political criteria for evaluating theology, throughout his career, to be by this time an established fact. The unity (not identity) which he saw between theology and ethics implied, among other things, that it was illegitimate to place theological and political criteria in fundamental opposition. Barth did not have nearly so abstract an understanding of God's Word as is sometimes ascribed to him. It was precisely because the Word of God as the central criterion was concrete that political criteria — in a relative and strictly subordinate, but still operative sense — were necessary. Failures in political judgment were characteristically

even the most doctrinally correct theologians were considered unworthy of their calling to the extent that they aligned themselves in practice with the forces of political reaction — or, to be more specific, with such forces as messianic nationalism, anticommunism, and capitalism.

Furthermore, Barth always considered some reactionaries to be worse than others. As Hans Frei reminds us, during the Third Reich the great danger to the church's witness was not, in Barth's eyes, the stupid and fanatical German Christians so much as it was the more sophisticated theologians (like Friedrich Gogarten) who tried to strike a compromise between God's self-revelation in Scripture and "the special vocation, culture and laws of particular nations at particular times."[10] But in either case Barth did not hesitate to apply elementary political tests in order to detect symptoms of a more fundamental theological failure.[11] Like today's liberation theologians, Barth believed that reactionary politics was a sign that the gospel had been left behind.

A second point which would align Barth with someone like Gutiérrez was his refusal to indulge in wholesale condemnations of communism. Barth was adamant in his insistence that the church should not let the fear of communism obscure the need for social justice. Western anticommunism generally struck him as self-righteous, hypocritical, irresponsible, and irrelevant. It was self-righteous to the extent that it assigned exceptional virtue to the West and extraordinary evil to the East;[12] hypocritical because it refused to condemn the West's own brutal and oppressive allies;[13] irresponsible when it provided an excuse for ignoring social injustice at home;[14] and irrelevant so far as the church was concerned, for why should the church alert anyone to a danger already so well-known?[15] Barth believed that in their quest for world domination, the two

---

traced by Barth as being related to failures in theological judgment (and, sometimes, vice versa). The reason, as he noted in 1939, was that "wherever there is theological talk, it is always implicitly or explicitly political talk as well" (quoted by Eberhard Busch, *Karl Barth: His Life from Letters and Autobiographical Texts* [Philadelphia: Fortress, 1976], p. 292). For further discussion see Ulrich Dannemann, *Theologie und Politik im Denken Karl Barths* (Munich: Chr. Kaiser Verlag, 1977), and George Hunsinger, ed., *Karl Barth and Radical Politics* (Philadelphia: Westminster, 1976).

10. Hans W. Frei, "An Afterword," in *Karl Barth in Re-View*, ed. H. Martin Rumscheidt (Pittsburgh: Pickwick, 1981), p. 106.

11. For a very late example of this procedure (1966), which in principle is no different from the one by which Barth found himself driven to theology in August 1914, see *Karl Barth and Radical Politics*, p. 123.

12. Karl Barth, *Against the Stream* (London: SCM, 1954), pp. 117, 146.

13. Barth, *Against the Stream*, pp. 117, 138, 139, 141.

14. Barth, *Against the Stream*, pp. 139-40, 170-71.

15. Barth, *Against the Stream*, pp. 116-17.

superpowers were the mirror image of one another,[16] and that the so-called totalitarian aspect of Soviet communism, which was the object of so much hysteria and alarm, was something to be explained in cultural more than ideological terms.[17] As an antidote to the excessive fear of communism, Barth proposed two solutions. The first was peace: "As Christians [the conflict between East and West] is not our concern at all. It is not a genuine, not a necessary, not an interesting conflict. It is a mere power conflict. We can only warn against the still greater crime of wanting to decide the issue in a third world war."[18] His second proposal was justice: "Anyone who does not want communism — and none of us does — should take socialism seriously."[19]

Finally, Barth stands with the liberation theologians against the neoconservatives on the crucial matter of capitalism. The salient point about capitalism for Barth was not, as neoconservatives would contend, that it decentralizes power and therefore stands as a bulwark against the totalitarian "drives" of society. On the contrary, Barth rightly insisted that capitalism generates enormous disparities in wealth and power, concentrating life-and-death decisions "in the hands of the relatively few, who pull all the strings . . . in a way completely outside the control of the vast majority."[20] Like the liberation theologians, on the other hand, Barth saw that capitalism fosters unwholesome collective relationships of exploitation and dependency — although, unlike the liberationists, the collective relationships he had in view seem to have been primarily domestic rather than international.[21] Barth went so far as to describe capitalism as an "almost unequivocally demonic process"[22] — largely because of the ways in which capitalism exacerbates the worst aspects of human nature, debases human culture, and, not least, obscures its own injustices.[23]

At the very minimum, therefore, Barth argued — and here is where in his view the neoconservatives would start to go wrong — that the Christian community cannot allow itself to "participate in the great self-deception" of capital-

16. Barth, *Against the Stream*, p. 129.

17. Barth, *Against the Stream*, pp. 138-39, 171.

18. Barth, *Against the Stream*, p. 131.

19. Quoted by Busch, p. 382.

20. Karl Barth, *Church Dogmatics* III/4 (Edinburgh: T. & T. Clark, 1961), p. 532, rev. For more on Barth's critique of capitalism, see George Hunsinger, "Karl Barth and Radical Politics: Some Further Considerations," *Studies in Religion/Sciences Religieuses* 7 (1978): 187-89. See also Dannemann, esp. pp. 184-201.

21. Barth, *Church Dogmatics* III/4, pp. 541-42. But on the international question, cf. pp. 451-52, 459.

22. Barth, *Church Dogmatics* III/4, p. 531.

23. On human nature, see Barth, *Church Dogmatics* III/4, pp. 537-41; on human culture, see pp. 532-33; on obscuring its own injustices, see pp. 540, 542.

ism concerning its supposed benefits, necessity, or even legitimacy as a system.[24] For example, the Christian community should not succumb to the false proposition that, although the wealth under capitalism is inequitably distributed, each person's income reflects how hard or valuably he or she has worked; for, in Barth's words, "the only choice which employees often have is between starvation and doing work which either does not benefit the cause of humanity, is detrimental to it, or is completely alienated, being performed in the service of a sinister and heartless and perpetually ambiguous idol" — namely, mammon in the guise of "capital."[25] By chronically forcing men and women to work for "meaningless ends and therefore dishonestly,"[26] capitalism will have only itself to blame should the communism it so greatly fears triumph over it. Given the terrible inhumanity of the capitalist system, "Is it not almost inevitable," asks Barth, "that the Marxist tyranny should finally overwhelm us, with its new and very different injustices and calamities, to teach us mores, true ethics" with respect to the meaning and purpose of human work?[27]

Much like the liberation theologians, therefore, Barth does not hesitate to specify capitalism as a system of disorder which the Christian community must oppose. The command of God, he wrote, "is self-evidently and in all circumstances a call for counter-movements on behalf of humanity and against its denial in any form, and therefore a call for the championing of the weak against every encroachment on the part of the strong."[28] Since the Christian community has been so slow in recognizing the meaning of God's command in a capitalist society, Barth felt that it was scarcely in any position to point its finger at the injustices of state socialism. Instead, he insisted that Christianity in the West has its work cut out merely to understand what he called "the disorder in the decisive form still current in the West, to remember and to assert the command of God in the face of this form, and to keep to the 'left' in opposition to its champions, i.e., to confess that it [Christianity] is fundamentally on the side of the victims of this disorder and to espouse their cause."[29] In view of state-

---

24. Barth, *Church Dogmatics* III/4, p. 541.

25. Barth, *Church Dogmatics* III/4, p. 532, rev.

26. Barth, *Church Dogmatics* III/4, p. 532.

27. Barth, *Church Dogmatics* III/4, p. 532.

28. Barth, *Church Dogmatics* III/4, p. 544.

29. Barth, *Church Dogmatics* III/4, p. 544. It might be pointed out that Barth quite naturally found some forms of capitalist society to be preferable to others. He was, after all, a democratic rather than a doctrinaire socialist. In practice he felt that one had to be pragmatic even while opposing capitalism in principle. In other words, he had no special wisdom concerning the central dilemma facing the nonideological left in western European societies: how to work for gradual improvements within capitalism while opposing capitalism itself.

ments like these, Barth would seem to have a very different idea than Neuhaus about what would make one an "apologist for oppression."

Let us turn now from the political solidarity between Barth and the liberationists (which is therefore also theological) to the much more difficult problem of the theological distance between them (which is therefore also political). The supreme difficulty at this point, it seems to me, is to find some road of access, some point of leverage, by which Barth and the Latin American theology can be meaningfully compared. When confronted by two such logically and materially diverse bodies of thought, is there any way to get around the impasse which so immediately and forcefully presents itself? Or must we settle in the end for the Barthian image of the elephant and the whale, whose modes of existence are so utterly alien that finally the most they can do is to stare at one another for a moment, quizzically and uncomprehendingly, before each turns and goes its separate way? One thing certain would seem to be that in this case no real parallel can be found to the happy solution of Dennis McCann, who in his excellent recent study of liberation theology and Reinhold Niebuhr was able to bring his comparison together by focusing on such material questions as their views of human nature and human history.[30] But when in such a study Karl Barth is substituted for Niebuhr, something more formative or rudimentary would seem to be needed as a focus if an adequate framework for discussion is to emerge. In this light I would suggest that, when viewed as a whole, what separates the Barthian and liberation theologies are two very different controlling passions.

The controlling passion of Barth's theology, it should come as no surprise, is to give unqualified precedence to the sovereign Word of God, whereas by contrast the controlling passion of liberation theology is most certainly to bring liberation to the oppressed. The operative word in this distinction, from which a great deal will be seen to follow, is the word "controlling." Of course, it would be just as false to suggest that the liberation theologians give no precedence to God's Word as it would be to suppose that Barth cared nothing about the oppressed and their needs. Nevertheless, in each case the universe of discourse, the very atmosphere, is strikingly different, and in no small part this difference can be traced respectively to the ruling theological passions.

When a theology's controlling passion is to give not just precedence but unqualified precedence to God's Word, as is the case with Barth, then the danger to be strenuously avoided will be for "the gospel to become an echo of what was present in our heart before we came to it, a rewording of what we had al-

---

30. Dennis P. McCann, *Christian Realism and Liberation Theology* (Maryknoll, N.Y.: Orbis, 1981).

ready thought."[31] If for no other reason than a recognition of sinful humanity's proclivity for self-deception, theology will attach itself fervently and exclusively to God's Word as the rich and complex event by which God shatters our self-deceptions and reveals to us what only God can reveal — God's true identity. This true identity will be found nowhere else than in Jesus Christ, as witnessed in all of Scripture, for he alone is the one Word of God and the only source for our knowledge of God.

Such a fervent and exclusive attachment to God's Word will therefore mean that theology reads Scripture, and especially its narrative portions, as an organic whole. Scripture will be regarded as possessing its own integrity despite all diversity, its own complex logic, and its own canons of meaning and truth. These canons will not be altered merely because they might seem at times to conflict with the canons of rationality in other fields, nor will the theological content they are designed to preserve require some more general or accessible conceptual framework in order to be understood. No such autonomous conceptual scheme, whatever it might be, will be allowed to function systematically as the precondition for theological meaning or truth.[32] Any correlations between theology and other fields of discourse will of necessity be eclectic, ad hoc, and indirect. The proximities will always have to be balanced dialectically by not losing sight of the even greater distances. How could it be otherwise when the Word to which theology bears witness is utterly unique? How could it be otherwise when this Word is the ever miraculous and mysterious event of God's free and sovereign grace?

When, on the other hand, a theology's controlling passion is to bring liberation to the oppressed, as is certainly the case with the Latin American theology, then the danger to be strenuously avoided will be the adoption of any ideas which might serve to advance or reinforce the interests of oppression's beneficiaries. If for no other reason than the church's historic readiness to assume precisely such an ideological role, a theology committed to liberation will find itself forced to wield a vigorous hermeneutic of suspicion. A gospel from which the great and powerful of this world would have little to fear and much to gain will no longer be acceptable. Poverty will no longer be tolerated as an inevitable historical fate, hope will no longer be deferred to some ethereal realm beyond the grave, and spirituality will no longer be interiorized within the essentially isolated individual. Instead, a Christian hope for this world will become the driving force behind a new collective and more authentic spiritual commit-

---

31. G. C. Berkouwer, "The Voice of Karl Barth," in *A Half Century of Theology* (Grand Rapids: Eerdmans, 1977), p. 73.

32. Frei, p. 108.

ment which aims to struggle in solidarity with the poor against the unnecessary shackles of their oppression.

Liberation praxis will therefore become the indispensable context in which theology must do its work. In a world where children are dying of hunger because of exploitation and oppression, theological neutrality will be impossible. Attention will be paid to the harsh reality of uneven development in which necessities are denied to the many while luxuries are delivered to the few; capitalism will not unreasonably be regarded as the engine which grinds out this wretched social result; and praxis will accordingly be organized around those social theories which seem to hold the most promise for eliminating the causes of oppression.

A theology rooted in praxis will be judged by functional criteria, for a gospel with no functional value for liberation would be no gospel at all. Theology's own conceptual integrity or epistemological fitness will thus be less important than its practical consequences. The important thing will be its capacity to clarify the struggle for a more humane future. Theology will present the truth of the gospel as something above all to be done. Scripture will be read as the story of God's liberation of the oppressed, and its exegesis will take place in deeds. The deed will be what counts, and so orthodoxy will be supplanted by orthopraxis. How could it be otherwise when Christ himself is the Liberator? How could it be otherwise when God has initiated a process of liberation whose goal will be the creation of a new humanity and in which theology is called to participate in solidarity with the oppressed?

Before going on to ask about the extent to which the theologies governed by two such different controlling passions might or might not be reconcilable, let us first examine them more closely by taking a representative test case. I propose that we do this by looking at what Barth and Gutiérrez have to say on the particular topic of poverty. Our texts for this brief study will be Barth's 1949 essay entitled "Poverty," supplemented by a snippet from his *Church Dogmatics* on the political meaning of faith in God's righteousness,[33] along with the final chapter of Gutiérrez's *Theology of Liberation*, entitled "Poverty: Solidarity and Protest."[34] In both cases it is explicitly claimed that a biblical view of poverty is being presented.

As might be expected from what we saw of their respective controlling passions, Barth's discussion of poverty accents those matters most distinctive to

---

33. Barth, "Poverty," in *Against the Stream*, pp. 243-46; *Church Dogmatics* II/1 (Edinburgh: T. & T. Clark, 1957), pp. 386-87.

34. Gustavo Gutiérrez, *A Theology of Liberation* (Maryknoll, N.Y.: Orbis, 1973), pp. 287-302.

the biblical tradition, whereas Gutiérrez's accents those most applicable to liberation praxis. Each sees things in Scripture which the other misses, and neither would be entirely satisfied with what the other has to say. Nevertheless, their two presentations not only partially overlap, but may finally be mutually corrective.

The span of distance between the two disparate statements on poverty may be gauged from the fact that Barth says almost nothing about oppression whereas Gutiérrez says almost nothing about grace. Indeed, on these scores some pointed objections would arise from both sides.

Gutiérrez would no doubt wonder, for example, why Barth chose to open his essay on such an apparently fatalistic note. Was it really necessary for Barth to contend that the existence of wealth and poverty "appears to be a kind of divine ordering of events" which has to be accepted "without question and without concerning ourselves with ideas of an essentially 'better future'"? Is this really such a dominant biblical note that one should choose to begin with it and then go on to insist that "without this starting point . . . we can comprehend nothing"?[35] And what does Barth mean when he goes so far as to speak of the "blessings of poverty"?[36] Does he really mean that poverty as such is "the mark of Heaven, the mirror of eternal salvation"?[37]

Doesn't Barth with such statements as these come all too close, Gutiérrez might ask, to making "material poverty a positive value, considering it almost a human and religious ideal"?[38] Doesn't he skate to the very edge of "sacralizing misery and injustice" and therefore of "preaching resignation to it"?[39] Shouldn't theology take special care to avoid any sentimental talk about poverty as a blessing "which in the last analysis justifies the status quo"?[40] Gutiérrez would undoubtedly acknowledge that such statements are only one part of what Barth has to say, and that elsewhere in the same essay Barth takes a strong stand on behalf of justice for the poor, not failing to make the biblically correct observation that poverty is against the will of God. But he might well go on to suggest that in the end Barth's essay cannot shake off a certain unfortunate ambiguity, for the "divine ordinance" Barth describes seems somehow to condone and yet not to condone poverty at the same time.

Gutiérrez could readily go on to agree with Barth that poverty is "not a natural condition," that it is "part of the evil which dominates" human life, and

---

35. Barth, *Against the Stream*, p. 243.
36. Barth, *Against the Stream*, p. 244.
37. Barth, *Against the Stream*, p. 246.
38. Gutiérrez, p. 289.
39. Gutiérrez, p. 298.
40. Gutiérrez, p. 290.

that it is "perhaps the most striking result of human sin."[41] Once again, however, Gutiérrez would find these statements, by going no further, to be inadequate. Can one leave it at that and really do justice to the force of what the Bible has to say? Doesn't the Bible consider poverty to be not merely unnatural but "subhuman"?[42] Doesn't it depict poverty as "a scandalous condition inimical to human dignity and therefore contrary to the will of God"?[43]

Why, then, should Barth in his essay pass by the scathing prophetic denunciation that poverty is "not caused by fate" but by "the injustice of the oppressors"?[44] Does not the Bible itself often testify that the rich are rich only at the expense of the poor, and that the poor are poor precisely because they are victims of oppression? Do the prophets hesitate to point the finger at those who are to blame?[45] But the Bible does not simply stop with denouncing poverty. It "speaks of positive and concrete measures to prevent poverty from becoming established among the People of God."[46] Yet again, we strangely hear nothing of this from Barth.

Finally, Gutiérrez might wonder why Barth spends so much time in his essay exhorting the rich to good works without once mentioning the "enormous proportions"[47] which the evil of poverty has assumed in our time. Surely Barth does not expect the rich themselves to rectify matters. Doesn't he realize that the poor will have to set in motion their own struggle for justice and that "to be with the oppressed is to be against the oppressor"?[48]

Barth, in turn, for his part would undoubtedly have some equally sharp questions to direct at Gutiérrez. He might begin by pointing out that in the opening theme of his essay, which I have imagined Gutiérrez would regard as fatalism, he states that in the Bible "those who possess and enjoy material wealth can be seen at a glance to be really very 'poor people.'"[49] Does not the Bible have something strong and incisive to say about the spiritual poverty which can and often does accompany material wealth? Is this not something quite different from the kind of spiritual poverty which Gutiérrez describes and rejects as a supposedly religious ideal?[50] More seriously, with this understand-

---

41. Barth, *Against the Stream,* p. 245.
42. Gutiérrez, p. 289.
43. Gutiérrez, p. 291.
44. Gutiérrez, p. 292.
45. Gutiérrez, p. 293.
46. Gutiérrez, p. 293.
47. Gutiérrez, p. 295.
48. Gutiérrez, p. 301.
49. Barth, *Against the Stream,* p. 243.
50. Gutiérrez, pp. 289-90.

ing of the spiritual emptiness of wealth, does not the Bible point to a far deeper and far graver source of human misery than Gutiérrez, with his single-minded focus on the oppressors and oppressed of this world, allows to come into view? Is it really within human powers to eliminate poverty in either the material or the spiritual sense of the term? Yet can anything other than the elimination of poverty in both senses be considered an essentially or qualitatively "better future"? Furthermore, even if it were possible to eliminate material poverty here and now, would not the other and ultimately more serious kind of poverty still remain? Why do we hear so little about this other kind of poverty from Gutiérrez?

Is not Gutiérrez's silence on the destitution of spiritual poverty, Barth might go on to ask, a symptom of the fundamental problem which seems to plague his entire work? Is it not finally all of one piece that Gutiérrez comes so close to absolutizing the distinction between rich oppressor and poor oppressed, that he regards the key to solving the apparently overriding soteriological problem of oppression not really a divine but a human action of liberation, and that therefore for him the chief importance of the divine praxis as attested in the biblical narratives is that it sets such a good example for the finally more urgent and decisive action of conscientized human beings? What else can one conclude when one reads such telling remarks from Gutiérrez as that our Christian action against poverty and oppression "means taking on humanity's sinful condition to liberate humanity from sin and all its consequences"?[51] In short, is not Gutiérrez's silence on the destitution of spiritual poverty a symptom of the fact that he has lost sight of the great and decisive dialectic between God's grace and human sin? But is it not precisely this dialectic which in the Bible is comprehensive and all-encompassing, so that it also embraces the lesser dialectic of liberation and oppression — not excluding or trivializing the latter, but certainly emphatically relativizing it?

Finally, Barth might conclude by redescribing what it means to affirm, as the Bible itself affirms, that God is on the side of the poor. "God stands," writes Barth, "at every time unconditionally and passionately on this and only on this side: always against the exalted and for the lowly, always against those who already have rights and for those from whom they are robbed and taken away."[52] This, and here he would agree with Gutiérrez, is the concrete political tendency of the biblical message; nor can this message be heard and believed, he continues, without awakening a sense of responsibility to follow in that direction today.

51. Gutiérrez, p. 301, rev.
52. Barth, *Church Dogmatics* II/1, p. 386, rev.

53

Unlike Gutiérrez, however, Barth goes on to ground these observations in a larger theological truth, namely, that God's righteousness is disclosed as mercy to all who are in distress, that God's grace — and this is decisive — triumphs precisely at the point where humanity has no means of triumphing.[53] It is precisely because God has acted once for all apart from us, against us, and for us in Jesus Christ — doing for us that which we most needed but were in no position whatsoever to do for ourselves — that we are in faith made responsible for all those who are poor and oppressed, that we are summoned to espouse the cause of those who suffer wrong. For in them it is manifested to us what we ourselves are in the sight of God. The living, gracious, and merciful action of God toward us consists in the fact that God alone in divine righteousness procures right for us, the poor and wretched. Therefore, we and all men and women stand in the presence of God as those for whom right can be procured only by God as such, and for whom right has indeed been procured in this way.[54] This is the theme of God's grace which Barth does not fail to make the dominant note even in this connection and of which we hear so little in any connection from Gutiérrez.

Where, then, does all this leave us? Are we finally left with an impasse between a theology of grace and a theology of liberation, between a theology which gives priority to the divine indicative and one which concentrates instead on the human imperative, between a theology which tends toward universalism and one which moves by contrast toward a kind of sectarianism? Are we left, in short, with an elephant and a whale?

I think not. Barth and Gutiérrez share too much common ground and have too much to learn from each other to allow them each to go unchanged their separate ways. What is at stake in the differing controlling passions which govern their theologies and in their contrasting approaches to the biblical teaching on poverty are, I think, two distinct orientations of love.

The controlling passion of Barth's theology can be read as a passion to love God and fear God above all else, whereas that of Gutiérrez's theology can be read as a passion to love one's neighbor as oneself. A passion to love God above all else can be discerned behind Barth's magnificent celebration of God's grace, whereas a passion to love one's neighbor as oneself can be discerned behind Gutiérrez's compelling incitement to liberation. It would finally be too simple, however, were we to allow the two theologies to be schematized in this way, for at bottom what is really at stake are two different elaborations of the relationship between love for God and neighbor-love. These different elabora-

---

53. Barth, *Church Dogmatics* II/1, p. 387.
54. Barth, *Church Dogmatics* II/1, p. 387.

tions are in themselves incompatible, but I think Barth is right in principle whereas the liberationists are right in practice.

When I say that the liberationists are right in practice with their passion for neighbor-love and hence for liberation, I mean that Barth would have something important to learn from them. While it is certainly true that one can find passages in Barth's theology where the radical political imperatives of the gospel sound forth, it is also true that these imperatives are often muffled by the extraordinary expanse of other themes which he so prodigiously sets forth. The result is perhaps a certain imbalance, despite all good intentions, in his work. For if one looks to the one documentary authority which Barth accepted as theology's primary source and criterion, then, as Ronald J. Sider has pointed out, "The sheer volume of biblical material that pertains to questions of hunger, justice and the poor is astonishing."[55] One could not say the same about the force of emphasis in Barth's theology, and the apparent thrust of Scripture may be due to what Helmut Gollwitzer has called "the bourgeois slant even to a theology antibourgeois in tendency."[56] Or perhaps it has something to do with what Hans Frei has described as the "almost aesthetic passion" which Barth felt for the traditional loci of Christian theology.[57] Regardless of how one explains it, however, the disjunction is obviously there, and the liberationists at least provide some useful and indispensable instruction on how to rectify it.

When I say, on the other hand, that Barth is right in principle with his passion to give unqualified precedence to God's Word and hence to God's grace, I mean that the liberationists themselves might learn something important from him. There is a strong tendency in liberation theology to define love for God almost exclusively in terms of neighbor-love. This tendency typifies the general pattern of thought in liberation theology as a whole. Barth has forcefully argued, however, that neighbor-love does not exhaustively or even predominantly define love for God. Despite the inextricable unity of the two loves, they remain irreducibly distinct, and neighbor-love is always something relative and subordinate to love for God. "If we try to love God as the neighbor," cautions Barth, "it will not be the God whom we are commanded to love. And if we try to love the neighbor as God, it will not be the neighbor we are commanded to love. If we are not to deviate from the divine revelation, if we really want to obey the one commandment of God, we can only love God and our neighbor."[58]

55. Ronald J. Sider, *Cry Justice* (New York: Paulist, 1980), p. 3.
56. Helmut Gollwitzer, "Kingdom of God and Socialism in the Theology of Karl Barth," in *Karl Barth and Radical Politics*, p. 106.
57. Frei, p. 110.
58. Barth, *Church Dogmatics* I/2 (Edinburgh: T. & T. Clark, 1956), p. 410.

What do these observations have to do with liberation theology? José Míguez Bonino has pointed to the problems posed by what he calls "the radical 'monism' of the new liberation theology."[59] This monism results, for example, when love for God collapses into neighbor-love, when it becomes increasingly difficult to differentiate liberation from salvation, or when, in Bonino's words, "reference to the history of divine revelation is secondary, merely exemplary, or even dispensable." He continues, "If we carry that tendency to its ultimate conclusion, we will end up wittingly or unwittingly deifying history or humanity itself. . . . There can be no doubt that contemporary Latin American theology has no such intention. But we must ask ourselves whether the formulations we have worked out so far do enough to rule out that possibility."[60] One especially thinks in this regard of the more recent work of Rubem Alves, who apparently has nothing better for the world these days than a few choice quotations from Feuerbach and Nietzsche.[61]

The dangerous tendency which Bonino identifies can only be resisted, in my opinion, by something like Barth's unqualified precedence for God's Word. This kind of precedence would go far toward dispelling the latent ambiguity, confusion, and reductionism of much liberation theology. Take, for example, Juan Luis Segundo's insistence that liberation praxis stands in what he calls "a causal relationship to the definitive kingdom."[62] Segundo argues for a relationship of "causality" between praxis and the coming kingdom on the strictly functional grounds that no one will dedicate his or her life to an "analogy," or die for an "outline," or be mobilized to act in the name of an "anticipation"[63] — thereby flatly rejecting the categories commonly used to differentiate God's praxis from even the most definitive human praxis. In view of this inflation of the human deed, it is perhaps not surprising that Segundo goes so far as to advocate what looks very much like the authoritarian political unit of the so-called revolutionary vanguard.[64] (By the way, Neuhaus is not wrong to notice such extremely disturbing trends in some liberation theologies, but he is culpably wrong in using those trends as a warrant for sweeping condemnations in the service of political reaction.)

59. José Míguez Bonino, "Historical Praxis and Christian Identity," in *Frontiers of Theology in Latin America,* ed. Rosino Gibellini (Maryknoll, N.Y.: Orbis, 1979), p. 263.

60. Bonino, p. 272.

61. Rubem Alves, "From Paradise to the Desert: Autobiographical Musings," in *Frontiers of Theology in Latin America,* pp. 284-303.

62. Juan Luis Segundo, "Capitalism versus Socialism: Crux Theologica," in *Frontiers of Theology in Latin America,* p. 257.

63. Segundo, "Capitalism versus Socialism," p. 247.

64. Juan Luis Segundo, *The Liberation of Theology* (Maryknoll, N.Y.: Orbis, 1976), pp. 208-37, esp. pp. 226-37. Cf. McCann, pp. 216-17.

What Barth has to offer liberation theology at such points, it seems to me, is a way of grounding and anchoring the admittedly necessary functional criteria in certain prior, determinative, and more fundamental theological criteria. For, as Bonino senses, the functional criteria will themselves all too readily become dysfunctional if they are not theologically anchored and well grounded. As Barth writes on the relationship of prayer to action, it cannot be the affair of those who pray for the coming of God's kingdom "to accomplish with their own deeds the act of God for which they pray." If we dare to regard ourselves as subjects who have authority and power to bring in with our own deeds that for which we pray, we will stumble into "an impossible enterprise foredoomed to failure," which can only "result in a further desecration of the name of God." "Those who try to do too much," warns Barth, "will in fact do too little, and in their wholly inappropriate identification with God they will not do what they are commanded to do in obedience to [God]." We must not forget that "since we cannot act as gods, what is required is from the very first a limited action both qualitatively and quantitatively."[65]

Those who pray for the coming of God's kingdom nonetheless declare at the same time "that in the matter about which they pray to God something will be done correspondingly by them." Such prayer "does not demand an occasional, tepid and sluggish movement in which we grow tired, are constantly pausing, or even stop altogether. It demands a movement analogous" — no more but no less — "to that for which we ask from God."[66] It is therefore foolish of someone like Segundo to suppose that "the limitation of the action required of us" in any way diminishes "the urgency with which it is required."[67] For as Barth says: "What is categorically demanded of us Christians is that we should take these steps of ours in all modesty as our responsibility in face of the coming glorifying of God's name by God [alone], . . . that they should be steps on the way to this goal, distinguished from the steps of other people by the fact that even though they are done here and now in the midst of others, they are done already with a view to this future act of God, and they thus bear witness to this act."[68]

This example, in which the precedence given to God's praxis serves to mobilize rather than detract from human praxis, may stand as an indication and suggestion of how a theology of liberation might be anchored more securely in a theology of grace. In this way the necessary passion for liberation

---

65. Barth, *The Christian Life* (Grand Rapids: Eerdmans, 1981), p. 171.
66. Barth, *The Christian Life*, p. 169.
67. Barth, *The Christian Life*, p. 172.
68. Barth, *The Christian Life*, p. 173.

would finally be grounded, oriented, and controlled by the distinctively and indispensably Christian passion to give unqualified precedence in all things to God's free and sovereign grace.

Postscript: Reply to Kamitsuka

In a wonderfully learned and lucid article, David G. Kamitsuka has challenged my critique of liberation theologies.[69] Not contesting the validity of my normative concerns, he argues that Gutiérrez, at least in his later theology, actually meets them. It would be wonderful if that were the case. Unfortunately Kamitsuka's argument does not convince me.

Despite his evident care in exposition, Kamitsuka does not adequately represent my concerns. I must assume that I have stated them too tersely. I will attempt to remedy the situation here. Kamitsuka rightly focuses on three points.

First, he notes my concern that liberation theology fails adequately to differentiate liberation from salvation. He interprets this concern as meaning that it fails to give proper priority to the indicative of divine grace. So far, so good. However, he thinks, wrongly in my opinion, that this concern can be met merely by allowing that "God's prevenient and gratuitous love for the poor" serves to ground the church's "liberating praxis" (p. 178). I would not contest that such ideas can be found in Gutiérrez and other liberation theologians. The problem is that these ideas are not to the point. The New Testament message, as I understand it, is that we have all sinned and fall short of the glory of God, that we are helpless to save ourselves, and that our only hope lies in God's gracious intervention for us in Jesus Christ. There is only one work of salvation. It has been accomplished by Jesus Christ. It is identical with his person. "If we confess our sins, [God] is faithful and just, and will forgive our sins and cleanse us from all unrighteousness" (I John 1:9). This promise is true because Christ died in our place and rose again to bring us into communion with himself (and just so into the communion of the Holy Trinity).[70] Victim-oriented soteriologies, such as we find among the liberationists, fail to do justice to this central truth. The fundamental human plight is that of sinners before God, not of victims before oppressors. How to maintain a properly sin-oriented soteriology so that a full if

69. David G. Kamitsuka, "Salvation, Liberation and Christian Character Formation: Postliberal and Liberation Theologians in Dialogue," *Modern Theology* 13 (1997): 171-89, on pp. 175-81.

70. Although with Gutiérrez Kamitsuka wishes to speak of salvation as communion with God, he does not place it on an adequate christocentric basis.

secondary place is accorded to the plight of victims is something we can learn better from Barth than from Gutiérrez or from any liberationist known to me.[71]

Doesn't liberation theology tend to define love for God too exclusively in terms of neighbor-love? Kamitsuka thinks this second concern, as raised by my critique, can be met merely by asserting that love for God is expressed through neighbor-love. Although this assertion is necessary, I would not regard it as sufficient. It still seems to presume that love for God never occurs apart from neighbor-love. It fails to acknowledge love for God as an independent activity in its own right, with independent modes of expression (such as worship). Commenting on Micah 6:6-8, Calvin got it right: "Nor is it strange that [the prophet] begins with the duties of love of neighbor. For although the worship of God has precedence and ought rightly to come first, yet justice which is practiced in human relations is the true evidence of devotion to God." This says everything Kamitsuka and the liberationists want to say in this regard without committing their mistake.

Finally, by failing adequately to distinguish God's redemptive activity from liberation praxis — by tending to conflate them — doesn't liberation theology tend to deify history or humanity? This concern is closely related to the first. Kamitsuka adopts the liberationist premise that what defines God's redemptive activity is liberation from oppression. This premise, however, displaces the centrality that belongs to Jesus Christ alone as the Savior of the world. It fails to acknowledge that what defines God's redemptive activity is our Lord's life, death, and resurrection — by which the world is saved from its sin. To meet the concern about "deifying" history or humanity, it is not adequate to state, as does Kamitsuka following Gutiérrez, merely that God's mystery transcends liberation. "Deification" will remain a danger for any theology that fails to regard human beings as sinners who are hostile to God and helpless to effect their own salvation (cf. Rom. 5:6, 8, 10). By placing divine prerogatives into human hands, it sows the seeds of destruction by giving the latter more than they can bear. Liberation praxis can surely be placed on a sounder theological footing.

71. For more on how a sin-oriented soteriology can do justice to the plight of victims, see my essay "Social Witness in Generous Orthodoxy," *Princeton Seminary Bulletin* 21, no. 1 (2000) (forthcoming).

CHAPTER 3

Barth, Barmen, and the Confessing Church Today

(1984)

Introduction

Fifty years ago, in response to an acute political and theological crisis, 139 delegates from nineteen territorial churches (Lutheran, Reformed, and United) gathered together in the German Rhineland city of Barmen. At the time the delegates could not have known they were about to take a historic stand for the faith of the church. Yet the implications of this stand would be decisive, not only for their encounter with National Socialism, but also far beyond that down to the present day. The delegates placed themselves in an exposed position. As articulated in the famous "Theological Declaration concerning the Present Situation of the German Evangelical Church," written primarily by Karl Barth and adopted unanimously by the synod, their confession of faith risked maximum fidelity to Scripture at a time when they could expect only minimum support from the prevailing culture. Indeed, the Barmen Declaration set them on a collision course not only with their government but also with the fundamental assumptions of academic theology as practiced for nearly two hundred years. The delegates audaciously believed that between what they had to oppose politically and what they had to oppose theologically there existed an intrinsic connection.

Today, as I shall argue, we too stand in an acute political and theological crisis. Our political situation is more ambiguous and more precarious than that faced by the church in Germany — more ambiguous because we are surrounded by the trappings of democracy, more precarious because we face the prospect not of persecution but of annihilation. The American theological situation, furthermore, both in the academy and in the congregations, is largely one of confusion, if measured by the standards of Barmen, and we would thus do well to refrain from publishing bold new professions of the faith.

We would not do well, however, to refrain from pondering what it might mean were some analogue to the German confessing church to emerge on the American scene. Could it be, for example, that despite our current limitations, a church might emerge which knew how to defend itself against temptation, to align itself with historic Christianity against the prevailing culture, and to draw the consequences in action? Is it still possible to hope for the emergence of a remnant church, a resisting church, a resilient church, a repentant church? I will pursue these questions under three headings: the need for a confessing church today, lessons from the confessing church of yesterday, and prospects for a confessing church tomorrow.

I. Our Unseen Crisis:
The Need for a Confessing Church Today

Our twofold crisis — political and theological — is all the more remarkable for going largely undiagnosed. Those who perceive the political dimension are often those perpetuating theological disarray; those with some inkling of the theological crisis are usually politically naive; and those who plumb neither the political nor the theological crises in their depths and underlying unity are doubtless the great majority. No truly confessing church will be possible for us today if we cannot find the courage to probe our twofold crisis to the end.

Executioners and Their Accomplices: The Political Need

In a recent issue of the *New York Review of Books*, Istvan Deak, a professor of history at Columbia University, published an essay under the title "How Guilty Were the Germans?"[1] The question has contemporary significance, Professor Deak believes, because large-scale acts of brutality are still sanctioned by ideology, and because the belief is still widespread that to correct perceived wrongs, any and every means is legitimate. As examples he cites cases from present-day Iran, North Korea, Zaire, Romania, and Northern Ireland. (With the partial exception of Zaire, his list consists of countries well beyond the sphere of official United States influence, a point to which we shall return.) With the contempo-

---

1. Istvan Deak, "How Guilty Were the Germans?" *New York Review of Books* 31, no. 9 (May 31, 1984): 37-42.

rary situation in mind, Deak focuses on two questions: whether ordinary Germans upheld the Nazi proposition that the Jews should be murdered and whether they possessed significant knowledge of Hitler's Final Solution. The first question is answered with a qualified no. Recent research has uncovered the extraordinary fact that most Germans (including Nazi Party members) had no desire to see Jews brutalized or killed. Widespread disapproval of brutality and killings seems to have been the main reason why persecution of the Jews had to be conducted in secret. Extreme anti-Semitism, Deak notes, was not a primary motive of people who voted for Hitler. They were more likely moved by the misery of the Depression, fear of communism, resurgent nationalism to avenge the Versailles Treaty, and other factors. However, if the Germans did not actively hate the Jews, does this mean they are absolved? Deak thinks otherwise: "What condemns the German population, in my opinion," he writes, "is not that they volunteered to kill, because generally they did not, but that they were indifferent."[2]

The second question concerns how much the Germans knew about Hitler's greatest crime — the slaughter of many millions of Europeans, most prominently Jews. Civilian awareness of Hitler's massacres is difficult to gauge, and Deak notes historical confusion about this question. He estimates that the mass extermination programs directed at the Jews must generally have been known but that their extent remained a secret. Moreover, that non-Jews were being indiscriminately murdered in eastern Europe must also have been public knowledge. "For example," writes Deak, "virtually every German soldier in the Eastern theatre of operations must have been aware that the Russian prisoners of war simply were not fed. This awareness must have been communicated to the Germans at home. After all . . . the Nazis starved to death or otherwise murdered three million non-Jewish Poles and 3,300,000 Russian prisoners of war."[3]

A communication such as Deak surmises must have been common can be found in Eberhard Bethge's biography of Dietrich Bonhoeffer.[4] One of Bonhoeffer's former theology students wrote him a letter from the eastern front which tells of liquidating fifty prisoners of war in a single day, of shooting women and children in the back of the neck for sneaking food to the captured, and of burning down entire villages. All those actions, which by Nuremberg standards would qualify as war crimes, are defended in anxious tones by Bonhoeffer's young correspondent as having been committed because of "military necessity."

2. Deak, p. 40.
3. Deak, p. 41.
4. Eberhard Bethge, *Dietrich Bonhoeffer* (New York: Harper & Row, 1970), p. 608.

Deak concludes with these words: "The German people in 1933 did not unanimously choose Hitler, nor did they, as a whole, obey him gladly and voluntarily. But most of them gave up the values of skepticism and freedom for the sake of immediate material benefits, revenge for Versailles, and national greatness. Even worse, they became or were casual, indifferent, and callous toward persecution."[5] Deak leaves us with a picture in which most Germans were guilty of unspeakable crimes not because they were executioners but because directly or indirectly they were the executioners' accomplices.

That there might be some dark continuity between our society and Nazi Germany is a deeply forbidden thought. Nazi extermination camps are, of course, in a class by themselves. Yet it would be a mistake to allow our moral grids to become so widespread that only the most enormous crimes could show up on our ethical screens.[6] An even worse mistake would be to allow Hitler's enormities to define the bare minimum for what sort of crime is to be condemned, as if anything less were now tolerable. Unconscionable criminal parallels can exist in a qualitative rather than quantitative sense.

If we turn to current U.S. relations to Third World countries, the relevant caption was penned by George Orwell: "The nationalist," he writes, "not only does not disapprove of atrocities committed by his own side, but he has a remarkable capacity for not even hearing about them."[7] Just as so-called necessity, military or otherwise, is the classic excuse of executioners, so ignorance is the classic plea of accomplices. Neither rationalization was accepted at Nuremberg, and still less should we admit them in the church. How much longer will the principle of military necessity or of national security be invoked to justify actions criminal from the standpoint of international law and sinful by canons of the church? How much longer can such actions as the systematic terror bombing of residential areas, torture on an administrative basis, mass murder by government-supported death squads, and other forms of state terrorism be condoned? The systematic slaughter of civilians can never be justified by the standards of Christian ethics, and a government engaging in such crimes, whether directly or by proxy, must be resisted as vigorously as possible.

Let us begin with current U.S. policy in Central America. In the fall of 1983 a disturbing article on our government's policies, entitled "Human Rights

5. Deak, p. 42.

6. I owe this metaphor to Theodore A. Gill, "What Can America Learn from the German Church Struggle?" in *The German Church Struggle and the Holocaust*, ed. Franklin H. Littell and Hubert G. Locke (Detroit: Wayne State University Press, 1974), p. 289.

7. George Orwell, "Notes on Nationalism," in *As I Please: The Collected Essays, Journalism, and Letters of George Orwell*, vol. 3 (New York and London: Harcourt Brace Jovanovich, 1968), p. 370.

Dehumanized," was published in *Foreign Policy* by Charles Maechling, Jr., a prominent international lawyer and a senior associate at the Carnegie Endowment for International Peace. Once again, as so often happened during the Vietnam War,[8] the specter of Nuremberg has come back to haunt us. "In El Salvador and Guatemala," Maechling writes, "the administration's acquiescence in practices of torture and mass murder by client governments comes perilously close to endorsement of offenses condemned at the Nuremberg War Crimes Tribunals — specifically, the indiscriminate killing, torture, and secret detention of unarmed civilians for their political sympathies or support of resistance movements."[9] Although abundant evidence may be obtained from virtually every independent human rights organization in the world, and although a summary of his article appeared prominently in the *New York Times* (September 4, 1983), Maechling's sober pronouncement, like others before and since, has vanished from public notice without a trace.

The Maechling example, which could be multiplied many times over, demonstrates that Orwell was right. Atrocities committed by our own side do not meet with our disapproval, and we have developed a remarkable capacity for not hearing about them. "There is no crime," Orwell wrote, "absolutely none, that cannot be condoned when 'our' side commits it. . . . Loyalty is involved, and so pity ceases to function."[10] Idolatrous loyalty, the will to believe patriotic truths, the lack of skepticism, and the fatal indifference of which Deak warned — these attitudes are so deeply ingrained in our culture (not least in our churches) that it seems as though nothing will ever shake our faith in America's benevolence toward the outside world. The very notion of American exceptionalism — that unlike other nations, wealth and power in our case somehow do not corrupt — is integral to the national myth. Whatever we do must be virtuous, simply because we do it.

Orwell, knowing that every imperial power has justified its actions on "idealistic" grounds, issued the corrective we ought to recall the next time we listen to a presidential press conference. "In our time," he notes, "political speech and writing are largely the defense of the indefensible. Thus political language has to consist largely of euphemism, question-begging and sheer cloudy vagueness."[11]

---

8. See Telford Taylor, *Nuremberg and Vietnam: An American Tragedy* (Chicago: Quadrangle Books, 1970). See also the critical discussion of Taylor's book, "Review Symposium: War Crimes," *Yale Law Journal* 80 (1971): 1456-1528.

9. Charles Maechling, Jr., "Human Rights Dehumanized," *Foreign Policy* 52 (fall 1983): 118.

10. Orwell, "Notes on Nationalism," p. 379.

11. George Orwell, "Politics and the English Language," in *A Collection of Essays* (San Diego: Harcourt Brace Jovanovich, 1946), p. 166.

Then, as if he were describing a scene from El Salvador today or Vietnam a decade ago, though he wrote in 1946, Orwell continues: "Defenseless villages are bombarded from the air, the inhabitants driven out into the countryside, the cattle machine-gunned, the huts set on fire with incendiary bullets: this is called *pacification*. . . . Such phraseology is needed if one wants to name things without calling up mental pictures of them."[12] "Political language," Orwell concludes, ". . . is designed to make lies sound truthful and murder respectable, and to give the appearance of solidity to sheer wind."[13]

Even if one approved of the ends that supposedly guide us, there still come moments, as Michael Waltzer points out, "when the sheer criminality of the means . . . overwhelms and annuls all righteous intentions."[14] The great unexamined question at the heart of our political crisis today is the question of the sheer criminality of the means. That is not to say the question of ends is unimportant. The ends for which the United States installs its clients and fights its wars in the Third World are matters of grave importance. Yet even if U.S. foreign policy were not governed by narrow business interests; even if it were not more concerned about markets, cheap labor, and investments than about human rights; even if it had not grown hard on communism only to become soft on fascism or subfascism such as one finds in South Korea, Chile, or Zaire; even if it had the best intentions in the world, the question would still remain about the sheer criminality of the means. The question extends from the sponsoring of torture on an administrative basis,[15] to the destruction of civilian populations as required by doc-

12. Orwell, "Politics," pp. 166-67.

13. Orwell, "Politics," p. 171.

14. Michael Waltzer, "Moral Judgment in Time of War," in *War and Morality,* ed. Richard A. Wassertom (Belmont, Calif.: Wadsworth Publishing Co., 1970), p. 61.

15. A recent example of how the U.S. government has provided clandestine sponsorship to those who torture on an administrative basis may be found in Allan Nairn, "Behind the Death Squads," *Progressive* 48, no. 5 (May 1984). Occasionally indications of such sponsorship surface in more establishment sectors of the mass media: see, for example, Seymour M. Hersh, "Ex-Analyst Says C.I.A. Rejected Warning on Shah," *New York Times,* January 7, 1979. Hersh quotes Jesse Leaf, the CIA's chief analyst on Iran from 1968 to 1973, as saying that the CIA conducted torture seminars for SAVAK, Iran's dreaded secret police, and that the seminars "were based on German torture techniques from World War II." A more systematic account may be found in Michael T. Klare and Cynthia Arnon, *Supplying Repression: U.S. Support for Authoritarian Regimes Abroad* (Washington, D.C.: Institute for Policy Studies, 1981). Also valuable is A. J. Langguth, *Hidden Terrors: The Truth about U.S. Police Operations in Latin America* (New York: Pantheon Books, 1978). Above all, however, mention must be made of the indefatigable, extensively documented, and largely ignored writings of Noam Chomsky and Edward S. Herman, especially their joint work, *The Political Economy of Human Rights,* vol. 1 (Boston: South End Press, 1979). I am greatly indebted to their analysis; the article by Seymour Hersh, mentioned above, which they cite on p. 364 n. 40, is typical of the kind of material they are able to glean from an assiduous reading of establishment

trines of counterinsurgency,[16] to the development of weaponry that cannot be used without slaughtering large numbers of noncombatants. These latter weapons, which threaten to unhinge the future, call for special consideration.

The United States has invested heavily in indiscriminate weapons of mass destruction.[17] It has also used them and sold them to other countries. Recall the kinds of weapons the United States used in Vietnam,[18] some of which are again being used in El Salvador today:[19] napalm, described by peasants as fire from the

---

sources. Apart from political considerations, which no doubt are dominant, perhaps one reason their work has not received the attention it deserves is the highly censorious tone in which they write, regardless of how justified it may be by the subject matter.

16. For a summary of these doctrines, see Waltzer, pp. 58-60.

17. For a critical survey of the U.S. arsenal, see the Boston Study Group, *The Price of Defense* (New York: Times Books, 1979). For the eroding difference between conventional and nuclear weapons, see Michael T. Klare, "Conventional Arms, Military Doctrine, and Nuclear War: The Vanishing Firebreak," *Thought* 59, no. 232 (March 1984): 55-63. For the way in which wars in recent decades have led to a progressive increase in civilian destruction, see Ruth Leger Sivard, *World Military and Social Expenditures* (Leesburg, Va.: World Priorities, 1982), p. 15.

George Kennan's recent comments are worth pondering:

I had always resisted the suggestion that war, as a phenomenon of international life, could be totally ruled out. . . .

I am now bound to say that while the earliest possible elimination of nuclear weaponry is of no less vital importance in my eyes than it ever was, this would not be enough, in itself, to give Western civilization even an adequate chance of survival. War itself, as a means of settling differences at least between great industrial powers, will have to be in some way ruled out; and with it there will have to be dismantled (for without this the whole outlawing of war would be futile) the greater part of the vast military establishments now maintained with a view to the possibility that war might take place. The weapons of this age — even the so-called conventional ones — are of such destructiveness that there can be no clear line between the discriminate ones and the weapons of mass destruction. . . .

No one could be more aware than I am of the difficulty of ruling out war among great states. (George Kennan, *The Nuclear Delusion* [New York: Pantheon Books, 1982], pp. xxviii-xxix)

18. See, for example, Frank Harvey, *Air War — Vietnam* (New York: Bantam Books, 1967). See also Robert Crichton, "Our Air War," *New York Review of Books* 9, no. 1 (January 4, 1968). These works are conveniently summarized in Phillip Slater, *The Pursuit of Loneliness* (Boston: Beacon Press, 1970), pp. 29-52.

19. See, for example, the interview with Charles Clements, an American medical doctor who has worked among Salvadoran peasants, in Alexander Cockburn and James Ridgeway, "On the Guapaza Front: Vietnam in El Salvador," *Village Voice*, May 3, 1983. See also Chris Hedges, "Salvadorans Allege Use of Napalm, Phosphorus Bombing Near Volcano," *National Catholic Reporter* 20, no. 28 (May 4, 1984): 19. For a description of Vietnam-style terror bombing, see Chris Hedges, "El Salvador War Escalates, Populated Areas Targeted," *National Catholic Reporter* 20, no. 27 (April 27, 1984): 1ff. Also Janis L. Zandel, "With the Peasants in El Salvador: Walking and Running, Hiding and Dying," *Christianity and Crisis* (July 22, 1985): 285-88.

sky, which rolls and splatters over wide areas, incinerating everything in sight, including homes, farms, even shelters; white phosphorus bombs, also indiscriminate, designed among other things to embed in human flesh burning pieces of phosphorus which cannot be extinguished by water; cluster bombs, perhaps the deadliest of "conventional" weapons, by which an area more than a mile long and a quarter-mile wide can be shredded by a million steel fragments. Recall also the clear and historic teaching of the church that the killing of noncombatants by direct intention — even if undertaken as a means to a much greater good — is equivalent to murder and a clear moral wrong. (Some moral theologians and ethicists, of course, attempt to legitimize indiscriminate weaponry on the grounds that its use does not kill noncombatants by direct but only by indirect intention. This is sometimes called "collateral damage," a term Orwell would have appreciated. To my mind, weaponry that cannot be used without violating the most minimal rules of warfare transcends any fine academic distinctions between "direct" and "indirect" intention. Certainly to the dead it is a distinction without a difference.)[20] Recall, finally, the church's long-standing inability to utter a clear and unequivocal *No!* to these developments in a way that commands consent and commitment from the pews, and you have a good picture of our crisis in its underlying unity and depths.

How can we as Christians avoid the conclusion drawn by George Kennan that "the great weapons of mass destruction — and nuclear weapons are not the only conceivable ones — should never be in human hands . . ."?[21] "The real problem at issue," he wrote as early as 1950, ". . . is the problem of our attitude toward weapons of mass destruction in general, and the role we allot to these weapons in our own military planning."[22] Kennan faces us with a great either/ or. "We cannot get away from it: either we approve of mass destruction as a means of warfare regardless of the disasters it holds for much of humanity, our own civilization included . . . or we disapprove of it, in which case we should . . . take the consequences . . . and . . . resolve that we shall not be the first to inaugu-

---

20. The distinction between "direct" and "indirect" intention when it comes to killing noncombatants is perhaps most strongly associated with the work of Paul Ramsey, especially in his book *The Just War* (New York: Scribners, 1968). An internal critique of Ramsey's logic, different from but compatible with my own, has been advanced recently by Douglas P. Lackey, *Moral Principles and Nuclear Weapons* (Totowa, N.J.: Rowman & Allanheld, 1984): ". . . Ramsey's insistence on the connection between the wrongfulness of X and the wrongfulness of intending X, his connection of intention with desire rather than with foreseeability, leads to the rather bizarre result that it is morally preferable to kill 10 million people unintentionally than one million people intentionally, even when the 10 million deaths are perfectly foreseeable" (p. 207). Lackey argues that our best moral alternative is the nonpossession of nuclear weapons.

21. Kennan, p. 72.

22. Kennan, p. 3.

rate this means of warfare — that we will find other means to assure our defense."[23] That is why from the very beginning of the nuclear age, Kennan has insisted on the principle of "no first use," which requires a completely different military structure than the one we developed, and on the eventual elimination of nuclear weapons themselves. "I see no solution to the problem," he writes, "other than the complete elimination of these and all other weapons of mass destruction from national arsenals; and the sooner we move toward that solution, and the greater courage we show in doing so, the safer we will be."[24] As things now stand, however, our government has planned to increase by 70 percent the total number of American nuclear weapons, from about twenty-five thousand to more than forty thousand, and to deploy a whole new generation of them.[25]

Too often in the past, especially in this terrible century in which we live, a century marked perhaps more than any other by the perpetration of unspeakable atrocities, Christians have remained silent, have not taken risks, have supported the status quo when their faith should have moved them to do otherwise. As professing and committed Christians, we can no longer afford to perpetuate this inaction and this silence. If Christians will not speak out and put themselves on the line while there is still time, then who will?

When I survey the great vault of corpses and mutilated bodies that begins with Hiroshima and Nagasaki, that stretches to the Indochinese corridor, where our government dropped the explosive equivalent of one Nagasaki bomb every week for seven and a half years,[26] and that extends now to the torture chambers and death-squad barracks of Central America and beyond; and when I contemplate the even greater vault of corpses that awaits us in the future and that will

---

23. Kennan, pp. 107-8.

24. Kennan, p. 160.

25. Andrew Winnick, "Rapid Deployment and Nuclear War: Reagan's New Military Strategy," *Socialist Review* 73 (January-February 1984): 21. Our government also plans, as things now stand, to pursue a massive research and development project designed to place vast numbers of weapons in outer space (the president's so-called Star Wars proposal). Apart from major questions of feasibility and cost, at least two others have been raised. The first concerns mere prudence. According to Richard Garwin and John Pike, a program for nullifying nuclear weapons from outer space would lead to an "inherently unstable" confrontation between the United States and the Soviet Union, "needing only the smallest spark to bring on a nuclear confrontation" (Garwin and Pike, "Space Weapons," *Bulletin of the Atomic Scientists* 40 [May 1984]). The other question, even more serious morally, has to do with the role of space-based weapons in a first-strike nuclear strategy. For background see chap. 8, "Space Warfare," in Robert C. Aldridge, *First Strike! The Pentagon's Strategy for Nuclear War* (Boston: South End Press, 1983).

26. Amory B. Lovins et al., "Nuclear Power and Nuclear Bombs," *Foreign Affairs* 58 (summer 1980): 1175.

surely signify the end of Western civilization and perhaps of life itself on earth, should something serious not soon be done to reverse the nuclear arms race; and when I remember Deak's strictures about a casual, indifferent, and callous people, then I am forced to the painful conclusion that today to be an American is to be an executioner or, what is much the same thing, an accomplice to the executioners.

It will immediately be objected that I have confined myself to the culpability of the United States and have neglected the crimes of other nations, especially those under communism. In reply I can only ask how the crimes of others in any way detract from our own. Furthermore, why concentrate on the crimes of others when they are constantly held aloft in this society for all to behold? Finally, why protest against crimes one can do almost nothing about instead of against those one might, in concert with others, still do something to rectify?

We do not expect to live in a world without murder, wrote Albert Camus in his essay "Neither Victims nor Executioners," but we can at least fight for a world in which murder is no longer legitimate. "All I ask," he said, "is that, in the midst of a murderous world, we agree to reflect on murder and to make a choice. After that, we can distinguish those who accept the consequences of being murderers themselves or the accomplices of murderers, and those who refuse to do so with all their force and being."[27] The need for a confessing church in America today, politically speaking, is the need for a grouping of Christians "resolved to speak out clearly and to pay up personally,"[28] who realize that Camus's "terrible dividing line" actually exists,[29] and who know on which side they are awaited by their Lord.

Protestantism without Reformation: The Theological Need

Our political crisis is so severe and plainly intractable that it may seem hard to imagine a theological crisis to match it. Two points can immediately be made: First, it is a symptom of the crisis itself — and one from which none of us are immune — to believe that the subject matter of theology is not a matter of life and death, that it does not make binding claims to truth, and that it does not finally force us to decisions of ultimate consequence. Second, our tendencies toward self-destruction, which could scarcely be writ larger than they are today,

27. Albert Camus, "Neither Victims nor Executioners," *Politics* (July-August 1947): 146-47.

28. Albert Camus, "The Unbeliever and Christians," in *Resistance, Rebellion, and Death* (New York: Modern Library, 1963), p. 53.

29. Camus, "Neither Victims nor Executioners," p. 147.

can be interpreted theologically as a drastic outcome of our underlying universal condition. To turn from God (sin) inevitably leads to self-destruction (death); that is the biblical diagnosis. Despite our abandonment of God, we are not abandoned in return (grace); that is the biblical hope. In these terms our political crisis is not autonomous, and to obscure either the diagnosis or the hope contributes directly or indirectly to our collapse. The theological crisis in America today may be summed up by saying that such contributions occur with breathtaking regularity.

Perhaps the definitive assessment of the American theological scene was produced by Dietrich Bonhoeffer in an essay called "Protestantism without Reformation."[30] Written five years after the Barmen Declaration at the end of Bonhoeffer's second American tour in 1939, it not only betrays the influence of Barmen but also analyzes the American religious character so cannily as to make Bonhoeffer our theological Tocqueville. The analysis covers six points: (1) the nature of a confessing church, (2) truth and tolerance, (3) the freedom of the gospel, (4) church and state, (5) black church vitality, and (6) the dislocation of doctrine. (No brief summary can do justice to the richness of Bonhoeffer's discussion.)

1. The Nature of a Confessing Church

Bonhoeffer had no interest in detailing ecclesiastical oddities, but he was deeply concerned to figure out why the American church struck him as alien and strange. Neutral observations of the historical, political, or sociological variety could not satisfy him. What he wanted was "a serious encounter," "a binding discussion," which to him could occur only on theological ground (p. 88). He found himself caught in an inward struggle to articulate as charitably as possible what he knew he finally had to say, yet his basic, most considered judgment could not help sounding severe: "God," he was to conclude, "has granted American Christianity no Reformation" (p. 112).

Bonhoeffer's first insight was that American churches do not understand themselves as churches; they understand themselves as "denominations." This is not a theological concept. It is not oriented toward the creed as the standard that determines the church's basic identity. Strictly speaking, therefore, denominations cannot be called confessing churches, for they exhibit little or no ur-

---

30. Dietrich Bonhoeffer, "Protestantism without Reformation," in *No Rusty Swords,* ed. Edwin H. Robertson (London: Fontana Library, 1970), pp. 88-113. References which follow in the text are to this work. (In this edition the title is misrepresented as "Protestantism with Reformation.")

gency about the question of theological truth. Members of denominations are likely to feel that the church's identity is more a matter of life and work than of confessions and creeds. There is a strength here as well as a weakness, but the basic orientation makes it difficult, Bonhoeffer observed, "for the American denominations to understand aright the struggle for a confessing church" (p. 97, rev.).

2. Truth and Tolerance

Although confessional stringency is conspicuous by its absence, tolerance and forbearance abound. In American denominationalism, Bonhoeffer notes, "the concept of tolerance becomes the basic principle of everything Christian. Any intolerance is in itself unchristian." Theology and church in liberal America are unlikely to press for a decision against clear distortions of biblical truth. Bonhoeffer connects the "peculiar relativism" of American Christianity to the country's history as a refuge from religious persecution (p. 99).

3. The Freedom of the Gospel

Praise for the nation's religious freedom resounds everywhere from America's pulpits. Yet freedom from state intervention is by no means essential to the church. Freedom in the deeper sense is not a possibility guaranteed by the state, but an event granted again and again by grace. "The essential freedom of the church is not a gift of the world to the church, but the freedom of the Word of God to gain a hearing" (p. 100). The church's true freedom is present only where it actually proclaims God's Word. It is not found where the church has possibilities, "but only where the gospel really and in its own power makes room for itself on earth, even and precisely when no such possibilities are offered to it. . . . But where thanks for institutional freedom must be rendered by the sacrifice of freedom of preaching, the church is in chains, even if it believes itself to be free" (pp. 100, 101, italics dropped).

4. Church and State

In America the principle of church/state separation has assumed "almost dogmatic significance" (p. 101). Yet nowhere is church participation in public life more pronounced than in this country with no state church. The explanation for this apparent paradox is that American separation of church and state rests not on the doctrine of two kingdoms, but on the doctrine that God's kingdom limits all earthly power. The church is thus free from any unbounded claim by the state but assumes responsibility for guiding formulation of state policy. Much of the secularization of American Christianity derives from the fact that in practice the church often adopts a highly secular role to the neglect of other matters and "from the enthusiastic claim of the church to universal influence on the world" (p. 104).

5. Black Church Vitality

The historic American discrimination against blacks, even to the point of segregated worship, indicates "a deep cleft in the church of Jesus Christ." "Black and white hear the Word and receive the sacrament in separation. They have no common worship" (p. 108). After sketching the origins of racial segregation in the church, Bonhoeffer sounds the most enthusiastic note in the essay: "One may also say that nowhere is revival preaching still so vigorous and so widespread as among the Negroes, that here the gospel of Jesus Christ, the savior of the sinner, is really preached and accepted with great welcome and visible emotion" (p. 109).

6. The Dislocation of Doctrine

It is appropriate to mention theology in last place, because that is more or less the position it occupies in American Christianity. The dislocation of doctrine by practice, or by "religion and ethics," is perhaps the most salient feature of American Christian life (apart from fundamentalist circles, which Bonhoeffer considered hidebound and uninteresting). Characteristic is the utter neglect of Christology. Even in the most significant and creative of American theologians, who certainly have something to offer (Bonhoeffer thinks especially here of Reinhold Niebuhr), a full-fledged doctrine of Jesus Christ's person and redemptive work is not found. (Niebuhr's Gifford Lectures, *The Nature and Destiny of Man*, had yet to be given — whether they would have satisfied Bonhoeffer is open to question.) The dislocation of doctrine in general and of Jesus Christ in particular is the chief reason, as Bonhoeffer saw it, for the "almost incalculably deep opposition" between American Christianity and the Continental Reformation (p. 110).

Bonhoeffer's closing statement deserves to be quoted at length:

> American theology and the American church as a whole have never been able to understand the meaning of "criticism" by the Word of God and all that signifies. Right to the last they do not understand that God's "criticism" touches every religion, the Christianity of the churches and the sanc-

tification of Christians, and that God has founded his church beyond religion and beyond ethics. A symptom of this is the general adherence to natural theology. . . . But because of this, the person and work of Jesus Christ must, for theology, sink into the background and in the long run remain misunderstood, because it is not recognized as the sole ground of radical judgment and radical forgiveness. (p. 113)

Throughout Bonhoeffer's essay, the imperiled situation of the confessing church in Germany is never far from his mind. Only by virtue of a vigorous contemporary declaration of faith, the Barmen Declaration, had this church survived the twin dangers of temptation from within and persecution from without. It was a church which knew that the Christian community lives only by the subject matter to which confession and creed bear witness. It knew how to rise above relativism to resist clear distortions of biblical truth. When faced with no possibilities, it had found that on earth God's Word creates its own possibilities and does not return empty. It was a church which had resisted the imposition of racial segregation within its ranks. Above all it was a church which, clinging to Jesus Christ as the center of its life, had separated itself from natural theology and attached itself for judgment and renewal solely to God's Word. "Culture shock" would probably be too tame to describe what Bonhoeffer, fresh from the church struggle in Germany, must have experienced in his final encounter with the American church.

Two recent publications show why it is still difficult for American Christians to understand what Bonhoeffer called "the struggle for a confessing church." No two books are likely to be regarded as more divergent, and even more at odds with each other, than Richard Neuhaus's *Naked Public Square: Religion and Democracy in America* (Eerdmans, 1984) and Harvey Cox's *Religion in the Secular City: Toward a Postmodern Theology* (Simon & Schuster, 1984). Few books dealing with theological topics have been accompanied by so much media promotion and advance praise. Here, apparently, are the books many people have been waiting for. Although we cannot examine the contents in detail, we can ask a basic question: Viewed separately and together, do these books contribute to or detract from the formation of a theologically vital confessing church in America today?

From a political conservative like Neuhaus, who sees in Jerry Falwell a potential hope for the future of democracy (p. 176) and who desires nothing more earnestly than an effacement of the memory of Vietnam (p. 184), one can reasonably hope for enlightenment only on matters of theology. It is at this point, however, that his book seems most confused. The argument in general is vague, repetitious, and self-contradictory, but nowhere more so than in its central thesis. Generally speaking, the thesis is that although democracy cannot long thrive without religious legitimation, religion in our society has been banished from the "public square" so that we are in danger of being overrun by communist totalitarianism if something is not soon done about it. The interesting part of this thesis has to do with what Neuhaus means by "religion" and "religious legitimation."

Three competing and mutually incompatible definitions of "religion" vie with one another in the text. Following Neuhaus, we may call them "particularist religion," "lowest-common-denominator religion," and the religion of a "community of virtue." The idea of a community of virtue is not incompatible with the idea of a confessing church. It implies a community whose religion cultivates the integrity or virtue of its members, however defined, and whose primary concern does not as such involve exerting direct influence on the public realm. Unfortunately, Neuhaus shows little interest in this form of religion and mentions it only vaguely in passing. Most of the book has Neuhaus swinging curiously back and forth between the other two religious forms. At a maximum he hankers for a "Christian America" — a term he actually uses (pp. 122ff.) — in which as a normal part of public discourse Christian symbols would be invoked to explain and sanctify the meaning of imperial America "within the larger purposes of God in world-historical change," much as Eusebius long ago provided the same benefit of clergy for imperial Rome (p. 61). ("Constantinianism" is explicitly endorsed; see p. 172.) At a pinch, however, Neuhaus settles for a religion of the lowest common denominator if it will do its duty of religious legitimation (p. 141); most of the time his preferred religious vocabulary is of the deracinated type which speaks nebulously of "the transcendent," "experiences of the absolute," and other assorted nonentities.

If one asks just what Neuhaus wants religion to legitimate, the answer is America's role in the world, but at this point (if not sooner) Neuhaus would vigorously object, insisting that what he wants religion to legitimate is not America's role in the world but democracy. He could appeal to many passages in the book which say just that. Unfortunately, however, democracy and America's role are so firmly combined in his mind that he seems incapable of imagining the former without the latter. The litmus test, furthermore, of just what Neuhaus wants to legitimate is whether he can countenance a systematic critique of America's role in the name of democratic ideals. The fact is that he cannot. Anyone with serious doubts about America's current influence for good is accused not of poor judgment but of disloyalty (p. 73). Neuhaus implies that such persons are guilty of betraying their country (p. 75). Denial of the overall benevolence of American influence is taken as though it were a betrayal of democracy itself. By resorting to rhetoric of disloyalty and betrayal at the crucial point, Neuhaus displays a striking incapacity to differentiate between the American system and democratic ideals, thereby indicating how thoroughly he equates them. In any case, whether the object is America or democracy or both, religion appears here strictly for purposes of legitimation. Neuhaus is quite right to suggest that any reduction of religion to the role of social utility is a form of blasphemy (p. 44), but all things considered, I cannot see what else he is doing in this book.

The clearest difference between Richard Neuhaus and Harvey Cox is in their political views. Whereas Neuhaus laments such things as "the runaway divorce rate, the pornography plague, the banning of God from the schoolhouse, the rise in homosexuality," "the disappearance of civility," and "the disease of secularization,"[31] Cox wants "a theology that affirms social justice, the rights of the poor, a communal understanding of salvation . . ." (*Religion in the Secular City*, p. 25). He endorses the idea of "class conflict" (p. 157) and underscores the nuclear peril of our age (p. 78).

Cox has also written the more engaging book. He is master of the vivid description, the telling detail, the well-honed phrase. Among theologians writing in English, he is perhaps the best stylist we have. The danger inherent in his brand of theological journalism, which he carries out at a very high level, is an almost unavoidable tendency toward glibness, as noted by more than one critic. Riding the crest of the latest trend can no doubt be exhilarating, but one always wonders what is left once the wave has hit the shore.

The trend this time is something called "postmodernism." The modern world is passing away, and the postmodern is struggling to be born. What this means for theology is a new conversation partner and a new set of problems. The old conversation partner was the skeptics, usually a highly educated, socially privileged group; the new conversation partner will be the poor in the struggle to throw off their chains. The new set of problems will be how to maintain liberating practices based on theological norms in the midst of an increasingly pluralistic world. Resources to solve these problems will be found only among those pockets of the theological community which have not bought into the modernist project. Cox therefore turns to the fundamentalists in the United States and the liberationists in Latin America to see if he can find what he is looking for. Much of the book is an account of this quest by way of de-

---

31. These phrasings are from Cox's discussion of contemporary conservatism (*Religion in the Secular City: Toward a Postmodern Theology* [New York: Simon & Schuster, 1984], p. 75), but they describe Neuhaus's positions well. See *The Naked Public Square: Religion and Democracy in America* (Grand Rapids: Eerdmans, 1984), pp. 75 (divorce); 111 (pornography); 147-48 (banning God from public school); 96-97, 111 (homosexuality); 55-77 (civility); passim (secularization).

lightful firsthand experiences. At the end the fundamentalists are found wanting for capitulating to that most modern of inventions, the electronic media,
and therefore (Cox thinks) to modernity; whereas the liberationists have yet to
appreciate the pressures exerted by pluralism on theology, though otherwise
Cox affirms their intent. Nor does the liberationist shortcoming seem to matter
much, since Cox concludes that what really counts is not one's theological beliefs so much as which side one takes in "the combat against social evil." "Sacred
stories" can only be judged by whether they do or do not serve this end; and re-
ligionists of all stripes are invited to put other differences aside by celebrating
"the promise of life" (p. 238), whatever that may be, and by appreciating one
another's "expressions of the same primal reality" (p. 249). (Whether the reality
they express is the same, primal, or even real is not discussed.)[32]

One problem with Cox's analysis, which many will be sure to note, is that
there really is nothing "postmodern" about it. At best it simply rearranges the
furniture in the old modernist room. Perhaps theology is just getting around to
appropriating Marx's insights about how the poor are exploited and Lessing's
insights in *Nathan the Wise* about the plurality and underlying unity of religions, but that hardly seems any reason to dignify the affair with an exalted
term like "postmodern." After all, why have modern skeptics been so skeptical if
not largely because their encounter with religious pluralism convinced them
that all religious truth claims are arbitrary? Nor are Cox's constructive proposals about how to cope with pluralism in any meaningful sense "postmodern."
The modernist theological strategy, when confronted with the fact of pluralism,
has always been to downgrade the cognitive element of religious truth claims in
favor of the affective dimension of religious symbols and the practical consequences one hopes to extract from them. Cox's appeal to "combat against social
evil" (practical) and to "expressions of the same primal reality" (affective) in no
way removes us from the familiar modernist rut.

Theologically speaking, what Cox and Neuhaus have in common is more
impressive and important than anything that sets them apart. In their com-
monality they typify the problems Bonhoeffer diagnosed in American theological discussion. Both, despite themselves, cannot help thinking of religion primarily in terms of social utility, though Cox is more candid about this than
Neuhaus; and both manifest much the same pervasive anxiety about influence
that is well-nigh inevitable when in a pluralistic society some type of culture

---

32. For a lively and provocative discussion which gives qualified support to a position
like Cox's, see Peter Berger, *The Heretical Imperative* (Garden City, N.Y.: Anchor Press/
Doubleday, 1980), esp. pp. 143-72. For a powerful counterargument, see George Lindbeck, *The
Nature of Doctrine: Religion and Theology in a Postliberal Age* (Philadelphia: Westminster, 1984),
pp. 30-72.

formation — whether imperialist or liberationist does not matter — is virtually the only meaningful role for religion. (Cox and Neuhaus would both deny that for them this is religion's "only" role; suffice it to say that this role seems to be the only thing that gets their juices flowing.)

What unites Cox and Neuhaus, in other words, is a common assumption that religion and culture are related by mutual immanence. Culture, as the saying goes, is the bearer of religion. For Neuhaus this means a symbiosis between the nation with the soul of a church and the church with the soul of a nation, whereas for Cox it means revolution ratified by religion and religion by revolution. Either way we are not far from the view that defines Christ by norms of culture. "The terms differ," wrote H. Richard Niebuhr, "but the logic is always the same: Christ is identified with what men conceive to be their finest ideals, their noblest institutions, and their best philosophy."[33]

The Christ of culture tends to be connotative and even derivative, to endorse but not to reign, precisely because he depends for his reality on our capacity to endow him with meaning. Where Jesus Christ is worshipped for reasons of cultural utility, he is not worshipped as Lord, and to that extent he is not worshipped at all. The Lordship of Jesus Christ over and beyond all relativities of human culture is, so far as the church is concerned, a matter of life and death, a binding truth and a decision of ultimate consequence. That is why Bonhoeffer insisted that "God has founded his church beyond religion and beyond ethics." That is why he stressed the meaning of "criticism" by God's Word and the importance of confession and creed. And that is why he worried so much about a relativism that could not resist distortions of biblical truth. Until we can move beyond "Protestantism without Reformation," we have little hope for the emergence of a theologically articulate confessing church.

II. The Clear and the Vague:
Lessons from the Confessing Church of Yesterday

The great lesson from the confessing church of yesterday is the Barmen Declaration itself, and one decisive lesson about the Barmen Declaration was the Stuttgart Confession of Guilt issued in October 1945. The Stuttgart Confession indicates that the Barmen Declaration was a peculiar mixture of the clear and the vague, of the theologically explicit and the politically all-too-implicit. It suggests that an explicit theology without an equally explicit corresponding politics will ill serve any future confessing church. "Unending suffering has

33. H. Richard Niebuhr, *Christ and Culture* (New York: Harper & Row, 1951), p. 103.

been brought by us to many peoples and countries," declared the confessing church leaders at Stuttgart — to the immediate and intense scandal of their fellow countrymen and countrywomen.[34] "We accuse ourselves," they continued, "that we did not witness more courageously, pray more faithfully, believe more joyously, love more ardently."[35] The church in America today might consider beginning with its own confession of guilt, even if its resources are scarce for a theological declaration of faith. In other words, perhaps this time it would be well if the sequence from Barmen to Stuttgart were reversed.

For his part, Karl Barth found even the Stuttgart Confession too vague. Without a more specific enumeration of crucial matters (such as anti-Semitism and unchecked militarism), he felt the Confession might dwindle to an exercise in unrepentance.[36] As early as 1935, Barth had warned the confessing church not to shrink from political consequences he considered to flow from Barmen. The confessing church, he wrote, "has fought hard to a certain extent for the freedom and purity of its proclamation, but it has, for example, remained silent on the action against the Jews, on the amazing treatment of political opponents, on the suppression of the freedom of the press in the new Germany and on so much else against which the Old Testament prophets would certainly have spoken out."[37] Even the confessing church's resistance to Nazi assimilation of its internal affairs had difficulty surviving the pressures of a state at war, and by 1941 Barth found himself writing to churches abroad that the German church struggle had "now almost come to a stop."[38]

Our purpose is not to blame the German confessing church for its shortcomings, especially considering the severity of its persecution for even limited resistance, and especially considering the great theological heritage it has bequeathed to us. If shortcomings cannot be overlooked, it is only because we cannot afford to ignore them for the sake of the future. As Barth himself pointed out in 1942, most members of the confessing church "thought they could agree to, or at least sympathize with, the political and social aims of National Socialism." "Up until the year 1934, while I was still in Germany," he ad-

---

34. See *Die Schuld der Kirche, Dokumente und Reflexionen zur Stuttgarter Schulderklärung vom 18./19. Oktober 1945*, ed. Martin Greschat (Munich: Chr. Kaiser Verlag, 1982). For a translation of the Stuttgart Confession, see Franklin H. Littell, "From Barmen (1934) to Stuttgart (1945): The Path of the Confessing Church in Germany," *Journal of Church and State* 3 (1961): 41-52, on p. 50.

35. Littell, p. 50.

36. Eberhard Busch, *Karl Barth* (Philadelphia: Fortress, 1976), pp. 329, 341.

37. Karl Barth, *The German Church Conflict* (Richmond: John Knox, 1965), p. 45.

38. Karl Barth, *A Letter to Great Britain from Switzerland* (London: Sheldon Press, 1941), p. 17.

mitted, "I myself thought I could relegate my political opposition to the background" and work only along the lines of resisting Nazi intrusion in church affairs.[39] Indeed, one cannot read through the history of the German confessing church without sensing the anxiety felt by its adherents that charges of disloyalty to the nation would be made to stick against them. In his book *The Nazi Persecution of the Churches,* historian John S. Conway identifies this anxiety as a decisive reason for failure. "With the refusal of most churchmen to follow a course of political and theological disloyalty," he writes, "hopes for a centre of resistance to Nazism quickly faded, while Luther's supposed teaching of obedience to the state was extended and misinterpreted to cover the submission of increasing numbers of Churchmen."[40] "Their attempts to create an effective opposition were doomed to failure from the start," he goes on, " — indeed considering the psychological obstacles in their way, it is perhaps surprising that an opposition existed at all. For most Germans, national loyalty dictated their political outlook, even in the Confessing Church."[41]

Karl Barth was convinced that our political outlook ought to be dictated by our loyalty to Jesus Christ. He was also convinced that the Barmen Declaration contained sufficient guidance and force to dispel from the church all political outlooks dictated by narrow national loyalties. Although history did not always bear out his second conviction in German confessing church practice, his first conviction remains unassailable; and his second conviction is, I believe, still correct in principle. Properly understood, Barmen lays a foundation for political resistance by the church. A brief glance at the political implications of the first article of the Barmen Declaration will back this claim.

The positive thesis of Article I runs as follows: "Jesus Christ, as he is attested for us in Holy Scripture, is the one Word of God which we have to hear and which we have to trust and obey in life and in death."[42] Stated more formally, this thesis can be interpreted to mean that in matters of faith and practice, the voice of Jesus Christ, as conveyed to us by the witness of Scripture, is both necessary and sufficient. Regarding faith, this is the one voice necessary and sufficient for us to trust and obey in life and in death. No other voice can carry this authority, for no other voice is the Word of God.

As is true for every article of Barmen, this positive thesis is followed by a negative. We may paraphrase it as saying that no other voice apart from or

39. Karl Barth, *The Church and the War* (New York: Macmillan, 1944), p. 8.

40. John S. Conway, *The Nazi Persecution of the Churches* (New York: Basic Books, 1968), p. 86.

41. Conway, p. 87.

42. English translation in Arthur C. Cochrane, *The Church's Confession under Hitler* (Philadelphia: Westminster, 1962), p. 239.

alongside the authentic, scriptural voice of Jesus Christ may become a source of authority for what the church proclaims and teaches. Here we have Barmen's famous rejection of natural theology. Two points about it are important to note.

First, it is primarily directed against natural theology in the form of culture-religion. Where Jesus Christ "no longer speaks the first and last word, but only at best an additional word," wrote Barth, an "assimilated and domesticated theology" will be the inevitable result.[43] Such domesticated theology may emerge in apparently agreeable and sophisticated forms, but once allowed in principle, it relativizes Christ's voice so that it is no longer understood as necessary, sufficient, and supreme. This relativizing is fatal partly because it undercuts any decisive defense against culture-religion in its more tribal and barbarous forms. The logic of the one admits the logic of the other. The Christ of natural theology is always openly or secretly the relativized Christ of culture. The trajectory of natural theology leads from the Christ who is not supreme to the Christ who is not sufficient and finally to the Christ who is not necessary. Culture-religion, relativization, and domestication or assimilation indicate that the Lordship of Jesus Christ is no longer believed in or understood. By rejecting all independent or second authorities, Barmen reaffirmed Christ's Lordship against the inroads of cultural self-assertion in the church.

Second, it is important to realize that Barmen's rejection of natural theology is epistemological in force. It does not imply that nothing good, beautiful, true, or worth noticing exists outside of Scripture or the church. "God may speak to us," wrote Barth, "through Russian communism or a flute concerto, a blossoming shrub or a dead dog. We shall do well to listen to him if he really does so."[44] No such object, however, can ever be allowed to become a source of authority for the church's preaching, for no such object can have independent revelatory or epistemological status. Only by criteria derived from the one authentic scriptural voice of Christ can we know if God might be speaking to us in those ways or not.

The political implications of the first article are spelled out, directly and indirectly, by the rest of the Barmen Declaration. Only the most cursory notice of their direction can be indicated here. Article II, which declares that no area of life can be said to be outside the Lordship of Jesus Christ, implies that christocentric theology may not be severed from politics or from political judgments in the church. Article III, which claims the church as the exclusive possession of Jesus Christ, carries the reverse implication that no christocentric

43. Karl Barth, *Church Dogmatics* II/1 (Edinburgh: T. & T. Clark, 1957), p. 163.
44. Karl Barth, *Church Dogmatics* I/1 (Edinburgh: T. & T. Clark, 1936), p. 60.

theology may be subordinated or reduced to political programs or ideals. In other words, whereas Article II implies that theology and politics may not be separated or divided, Article III implies that they may not be confused or mixed. Article IV rejects any imposition on the church of an alien form of polity and implies the nonconformity of the church to the world. Article V interprets the traditional two-kingdoms doctrine in a christocentric way so that our hierarchies of loyalty are clear and so that, in the church's eyes, only conditional loyalty is enjoyed by the state. Finally, Article VI, which rejects any "arbitrarily chosen desires, purposes and plans" while affirming service to the message of God's free grace, implies that all political activity engaged in by the church will carry the basic status of a witness to grace.

Of these several themes, two are most important: Barmen's interpretation of the two-kingdoms doctrine and Barmen's overall suggestion that theology and politics stand in a pattern of differentiated hierarchy and unity.

Two competing understandings of the status of state authority have contended with one another in the history of the church.[45] The one view, which held sway in German Protestantism right down to the confessing church (as well as elsewhere), believed Scripture to teach that, being instituted by God, the state could command unconditional loyalty within its sphere of competence and was to be resisted by noncompliance only if it sought to meddle with church affairs and beliefs. Perhaps more rightly than wrongly, this view is associated with Luther and Augustine. The other view agreed completely about the state's limited sphere of competence and about the measures to be taken when the state overstepped itself relative to the church. Where it differed from the first view was in its belief that Scripture did not teach a requirement of unconditional obedience to any state so long as it merely respected ecclesiastical bounds. Rather, this view understood Scripture to mean that, being instituted by God, the state had obligations to fulfill, such as rewarding good and punishing evil. If these obligations were flagrantly and systematically violated so as to establish an unmistakable pattern of malfeasance, the state would forfeit its status as a state and therefore its mantle of divine legitimacy. This view is associated with Calvin and Aquinas. The difference between the two views is clear: the one holds that to obey the state, even the radically unjust state, is to render obedience to God; the other holds that times may come when obedience to God requires political disobedience and resistance to the state.

The fifth article of Barmen is compatible with the second view. It is a novel

---

45. Compare the relevant sections in the discussions of Augustine, Aquinas, Luther, and Calvin in A. J. Carlyle and R. W. Carlyle, *A History of Medieval Political Thought in the West*, 6 vols. (Edinburgh: William Blackwood & Sons, 1903-36).

version of that view to the extent that the question of obligations is stated, though only indirectly, in terms of a hierarchy of loyalties culminating in our loyalty to Jesus Christ. The state is assigned the task of "providing for justice and peace." Of course, the peace and justice it provides will never be more than rough, since we live in "the as yet unredeemed world." Should the state systematically violate its appointment, the article implies that the church is then to trust and obey "the power of the Word of God by which God upholds all things." For although the emperor is to be honored, when warranted, God alone is the one to be feared.[46]

In his writings during the Nazi period, especially after 1935, Barth always interpreted these ideas as a mandate for political resistance, for the National Socialist state was clearly guilty of a systematic pattern of crimes against justice and peace. However, while Barth's interpretation is most apt considering Barmen's overall spirit and the crisis of the times, neither Article V nor the Declaration as a whole sufficiently rules out the possibility that the opposite interpretation might also be regarded as compatible with the wording of the fifth article. Article V, in other words, does not unequivocally reject a reading along the lines of the other traditional, deeply ingrained view that the state within its sphere of competence must be obeyed unconditionally. Barmen V clearly sets forth the state's basic obligations, but not the church's duty to resist should those obligations be grievously transgressed. Be that as it may, the text certainly seems to imply that even in its own sphere the state's legitimacy is not unconditional. Moreover, it is hard to see how a state sponsoring systematic human rights violations and proliferating the indiscriminate weaponry of mass destruction could reasonably be regarded, under a Barthian reading of Article V, as not inspiring a similar mandate to resistance.

Several Barmen articles, when taken together, imply a relationship between theology and politics involving unity, hierarchy, and differentiation. This "Chalcedonian" relationship is at the heart of Barth's political theology, but it has not always been an easy one to grasp. In fact, it has commonly driven Barth's critics to exasperation. Some, for example, have noticed the hierarchy and differentiation but not the unity. Thus Reinhold Niebuhr accused Barth of soaring above political reality in "an eschatological airplane" which never came down to earth.[47] Others, on the other hand, have experienced the unity Barth assumed at full blast. Thus the great church historian Hans von Campenhausen is said one time to have "quivered with anger because Karl Barth gave his politi-

---

46. For a similar line of interpretation, see Wolfgang Huber, "Gebot für den Staat, Zur Aktualität des Barmer Bekenntnisses," *Evangelische Kommentare* 17, no. 2 (February 1984): 67-70.

47. Reinhold Niebuhr, "Why Is Barth Silent on Hungary?" in *Essays in Applied Christianity* (New York: Meridian Living Age Books, 1959), p. 186.

cal views in such a way that those who differed were necessarily put into question." To which Barth is said characteristically to have retorted: "Why don't you put forward your view with the same (Christian) commitment?"[48] (The issue on which they divided was postwar German rearmament, Barth being vehemently against it.) How is it possible for the same man to have so coolly proposed in the midst of the 1933 Nazi crisis that theology and church should proceed "as if nothing had happened,"[49] while at other times he seemed to make political decisions into virtually a *status confessionis?*

Part of the answer lies in Barth's belief that the necessary political implications would follow indirectly and of their own accord if the church would simply pursue its proper tasks such as Bible study, prayer, and theological reflection.[50] "It must be clear," he once wrote in 1942, "that our resistance can have meaning only to the extent that it is able to nourish itself from its own roots."[51] Or as he insisted much earlier in 1934: "Let theology at last become primary for us and Church politics only secondary, so that in this properly ordered relationship it may become good politics!"[52] Statements like these underscore the sense of hierarchy and proper differentiation Barth strove to write into the Barmen Declaration.

One of Barth's most suggestive treatments of this question appears in an article solicited by the American journal *Foreign Affairs* which appeared in January 1943.[53] At one point Barth contrasts the churches in Holland, Norway, and Britain and the confessing church in Germany. The former he regards as politically progressive but theologically lacking, for they resist Nazism but not culture-bound theology. The latter is just the reverse, theologically progressive but politically lacking, and for the opposite reason. Despite its praiseworthy theology, it does not see that to Nazism, Christian belief has no choice but to utter a wholehearted and unequivocal "No!" Those who do otherwise have failed to understand National Socialism, have failed to think through the mes-

---

48. Busch, p. 405.

49. Karl Barth, *Theological Existence Today!* (Lexington, Ky.: American Theological Library Association Committee on Reprinting, 1962), p. 9. Cf. what Barth says later in the essay: "In this way, perhaps, there might even be created a centre of resistance, which, because unsought, might one of these days possess an outstanding 'political' importance for the Church and be effective against the danger impending over the Church today" (pp. 75-76). Cf. also what Barth says about theology and politics in the foreword to *Church Dogmatics* I/1, p. xiii.

50. For a critique of this assumption, see George Hunsinger, "Karl Barth and Radical Politics: Some Further Considerations," *Studies in Religion/Sciences Religieuses* 7 (1978): 181-83.

51. Barth, *Church and the War*, p. 14.

52. Barth, *The German Church Conflict*, p. 39.

53. Karl Barth, "The Protestant Churches in Europe," *Foreign Affairs* 21 (January 1943): 260-75. Reprinted in *Church and the War*, pp. 1-18. German original in *Einer Schweizer Stimme, 1938-1945* (Zürich: Evangelischer Verlag A. G. Zollikon, 1948), pp. 251-71.

sage of the Bible, or "have developed a kind of schizophrenia in which totally divergent yardsticks are adopted for the inner and the external life"[54] — an allusion not only to the traditional German two-kingdoms doctrine, but also to the false separations and divisions rejected by Barmen Article II.

Then, with the confessing church still in mind, Barth drives home the unity he believed inexorably to obtain between theology and politics: "No matter how far they (the confessing church) may have progressed in other directions, they will have to learn from the other churches that there are a Christian center and a Christian periphery, that the Christian substance and its political application are indeed two different things, but that there is only one truth and one justice — and that no one can serve two masters."[55]

Barth contends here that there are a center and a periphery, the gospel and its political application, and that they need to be kept eternally distinct. Yet just as the periphery cannot be had without the center, so the center cannot be had without the periphery. Together, gospel and political application form one circle, one unitary whole. When to stress their distinction and when to stress their unity depends almost entirely on the situation. Not every political issue of the day demands a decision from the church, but for those like National Socialism that do, the decision must be forceful and clear-cut.

No periphery without the center! That is what Barth insisted to politically progressive Christians who wanted to stress their politics at the expense of the gospel, or to sacrifice the gospel's uniqueness by reinterpreting it in political terms, or perhaps in their zeal to dispense with the gospel altogether. Without the vital center, Barth insisted, without the gospel's utter uniqueness, the prospects for the periphery — for vibrant and chastened social action — are not good. To have the periphery without the center, the ethics without the doctrine, is the impossible modernist dream that sooner or later becomes a nightmare.

No center without the periphery! That in turn is what Barth urged upon the politically timid confessing church and upon all theologically traditional Christians who wanted the gospel at the expense of progressive politics[56] —

---

54. Barth, *Church and the War*, p. 12.

55. Barth, *Church and the War*, p. 12, rev.

56. For a discussion on the relationship Barth saw between the gospel and progressive politics, see Ulrich Dannemann, *Theologie und Politik im Denken Karl Barths* (Munich: Chr. Kaiser Verlag, 1977). See also *Karl Barth and Radical Politics*, ed. George Hunsinger (Philadelphia: Westminster, 1976); and George Hunsinger, "Karl Barth and Liberation Theology," chapter 2 above. For a brilliant discussion of how Barth's theological anthropology mediates between his theological and political views, see the unpublished doctoral dissertation by William Werpehowski, "Social Justice, Social Selves: John Rawls's *A Theory of Justice* and Christian Ethics" (Yale University, 1981), chap. 1.

who wanted to avoid the gospel's political imperatives by quietly diluting them or by expunging them completely. Without the progressive periphery, he believed, the doctrinal center not only appears rather dubious, but is inwardly debased. A circle's center without its periphery is a contradiction in terms. Where Christian doctrine is held while the imperatives of peace and justice are denied, questions arise whether the gospel has been encountered or understood at all. Happily, however, between evangelical truth and social justice we need not choose, for in the unity of the Lordship of Jesus Christ, "there is only one truth and one justice — and no one can serve two masters."

Note that two kinds of argument are in play here. First is that the gospel is intrinsically true and self-authenticating in its radical uniqueness beyond all cultural possibilities. Second is that the gospel has salutary political consequences which at times are directly to be pursued, consequences that will be subverted should gospel *qua* gospel cease to be the core. The first argument might be described as axiomatic, the second as functional. The salient point is that Barth employs both arguments dialectically, according to the pattern of thought just described. To put it another way, he has nothing against politically functional arguments so long as one brings out in strong relief that the functional is not central, that the axiomatic is not peripheral, and that, finally, neither can be had without the other.

The great lesson from the confessing church of yesterday, therefore, with its theological successes and its political failures, as each in its own way is indicated by the Barmen Declaration, is that we can no longer afford to be satisfied with mixtures of the clear and the vague. Loyalty to Jesus Christ, as he is attested for us in Holy Scripture, is the one standard by which we are to abide in all theological and all political decisions. Our fear of disloyalty to any human cause, even when nationalist or revolutionary, may never be greater than our fear of disloyalty to him, for he alone is to be loved and feared above all things. Loving and fearing only him in this way, we will not be surprised if times should come when loyalty to some particular human cause, especially in the political realm, must be met with a clear and vigorous "No!"

III. Resistance and Suffering:
Prospects for a Confessing Church Tomorrow

If our present need can be granted and yesterday's lessons are clear, are there prospects for a confessing church tomorrow? Might a church grounded in biblical witness and committed to justice and peace be emerging on the horizon?

Dare we hope for a grouping of Christians prepared in theology and politics to resist our more disturbing trends?

Perhaps the first thing to keep in mind is the vitality of the black church to which Bonhoeffer called our attention. No doubt a strong case could be made that the black church in America has always been close, both politically and theologically, to the kind of confessing church we are considering. The white church in America, to the extent that it split into an unfortunate, self-perpetuating, and ugly division between fundamentalists without justice and liberals without doctrine, could then be regarded as living in two forms of a single apostasy, which the black church with its surer historic grasp of these matters might still help the white church overcome. Certainly no confessing church tomorrow, fighting for human rights and nuclear disarmament, could ignore today's racism and injustice at home. The black church within any larger confessing church would do what it has always done to keep the rest of us honest.

A second point to bear in mind is that the best parallel between the confessing church of yesterday and the one possible tomorrow may already exist to the south. In Latin America the church is enjoying an unprecedented spiritual renewal through the formation of small groups centered on Bible study, Eucharist, and prayer. At the same time, across the entire continent, this church is suffering a persecution of historic proportions, directed at those who stand up for the most elemental human rights. Once again, as in Hitler's Germany, the church has become the last institutional refuge against state terror and repression. Also bearing comparison to the Nazi period in Europe is the flight of the persecuted. Nowhere is this reality more heartrending today than in the flight from Central America. Rather than welcoming these refugees, our government seeks to deport them, sending them back to a fate uncertain or perhaps all-too-certain.

The growing resistance to this deportation now under way in the American churches is one of the most hopeful signs for a confessing church tomorrow.[57] Sanctuary is offered to the refugees even to the point of breaking what our government interprets as the law. No confessing church tomorrow can afford to ignore its persecuted sisters and brothers to the south. If developments like the sanctuary movement deepen, perhaps we will not need to say of our country what after the war Karl Barth said of his: "The Rhine will not wash away our guilt for having turned away ten thousand fugitives and having treated unworthily those whom we did accept."[58]

57. See Geraldine Brooks, "Offered Sanctuary: Scores of U.S. Churches Take in Illegal Aliens Fleeing Latin America," *Wall Street Journal*, June 21, 1984, pp. 1ff.
58. Busch, p. 318.

Finally, the sanctuary movement points us to a great but still uncertain trend: spiritually grounded civil disobedience. Forces of spiritual renewal — among Roman Catholics, groups like Pax Christi; among Protestants, groups like World Peacemakers — bear fruit in actions of resistance. Good Friday vigils through the streets of Manhattan ending in civil disobedience at nuclear-weapons research institutes; Peace Pentecosts in which Christians singing gospel songs and praying for peace are dragged in arrest from the rotunda of the Capitol building while within earshot Congress debates funding for the MX missile program — these could be seeds of a confessing church tomorrow.

Although for the historic reasons mentioned, a renewed and resisting church in America is not likely to emerge on an explicitly confessional basis, our traditional American activism, as Bonhoeffer recognized, could still be an asset. As an example of the best in American Christian renewal that might inform a confessing church tomorrow, I offer these words from a Roman Catholic woman named Helen Woodson, who on September 2, 1982, was arrested for pouring blood on the floor of the White House. At her trial she read these words to the judge:

> For the past 18 years my life has been children — one birth child, 7 adopted children and 3 foster children. 10 of my kids are mentally retarded. We also share our home with a paraplegic Cuban refugee and with ex-prisoners and others who need shelter. All of these people are considered of little value by society. My children will never contribute to the Gross National Product, they will never pay taxes to the war machine, they will never cast a vote for corporate political interests, they will never turn their bodies and minds over to Selective Service. They are of no value in a society based on competition, profit and war, and yet it is these useless people who have taught me what I know of the preciousness of human life, the sacredness that transcends damage and imperfection. . . .
>
> Tragic death cannot always be prevented. Accident or disease may kill our children while we stand helpless to do anything. But death in nuclear war is preventable. It can happen only if we allow it, and if we allow it, we will come for judgment not before the Superior Court of the District of Columbia but before God and the murdered innocents.
>
> It is morally incumbent upon us to defend the children. I have done so at home for 18 years. I did so on September 2nd at the White House, pouring my blood to speak against the death of nuclear weapons and for the life we could have instead — a life of reconciliation and peace. The acts through which I serve life at home are considered exemplary and noble; my nonviolent witness at the White House is considered to be criminal. After more than two years of prayer and the thought which preceded my civil

disobedience and after the 76 days I have spent in the DC Jail, I cannot, in all good conscience, see the difference between the two.[59]

A confessing church in America tomorrow is at first more likely to be grounded in prayer than in any kind of doctrinal renewal, as sorely as the latter may be needed. Prayer is among the church's highest responsibilities and privileges, even from a political standpoint. "Prayer will not lead us away from political thought and action of a modest but definite kind," wrote Karl Barth, "but will rather lead us directly into conflict where we are conscious of our goal."[60] Prayer does not mean shoving on God what we are unwilling to tackle ourselves, but it does mean relying wholly on an ethic of witness and faithfulness that resists all anxieties about influence. Influence will be sought and welcomed should it come, but witness and faithfulness will be the overriding goal. Prayer is not a sterile retreat to an enclave beyond secular involvements. It is the first step toward renewing and preserving the church and hence, directly and indirectly, the world. Knowing, therefore, that prayer without action is empty and that action without prayer is blind, finding joy in the midst of suffering and life in the midst of death, being convinced above all that he who has suffered will conquer and that at his name every knee shall finally bow, perhaps a confessing church tomorrow will find it has been granted not to produce a new confession of its own but to be gathered and sustained by one it has already received: "Jesus Christ, as he is attested for us in Holy Scripture, is the one Word of God which we have to hear and which we have to trust and obey in life and in death."[61]

---

59. Helen Woodson, "Statement of November 15, 1982," *Harvest of Justice, Newsletter of the Gaudete Peace and Justice Center* (December 1982): 2. Cf. the document, "Statement on Peace and Justice," adopted by the Sixth Assembly of the World Council of Churches (Vancouver 1983), which includes these words: "We believe the time has come when the churches must unequivocally declare that the production and deployment as well as the use of nuclear weapons are a crime against humanity and that such activities must be condemned on ethical and theological grounds . . . we believe that Christians should give witness to their unwillingness to participate in any conflict involving weapons of mass destruction or indiscriminate effect."

60. Barth, *Letter to Great Britain*, p. 51, rev.

61. Since my original essay, a number of books have appeared about the Barmen Declaration and the confessing church: Rolf Ahlers, *The Barmen Theological Declaration of 1934* (Lewiston, N.Y.: Edwin Mellen Press, 1986); Shelly Baranowski, *The Confessing Church, Conservative Elite and the Nazi State* (Lewiston, N.Y.: Edwin Mellen Press, 1986); *The Barmen Confession: Papers from the Seattle Assembly,* ed. Hubert G. Locke (Lewiston, N.Y.: Edwin Mellen Press, 1986); *The Church Confronts the Nazis: Barmen Then and Now,* ed. Hubert G. Locke (Lewiston, N.Y.: Edwin Mellen Press, 1984); Klaus Sholder, *The Churches and the Third Reich* (Philadelphia: Fortress, 1987).

CHAPTER 4

Where the Battle Rages:
Confessing Christ in America Today

(1987)

"If," wrote Martin Luther, "I profess with the loudest voice and clearest exposition every portion of the truth of God except precisely that little point which the world and the devil are at that moment attacking, I am not confessing Christ, however boldly I may be professing him. Where the battle rages, there the loyalty of the soldier is proved, and to be steady on all the battlefield besides is mere flight and disgrace if he flinches at that point."[1]

With these characteristically vivid words, Martin Luther stresses that biblical confession is always situational. Confessing Christ, Luther urges, is not a matter of parroting biblical truths. It is possible to say all the right things, to be impeccably orthodox in one's theology, and still to be fatally disloyal. Loyalty to Jesus Christ occurs only when our confession of him is concrete, and our confession of him is concrete only when offered where it counts — in the pitch of battle, where confession really costs something, not from the safety of some remote enclave, where confession may be true but costs nothing. We will be sorely tempted, Luther implies, to scurry from the front of battle rather than subject ourselves, for the sake of Jesus Christ, to attack by the devil and the world. We will even be tempted to confess all the more loudly and clearly once the retreat to safety has rendered our confession irrelevant.

Luther's battlefield imagery is stirring, and I would not wish to detract from it. But what if there is a sense in which the image of raging battles fails to illumine our concrete situation? For what are we to do if the battle has ceased to

---

1. *D. Martin Luthers Werke. Briefwechsel,* 18 vols. (Weimar, 1930-), 3:81f.

rage? What if, instead of raging battles, what we actually have to contemplate is a string of irretrievable defeats? Where the battle rages, the outcome still hangs in the balance. But what if, by now, the outcome is all too clear and our forces are lost and dispersed? What if, at last, the tide has turned so irrevocably against us that, for the few skirmishes which remain, our options are forced and severe? What if we have no choice but to fight a losing battle on diminishing terrain, a last battle to the bitter end from which there will be no escape? It is from this admittedly bleak perspective that I want to sketch our current political and theological situations.[2]

I. Where Battles Once Raged: A Survey of Political Carnage

Mother dragged away some of the burning boards and wood and got me out. I can never forget how happy I felt at that moment. . . . But everything was so changed that I was utterly amazed. As far as I could see, almost every building was destroyed and in flames. There were people whose skin was peeling off, leaving their bodies red and raw. They were screaming pitifully, and others were already dead. The street was so covered with the dead, the seriously injured, groaning, and collapsed buildings that we couldn't get through. I didn't know what to do, then to the west I saw flames coming nearer.[3]

These are the words of Hisato Itoh, a survivor of Hiroshima, describing what he saw as a fifth-grade boy at the time. Let them stand for us as a warning from the past to the future. If we fail to heed this warning, the future will surely be an enlargement of this past. Let these words stand as an icon of the future. Let them disclose the meaning of every relentless preparation for nuclear war. Even now the streets are covered with carnage and collapse, and we don't know how to get through. Even now we can see the flames coming nearer.

Returning home from the Potsdam conference, Harry Truman, on August 6, 1945, was aboard the cruiser *Augusta*. As he paced the deck, he was handed an anxiously awaited note. The first atomic bomb ever used in warfare had been dropped on a Japanese city. Turning to a group of sailors, Truman buoyantly exclaimed: "This is the greatest thing in history." Soon thereafter, Truman warned the Japanese that the United States was "now prepared to oblit-

2. Cf. C. S. Lewis, *The Last Battle* (New York: Macmillan, 1956), a children's story which may be read as a tract for the times.

3. *Children of Hiroshima*, ed. Arata Osada (New York: Harper & Row, 1982), p. 162.

erate more rapidly and completely every productive enterprise the Japanese have above ground in any city. We shall destroy their docks, their factories, and their communications." Reflecting back after ten years, Truman would remark: "I regarded the bomb as a military weapon and never had any doubt that it should be used."[4]

Harry Truman, who has been described as "an outstanding Baptist layman," was voicing the sentiments not only of the American people, but of most American Christians.[5] The atomic bomb, that greatest historical thing, had been used, once the fact was known, with few Christian misgivings. It would then be refined and stockpiled with overriding Christian consent. To this day, most American Christians would have no doubt that the bomb should have been used as it was against Japan. Even today, the Christian community cannot bring itself to enter into unequivocal opposition to a depraved reliance on nuclear threats. Thus, as we contemplate the once and future nuclear carnage, we must also grapple with an overwhelming spiritual collapse.

It is a collapse in which we have lost touch with even the minimal standards of morality. I am myself convinced that much more than the mere minimum is expected of us, but what needs to be noted is that even the minimum suffers massive defection. The prevailing sense seems to be that, if the demands of biblical morality contradict the dictates of national security, so much the worse for biblical morality. Thus, even the minimalist logic of the just-war theory has vanished from popular consciousness. No longer is there any sense that the strategic bombing of civilian populations can never be justified. No longer is there any inkling, as recent events in Libya have only served to show, that no ethics — least of all Christian ethics — gives us leave to kill another man's children directly as a means of weakening his supposedly murderous intent.[6] No longer is there any awareness that it would be better to suffer wrong than to commit mass murder, and that even the very threat to commit mass murder, backed by convincing preparations,

---

4. The quotations from Harry Truman may be found in Sidney Lens, *The Day before Doomsday* (New York: Doubleday, 1977), pp. 1-2; and Paul Ramsey, *War and the Christian Conscience* (Durham, N.C.: Duke University Press, 1961), pp. 149-50.

5. The description is Ramsey's, p. 149.

6. I am here closely paraphrasing Ramsey, p. 11. Ramsey, who could not have anticipated such a literal fulfillment of his image as recently took place in Libya, has been an eloquent spokesperson for the just-war tradition, especially insofar as it excludes direct assaults on civilians. (See, for example, his indirect but powerful condemnation of the atomic bombing of Hiroshima and Nagasaki; p. 295.) Of course, Ramsey also goes on to designate certain nuclear-weapons targeting strategies as fulfilling the conditions for "counterforce" — a designation I regard as a category mistake of the first order. For a careful survey and critique of Ramsey's changing arguments about nuclear weapons over the years, see Edward J. Laarman, *Nuclear Pacifism: "Just War" Thinking Today* (New York: Peter Lang, 1984).

is intrinsically and monstrously evil. The moral incapacitation of the Christian community in the nuclear era is a sign of grievous defeat.

It was not always so. When, in 1937, Franco's forces bombed and strafed the Spanish town of Guernica, killing hundreds of unarmed civilians, the civilized world was shocked at what it considered to be a sickening atrocity. When, in the same year, the Japanese bombed the city of Nanking, the United States government issued a formal diplomatic protest against the direct targeting of noncombatants. On the first day of World War II, President Roosevelt issued an urgent appeal to every government engaged in hostilities. He implored them to make public a declaration that under no circumstances would they bomb civilian populations or directly target cities. The following year he reaffirmed this stand. "The bombing of helpless and unprotected civilians," he said, "is a strategy which has aroused the horror of all mankind. I recall with pride that the United States consistently has taken the lead in urging that this inhuman practice be prohibited." Hitler's vicious bombing of Warsaw and Rotterdam was widely condemned as a sign of his treachery and ruthless militarism. "Until well into 1940 civilized opinion was unanimously against the bombing of civilians; this form of attack was considered fit only for totalitarian dictators."[7] It used to be only fascists and their ilk who bombed civilians.

By 1942, however, a sea change would occur in Allied policy. Robert C. Batchelder attributes this change to two main factors: a desire for revenge after the German bombing of British cities and a sincere adherence to the idea that a direct assault on German civilians would shorten the war. Thus, Winston Churchill came to speak of the "systematic shattering" of German cities and of "beating the life out of Germany." He told the House of Commons that "there are no lengths in violence to which we will not go." The new policy came to be formulated like this: "Our plans are to bomb, burn, and ruthlessly destroy in every way available to us the people responsible for creating the war."[8] "What was universally condemned by church members and decent people generally in 1937, and considered fit only for dictators in 1939, was between 1940 and 1944 accepted as a 'military necessity' and a normal part of the procedure of war, both by the general public and by the large majority of church people, both Protestant and Roman Catholic."[9] Having enlisted in the aims of the war, Christians lost all will to resist, all sense that there even was something to resist, when the conduct of the war became wantonly immoral.

7. Robert C. Batchelder, *The Irreversible Decision: 1939-1950* (Boston: Houghton Mifflin, 1961), pp. 172-73. The Roosevelt quotation and the other historical material in this paragraph are from these pages.

8. The quotations are from Batchelder, p. 175.

9. Batchelder, p. 181.

The decision to use the atomic bomb was made in this context. Obliteration bombing had gradually come to be accepted as a military necessity. The mass bombing of Japanese cities soon became standard procedure. It was this erosion of moral constraints which largely determined that the atomic bomb, once developed, would be dropped on the center of a large city — "despite the professed concern of our leaders to avoid the killing of undefended civilians."[10] It was by this process of moral erosion in a time of war that most Americans, including most American Christians, came to believe that it can be right to perform an enormously immoral act in order to achieve a good or desirable end and to avoid the suffering of harm. It was by this process that matters of military necessity came to be regarded as exempt from moral scrutiny. And it was by this process that there thus came to be confirmed the prediction made by Joseph Goebbels, Hitler's trusted assistant: "Even if we lose, we shall win," he wrote, "for our ideals will have penetrated the hearts of our enemies."[11]

The extent to which our hearts are penetrated by unspeakable ideals can be gauged by noting the extent to which we have consented to live in an Orwellian universe. For have we not become accustomed to a world in which we hear a great deal about atrocities committed by our enemies but never anything of our own? Is it not a world in which our government will always be regarded as benevolent no matter how many nuclear weapons it builds, no matter how many overtures for peace it spurns, and no matter how many brutal dictatorships it supports? Dungeons of disease, exploitation, malnutrition, torture, and death are described as belonging to the free world. Terrorists, rapists, and fascists we train and supply are passed off as champions of democracy. War criminals in high places we honor as laureates of peace. Acts of aggression against nations of peasants we celebrate as our noble deeds of self-sacrifice or of preemptive self-defense. Orwell has become our destiny.[12]

We are entangled in webs of endless deceit from which we show little inclination to extricate ourselves. The passive acquiescence of a Christian community which has lost its moral conscience in matters of state contributes substantially not only to misery and oppression, but perhaps, eventually, to global destruction.[13] "The most urgent necessity of our time," wrote Thomas Merton, "is not merely to prevent the destruction of the human race by nuclear war.

---

10. Batchelder, p. 211.

11. Quoted by Dale Aukerman, *Darkening Valley: A Biblical Perspective on Nuclear War* (New York: Seabury Press, 1981), p. 85.

12. See Noam Chomsky, "Notes on Orwell's Problem," in *Knowledge of Language* (New York: Praeger, 1985).

13. Cf. Chomsky, *Turning the Tide: U.S. Intervention in Central America and the Struggle for Peace* (Boston: South End Press, 1985).

Even if it should happen to be no longer possible to prevent the disaster (which God forbid), there is still a greater evil that can and must be prevented. It must be possible for every free man and woman to refuse consent and deny cooperation to this greatest of crimes."[14] Is it still possible for the larger Christian community in America today to become a confessing church — a church whose loyalty to Jesus Christ will lead it to refuse consent to and cooperation with the greatest of crimes? Can it cease to be a church of acquiescence by, at last, placing itself precisely at that one little point where real battles might commence to rage?

II. Where Skirmishes Remain: A Survey of Theology in Crisis

"I am the way, and the truth, and the life; no one comes to the Father, but by me" (John 14:6).

"Truly, truly, I say to you, anyone who does not enter the sheepfold by the door but climbs in by another way, that person is a thief and a robber. I am the door, if anyone enters by me, they will be saved" (John 10:1, 9).

Jesus Christ, as he is attested for us in Holy Scripture, is the one Word of God which we have to hear and which we have to trust and obey in life and in death.

We reject the false doctrine, as though the Church could and would have to acknowledge as a source of its proclamation, apart from and besides this one Word of God, still other events and powers, figures and truths, as God's revelation."[15]

These are the words of the first article of the Barmen Declaration, written by Karl Barth and adopted on May 31, 1934, by the confessing church in Nazi Germany. Let them stand for us as a cry of need and a cry of joy. Let them rise as a cry of need. Let them tell how we would not enter by the door, but climb in by another way. Let them judge our lives as ruled by other events and powers, other figures and truths. And let them be a cry of joy. Let them gladden our hearts at the grace which does not desert us. Let them guide us in distress, showing the way beyond our impasse, the truth beyond our doubt, and the life

14. Thomas Merton, "Nuclear War and Christian Responsibility," *Commonweal* 75 (1961-62): 513 (quotation slightly emended).

15. Translated by Arthur Cochrane, *The Church's Confession under Hitler* (Philadelphia: Westminster, 1962), p. 239.

which overcomes death. Let them clear the barriers and quench the engulfing flames.

In his short commentary on Article I of Barmen, Karl Barth makes four main points. First, as the one Word of God, Jesus Christ demands our exclusive loyalty. "The church lives," writes Barth, "by the fact that it hears the Word of God to which it can give entire trust and entire obedience. And it can do so in life and in death — that is, in the certainty that it will be sustained in this trust and obedience for time and in eternity." Either Jesus Christ confronts us with this exclusive claim or he does not confront us at all. When we bind ourselves to him as he has bound himself to us, no other power need be honored and feared as way, truth, life, or door.[16]

Second, compromises of loyalty will slowly devastate the church. The church prepared to offer binding loyalty to Hitler was a church which had died the death of a thousand smaller compromises. For more than two hundred years, it had been trying to divide its loyalty between Jesus Christ and other supposed sources of divine revelation. Whether reason, conscience, the emotions, history, nature, or culture, some second authority was continually proposed and ratified alongside the first. But no claim of exclusive loyalty can tolerate an external loyalty that is equally binding and obligatory. The attempt to turn an either/or into a both/and could only mean that the church's loyalty was compromised and divided. For whether the church realized it or not, no second authority, however apparently benign, could represent anything other than an exclusive and competing counterclaim to that of God's Word. By the time Hitler came along, the church was incapacitated by its history of compromise. When the majority of Christians in Germany wanted to place loyalty to Hitler on the same plane with loyalty to Jesus Christ, "it was about two hundred years too late to make any well-founded objection" (II/1, p. 174). In face of all the precedents, "there could be no basic reason for silencing this new nationalism of race" (II/1, p. 174). Humanly speaking, it was inevitable that, in 1933, the church should consent to the demand posed by Hitler "with exactly the same abandon as it had done to so many other demands" (II/1, p. 175).

Third, in spite of the history of compromise, the Word of God remained. What might have been expected was that, having so often compromised in smaller ways, "the church would now be tired and its eyes blurred and it would be inwardly exhausted, so that it would succumb all the more easily and this time for good to the assault of the blatant temptation. But the fact is that this did not happen. The Word of God still remained, in spite of everything, in the

16. Karl Barth, *Church Dogmatics* II/1 (Edinburgh: T. & T. Clark, 1957), p. 177. References which follow in the text are to this work.

same church in which it had been so often denied and betrayed" (II/1, p. 176). The Word of God who is called Jesus Christ remained, calling forth a confessing church as if from an abyss, a church which could and did take a new stand. Often inconspicuous, and rarely more than inconvenient to the prevailing powers, it was at least a church which had recovered its true identity by repudiating the history of compromise. For by adopting the first article of the Barmen Declaration, it had named and rejected "the great modern disorder" (II/1, p. 176). It had broken with the division of loyalties between God's Word and other supposedly revelatory authorities. Terrified at the specter of a nationalist god and his fascist messiah, it had learned in the midst of grave temptation that "what helps, when every helper fails, is only the miracle, power and comfort of the one Word of God" (II/1, p. 177).

Finally, in actual practice the confessing church stood or fell by whether loyalty was maintained to Jesus Christ as the one Word of God. The history of the confessing church is itself a history of accumulated errors and sometimes tragic vacillations. Even within its ranks, many lived in mortal fear that they would be accused of disloyalty to the nation. The history of the confessing church is, thus, the history of a struggle to become the confessing church. Where this struggle was relaxed, "no other attitude could be reached in practice than that of continual partial retreats and compromises." But where the church lived not by fear of disloyalty to the nation but by faith in Jesus Christ as the one Word of God, "it carried with it automatically the will and power to resist" (II/1, p. 175).

Karl Barth's insights cannot be applied to America today unless we see that what he has to offer is a very nonutilitarian version of Christianity. Loyalty to Jesus Christ is not the means to an end. It is, rather, the supreme end by which all other ends are judged and in which all worthy ends are included, though in practice there may be times when even worthy ends will need to be sacrificed for the sake of the supreme end. Loyalty to Jesus Christ as the one Word of God is to be sought for its own sake, for nothing can surpass the importance of faithfulness to him. Faithfulness regardless of cost is the highest (indeed, the only) virtue, and unfaithfulness the deepest sin. The paradox is that those who lose their life for the sake of Jesus Christ will find it, and that, when God's kingdom is sought for its own sake, all else will be added as well. But this paradox is itself a matter of faith far more than of sight. Faithfulness often means holding to the paradox despite all contrary appearances. In plain English, faithfulness means readiness to entail the risk of hurt, sacrifice, or loss. Since the servant is not greater than the master, faithfulness can expect to mean voluntary suffering, with the promise that, even in the midst of suffering, we will not be bereft of God's grace. Faithfulness to Jesus Christ is, therefore, the very opposite of the temptation with which it is often confused — losing for the sake of finding, and seeking for the sake of benefits, as though God were the means to an end.[17]

This nonutilitarian (i.e., biblical) version of Christianity stands in sharp contrast to the prevailing mores of our culture. As Robert Bellah and his co-workers have pointed out in *Habits of the Heart,* their fascinating study of the contemporary American middle class, utilitarian modes of thought run rampant. Although in respectable ethical theory utilitarianism is associated with a quest for the common good, in popular American consciousness the notion of the common good, if our researchers are to be believed, has all but disappeared. What one finds instead is a utilitarianism of private interest. White middle-class Americans describe their ethical and religious choices as depending on little more than a shifting set of personal wants and inner impulses. "Seek your own welfare above all else" has become the maxim of the day. Whether one's welfare is defined in terms of wealth, status, and power or in terms of inner psychic satisfactions, either way one's choices are grounded in virtually nothing more than a sense of the solitary, autonomous self.

Bellah circles around this problem again and again. For many, he writes with dismay, "there is simply no objectifiable criterion for choosing one value or course of action over another. One's own idiosyncratic preferences are their own justification, because they define the true self."[18] Reliance on mere preference to define the self is something Bellah regards as symptomatic of the therapeutic style which has pervaded the values of our culture. At the center of the therapeutic style is "the autonomous individual, presumed to be able to choose the roles he will play and the commitments he will make, not on the basis of higher truths, but according to the criterion of life-effectiveness as the individual judges it."[19] The ordering of all other goals to the goal of self-fulfillment, as determined by need and preference, is the hallmark of the therapeutic style.

What troubles Bellah is the stunning loss of any other criterion, any higher truth, for moral judgment. "The right act," he comments, "is simply the one that yields the agent the most exciting challenge or the most good feeling. . . . In the absence of any objectifiable criteria of right and wrong, good and evil, the self and

17. See the seminal essay by H. Richard Niebuhr, "Utilitarian Christianity," in *Witness to a Generation,* ed. Wayne H. Cowan (Indianapolis: Bobbs-Merrill, 1966), pp. 240-45. The essay first appeared in *Christianity and Crisis* (July 8, 1946).

18. Robert N. Bellah, Richard Madsen, William M. Sullivan, Ann Swidler, and Steve M. Tipton, *Habits of the Heart: Individualism and Commitment in American Life* (Berkeley: University of California Press, 1985), p. 75.

19. Bellah et al., p. 47.

its feelings become our only moral guide."[20] The ethic of arbitrary self-interest, in other words, which so many of our contemporaries have espoused as their own, is largely sponsored by a pervasive sense of relativism — a sense that no values are ever more than arbitrary preferences grounded in the autonomous self. Bellah connects the seepage of relativism into our culture with a massive flight from communally transmitted authority and tradition as the vehicles of objectifiable moral criteria. The ethic of arbitrary self-interest and its connection with our surrender to relativism are nicely captured by a line which sums up the distress of Bellah's book: "Utility replaces duty," he writes, "self-expression unseats authority."[21]

The moral crisis Bellah describes has a religious and theological counterpart. At both popular and sophisticated levels of discourse, Christianity is widely regarded as instrumental to the attainment of various benefits or satisfactions. Biblical truth is sought not as an intrinsic good in itself, but as a pragmatic device for fulfilling wishes and desires shaped independently of faith. And utilitarian Christianity, in turn, is sponsored openly or secretly by an unhappy surrender to relativism — that is, by such an extreme departure from Jesus Christ, as he is attested for us in Holy Scripture, that we regard him as an object not of obedience, love, and awe, but of our control and manipulation. The severity of our disorder can be illustrated by three examples.

First, there is what James Davison Hunter, in his book *American Evangelicalism*, calls "psychological Christocentrism." Through a study of books released by the eight largest publishers of evangelical literature, Hunter finds that, beginning in the 1960s and reaching dominance in the 1970s, an important shift occurred in conservative evangelical piety. Suffering, sacrifice, and the obligations of the Christian life were increasingly downplayed. On the upswing were promises of happiness, fulfillment, and "a new zest for living." "Jesus meant for the Christian life to be an exciting, abundant adventure" is the theme of many variations. When Jesus is presented as little more than a means of coping with psychological problems, what we have is a triumph of the therapeutic.[22]

---

20. Bellah et al., p. 76.

21. Bellah et al., p. 77. It seems plausible that the moral situation Bellah describes has something to do with the ethos of late capitalist society (not that this ethos is the "cause" of the situation, but that it is a factor which cannot be ignored). "It is not surprising," writes Terry Eagleton, "that classical models of truth and cognition are increasingly out of favor in a society where what matters is whether you deliver the commercial or rhetorical goods. The goal is no longer truth but performativity, not reason but power." Eagleton, "Capitalism, Modernism and Postmodernism," *New Left Review*, no. 152 (July/August 1985): 63.

22. James Davison Hunter, *American Evangelicalism: Conservative Religion and the Quandary of Modernity* (New Brunswick, N.J.: Rutgers University Press, 1983), pp. 91-101. Cited by Bellah et al., pp. 324-25.

The therapeutic style, unfortunately, has also infected a great deal of recent feminist argument in theology. Religious symbols are voted up or down on the basis of their putative therapeutic content or lack thereof. Even the case for retaining biblical language about God as Father is made in therapeutic terms. Images of God as Father are not to be jettisoned, we are told, because they provide such important psychological compensation for women's experiences of male abandonment.[23] Surely, promoting the full humanity of women in the church and understanding our relationship to God are both far too important to be argued on therapeutic, utilitarian grounds.[24]

Second, at a very sophisticated level of theological discourse, a mounting attack is being waged against the biblical depiction of Jesus Christ. The worst sins ever committed by the church in history are being laid at the door of the New Testament itself. These sins are not regarded as a defection from the way of the cross. They are regarded as a consequence of the message that Jesus Christ demands and deserves our exclusive loyalty. Instead of Jesus Christ as depicted in Scripture — which some theologians are now calling "Christofascism" — what we are offered as an alternative is the promise of a "nonnormative Christology." But this Christology without norms only exacerbates the problems noted by Bellah and Barth. Despite the vigorous morality which its theological advocates would like to maintain — a morality which, I suspect, owes much more to the authority of Scripture and its depiction of Jesus Christ than they will admit — Jesus Christ is consistently reduced to an object of mere personal preference and cultural location. It is hard to see how this extreme relativism can logically avoid undermining any sense of objectifiable moral criteria, and therefore it is hard to see how it does not itself massively contribute to the compromises of loyalty which Barth believed devastated the church in Germany and which devastate our churches today.[25]

23. Diane Tennis, *Is God the Only Reliable Father?* (Philadelphia: Westminster, 1985), p. 21. For a very different mode of argument, see p. 107.

24. I am making a logical point that is both limited and friendly. The point is limited. I do not mean to imply that only therapeutic, utilitarian arguments are found in feminist theological writing. Other, stronger arguments may be found there. Nor do I mean to imply that such utilitarian arguments are made only there. Such modes of argument appear to far worse effect in antifeminist and patriarchal writings. I mean to say merely that such modes of argument currently pervade much feminist theological discussion. The point is friendly, because feminist argument itself, if I do not misunderstand it, is essentially opposed to the kind of calculating and manipulative sensibility which utilitarian argument in theology represents. The utilitarian, therapeutic style is, in other words, quintessentially "patriarchal."

25. See Paul F. Knitter, *No Other Name! A Critical Survey of Christian Attitudes toward the World Religions* (Maryknoll, N.Y.: Orbis, 1985), and the literature there cited. For a discussion of relativism from within the stance of "nonnormative Christology," see Tom F. Driver, *Christ in a Changing World* (New York: Crossroad, 1981), pp. 66-74.

My last example of the severity of our crisis is the presidential address delivered in 1982 to the American Academy of Religion (AAR) by Gordon D. Kaufman, titled "Nuclear Eschatology and the Study of Religion."[26] Kaufman's argument is a nearly classical combination of historical relativism and utilitarian religion. The argument moves in essentially two directions. The one proceeds from the nuclear threat to biblical religion. The nuclear threat is not regarded as the epitome of sinful rebellion, nor as an extreme manifestation of the mystery of evil. It is, rather, regarded as an occasion to deny the love and sovereignty of God. Human beings are now totally responsible for the future of humanity, we are told, because they hold the power to exterminate the human race. Since neither God's love nor God's power can be reconciled with this concept of total human responsibility, the former (God's love and power) will have to go. This is the relativistic side to Kaufman's argument.[27]

The other proceeds from religion to the nuclear threat. The nuclear threat is to be condemned, not because it violates our loyalty to God, but because it imperils the survival of the human race. Without prospect that the race will survive, there would be nothing to give meaning to our lives. The event of nuclear extermination would obliterate all human meaning. Every human re-

---

26. Gordon D. Kaufman, "Nuclear Eschatology and the Study of Religion," *Journal of the American Academy of Religion* 51 (1983): 3-14. An expanded version of Kaufman's argument may be found in his *Theology for a Nuclear Age* (Philadelphia: Westminster, 1985).

27. In *Relativism, Knowledge, and Faith* (Chicago: University of Chicago Press, 1960), Kaufman argues that relativism is not self-refuting. I do not find the argument convincing. Faith is presented as a necessary condition for the overcoming of relativism, and this necessity is regarded as both logical and existential. The argument never explains, however, how this essentially analytical point is to acquire prescriptive force. It never explains why relativism ought to be overcome by faith, and thus why nihilism as the final consequence of relativism is not still logically and existentially inevitable within the bounds of relativism itself. Relativism in itself thus remains self-refuting, for, apart from some act of faith, it lands in the abyss of nihilism. Nevertheless, Kaufman considers it to be an act of faith that "our knowledge somehow participates in that which transcends the relativities of our situation" (p. 86), and I would agree, at least insofar as our knowledge of God is concerned. But he evacuates his affirmation of content when he goes on to argue that we can have "no clear idea" of what this transcendence finally means (p. 124). Thus, in effect, relativism as such remains in force. The difficulty of opposing the acids of modernity with little more than the thought forms and the emotions of Christianity as expressed in religious symbols is nicely illustrated by the increasingly skeptical turn taken in Kaufman's later works. No matter how imaginative the constructions, relativism of the mind is not likely to be counteracted by an appeal to the formal concepts of theology in conjunction with reasons of the heart. For recent discussions of relativism and nihilism, see *Relativism, Cognitive and Moral*, ed. Jack W. Meiland and Michael Krausz (Notre Dame, Ind.: University of Notre Dame Press, 1982), and Stanley Rosen, *Nihilism: A Philosophical Essay* (New Haven: Yale University Press, 1969).

source, including religion, must be used to challenge this terrible possibility. Guidance will come not from traditional communities with their outmoded versions of faith, but — *mirabile dictu* — from departments of religious studies, with their wellsprings of expertise. Survival is the overriding end, and religion, when academically purified, is the indispensable means. This is the utilitarian side to Kaufman's argument.[28] Needless to say, Kaufman does not explain how the relativism endemic to the first side of his argument can be kept from undermining even the improbable utilitarianism of the second.

The examples we have just reviewed — psychological christocentrism, therapeutic feminism, nonnormative Christology, utilitarian religion — are all instances of what Karl Barth described as "the great modern disorder." In one way or another they all exhibit "the specifically modern self, the self that . . . finds no limits to set to that on which it may pass judgment,"[29] the self which does not hesitate to pass judgment even on the one Word of God. Whether by subjecting God's Word to the quest for therapeutic satisfactions or by gutting it through abstract standards divorced from the world of biblical particularity, either way what we have is the assertion of an autonomous, protean self for whom there is finally nothing to faith but expressions of will, and for whom God can only be what faith chooses to create.[30] It is a self "to which the notion of authority is alien and repugnant, so that appeals to authority appear irrational."[31] The flight from authority is essentially a flight to autarky. The self without limits becomes an absolute unto itself, the final arbiter of meaning and truth, dismissing all appeals to higher authority with sovereign contempt.

When Karl Barth wrote the first article of the Barmen Declaration, it was this enclosed, exaggerated self against which he wanted to warn, for this was the self which, for two hundred years, had been claiming to be equally binding and

---

28. My critique of utilitarian argumentation does not impute motives of self-interest (cf. Kaufman's *Theology*, p. 59). The critique rather concentrates on the logic of any attempt to commend the Christian faith or Christian symbols on grounds of their supposedly salutary function in our lives. To commend the Christian faith because it is functional is to commend it not for its own sake but for the sake of its supposed utility. Kaufman's AAR address commends Christian and other religious symbols for the sake of their possible utility in securing the survival of the human race as threatened by nuclear extinction. For a critique of such "survivalism" as is found in Jonathan Schell's *The Fate of the Earth* (New York: Knopf, 1982) — a work on which Kaufman draws heavily — see Stanley Hauerwas, *Against the Nations* (Minneapolis: Winston Press, 1985), pp. 140-46.

29. Alasdair MacIntyre, *After Virtue* (Notre Dame, Ind.: University of Notre Dame Press, 1981), p. 30. Bellah's *Habits of the Heart* is essentially a sociological footnote to MacIntyre's *After Virtue*.

30. Cf. MacIntyre, p. 107.

31. MacIntyre, p. 41.

obligatory alongside the one Word of God, yet all the while harbored within itself pretensions to exclusive authority. It was this self which secretly lurked in wait behind what Barth rejected so vehemently as "natural theology," which reached demonic culmination in Adolf Hitler, and which reaches new culmination, potentially worse than the first, in the nuclear-weapons state today. The self without limits is essentially catastrophic.

Barth's warning was not much heeded. Theology and church in the postwar period continued to take a different path. Even those who followed Barth, with a few honorable exceptions, failed to appreciate the political thrust of his theology. They failed to see that the one Word of God, believed in for nothing but its own sake, "carried with it automatically the will and power to resist." They failed to see what Barth always knew, that where resistance does not occur, the Word of God itself has been rejected or misunderstood. Hence, the one great chance for renewal in theology and church was more or less everywhere passed by. But there were those honorable exceptions. There were those who withstood the modernist temptation and those who refused to forget. Can it be that, once again faced with the terrifying specter of the self without limits, their forces will gather and grow? Can it be that the church will, once again, find itself delivered from the brink, to resist by confessing and, in confessing, to resist? Can it be that a confessing church will be raised from the dead and regrouped for the skirmishes that remain?[32]

III. Finding Our Field Map:
From Barmen to the Free Church Tradition

A very vivid dream came to me one night after I had spent hours perusing statistics on nuclear proliferation; before going to bed, I had leafed through baby pictures of our three children to find a snapshot for my daughter's high-school yearbook.

In my dream I behold the three of them as they appeared in the old photos, and I am struck most by the sweet wholesomeness of their flesh. My husband and I are journeying with them across an unfamiliar landscape. The land is becoming dreary, treeless and strewn with rocks; Peggy, the youngest, can barely clamber over the boulders in the

---

32. I am assuming here not only that the church's resistance is internal to its confession of Jesus Christ as the one Word of God but also that the church's confession is its primary form of resistance. "The power against which it stands," writes Barth, "is too great for it to meet it otherwise than with the weapon of this testimony" (*Church Dogmatics* II/1, p. 177).

path. Just as the going is getting very difficult, even frightening, I sud-
denly realize that, by some thoughtless but unalterable prearrange-
ment, their father and I must leave them. I can see the grimness of the
way that lies ahead of them, bleak and craggy as a moonscape and
with a flesh-burning, sickly tinge to the air. I am maddened with sor-
row that my children must face this ordeal without me. I kiss each of
them and tell them we will meet again, but I know no place to name
where we will meet. Perhaps another planet, I say. Innocent of terror,
they try to reassure me, ready to be off. Removed, from a height in the
sky, I watch them go — three small solitary figures trudging across
that angry wasteland, holding one another by the hand and not stop-
ping to look back. In spite of the widening distance, I see with a surre-
alist's precision the ulcerating of their flesh. I see how the skin bubbles
and curls back to expose raw tissue, as they doggedly go forward, the
boys helping the little sister across the rocks.[33]

These are the words of Joanna Rogers Macy, author of writings and leader of workshops on how to deal with despair. Let them honor pain, let them pierce to relinquishment, and let them whisper of hope beyond hope. Let them honor our pain. Let us honor it in ourselves and in others. Let us acknowledge that which we feel for ourselves and our children, our pain for the world, for the whole creation groaning. May we not deny its reality nor trivialize its meaning with hollow words of cheer nor foster its repression. May we hear and accept the pain.[34]

And let these words pierce to the point of relinquishment. May they open us to letting go. May they move us through pain to prayer — prayer that the facts will speak a different language, prayer that this future should not become the present, prayer that God's sovereignty should not be concealed in this hideous way under the sovereignty of evil and evil human beings.[35] Yet, in this prayer let us come to relinquishment. Let us relinquish the future. Let us relinquish it to God, who upholds us in our pain, who frees us for doing what is faithful, but who frees us from the need to prevail.

And let these words speak of hope, however faintly, of hope beyond hope. Let them whisper of that hope which only relinquishment makes possible. May we join pessimism of the mind with optimism of the will, and both with faith-

---

33. Joanna Rogers Macy, "How to Deal with Despair," *New Age* 4 (June 1979): 40-45.

34. Cf. Macy, *Despair and Personal Power in the Nuclear Age* (Philadelphia: New Society, 1983), p. 37.

35. Cf. Barth, *Church Dogmatics* IV/1 (Edinburgh: T. & T. Clark, 1956), pp. 269-71.

fulness of the heart. Let us name in freedom the unnamed place where we will meet, the place which gospel knows better than dream.

> Then I saw a new heaven and a new earth; for the first heaven and the first earth had passed away, and the sea was no more. And I saw the holy city coming down out of heaven from God, prepared as a bride adorned for her husband; and I heard a loud voice from the throne saying, "Behold, the dwelling of God is with women and men. God will dwell with them, and they shall be God's people, and God will be with them; God will wipe away every tear from their eyes, and death shall be no more, neither shall there be mourning nor crying nor pain any more, for the former things have passed away." (Rev. 21:1-4)

I must confess that I do not know if there will be an American confessing church and, if there should be, just what form it will take. What should be the scope of its activities, and what disciplines should it incorporate? Should it be centralized or decentralized? Should its resistance be active or passive? Should it work within existing church structures or outside them? "We do not know what to do, but our eyes are on thee" (II Chron. 20:12).[36]

In a little-known but extremely important essay, John Howard Yoder has described the essential structure of any future American confessing church. Although he does not use these terms, Yoder's essay is built around a distinction between the activist church, the conversionist church, and the confessing church. In closing, let me summarize his argument.[37]

The social-activist church is not unconcerned with ecclesiastical renewal, but in practice it seems to believe "that what ultimately matters in God's purpose is the building of a better society" (p. 273). It wants to humanize social structures to the greater glory of God, and it calls the church to discern God as the agent behind movements for social change, so that Christians will join God in accomplishing justice and peace. Thus, the activist church is preoccupied "with making world history come out right and making the secular city be the city of God" (p. 274).

By contrast, the personal-conversionist church "argues (rightly as far as that goes) that no juggling of the structures of society can do away with the ef-

---

36. For a discussion of the emerging signs of a possible confessing church in America today, see Jim Wallis, "The Rise of Christian Conscience," *Sojourners* 14, no. 1 (January 1985): 12-16. See also George Hunsinger, "Barth, Barmen and the Confessing Church Today," chapter 3 above.

37. John Howard Yoder, "A People in the World: Theological Interpretation," in *The Concept of the Believer's Church*, ed. James Leo Garrett, Jr. (Scottdale, Pa.: Herald, 1969), pp. 252-83. References which follow in the text are to this work.

fects of human sinfulness, so that the promises of a new secular optimism are deceptive, in addition to being less than the New Testament gospel, because they bypass the element of personal guilt and reconciliation" (p. 276). The conversionist church thus shifts the locus of historical meaning from without to within, from society to spirit. Leaving social and ecclesiastical structures as they are, it works instead for inward renewals of the heart. But this means that it does not have "an alternative social ethic of its own" (p. 276). It merely shifts the problem from a "religiously glorified revolution" to a "religiously glorified conservatism" (p. 277).

The confessing church is not a synthesis of the previous views. It is a radical alternative. It rejects the individualism of the conversionists, the secularism of the activists, and a matter peculiar to them both: the equating of faithfulness with effectiveness (or with working for effectiveness). By contrast, a confessing church finds the locus of historical meaning neither in the transformed social structure nor in the strangely warmed heart but in the congregation's loyalty to Jesus Christ. The confessing church is itself the work of God which locates historical meaning, the primary unit from which personal conversion (which calls people into this community) and social witness are derived. It strives to be as effective and as faithful as possible, but it relinquishes effectiveness as the overriding goal. It is committed first of all to restructuring neither society nor the heart but the church according to the will of God (p. 271). The church restructured will be a church of reconciliation, a church of nonconformity, and a church of the cross.

The confessing church will be a church of reconciliation. Just as Jesus Christ reconciles the world to God, so in the faithful community social divisions are overcome. In the world of the Bible, the great social division is the one between Jews and Gentiles. If that division falls, they all fall — whether based on race, gender, class, nation, or some other social distinction — so that all are one in Christ Jesus. The social novelty of the confessing church is essential to the proclamation of the gospel. For the mystery of reconciliation, once hidden but now revealed, is part and parcel of the message to be proclaimed. No church organization around existing social divisions can meaningfully proclaim the gospel (p. 274).

The confessing church will be a church of nonconformity. Its social novelty and moral integrity will distinguish it from the surrounding world. Its inner communal life and outward communal mission will reflect the difference it makes that Christ, not Mars or mammon, is Lord. "If the Church is visible in that these people keep their promises, love their enemies, enjoy their neighbors, and tell the truth, as others do not, this may communicate something of the reconciling, i.e., love of God" (pp. 264-65). Likewise, active participation in secular movements against injustice, hunger, imperialism, and war can be part of the community's "necessary proclamatory action" (p. 265). No church, however, whose inner communal life is at conflict with God through conformity with the world can expect its proclamatory deeds to be taken very seriously.

Finally, the confessing church will be a church of the cross. The emphasis in confessing falls not simply on proclaiming a message, "but on the readiness to do so in the face of hostility from the world. . . . What is central is that the witness be proclaimed without compromise in the face of opposition" (p. 267). Witness without compromise will have a revolutionary social impact and will lead to suffering. This suffering results not from misbehavior (though it may involve civil disobedience), but from conformity to the crucified Christ. The cross is not a resigned acceptance of limitations or of injustice in an imperfect world but the cost of nonconformist existence. It is, thus, not simply regrettable but unavoidable. "It is rather a participation in the victory of Christ over the powers of this age" (p. 270). It means reflecting the essence of Christ's saving work and partaking in it. It means joyfully doing in the world, come what may, the will of God. No church which compromises its witness, either for the sake of avoiding suffering or for the sake of supposed effectiveness, can be truly faithful to its calling.

The one who is Lord of the universe, writes Dale Aukerman, "died defenseless at the hands of his enemies, but precisely because he stood obediently defenseless at the chaos, madness, and doom of rebelling human beings and institutions, God raised him as a victor over that darkness."[38] The church in any age, Aukerman continues, is called to utter an emphatic No to the prime negation of the gospel within its period and setting. For Christians in the most powerful nations, "the prime negation currently is that of reliance on violence, war, nuclear weapons," because of idolatrous loyalty to the nation-state.[39]

Therefore, the emphatic No of any future American confessing church might sound something like this:

"I am come that they might have life and have it abundantly" (John 10:10).

"In the world you have tribulation; but be of good cheer, I have overcome the world" (John 16:33).

Jesus Christ as he is attested for us in Holy Scripture, is the one true

---

38. Aukerman, p. 200.

39. Aukerman, p. 200. Although my argument is directed primarily toward clarifying a proper response from the church to our country's commitment to nuclear weapons, the argument implies that nonpossession of nuclear weapons would be morally the best policy for our government to adopt. A case for nonpossession may be found in Douglas P. Lackey, *Moral Principles and Nuclear Weapons* (Totowa, N.J.: Rowman & Allanheld, 1984).

Prince of Peace, whose gift of new life we are joyfully to receive, and whose way of the cross we are faithfully to take up, as our supreme security in this world.

We reject the false teaching that it is not a sin to seek security in nuclear weapons — to build, possess, test, deploy, brandish or launch them. The moral and theological justification of such activities is a travesty of the gospel. Any cooperation with them, whether open or tacit, is a clear form of heresy and a betrayal of Jesus Christ.

We therefore call upon all Christians to refuse consent and cooperation with preparations for nuclear war. We call upon them to examine, confess and repent of their complicity with such preparations, to meet together for prayer, reflection and mutual support, and to enact faithful, creative patterns of noncooperation, both as individuals and as communities.[40]

The emphatic No, in other words, will need to be couched, as were the protests of Barmen, in terms of an even more emphatic Yes. Where Barmen stressed the one Word of God, a confessing church today will stress the true Prince of Peace. Beyond Barmen, a confessing church today will need to spell out its protest with definite ethical directives. The Yes indicates that a confessing church cannot properly be mobilized by the nuclear peril alone. But the directives suggest that God can use that peril, as in Germany God once used the peril of Nazism, to gather and renew the church.

Humanly considered, little prospect can be offered of halting the drift to nuclear war. But a confessing church will not, because of that, be frozen by fear or impelled into frantic activism. Nuclear catastrophe is not inevitable. God in Jesus Christ, as attested in Scripture, continues to hold back the chaos, giving us

---

40. In March 1958 a group called the *Bruderschaften* petitioned the Synod of the Evangelical Church in Germany with a series of propositions on the Christian faith and nuclear war. The petition proposed that, being faced with a *status confessionis*, the church is called to noncooperation with nuclear war and its preparation. Christians "may not and cannot participate in the design, testing, manufacture, stocking and use of atomic weapons, nor in training with these weapons." "We challenge all those who seriously want to be Christians to renounce, without reserve and under all circumstances, any participation in preparations for atomic war." Christians who would argue otherwise or who tried to remain neutral were regarded as denying "all three articles of the Christian faith." A translation of the *Bruderschaften* petition may be found in Yoder, *Karl Barth and the Problem of War* (Nashville: Abingdon, 1970), pp. 134-36. The petition was written anonymously by Karl Barth, who had occasion to associate himself publicly with it and in particular with the proposition about denying all three articles of the Christian faith. (See Eberhard Busch, *Karl Barth* [Philadelphia: Fortress, 1976], p. 431.) For an important and very full discussion of the concept of *status confessionis*, see D. J. Smit, "What Does *Status Confessionis* Mean?" in *A Moment of Truth*, ed. C. D. Cloete and D. J. Smit (Grand Rapids: Eerdmans, 1984), pp. 7-32.

time for serious repentance. Even today, the Word of God remains. Even today, God's sovereignty is "a sovereignty of surprises."[41] Gathered around Word and sacrament, fellowship and prayer, a confessing church "will be able to discern the forms and acts of witness God wants of it." In the midst of encircling chaos, it will stand in the name of God's peace. A community of reconciliation in the midst of division, of the cross in the midst of compromise, and of joy in the midst of despair, it will play its part by bearing witness to Jesus Christ, crucified and risen; and in so doing, it will be there where the battle rages.[42]

IV. Postscript: Meditation on Le Chambon: How *Did* Goodness Happen?

By his own account Philip Hallie, a philosopher of ethics at Wesleyan University, had devoted his life's work to investigating human cruelty. "I had studied," he writes, "the tortures white men inflicted on native Indians and then upon blacks in the Americas, and now I was reading mainly about the torture experiments the Nazis conducted upon the bodies of small children in [the central European] death camps."[43] Throughout it all, as he watched for recurring patterns of persecution, Professor Hallie strove to maintain an attitude of strict scientific detachment. And as he did so, over the course of years, his soul seemed to have passed, he tells us, from an initial stage of shock and outrage into one of little more than boredom and numbness. One day, as he was reading in an anthology of documents from the Holocaust, he came across a short article about a little village in the mountains of southern France.

> As usual, I was reading the pages with an effort at objectivity. . . . About halfway down the third page of the account of this village, I was annoyed by a strange sensation on my cheeks. The story was so simple and so factual

41. Aukerman, p. 205. I am indebted to Aukerman throughout these final paragraphs.

42. I would like to thank Deborah van Deusen Hunsinger for her valuable editorial assistance. This essay was originally presented to a conference entitled "The Confessing Church in America, Conscientious Objection to Conscription of the Heart and Mind," sponsored by the Mennonite Central Committee, U.S. Peace Section, in Wichita, Kansas, on April 25-26, 1986. It was also presented at a conference celebrating the centenary of Karl Barth's birth, "Karl Barth: Confessional Theology and Political Crisis," sponsored by the Christic Institute, the Global Theology Project, and the Karl Barth Society of North America, in Stony Point, New York, on May 2-4, 1986.

43. Philip P. Hallie, *Lest Innocent Blood Be Shed: The Story of the Village of Le Chambon and How Goodness Happened There* (New York: Harper & Row, 1979), p. 2. References which follow in the text are to this work.

that I had found it easy to concentrate upon it, not upon my own feelings. And so, still following the story and thinking about how neatly some of it fit into the old patterns of persecution, I reached up to my cheek to wipe away a bit of dust, and I felt tears upon my fingertips. Not one or two drops; my whole cheek was wet. (pp. 2-3)

What Philip Hallie had encountered was the story of Le Chambon and its French Reformed pastor, André Trocmé. During the darkest days of World War II, in full view of the Vichy government and a nearby division of the Nazi SS, Le Chambon's villagers, under the leadership of André Trocmé, organized to do something beyond all telling, namely, to save thousands of Jewish children and adults from certain death. Professor Hallie thereupon resolved to put aside his investigation of human cruelty in order to pursue a very different sort of work, which eventually appeared as *Lest Innocent Blood Be Shed*. The subtitle of this remarkable volume is *The Story of the Village of Le Chambon and How Goodness Happened There*.

The basic question which Hallie raises — how *did* goodness happen there? — is not only exceedingly complex, but is also finally so elusive as to defy all attempts at a definitive answer. Perhaps such happenings of goodness, rare and unpredictable as they are, must inevitably remain mysterious in the face of all attempts to explain them. Certainly Hallie's own efforts at explanation vary widely in quality and force. In any case, what follows can be only the briefest of sketches. Without hoping to be in any way exhaustive, I will not try to explain so much as merely to describe certain significant features which seem to emerge from Hallie's account of what goodness actually looks like under such trying circumstances when it happens.

1. An Ethic of Watchfulness

Goodness could not have happened in Le Chambon, as Hallie makes abundantly clear, if the villagers had not adopted an ethic of watchfulness. Their own long, bloody, and vividly remembered history as a persecuted minority — for these people were Huguenots in overwhelmingly Catholic France — had undoubtedly heightened their sensitivity to government-sponsored lies and violence. They staunchly refused to believe the propaganda that was being disseminated all about them, choosing instead to remain watchful and alert to the plight of those in need. The Jewish children who showed up on their doorsteps were not at all what vile Nazi propaganda, reinforced by centuries of disastrous Christian anti-Semitism, made them out to be. They were, as far as these villagers were concerned, simply fellow human beings in jeopardy of their lives. They were therefore to be given refuge and help, regardless of the risks for those who helped them. In this matter the villagers had been influenced by Pastor Trocmé. As Hallie observes, Trocmé "believed that 'decent' people who stay inactive out of cowardice or indifference when around them human beings are being humiliated and destroyed are the most dangerous people in the world" (p. 266).

We may pause here to ask some simple if disturbing questions. Where is it today that human beings around us are being systematically humiliated and destroyed? Are there perhaps sources of propaganda and violence, not excluding our own government or even our own tradition, which might be turning us ourselves into some of the most dangerous people in the world — people who stay inactive out of cowardice or indifference? And if we would somehow resolve to lay aside an ethic of indifference in favor of an ethic of watchfulness and action, how can it really be done? How might that goodness which seems once to have happened in Le Chambon happen again in our churches and in our own lives even today?

2. An Ethic of Noncompliance

Goodness could not have happened in Le Chambon, as Hallie's account also makes clear, if the ethic of watchfulness had not been supplemented by an ethic of noncompliance. For the villagers, noncompliance meant, again under the leadership of Pastor Trocmé, a commitment to nonviolent resistance. Trocmé's sermons, says Hallie,

> emphasized the need to obey one's own conscience when there is a conflict between it and the laws and commands of governments. He often talked about the "power of the spirit," which he described as being a surprising power, a force which no one can predict or control. He offered no systems or methods — this would be to violate the surprising force of the spirit — but he had one principle which he never forsook: the obligation to help the weak, though it meant disobedience to the strong. (p. 170)

Hallie's book contains many stories of how the people of Le Chambon had to disobey the strong if they were to fulfill their obligation to help the weak. One of the most memorable concerns a time when Pastor Trocmé was confronted by a top leader from the Reformed Church of France (p. 143).

Church official: What I want to say is this: you must stop helping refugees.
Trocmé: Do you realize what you are asking? These people, especially the

Jews, are in very great danger. If we do not shelter them or take them across the mountains to Switzerland, they may well die.

Church official: What you are doing is endangering the very existence not only of this village but of the Protestant church of France! You must stop helping them.

Trocmé: If we stop, many of them will starve to death, or die of exposure, or be deported and killed. We cannot stop.

Church official: You must stop. The marshall will take care of them. He will see to it that they are not hurt.

Trocmé: No.

André Trocmé and the remarkable villagers he led refused to abide by such an ethic of safety-first as urged by this ranking official of the church. The higher allegiances by which they felt themselves bound not only made them watchful over against all official lies and propaganda for the sake of the abused, the vulnerable, and the oppressed, but those same allegiances also made them noncompliant over against all official sources of pressure and threats at considerable risk to themselves. But now perhaps we come closer to the heart of the matter. Just what exactly were those higher allegiances by which the Chambonnais felt themselves to be bound?

3. An Ethic of Fidelity and Witness

The ethic which informed and shaped the life of André Trocmé, and through him the life of his entire village of parishioners, was above all an ethic of fidelity to Jesus Christ. And for Trocmé this ethic of fidelity involved a steadfast commitment to the way of nonviolence. In an interesting contrast to Dietrich Bonhoeffer, Trocmé once considered and then rejected entering into a plot to assassinate Hitler. "It is because [he] feared separating [himself] from Jesus Christ," Trocmé later reflected, that he decided against such a course of action, remembering that Jesus himself had "refused to use arms to prevent the crime that was being prepared for him" (p. 265). Trocmé's obedience to Jesus, Hallie comments, "was not like the obedience of a soldier to a military leader; it was more like the obedience of a lover to his beloved" (p. 161). In other words, Trocmé's commitment to nonviolence was grounded not in the law but in the gospel. It was not the rigid adherence to a principle, but the response of love and fidelity to a person. It was a matter not of necessity and coercion, but rather of freedom and grateful devotion. "Trocmé would not separate himself from Jesus," writes Hallie, "by hating and killing his fellowman" (p. 84).

This ethic of fidelity was very closely connected in Trocmé's mind with an ethic of witness to the cross. André Trocmé confessed the traditional faith of the church, from which he drew some remarkably untraditional conclusions. He affirmed the incarnation and the atonement. That is, he affirmed, as Hallie points out, that God had shown us how precious humankind was to him by taking the form of a human being and coming down to help us in our deepest need. Jesus Christ had enacted our salvation by dying in our place on the cross. "In short," says Hallie, "Jesus was for Trocmé the embodied forgiveness of sins, and staying close to Jesus meant always being ready to forgive your enemies instead of torturing and killing them. Trocmé could not bear to separate himself from Jesus by ignoring the precious quality of human life that God had demonstrated in the birth, the life, and the crucifixion of His son" (p. 34). In other words, Trocmé believed, in the words of St. Paul, that "one had died for all," or, in the words of Isaiah, that "he was wounded for our transgressions" and that "with his stripes we are healed." And Trocmé also believed, again in the words of St. Paul, that in consequence Christians were called to a passionate ethic of fidelity and devotion, living "no longer for themselves but for him who for their sake died and was raised."

The practical conclusion Trocmé drew from this confession of faith determined not only his thought but also his life and ministry. "By choosing to save [humankind] at the price of his life," Trocmé wrote in his book *Jesus and the Nonviolent Revolution*, "Jesus forever joined two facts: redemption and nonviolence. Because Jesus is the Redeemer no one can any longer save by killing or kill to save. Life alone, life given, not exacted from others, can save a [person's] life."[44] Here is where the ethic of fidelity and devotion crosses over into an ethic of witness. "Nonviolence is above all," Trocmé wrote, "a witness to God" (p. 168). It is not a mere technique for social change, which would make it into little more than a means to some higher end. For Trocmé nonviolence was more nearly an end in itself, for Christian believers could have no higher goal than to bear witness in the world to God's love for the world in Jesus Christ, who sacrificed himself on the cross that we might be redeemed from death to life. The function of God's people on earth, Trocmé wrote, "is to be God's witnesses of the cross and redemption" (p. 166). "The object of nonviolence," he continued — whether it be the enemy who means us harm or the neighbor who claims our help in need — "the fabric of which it is knit, is the human being as person, always unique in the sight of God's person, since the unique Son of God sacrificed His life for this person" (p. 172).

Space does not permit further exploration of how this ethic of nonvio-

---

44. André Trocmé, *Jesus and the Nonviolent Revolution* (Scottdale, Pa.: Herald, 1973), p. 147. References which follow in the text are to this work.

lence — of watchfulness, noncompliance, fidelity and witness — may have enabled goodness to happen as it did in Le Chambon. Pastor Trocmé not only practiced this ethic for himself, he also conveyed it to the hearts of his parishioners so that when the time came they were ready. Although more might be contemplated, when all is said and done one thing remains clear. When the time came, they did not fail to act on behalf of so many persecuted children and adults.

CHAPTER 5

Karl Barth and the Politics of Sectarian Protestantism: A Dialogue with John Howard Yoder

(1980)

Whatever else might be said about the controversial volume by Friedrich Wilhelm Marquardt, *Theologie und Sozialismus: Das Beispiel Karl Barths* (Munich, 1972), two points would seem beyond dispute.

First, Marquardt served effectively to dispel the illusion that Barth's theology was done in splendid isolation. No longer could Karl Barth be so safely imagined (whether by his critics or by his adulators) as a man squirreled away in his cubicle with a Bible, surrounded by musty theological texts, and absorbed in some strangely scholastic enterprise. Instead, as Dieter Schellong has pointed out, Marquardt managed to place Barth's theology once again in the midst of contemporary political debate, where it had always been during Barth's lifetime.[1] The Barth who had repeatedly insisted that "It is a bad sign when Christians are frightened by 'political' sermons — as if Christian preaching could be anything but political!"[2] — or that "Whenever there is theological talk, it is always implicitly or explicitly political talk as well,"[3] this Barth had to be given another look and taken much more seriously. The standard view made popular by Reinhold Niebuhr, that Barth's theology "disavows political responsibility in principle,"[4] seemed certainly to be foiled and sent well down the road toward the obscurity it deserved.

---

1. Dieter Schellong, "On Reading Karl Barth from the Left," in *Karl Barth and Radical Politics,* ed. George Hunsinger (Philadelphia: Westminster, 1976), p. 141.

2. Karl Barth, "The Christian Community and the Civil Community," in *Community, State, and Church,* ed. Will Herberg (Garden City, N.Y.: Doubleday, 1960), p. 185.

3. Barth, as quoted by Eberhard Busch, *Karl Barth* (Philadelphia: Fortress, 1976), p. 292.

4. Reinhold Niebuhr, *Essays in Applied Christianity* (New York: Meridian, 1959), p. 187.

The second point about Marquardt's volume is that it aroused the tiny world of Barthian scholarship from, as it were, its dogmatic slumbers. Defenders and detractors jumped up from all sides to join in the fray about whether or not Marquardt had distorted, or even obliterated, the intentions and teachings of the master. The positions argued in the course of that controversy need not be reiterated here. Suffice it to say that despite some brilliant flashes of insight, Marquardt left the unfortunate impression that for Barth theology was something like a predicate of socialism, rather than the other way around, and that thus Marquardt made things too easy for his detractors.

Now that the dust has more or less settled, an interesting phenomenon may be observed. The discussion is entering a new and second phase — one no longer centered on Marquardt's work although deeply influenced by the questions it raised. Participants in this more recent discussion are taking it for granted that Barth's theology combined with some sort of left-wing politics, but they are attempting to define that politics and its theological basis with renewed precision.

In what follows, one important voice in the new discussion will be singled out for a careful hearing — that of John Howard Yoder. However, there are two others I should like to mention at least in passing, Dieter Schellong and Ulrich Dannemann, both of whom have made substantial contributions. Yoder argues that Barth represents the political stance not of a reformed but of a sectarian Protestant; Schellong interprets Barth as a thoroughgoing critic of bourgeois culture;[5] and Dannemann retraces in a full-length study the ground covered by Marquardt to show that the mature Barth ended up as a proponent of democratic socialism.[6] Although it would be interesting to study these three positions in relation to each other, time and space do not permit. Therefore, let us take what is perhaps the most provocative of the three — the position of Yoder — and examine it in some detail.

Yoder's contribution has been brief but pithy. In a paper[7] delivered to this

---

5. See Dieter Schellong, "A Theological Critique of the 'Bourgeois' World-View," in *Christianity and the Bourgeoisie*, ed. J. B. Metz (New York: Seabury, 1979), pp. 74-82; Schellong, *Bürgertum und christliche Religion* (Munich: Chr. Kaiser, 1975), pp. 96-115; Schellong, "Karl Barth als Theologe der Neuzeit," in K. D. Steck and D. Schellong, *Karl Barth und die Neuzeit* (Munich: Chr. Kaiser, 1973), pp. 54-68.

6. Ulrich Dannemann, *Theologie und Politik im Denken Karl Barths* (Munich: Chr. Kaiser, 1977); Dannemann, "Karl Barth und der religiöse Sozialismus," *Evangelische Theologie* 37 (1977): 127-48.

7. John Howard Yoder, "The Basis of Barth's Social Ethics" (unpublished manuscript of a lecture delivered at Elmhurst College in September 1978 to the Midwest chapter of the Karl Barth Society of North America).

society and in a review of a book on the Marquardt controversy,[8] Yoder has attempted to direct our attention to some previously neglected matters. If I understand him correctly, he makes essentially three points. The first is methodological. Yoder warns sharply against the temptation to overevaluate the seminal when tracing the relation of theology to politics in Barth's thought. He contends that Marquardt and others have succumbed to this temptation, which in general he sees as typical of much German theological scholarship. Yoder's point here would seem to be essentially negative — telling us what the relation of theology to politics is not — and he uses a variety of images to express it. Theology is not a railroad's switching yard or an opening move in a chess game which determines the political and ethical outcome by virtue of a few foundational moves. Nor is it like an inertial guidance system in which the entire political course of the missile, so to speak, is determined by the data fed in at the outset. What Yoder seems to be driving at is that, for Barth, political praxis was never a matter of sheer deduction from first principles, never something mechanistic or automatic. Therefore, one can make no blanket statements on the basis of Barth's theology alone, but one must rather attend to the way Barth actually developed his political ideas over the course of time.[9]

At the general level at which this point is made, I don't see how anyone could disagree with it. Certainly Yoder is right that no rigid determinism governs the move from theology to politics, not even for Barth, and perhaps he is also right to detect a tendency in Marquardt to interpret Barth in this way. I have two reservations about Yoder's methodological point, however. First, when one attends to the way the mature Barth actually developed his political ideas, one discovers that there was a hard side and a soft side to his theological concept of political praxis, or to put it another way, a fixed side and an open-ended side. The fixed side was what he called the "one unswerving direction and one continuous line," the "constant direction"[10] which he believed derived from the gospel and should be binding on the church. Then, within these relatively fixed boundaries came the open-ended side, which allowed a great deal of latitude for dealing with any particular political decision on the basis of communal deliberation and prayer. As I have argued elsewhere,[11] Barth was never entirely clear about just exactly how he thought the fixed side was to be theologically derived and grounded, but he was quite clear about the fact that,

8. Yoder, review of *Karl Barth and Radical Politics*, in *Journal of Church and State* 10 (1978): 338f.; hereafter referred to as "Review."

9. Yoder, "Basis," p. 2; "Review," pp. 238f.

10. Barth, "Christian Community," p. 180.

11. George Hunsinger, "Karl Barth and Radical Politics: Some Further Considerations," *Studies in Religion/Sciences Religieuses* 7 (1978): 165-91.

among other things, he considered it to be broadly socialist. (Dannemann throws some interesting light on this question, which cannot here be pursued.)[12] So, while Yoder is right that Barth does not represent a rigid determinism, it is also the case that he does not represent a flaccid pragmatism either. The really important questions only begin to arise once one has ruled out these two extremes.

My second reservation goes beyond noting that Yoder's methodological point doesn't tell us very much. Yoder charges that Marquardt and others have overemphasized the early developments in Barth's theology at the expense of later ones. By contrast, Yoder wants to insist that Barth's way of expressing his socialism changed greatly over time and that there are some highly important later developments in Barth's thought which need to be recognized and accounted for. Again, at a general level there would be nothing here to quarrel with. In Barth's socialism there was not only continuity but also change. Because the continuity itself had been in question, Marquardt, Gollwitzer, and others had felt it necessary to emphasize, each in his own way, the element of continuity. Now Yoder comes along, apparently presupposing the element of continuity, at least to some extent, and wants to emphasize the magnitude of the changes. As long as Yoder gives the element of continuity its due, no objections are in order and what he insists on is much to the point.

Yet we have moved onto very different terrain when Yoder comes to his central thesis, in which he claims that "despite the variations of time and setting, Karl Barth's social stance was in theory and practice that of a free churchman. . . ."[13] At this point Yoder seems in danger of falling off the other side of the log — that is, of overestimating the magnitude of Barth's later developments. Only on the basis of a radical discontinuity in his development — a discontinuity which would have arguably placed him in contradiction to some of his most basic theological convictions — can a case be made that Barth came to espouse toward the end of his career the politics of sectarian Protestantism.

Yoder's other two points are more nearly substantial than methodological. One of these raises the question as to just what constitutes radical politics for Barth. Here Yoder insists that Marquardt and others have construed the term too loosely, on the one hand, and too narrowly, on the other. "Radical politics" is construed too loosely when every kind of consideration is made to count as evidence that Barth's politics were radical. Yoder thinks the term loses its meaning when it encompasses such disparate things as being to the left of the political center, belonging to a socialist party, criticizing capitalist society,

12. Dannemann, *Theologie und Politik im Denken Karl Barths*, pp. 184-229.
13. Yoder, "Review," p. 239.

not being stridently anticommunist, etc.[14] Here it seems that Yoder misses the point rather widely. Not only, as Yoder also wants to stress, did Barth's way of expressing his socialism change from one situation to the next, but what Barth was actually expressing in and through these changes was precisely his socialism. The problem in Marquardt at this point, it seems to me, is not that he is conceptually loose, but that he does not make his working definition of socialism more explicit. Helmut Gollwitzer's comment here is germane:

> Marquardt has clearly worked out what content and what nuances the concept had for Barth. The lack of consistency about it is not as great as it appears in the face of the conflict of the many socialisms. For they are all close together when it comes to the notion and promise of the goal: Socialism means not merely certain social reforms, certain improvements within the capitalistic system of production, but rather a society in which all members are assured of an equal share in the commonly produced social product, and in which the control of production is in the hands of the producers — a society which is thus as egalitarian as possible; one which is constantly destroying the material privileges that continually accumulate and which is constantly building up a material democracy. . . . Karl Barth knew what he was saying when he spoke of socialism.[15]

This definition of the socialist dimension to Barth's radical politics would seem to suffice for general purposes. The supposedly disparate elements which Yoder cites are all varying expressions of a single political vision. If any lingering doubt should remain that this vision is exactly the sort of thing Barth had in mind, it ought to be dispelled by the work of Dannemann, who shows in considerable detail that Barth was especially interested in the socialist goal of production for humane use rather than for profit, and in extending democratic practices and control to the economic order so as to eliminate class privileges of wealth and income in favor of economic and therefore political equality.[16]

The other half of Yoder's point — that in Barth's case the term "radical politics" must not be construed too narrowly — would seem to hold considerable merit.[17] Barth's radical politics was nothing less than socialist, but certainly it was also something more. I know of no one who has made this point

14. Yoder, "Basis," pp. 1f.

15. Helmut Gollwitzer, "Kingdom of God and Socialism in the Theology of Karl Barth," in *Karl Barth and Radical Politics*, p. 100.

16. Dannemann, *Theologie und Politik im Denken Karl Barths*, pp. 207-16.

17. Yoder, "Review," p. 238.

more forcefully than Yoder. Barth's practical rather than ideological socialism found its counterpart in a practical rather than ideological pacifism. Whether one takes his socialism or his pacifism, it would seem that Barth's conception was characterized by what I earlier described as a "fixed" and an "open-ended" side. The difference was, however, that Barth hedged considerably when it came to embracing the fixed side of the pacifist implications of his own theology — even toward the end of his career — in a way that he did not when it came to the fixed side of the socialist implications. As I think Yoder has brilliantly demonstrated in *Karl Barth and the Problem of War* (Nashville: Abingdon, 1970), Barth's more tentative and equivocal relation to pacifism stands in contradiction to the thrust of his theology. Hence the radicalism of Barth's theology includes pacifist as well as socialist dimensions. In other words, just as the question his theology poses is not whether but how to be socialist, so also is its question not whether but how to be pacifist.

Besides the practical pacifism, Yoder calls attention to other radical elements in Barth's political vision[18] — namely, to the disestablishmentarian tendency in his later writings on the church, to the stance taken against all forms of authoritarianism, and to what Yoder calls Barth's radical approach to the doctrine of the state. In the latter instance Yoder seems to be using the term "radical" in the sense of "sectarian Protestant." I will argue, however, that there is nothing even in tendency in Barth's later writings in which he approaches a sectarian Protestant doctrine of the state and that, in fact, the tendency of his thought runs very much in the opposite direction. For now, however, it is enough simply to underscore Yoder's point that Barth's radical politics includes more than just his socialism.

The last of Yoder's three main points concerns the question I have already had occasion to broach — the question of free church elements in Barth's theology and politics. Here I think Yoder is at his most penetrating and his most shortsighted. In other words, I think this is the most interesting and important proposal that he makes, and that the results are mixed.

Let me try to sort out the various strands which constitute the proposal. If I understand him correctly (and let me add that I do not always find him to be as clear as might be hoped), Yoder's case for the claim that Barth's political theology ended up in the free church tradition seems to rest on three separate prongs. First, Barth developed what was essentially a free church ecclesiology. Second, he moved from an establishment to a nonconformist social ethic. And finally, he was implicitly headed toward a sectarian Protestant view of the secular realm. The warrant Yoder supplies for the second two prongs is the claim

18. Yoder, "Basis," pp. 7-10; "Review," p. 239.

that Barth's supposedly free church ecclesiology provides a clue to his emerging social stance as a whole. Barth's supposedly new understanding of Jesus as an ethical example for the church[19] and his development of the ethics of sanctification (toward practical pacifism) were leading him onto unanticipated turf in which he had become a sectarian Protestant without actually realizing it.

I think Yoder is largely right about a sectarian dimension in Barth's later doctrine of the church, that he is only half right about the ethic of nonconformity, and that he is mostly wrong about Barth's attitude toward the civil community or the secular realm. This means that I do not think the free church dimension to Barth's later ecclesiology supplies the key to his social stance as a whole or that Barth's social ethics can be reduced to a matter of nonconformity.

It is obviously true that Barth's later doctrine of the church shows some strong affinities with the free church tradition. One need only be familiar with Barth's rejection of infant baptism and his "low" view of the Eucharist to realize that. Yet Yoder draws out some other rather interesting parallels: Barth presupposes such a separation between the church and the world that he poses the question of how those who confess Christ can find a common language with those who do not; by deriving the order of the gathered community from Christology itself, he is led to prefer the word *Gemeinde* to the word *Kirche* and to develop a concept of church order based on service and noncoercion rather than hierarchy; he allows for discontinuities and new beginnings in the history of the church as opposed to stressing a necessary continuity as the basis for ecclesiastical legitimacy; he rejects the idea that there is only one pattern for the church valid at all times and places; finally and most importantly, he argues

---

19. I have my doubts about Yoder's claim ("Basis," p. 7) that the emphasis in Barth's Christology shifted from a more nearly symbolic to a fully human Jesus. (Yoder thinks that in the earlier volumes of the *Church Dogmatics* Jesus was some sort of cipher for revelation.) I think it would probably be safer and fairer to say something like this: From the earlier to the later volumes of the *Church Dogmatics,* there is a general tendency for Barth to move in the direction of a narrative Christology, or at least a Christology with strong narrative aspects. Elements of it appear as early as *Church Dogmatics* II/2, while it emerges in full bloom in IV/1, continuing throughout vol. IV. What Yoder sees as a radical departure for Barth (the discussion of Jesus as the Holy One to be followed in discipleship by the members of the sanctified community) seems to me to be more like a special instance and consequence of the narrative turn in his Christology rather than something fundamentally new in its own right. What Yoder sees as christologically "programmatic" in the earlier volumes would seem to me to be programmatic mainly in the sense that it anticipates at a general level, in embryo, so to speak, the narrative aspects of the Christology in the later volumes. On the other hand, I do not think Yoder is entirely wrong about the so-called *Chiffre*-effect which sometimes comes through in Barth's earlier christological discussions. The point here, however, is that once again Yoder would seem to be overstating the discontinuity of the later from the earlier Barth.

that the proper order of the church ought to serve as an example for the proper ordering of the civil community.[20]

It is this latter point about the exemplary character of communal order which I find most fascinating. Here Yoder has indeed discerned something that others have neglected. Barth had always believed in his later years that the Christian community ought to serve as a model and prototype for the civil community, but apparently his thinking underwent a subtle shift. He was apparently somewhat more tentative in 1946 when he wrote "The Christian Community and the Civil Community" than he was in 1955 when he wrote "The Upbuilding of the Christian Community" in *Church Dogmatics* IV/2. The church's proper shaping of its own internal life shifted from being described as "perhaps the most important contribution" (1946) to being indeed "the decisive contribution" (1955) which the Christian community can make in its social witness to the larger world.[21]

This is precisely the trend that Yoder is interested in identifying — a trend in which Barth increasingly emphasizes the uniqueness, separateness, and primacy of the church. Although, as I will explain, I think this trend can be overestimated, Barth's conviction that the Christian community will make its greatest contribution to society not directly but indirectly through the creative ordering of its own gathered life did seem to grow in intensity. One might underscore this point by suggesting that a church which is indifferent or self-satisfied with regard to the current form of its own order will hardly be in a position to speak convincingly about what Barth called "that great alteration of the human situation"[22] to which the church is called to bear witness, nor will the church be in a very good position to draw any implications from that great alteration for the secular realm. To put it bluntly: Ought not the socialism and pacifism implied by the gospel find their primary application in the church's arrangement of its own internal affairs — including matters of racial and ethnic composition in its individual congregations, of gender equality in matters of governance, and of socially responsible financial investments?[23]

This emphasis on applying the social implications of the gospel first of all to the common life of the church rather than immediately to society at large is not always a popular one today, and it is to Yoder's credit to have called attention to

---

20. Yoder, "Basis," pp. 7-9.

21. Barth, "Christian Community," p. 186.

22. Karl Barth, *Church Dogmatics* IV/2 (Edinburgh: T. & T. Clark, 1958), p. 721.

23. Cf. Barth: "How can the world believe the gospel . . . if . . . the church shows that it has no intention of basing its own internal policy on the gospel? . . . The church must not forget that what it is rather than what it says will be best understood, not least in the State" ("Christian Community," pp. 186, 187).

this theme in Barth. It is at this point that I think Yoder is largely right about the free church aspect to Barth's later doctrine of the church. Yet it is precisely from this point forward that I think Yoder begins to go wrong. He mistakes Barth's movement in the direction of a free church ecclesiology with a movement in the direction of a free church self-understanding, as if the two were the same thing. In other words, Yoder begins to mistake the part for the whole. An ecclesiological aspect is one thing, a self-understanding quite another.[24]

Take, for example, what Yoder says about Barth's supposed movement from an establishment to a nonconformist social ethic. According to Yoder, the establishment ethic concentrated on the shape of secular society and saw the order of the community as derivative, whereas the later nonconformist ethic concentrated on the Christian community's order, from which, then, the order of society was to devolve.[25] It is a matter of some consequence, however, that for the mature Barth this whole conceptuality was decisively transcended, that neither the order of secular society nor the order of the Christian community stood at the center, but that both of them were seen instead as derivative from something else, from something much more central, from something they both had in common. Consequently, the primacy of the Christian community over the civil community in Barth's thought was highly relativized, and it is this very relativization — in form and content — which gave his social thought its irrevocably nonsectarian tenor and thrust.

Yoder is only half right about the ethic of nonconformity in Barth, because he misses its essential connection to an ethic of solidarity. He thus ends up elevating into a position of priority a concept which in Barth's mature thought occupies a position of subordination. It is true that Barth describes the community as standing against the world and as needing to be upheld by Word and Spirit because it is endangered by the world. It is not true, however, that Barth rigidifies this opposition into what Yoder calls a polar encounter.[26] For Barth nonconformity takes place for, and only for, the sake of solidarity. He thinks there can be no solidarity without nonconformity, but he never sees nonconformity in isolation or as an end in itself. It is only because the church is for the world that it must also be against it. The human No of the church, like the divine No to church and world, is a No which always originates from and always tends toward a more fundamental Yes. In Barth nonconformity is always instrumental and subordinate to solidarity; the church separates itself from the world only in order to participate in it.

---

24. Yoder seems to use the terms "free church ecclesiology" and "free church self-understanding" as if they were virtually synonymous on p. 10 of "Basis."

25. Yoder, "Basis," p. 10.

26. Yoder, "Basis," p. 8.

It is the note of solidarity with the world, with all that implies — it is the note of affirmation — which separates Barth's ecclesiology and politics from all forms of sectarianism in Christian thought. Barth writes: "Solidarity with the world means full commitment to it, unreserved participation in its situation, in the promise given it by creation, in its responsibility for the arrogance, sloth and falsehood which reign within it, in its suffering under the resultant distress, but primarily and supremely in the free grace of God demonstrated and addressed to it in Jesus Christ, and therefore in its hope."[27]

There is an important sense for Barth in which the church is not to be seen as more sanctified than the world, nor the world as less sanctified than the church. The church shares with the world a solidarity in both sin and grace. This inclusive solidarity meant that Barth found what the church had in common with the world to be always more fundamental than any polarity which might arise on the basis of the church's human response to Jesus Christ.

Up to this point I have affirmed two things, that a certain sectarian aspect may be found in Barth's doctrine of the relationship between ecclesiastical and civil order, but that such a tendency may not be found in his broader understanding of the relationship between the church and the world. Neither of these affirmations, however, is sufficient to settle the question of whether Barth adopted, as Yoder claims, the social stance of a sectarian Protestant. That question can only be resolved by looking at the point where the previous two affirmations converge, that is, at the doctrine of the civil community and the state. Barth's doctrine of the civil community as governed by the state is the crux of the matter, as I think Yoder rightly senses, because it brings the relation of nonconformity and solidarity to a head. If the sectarian tendency in Barth's doctrine of the church prevails, then his attitude toward the state will be one in which the church's nonparticipation is predominant. On the other hand, if the nonsectarian tendency prevails, then his attitude will be one in which the active solidarity of Christians in the tasks of the state is taken as a matter of course. Furthermore, if the sectarian tendency prevails, two other attitudes are to be expected: a sharp priority assigned to the church over the civil community in the scheme of redemption, and a sharp institutional polarity between church and state due to the state's being implicated in the mechanisms of coercion.

To show that Barth's understanding of the state runs directly counter to the sectarian view, I will contrast Barth's stance at certain decisive points to one taken by an unimpeachable representative of the sectarian Protestant view —

27. Karl Barth, *Church Dogmatics* IV/3, second half (Edinburgh: T. & T. Clark, 1962), p. 773; hereafter cited as IV/3.

John Howard Yoder. In his book *The Christian Witness to the State*,[28] Yoder presents views which at key points diverge significantly from those advanced by Barth in his essay "The Christian Community and the Civil Community" — an essay, by the way, which Yoder has untenably classified as sectarian.[29]

A first point of divergence is this: whereas Yoder proceeds from the assumption that a predominantly negative relationship underlies any positive connections between the Christian community and the state, Barth's assumption is exactly the reverse, that any negative relationship between the two communities is always undergirded by one that is fundamentally positive. As far as Yoder is concerned, the fundamental *diastasis* between church and state is based on the fact that the church is a community of love which has renounced all means of coercion, in contrast to the state, which by its very nature is grounded in force.[30] Barth, on the other hand, sees the fundamentally positive relationship between the two communities as grounded in the fact that they are both exponents of the kingdom of God independently of their relationship to one another.[31]

Here we have come to a difference of major proportions. Because the state is by nature implicated in violence, Yoder can find no positive and independent relationship of the state to God's kingdom. The only positive relationship which Yoder describes between the state and God's kingdom is mediated through the state's relationship to the church. It is only through its relationship to the church that the state makes any positive contribution to the order of redemption. By means of force the state maintains social order and preserves the fabric of society so that the church's work, the work of redemption, can be carried on. The state can only play a role in God's redemptive plan through this, its service to the church. In and of itself it does not represent in any sense the order of redemption; rather, compromised by coercion, it stands beside, and therefore outside, the order of redemption, by representing the order of providence through which evil and chaos are restrained. The coercive state could not possibly have a positive relationship to God's kingdom unmediated by its relationship to the church, for by definition it represents the old aeon of sin.[32]

---

28. It is possible that in his later writings Yoder modified the views stated in this work. To what extent those possible modifications would qualify my analysis is beyond the scope of this paper. My analysis would at least hold good for a certain variety of sectarian Protestantism, a variety that it is unlikely Yoder ever completely left behind.

29. Yoder, "Basis," pp. 7f.

30. Yoder, *The Christian Witness to the State*, 3rd ed. (Newton, Kans.: Faith and Life Press, 1973), pp. 6f.

31. Barth, "Christian Community," pp. 154, 156, 160, 164, 169, 170, etc.

32. Yoder, *Christian Witness*, pp. 8-13.

For Barth, on the other hand, the civil order may stand in a positive relationship to God's kingdom which is not directly dependent on its relationship to the church. It has its own independent and ultimately indissoluble connection with the order of redemption. To be sure, Barth also says the ultimate purpose of the state is to make possible the existence and work of the church, but for him that does not exhaust the state's positive relation to the order of redemption. For Barth the civil order not only restrains evil; in its own limited but still significant way it bears witness in a positive sense to God's kingdom to the extent that it fosters humanization in the world through such things as establishing justice and safeguarding freedom and peace. The state itself, its coercive aspects notwithstanding, can be molded into a positive likeness, however distant, to God's kingdom. Barth can even go so far as to say what is completely unimaginable from Yoder, that through the very exercise of political power and order, the activity of the state brings about the unhallowed world's "relative sanctification."[33]

A second major point of difference between Yoder and Barth is close to the first. The polarity Yoder posits between church and state finds its conceptual counterpart in the sharp priority he assigns to the church in the scheme of redemption. Yoder can speak of "the absolute priority of church over state in the plan of God," of God's kingdom as representing "the victory of the church and the overcoming of the world,"[34] and finally, in the supreme example of this theme: "The meaning of history — and therefore the significance of the state — lies in the creation and work of the church."[35] From Barth's point of view, none of these statements would be possible. Where Yoder finds himself speaking of the church, Barth would insist on speaking of Jesus Christ. He would say that it is not the church which has "absolute priority" over the state in the plan of God, but Jesus Christ. He would deny that God's kingdom represents the victory of the church in any exclusive sense, for it first and foremost represents the victory of Jesus Christ, whose redemptive work is focused on the church but not restricted to it. Finally, Barth would insist that the very meaning of history — and therefore the significance of (among other things) the state — lies not in the creation and work of the church, but in the obedience and Lordship of Jesus Christ.

These are not just idle points. They contain the essence of Barth's difference from the free church tradition. Barth places the civil community in general and the state in particular in the order of redemption rather than in the order of the unredeemed creation. For the free church tradition, and here of

33. Barth, "Christian Community," p. 157.
34. Yoder, *Christian Witness*, p. 17.
35. Yoder, *Christian Witness*, p. 13.

course it is certainly not alone, the civil community and the state represent the unredeemed creation par excellence. But for Barth there is no unredeemed creation. Therefore, at bottom, even the most tyrannical state cannot lose its positive connection to Jesus Christ. Therefore, the Christian community cannot cease to be actively involved in the affairs of the civil community and the state. And therefore, the difference between church and world will always be more relative for Barth than for any truly sectarian Protestant view.

It was this point — the positive and independent, if still limited, participation of the civil community and the state in the order of redemption — which I had in mind earlier when I said that Barth could not have adopted the social stance of a sectarian Protestant without contradicting some of his most basic theological convictions. The fact that Barth may in some ways have been moving in a free church direction with regard to ecclesiology — a fact which I think no one could doubt — implies nothing about a corresponding movement with regard to his understanding of the secular realm itself. To suggest that, had he lived, he would have developed a sectarian understanding of the state, is surely to have misunderstood the whole tenor of Barth's thought on this particular point. Even with regard to church order the later Barth did not imagine only a one-way street. He wrote:

> If the community were to imagine that the reach of sanctification of humanity accomplished in Jesus Christ were restricted to itself and the ingathering of believers, that it did not have corresponding effects *extra muros ecclesiae,* that would be in flat contradiction to its own confession to its Lord. . . . In its encounter with the world it may sometimes happen that in this particular field the children of the world prove to be wiser than the children of light, so that in the question concerning its law the church has reason to learn from the world . . . receiving from it the witness which it ought to give. (IV/3, pp. 723, 725)

It was neither the Christian community nor the civil community which stood at the center of Karl Barth's social thought. What stood at the center was Jesus Christ and therefore the kingdom of God. It was Jesus Christ and God's kingdom which Barth believed that both communities — and not just one of them — had in common. It was Jesus Christ and God's kingdom — not one another — from which their mutual relations were derived. And therefore it was Jesus Christ and God's kingdom which relativized all differences between these two communities on earth in a way which runs counter to the basic impulses and emphases not only of Yoder but of sectarian Protestantism in general.

Now at this point, I suspect, John Howard Yoder would still not be convinced. He would return to the methodological point mentioned at the outset and contend that Barth's ethics of sanctification had led him to develop themes for which he had not made programmatic provision. As evidence he might well go on to cite the following passage from *Church Dogmatics* IV/2, in which Barth says the kingdom of God puts an end "to the fixed idea of the necessity and beneficial value of force." Barth continues:

> The direction of Jesus must have embedded itself particularly deeply in the disciples in this respect. They were neither to fear force nor to exercise it. They were not to fear it as brought to bear against themselves, for at the very worst their enemies could kill only the body and not the soul. . . . On the other hand, those who have no need to fear the exercise of force against them by others because it cannot finally harm them can hardly expect to apply force to others. (IV/2, p. 549)

Barth then concludes by saying that this is "a concrete and incontestable direction which has to be carried out exactly as given" (IV/2, p. 550).

In light of such a passage as this, Yoder might ask, how could Barth possibly be conceived as making provision for a Christian participation in the coercive tasks of the state? He would again insist, in light of all the other sectarian strands he has isolated in Barth, that the conclusion is still irresistible when all things are considered that Barth had unconsciously become a sectarian Protestant in his concept of political praxis. And he might drive this conclusion home by asking how at this point — the point of participating in the civil and political exercise of force — Barth could have moved in any other direction than toward an ethic of nonconformity and noncooperation rather than toward an ethic of solidarity and involvement. Would it not be only a bogus sort of solidarity which would allow the Christian to be implicated in the exercise of force?

My reply to this line of reasoning, which I have taken the liberty to surmise that Yoder might pursue, would be this, and with these remarks I conclude. First, I think Yoder is on to something here. In the course of reflecting on the meaning of sanctification, Barth did move very far in a pacifist direction; he did so in a way for which it would seem he had not always programmatically anticipated; and he did so in a way which would probably have required him to revise or supplement some of his ideas about political praxis. I cannot imagine Barth repeating his 1938 saying about Czech soldiers against Germany dying for the sake of Christ, nor can I quite imagine him enlisting so enthusiastically in the Swiss border guard if he were to remain true to the statement cited on the use of force.

On the other hand, I have my doubts that Barth would have been carried to the point of developing a sectarian view of the state and of rejecting all

Christian participation in the civil and political exercise of force. There is, after all, more than one way of being a practical pacifist. But as Yoder and I would both have to agree, at this point we are entering onto speculative ground, for the later Barth simply did not develop a full-fledged doctrine of the state, or of Christian participation in its administration. For the theological reasons I have already given, I suspect Barth would have remained within the broad outlines of "The Christian Community and the Civil Community" — an essay which I think it would be mistaken to regard as sectarian. At any rate, it is always a risky business to isolate one line of thought in Barth — even when it is dominant — without watching for the qualifications which he derives from a consideration of its opposite. As Robert Jenson once remarked, it is astonishing how many wheels within wheels Barth's dialectical engine could keep spinning. On the matter of Christians exercising force in some civil and political contexts, I even suspect that one of those wheels within wheels would go something like this: "[The church] manifests a remarkable conformity to the world if concern for its purity and reputation forbid it to compromise itself with it. . . . As distinct from all other circles and groups, the community of Jesus Christ cannot possibly allow itself to exist in this pharisaical conformity to the world. Coming from the table of the Lord, it cannot fail to follow his example and to sit down at table with the rest, with all sinners" (IV/3, p. 775).[36]

36. I cite this passage to make a point about Barth, not to imply anything about the position taken by Yoder. It is a peculiarly (though not exclusively) Christian insight that power cannot be exercised without incurring guilt. On this point I think Barth and Yoder would agree. But for Yoder, at least in his early writings, there is such heterogeneity between love and political force, and between the communities organized on those respective bases, that it is virtually impossible to conceive of direct Christian involvement in power politics. I suspect that Barth would have acknowledged the same heterogeneity, but would have then gone on to make some dialectical qualifications. I think he would have left room for some Christian participation in civil matters and thus for some Christian wielding of the instruments of coercion. Among other things, I think Barth would have complicated the heterogeneity and relativized it on the basis of human solidarity in sin. The passage cited suggests that there may be a basis for this interpretation in Barth's mature published work.

PART II

DOCTRINAL THEOLOGY

Karl Barth's Christology: Its Basic Chalcedonian Character

(1999)

"In Christ two natures met to be thy cure."[1] When George Herbert wrote these words, he captured the essence of Chalcedonian Christology, with all its strange complexity and simplicity, in a single elegant line. It is sometimes overlooked that the interest behind Chalcedonian Christology has always been largely soteriological. Herbert's line, however, makes the point very well. It is the saving work of Christ — *to be thy cure* — which serves as the guiding intention behind the Chalcedonian definition of Christ's person, just as the definition of his person (following Herbert) — *in Christ two natures met* — serves as the crucial premise of Christ's saving work. Change the definition of Christ's person — make him less than fully God and fully human at the same time — and the saving cure Christ offers changes drastically as well. In other words, just as it makes no sense to have a high view of Christ's person without an equally high view of his work, so a high view of Christ's work — in particular, of his saving death — cannot be sustained without a suitably high view of his person. The work presupposes the person just as the person conditions the work.[2]

---

1. George Herbert, "An Offering," in *The Life and Works of George Herbert*, vol. 2, ed. G. H. Palmer (Boston: Houghton Mifflin, 1905), p. 393, italics added.

2. This latter sentence, by the way, states a basic rule of all Christology, although as applied here it sheds light on a particular type, namely, the Chalcedonian. In any Christology, at least when internally coherent (which cannot always be presupposed), the person *(p)* and the work *(w)* of Christ mutually imply each other: If *w*, then *p*; and if *p*, then *w*. Insofar as modern Christology has typically abandoned a high view of Christ's person, it has also abandoned the correspondingly high conception of Christ's saving work that Chalcedonian Christology is

Much in this saving work depends, furthermore, on how *in Christ two natures met,* in other words, on how his natures are defined and related. It has not always been appreciated just how minimalist the historic Chalcedonian Definition really is in this respect. Chalcedonian Christology does not isolate a point on a line that one either occupies or not. It demarcates a region in which there is more than one place to take up residence. The region is defined by certain distinct boundaries. Jesus Christ is understood as "one person in two natures." The two natures — his deity and his humanity — are seen as internal to his person. He is not merely a human being with a special relationship to God, nor is he merely a divine being in the guise of a phantom humanity. He is, in the language of Chalcedon, a single person who is at once "complete in deity" and "complete in humanity." The restraint in these predications, astonishing as they are, is significant. No definition is given of either Christ's deity or his humanity except that, whatever else they might entail, they are present in him in a way that is unabridged, perfect, and complete. Further specifications of his "deity" and his "humanity" are not ruled out, but neither are they supplied.[3]

Two observations are in order here. First, from a Chalcedonian point of view, any definition of Christ's two natures that does not meet this minimal standard will fail, because it will not be sufficient for understanding Christ's saving work. Other features of his humanity and his deity will no doubt prove also to be greatly important, but unless both of the natures in Christ's person are seen as complete and unabridged in themselves, no adequate account can be given of his saving significance. Second, this minimalism suggests that the Chalcedonian Definition is not determined exclusively by soteriological inter-

---

meant to sustain. Only a high Christology can state without equivocation, for example, that Jesus Christ is "the Lamb of God who takes away the sin of the world" (John 1:29). If Christ's saving work consists in no more than his functioning as a spiritual teacher, a moral example, a symbol of religious experience, or even a unique bearer and transmitter of the Holy Spirit, a high or Chalcedonian view of Christ's person is *logically* unnecessary. As modernist Christologies typically evidence (though not always forthrightly), such a saving figure need only be "fully human" without also being "fully God."

3. The wording of the Chalcedonian Definition, of course, includes certain elaborations that analytically unpack what it means to say that Christ's deity and his humanity are each "true" *(alethos)* and "complete" *(teleios)* in themselves. His deity is said to be "consubstantial" *(homoousios)* with the Father, just as his humanity is said to be "consubstantial" *(homoousios)* with us. His deity is properly eternal, since he was "begotten before all ages of the Father," whereas his humanity is properly temporal, since he was "born of the Virgin Mary" (who is "the Mother of God" in his humanity). Since his humanity is complete, it consists in "a reasonable soul and a body" (not in a body alone), and he is "in all things like us, except without sin." For the full text of "The Symbol of Chalcedon" in Greek, Latin, and English, and with notes, see Philip Schaff, *The Creeds of Christendom,* vol. 2 (New York: Harper & Row, 1931), pp. 62-65.

ests. It is also largely a hermeneutical construct. It attempts to articulate the deep structure of the New Testament in its witness to the person of Christ. It arises from an ecclesial reading of the New Testament, taken as a whole, and then leads back to it again. It offers a framework for reading to guide the church as it interprets the multifaceted depiction of Jesus Christ contained in the New Testament.

The minimalism of Chalcedon, in other words, is not only constitutive but also regulative. It is constitutive with respect to salvation and regulative with respect to interpretation. More precisely, it is constitutive regarding Christ's person in the work of salvation and regulative for the church in its interpretation of Scripture. As a hermeneutical construct in particular, Chalcedon offers no more and no less than a set of spectacles for bringing the central witness of the New Testament into focus. It suggests that just because Jesus was fully God, that does not mean he was not also fully human; and that just because he was fully human, that does not mean he was not also fully God. When the New Testament depicts Jesus in his divine power, status, and authority, it presupposes his humanity; and when it depicts him in his human finitude, weakness, and mortality, it presupposes his deity. No interpretation will be adequate which asserts the one at the expense of the other.

A Chalcedonian reading is guided not only by a minimalist definition of Christ's two natures in themselves, to be fleshed out more thoroughly by attending to the New Testament itself, but also by a certain conception of how these two natures are related in one and the same person. Chalcedon proposes that when Christ's two natures met, they did so "without separation or division" and "without confusion or change." Neither his deity nor his humanity surrendered their defining characteristics, and yet they converged to form an indissoluble unity. Again the Chalcedonian formulations are notable for their open-textured reticence. Note that they are negatively rather than positively phrased. Neither separation nor confusion is tolerable. No more is said about how Christ's two natures are related than to rule out these unacceptable extremes. Each nature retained its integrity while engaging the other in the closest of communions. The relation of Christ's two natures, as stated by Chalcedon, suggests an abiding mystery of their unity-in-distinction and distinction-in-unity.

In short, any Chalcedonian Christology that is true to type will display certain basic features. It will see Jesus Christ as "one person in two natures." It will regard him as at once "complete in deity" and "complete in humanity." And it will hold that when these two natures met in Christ, they did so "without separation or division" and yet also "without confusion or change."

Although Karl Barth offers one of the most fully elaborated Chalcedonian

Christologies ever to have appeared in Christian doctrine, his Christology has been regularly classified otherwise, and indeed in diametrically opposite ways. The two basic alternatives to Chalcedonian Christology are, of course, the Alexandrian and the Antiochian types. At this point matters become tricky, because there are in fact relatively Alexandrian ways to be Chalcedonian, as there are also relatively Antiochian ways. The categorical boundaries, in other words, are fluid and can shade off into matters of degree. The centrifugal force involved in Chalcedon's key affirmations makes a certain gray area seem inevitable. "Complete in deity" and "complete in humanity," after all, repel one another like two identical magnetic poles. Even the most conscientious Chalcedonian effort is likely to veer off at some point in an Alexandrian or an Antiochian direction. Nevertheless, there are Alexandrian and Antiochian extremes that Chalcedon was designed to avoid. It is often thought, however, that these extremes represent in a blatant form certain tendencies endemic to the types as a whole. When Barth's Christology has been classified as other than Chalcedonian, it is alleged that he succumbs to one or another of these tendencies or extremes.

Chalcedon, as has been shown, basically sets forth two terms and a relationship. The terms are "deity" and "humanity," and their relationship is one of "unity-in-distinction" within one and the same person. Extreme versions of Alexandrian and Antiochian Christology (at least when seen from a Chalcedonian point of view) define at least one of the terms deficiently, or their relationship deficiently, or both. For our purposes it will not be necessary to explore every single area and degree of possible deficiency. Only two are relevant for understanding the existing allegations that what we have is a non-Chalcedonian Barth.

"Docetism" is the extreme or subtle Alexandrian tendency that stresses Jesus' deity at the expense of his humanity. His humanity is in effect no longer real but merely apparent. It is so overpowered by its union with his deity that it ends up being less than "complete." The union between the two natures finally obliterates their distinction. Jesus becomes the kind of divine being with a phantom humanity that Chalcedon wanted to rule out. When Barth's Christology is classified as "Alexandrian," or when is it criticized for being "docetic," the allegation is that Barth's conception of Christ's humanity is deficient.

"Nestorianism," on the other hand, is the extreme or subtle Antiochian tendency that has much the opposite result. It stresses Jesus' humanity at the expense of his deity. Although it thinks of Jesus as in some sense "divine," it does not think of him as "complete in deity." It does not see the union of his two "natures" as being internal to his "person." Rather it sees the "divinity" of Jesus as arising from the special character of his union as a human person with God. His "divinity" is more nearly adjectival than substantive, not intrinsic but participatory.[4] His union with God is fundamentally extrinsic to the constitution of his person, for his person is that of a human being. No matter how elevated by virtue of this union he may be, no matter how "divine," he is in himself never more than "fully human," and thus never also "fully God." When Barth's Christology is classified as "Antiochian," or when it is criticized for being "Nestorian," the allegation is that Barth's conception of Jesus' union with God, and thus of Jesus' complete and intrinsic "deity," is deficient.

No brief essay such as this could possibly sort through all the relevant texts and all the relevant issues, which are often finally quite technical, in order to demonstrate that the charges against Barth for being non-Chalcedonian do not stand up. Only some fairly general points of clarification and orientation can be offered. One point, however, has been almost universally overlooked. Barth is probably the first theologian in the history of Christian doctrine who alternates back and forth, deliberately, between an "Alexandrian" and an "Antiochian" idiom. The proper way to be Chalcedonian in Christology, Barth believed, was to follow the lead of the New Testament itself by employing a definite diversity of idioms. Any other strategy for articulating the Chalcedonian mystery would inevitably have unbalanced or one-sided results. Because Barth wanted to do justice to the whole mystery of Christ's person, as complete no less in deity than in humanity, he boldly set out to construct a large-scale collage, so to speak, out of seemingly incompatible materials.

The point of Christology, Barth believed, is to comprehend the incomprehensibility of the incarnation precisely in its incomprehensibility. The New Testament, he suggested, directs us to this incomprehensibility by the very way it juxtaposes two different modes of depiction. On the one hand, Jesus of Nazareth is depicted as the Son of God; and on the other, the Son of God is depicted as Jesus of Nazareth. The one mode is illustrated by the synoptic tradition; the other, by the Johannine tradition. The conclusion Barth drew is significant: "It is impossible to listen at one and the same time to the two statements that Jesus of Nazareth is the Son of God, and that the Son of God is Jesus of Nazareth. One hears either the one or the other or one hears nothing. When one is heard, the other can be heard only indirectly, in faith."[5] No harmonization of these different statements is either possible or appropriate. Although both, it is important to note, speak of the humanity and deity of Jesus Christ, they do so "with such varying interests and emphases" that we can only "misunderstand

---

4. This way of understanding Antiochian Christology follows the view taken by Richard A. Norris, *Manhood and Christ: A Study in the Christology of Theodore of Mopsuestia* (Oxford: Clarendon, 1963), esp. pp. 201, 213-16, 235-36.

5. Karl Barth, *Church Dogmatics* I/1 (Edinburgh: T. & T. Clark, 1936), p. 180; hereafter cited as I/1.

both" if we try to select merely the one while discarding the other, or else to smooth away the unresolved tensions between them (I/1, p. 180). The alternative that Barth proposed was actually to retain and uphold the tensions through a strategy of juxtaposition (thus emulating the strategy of the New Testament itself).

Adopting a strategy of juxtaposition meant surrendering the deeply ingrained expectation that the mystery of the incarnation could be contained by a conceptual scheme. The name of Jesus Christ, Barth commented, "is not a system representing a unified experience or a unified thought; it is the Word of God itself" (I/1, p. 181).[6] It points to a *Novum* in human experience and human history which cannot be understood on the basis of what is generally the case, but only on the basis of itself. The *Novum* of the incarnation is so unique that (contrary to someone like Kierkegaard) it cannot even be explained as an absurdity, for that would imply not only that the limits of our minds can circumscribe God's rationality, but also that we are in a position to know in advance what is possible or impossible for God. "The Incarnation is inconceivable," Barth wrote, "but it is not absurd, and it must not be explained as an absurdity."[7] It is rather to be understood as something that, for all its inconceivability, actually took place in and by the freedom of God.

What makes Barth's Christology different from Alexandrian and Antiochian Christologies is mainly that these two alternatives, each in its own way, tend to resolve the incarnational mystery into something more nearly conceivable on the basis of ordinary experience and history. They opt for the unified thought at the expense of the ineffable actuality. Yet once the project of constructing a fully cohesive system is abandoned, the relative value of each can be appreciated and retained. "The christologies of Alexandria and Antioch," Barth stated, ". . . mutually supplement and explain each other and to that extent remain on peaceful terms." "We are dealing with testimonies to one reality, which though contrary to one another, do not dispute or negate one another." In their original New Testament forms, "their relations are so interlocked, that if we are to understand one we must first do justice to the other and *vice versa*" (I/2, p. 24). Certainly no "systematic unity or principle" can be found that will

---

6. The "name" of Jesus Christ differs from any theoretical or "systematic" conception of his person, Barth believes, for "only by this name" can the two antithetical statements (that the man Jesus is fully God and that the eternal Son is fully human as this man) be spoken together (I/1, p. 181). For Barth the "name" (and thus the narrative in which it is embedded and from which it is inseparable) functions to embrace the whole ineffability of Christ's person in a way that no system or conception possibly can.

7. Karl Barth, *Church Dogmatics* I/2 (Edinburgh: T. & T. Clark, 1956), p. 160; hereafter cited as I/2.

eliminate the antithesis at stake in saying that Jesus was "complete in deity" and "complete in humanity" at the same time (I/2, p. 24). But by speaking now in an "Alexandrian" idiom, and now again in an "Antiochian" idiom, by switching back and forth between them dialectically, Barth hoped to provide as descriptively adequate an account as might be possible of an event that was, by definition, inherently ineffable.

The reason why a non-Chalcedonian Christology has been imputed to Barth, one way or the other, would seem to be rooted mainly in a failure to appreciate that he employs a dialectical strategy of juxtaposition.[8] The discussion is always jinxed when one or the other prong in Barth's two-sided dialectic is seized upon in isolation as if it could stand for his Christology as a whole.[9] However, it might still be wondered whether Barth did not finally leave us with the worst of both worlds. When speaking in an Alexandrian idiom, did he not offer a deficient view of Christ's humanity; and when speaking in an Antiochian idiom, did he not in turn offer a deficient view of Christ's deity? Although at some point these become questions with complex ramifications, at least something can be said in response without foreclosing the need for a fuller and more technical discussion.

The charge that Barth's Alexandrian idiom offers a deficient view of Christ's humanity does not, at first, seem to rest on especially technical considerations. It seems to rest mainly on an intuition that Jesus' humanity cannot really be "complete" if Jesus is also "complete in deity." Jesus' humanity, it is said, cannot be "complete" unless his will is "independent" of God's will. If the relation of Jesus' will to God's will is seen as one of "absolute dependence," and if this relation is seen as internal to Jesus' constitution as a "person," then Jesus

8. Whereas most of the massive christological discussion in *Church Dogmatics* IV/1 speaks in an "Alexandrian" idiom offset by the occasional "Antiochian" counterpoint, the proportions in the equally massive IV/2 are more or less reversed, while the proportions in IV/3 are perhaps about equal. In this way Barth attempted to carry out his announced procedure for using the two "idioms": "Our task is to hear the second in the first, and the first in the second, and, therefore, in a process of thinking and not in a system, to hear the one [Jesus Christ] in both" (I/2, p. 25). Note that the ground on which Christology takes shape here is much closer to "narratology," or the study of narrative structures and strategies, than it is to metaphysics.

9. Although Charles T. Waldrop pays close attention to both strands in Barth's Christology, he thinks that only one of them (the Alexandrian) is basically characteristic. He remains at a loss to account for the other massive strand (the Antiochian) that he cannot deny is also there. Significantly, he never once takes Chalcedon seriously as a christological type. He simply contents himself with a forced option between Alexandria and Antioch. Being essentially a systematizer of the Antiochian type (like so many other modernists), he not only ignores Barth's repeated, explicit avowals of Chalcedon, but also the dialectical strategy that Barth uses for implementing it. See Waldrop, *Karl Barth's Christology: Its Basic Alexandrian Character* (Berlin: de Gruyter, 1984).

cannot possibly be "complete in humanity."[10] There are at least two questions here. One is how to conceive of the relation between divine and human agency in general, and of their relation in the incarnation in particular; the other is how we can know what really constitutes "complete" humanity.

Barth's answer involves the rejection of a hidden premise. If "two-natures" Christology is valid, as Barth assumes, on the basis of the New Testament as interpreted by the Fourth Ecumenical Council (Chalcedon), then it does not seem unreasonable to give up the expectation that the "person" of Christ can be grasped by a "unified thought." Yet the objection seems to cling to such an improper expectation, for in effect it demands a "principle" that will "explain" just how Jesus can be the kind of person that Chalcedon describes. By definition, Barth holds, no such principle is either possible or necessary, except for the freedom of God, which makes the incarnation possible in such a way that Jesus' full humanity is in fact upheld rather than compromised (as the New Testament narratives themselves plausibly attest). Moreover, on the same grounds (Chalcedon), it does not seem unreasonable to suppose that we do not know in the abstract what "deity" and "humanity" really mean, but that we must learn to understand them in light of the incarnation itself, which first shows us what true deity and true humanity really are in their fullness, rather than the reverse (i.e., understanding the incarnation in light of prior definitions of "deity" and "humanity"). While much more could be said, these are the main lines of response. "Complete in humanity," Barth contends, needs to be defined on the basis of the incarnation itself, and no conception of divine and human agency will be adequate which rejects seeing their unified relation (with the integrity of each term) as a fully ineffable actuality, grounded in the freedom of God.[11]

The diametrically opposite charge — that Barth is "Nestorian" in Christology — has also been alleged. Barth is said to be "Nestorian" on the grounds

10. Waldrop uses the terms "complete" and "independent" interchangeably in this respect. He assumes that no "person" can be "complete in deity" and "complete in humanity" at the same time, on the (question-begging) grounds that no humanity can be complete unless it is constituted as a "person" that is other than God. See Waldrop, passim, but esp. pp. 172-75.

11. For Barth's principled refusal of "explanation" in favor of "description," and for his programmatic allowance for God's freedom by way of dialectical juxtaposition (as opposed to a unified explanatory "system"), see I/1, pp. 8-9. For some indications of how "deity" is defined in light of the incarnation, see Church Dogmatics IV/1 (Edinburgh: T. & T. Clark, 1956), pp. 129, 159, 177; hereafter cited as IV/1. For a corresponding way of defining "humanity," see IV/1, p. 131, and Church Dogmatics III/2 (Edinburgh: T. & T. Clark, 1960), pp. 203-22; hereafter cited as III/2. For a summary of how Barth views divine and human agency, see George Hunsinger, How to Read Karl Barth: The Shape of His Theology (New York: Oxford University Press, 1991), pp. 185-224. It should be noted that Barth generally writes of Wesen rather than Natur when translating the Chalcedonian term "nature" (physis).

that he offers a deficient view of Christ's deity in which the union of Christ's humanity with God is seen as external to the constitution of Christ's person. This charge, too, seems to rest mainly on a failure to appreciate Barth's dialectical strategy of juxtaposition.[12] Barth ventures that, from *one* perspective, Jesus of Nazareth, who is in himself no less "complete" in deity than in humanity, can nonetheless be described in his humanity as the perfect covenant partner of God. Although Barth never deploys this perspective without careful qualification and supplementation, he does expound it by speaking of Jesus in his humanity as "attesting," "corresponding to," "representing," or otherwise standing in "analogy" to God. When all Barth's dialectical and substantive countermoves are disregarded, his discourse in this idiom can be flattened into "Nestorianism." Taken in isolation, this way of foregrounding Christ's humanity can be construed (or better, misconstrued) as though his humanity stood for a "person" who was separate from and other than God.

When everything is taken into account, however, it is hard to see how Barth could reasonably be charged with teaching that the relation of Jesus Christ to God, and thus of Christ's two natures, is "exclusively analogical."[13] Such a criticism would be something like wresting a postcard from a stereoscope and declaiming, "See! It's not really three-dimensional after all!" In a way that seems compatible with the Sixth Ecumenical Council (which affirmed that Christ's having two "natures" entailed his also having two "wills"),[14] Barth teaches: "In the work of the one Jesus Christ everything is at one and the same time, but distinctly, both divine and human."[15] The relation of double agency,

12. Although Regin Prenter sees that Barth's strategy is dialectical, he lacks the kind of sympathy and imagination that would be required for understanding it. He discerns neither its underlying rationale nor its actual function. There is perhaps something tone-deaf about the way he typically notices and yet misreads Barth's dialectic. He insists on seeing divisions where Barth posits unities, and on seeing fusions where Barth posits distinctions. His argument that the Antiochian strand in Barth's Christology is "Nestorian" may be found in "Karl Barths Umbildung der traditionellen Zweinaturlehre in lutherischer Beleuchtung," *Studia Theologia* 11 (1958): 1-88, on pp. 10-43.

13. Prenter repeatedly makes this charge. See, for example, p. 41. Yet when Barth foregrounds the humanity of Jesus as God's perfect covenant partner, he always presupposes (and does not retract) the dialectical aspect of truth that from this perspective he keeps in the background: "[Jesus Christ] is God as such. He is not a mere analogy of God, even the highest, in a sphere of reality distinct from God. He does not signify God himself; he is God himself" (I/1, p. 426, rev.).

14. See Patrick T. R. Gray, *The Defense of Chalcedon in the East (451-553)* (Leiden: Brill, 1979); Karl Joseph von Hefele, *A History of the Christian Councils*, vol. 5 (Edinburgh: T. & T. Clark, 1896).

15. Karl Barth, *Church Dogmatics* IV/2 (Edinburgh: T. & T. Clark, 1958), p. 117; hereafter cited as IV/2.

of divine and human willing, in the person of Christ is thus not only one of "coordination in difference" (IV/2, p. 116), but also of one of "mutual participation" for the sake of a common and single work *(communicatio operationum)* (IV/2, p. 117). When in Christ's one divine person two natures, and thus also two wills or operations, met, they did so not merely analogically or externally, but in a relation of mutual participation, indwelling or *koinonia,* and thus in a Chalcedonian unity-in-distinction and distinction-in-unity (IV/1, p. 126).

Barth counts on it that his readers will understand him only if they read dialectically. Fair-minded readers will grant his premise, at least for the sake of argument, that a "systematic conspectus" of the incarnation is impossible. They will not discount him when he posits that although two different statements are equally necessary (that "Jesus of Nazareth is the Son of God" and that "the Son of God is Jesus of Nazareth"), we are simply incapable of listening "to both at the same time," but can only listen "either to the one or the other at the one time" (I/1, p. 180). Whether agreeing with him or not, they will at least take seriously the special nuance that he finds in the New Testament understanding of faith. Faith, he remarks, means seeing "the validity of each [statement] in the other." Faith means "the perception either way of what is not said" (I/1, p. 180). "We can listen only to the one [statement] or the other," he reasons, "registering what is said by the one or the other, and then, in and in spite of the concealment, we can in faith hear the other in the one" (I/1, p. 181, rev.). Judicious readers will at least appreciate that Barth has made a fresh, thoughtful, and distinguished attempt to be Chalcedonian in Christology precisely by speaking now in an Alexandrian, and now again in an Antiochian, voice.[16]

In conclusion, at least something might be said, however sketchily, about certain other far-reaching innovations that Barth made in constructing Christology within the premises of Chalcedon. First, he actualized the traditional conception of the incarnation. Second, he personalized the saving significance of Christ's death. Finally, he contemporized the consequences of Christ's resurrection.

---

16. For a recent technical assessment of Barth's Christology as "Chalcedonian," see Gregor Taxacher, *Trinität und Sprache* (Würzburg: Echter, 1994), pp. 349-71. The basically Chalcedonian character of Barth's Christology emerges in an especially clear and succinct way when he writes: "But God is himself this man Jesus Christ, very God and very man, both of them unconfused and unmixed, but also unseparated and undivided, in the one person of this Messiah and Savior" (*Church Dogmatics* II/1 [Edinburgh: T. & T. Clark, 1957], p. 486; hereafter cited as II/1). From this Chalcedonian standpoint Barth typically critiques what he regards as Alexandrian and Antiochian excesses (II/1, pp. 487-88). For an excellent contemporary discussion of Chalcedon, see Dorothea Wendebourg, "Chalcedon in Ecumenical Discourse," *Pro Ecclesia* 7 (1998): 307-32.

1. The incarnation, Barth argued, is best understood as a concrete history, not as an abstract state of being. The person of Jesus Christ, who is at once truly God and yet also truly human, does not exist apart from his work, nor his work apart from his person. Rather, his unique person is *in* his work even as his saving work is *in* his person. "His being as this One is his history, and his history is this being" (IV/1, p. 128). The incarnation is the event which occurs in the "identity" of his truly human action with his truly divine action (IV/2, p. 99). "He acts as God when he acts as a human being, and as a human being when he acts as God" (IV/2, p. 115, rev.). The incarnation, the meeting of two natures in Christ, is what occurred as he enacted his saving history. Although his deity and his humanity were actual from the very outset *(conceptus de Spiritu Sancto!)*, their union was never essentially static. It was a state of being in the process of becoming.

This apparently simple thesis illustrates how Barth's Chalcedonian Christology managed to be resoundingly traditional and brilliantly innovative at the same time. The divine and human identity of Jesus Christ in its historical enactment had to be taken seriously, Barth urged, as a qualitative and indivisible whole. It would not do to understand the significance of Christ's singular identity by dividing it up into parts. The humiliation of Jesus Christ, to take a key example, was not to be separated, whether chronologically or ontologically, from his exaltation. Rather, both were to be conceived as occurring together simultaneously in the course of their enactment. The humiliation of the Son of God took place in and with the exaltation of the Son of man.[17] Humiliation and exaltation were regarded as two ways of looking at the incarnation as a whole, not as two different stages in sequence. "It was God who went into the far country, and it is the human creature who returns home. Both took place in the one Jesus Christ" (IV/2, p. 21, rev.). God was in Christ, humbling himself for the good of the creature, even as the human creature was exalted on the basis of that self-humiliation. "It is not . . . a matter of two different and successive actions, but of a single action in . . . the being and history of the one Jesus Christ" (IV/2, p. 21). But since this simultaneity could not be grasped by a "unified thought," Barth again resorted to his dialectical strategy of juxtaposition.[18]

17. In Barth's parlance the term "Son of God" is a kind of shorthand for "the Son of God was Jesus of Nazareth," while the term "Son of man" stands for the reverse statement that "Jesus of Nazareth is the Son of God."

18. The humiliation of the Son of God is the theme of IV/1, and the exaltation of the Son of man is the theme of IV/2. Note that Barth made a similar move regarding the tradition of Christ's threefold office as prophet, priest, and king. Although the human mind is only capable of considering them *ad seriatum*, each is always included in the others in such a way that they each pertain simultaneously to Christ's person and work as a whole. Barth took them up one by

The received tradition of Christ's two "states" (humiliation and exaltation) was thereby subjected to a powerful and ingenious restatement whose strengths and weaknesses have yet to be adequately assessed.[19]

The history of Christ's humiliation and exaltation culminates in his death. "His death on the cross was and is the fulfillment of . . . the humiliation of the Son of God and exaltation of the Son of man" (IV/2, pp. 140-41). It is the moment of their supreme simultaneity. "It is only then — not before — that there did and does take place the realization of the final depth of humiliation, the descent into hell of Jesus Christ the Son of God, but also his supreme exaltation, the triumphant coronation of Jesus Christ the Son of man" (IV/2, p. 141). As he died the death of the sinner, the Son of God entered the nadir of his humiliation for our sakes, even as his exaltation as the Son of man attained its zenith in that sinless obedience which, having freely embraced the cross, would be crowned by eternal life. His humiliation was always the basis of his exaltation, even as his exaltation was always the goal of his humiliation, and both were supremely one in his death on our behalf. "It was in this way that the reconciliation of the world with God was accomplished in the unity of his being" (IV/2, p. 141, rev.).

2. The saving significance of Christ's death cannot be adequately understood, Barth proposes, if legal or juridical considerations are allowed to take precedence over those that are more merciful or compassionate. Although God's grace never occurs without judgment, nor God's judgment without grace, in Jesus Christ it is always God's grace, Barth believes, that is decisive. Therefore, although the traditional themes of punishment and penalty are not eliminated from Barth's discourse about Christ's death, they are displaced from being central or predominant.

> The decisive thing is not that he has suffered what we ought to have suffered so that we do not have to suffer it, the destruction to which we have fallen victim by our guilt, and therefore the punishment which we deserve. This is true, of course. But it is true only as it derives from the decisive thing that in the suffering and death of Jesus Christ it has come to pass that in his own person he has made an end of us as sinners and therefore of sin itself by going to death as the one who took our place as sinners. In his person he has delivered up us sinners and sin itself to destruction. (IV/1, p. 253)

---

one, devoting a massive discussion to each: the priestly office in IV/1, the royal office in IV/2, and the prophetic office in IV/3.

19. Barth's moves here would need to be compared carefully to Reformed and Lutheran orthodoxy as well as to Luther and Calvin and to patristic theologians like Athanasius and Cyril. Although Prenter makes an interesting start in this direction, he is not careful enough to be useful.

The uncompromising judgment of God is seen in the suffering love of the cross. Because this judgment is uncompromising, the sinner is delivered up to the death and destruction which sin inevitably deserves. Yet because this judgment is carried out in the person of Jesus Christ, very God and very man, it is borne only to be removed and borne away. "In the deliverance of sinful man and sin itself to destruction, which he accomplished when he suffered our punishment, he has on the other side blocked the source of our destruction" (IV/1, p. 254). By taking our place as sinners before God, "he has seen to it that we do not have to suffer what we ought to suffer; he has removed the accusation and condemnation and perdition which had passed upon us; he has canceled their relevance to us; he has saved us from destruction and rescued us from eternal death" (IV/1, p. 254). The cross reveals an abyss of sin swallowed up by the suffering of divine love.

By virtue of his unique person, Christ was in a position to take our place in both a positive and a negative sense. As the Son of man he effected our reconciliation with God by living as the true covenant partner whom God had always sought but never found. He thus fulfilled the meaning of human existence as intended in the election of Israel. As the Son of God, on the other hand, he gave a universal significance and depth to his reconciling work that would not have obtained had he been no more than a human being. As the Son of God incarnate, "he has the omnipotence in the power of this work to bear our sins, to bear them away from us, to suffer the consequences of our sins, to be the just One for us sinners, to forgive us our sins" (IV/1, p. 235). Barth thus retains the tradition of Christ's "active" and "passive" obedience. They, too, occur simultaneously and pertain to Christ's history as a whole. As the Son of man, Christ did right at the very place where we had done wrong (active obedience). As the Son of God, he suffered our punishment in order to remove it once and for all (passive obedience) (IV/1, p. 237). The righteousness fulfilled in his death, through his active and passive obedience, secured the triumph of grace.

The reconciling work of Christ is thus presented from two perspectives, both of which are rooted in the unique constitution of his enacted person as complete in deity and complete in humanity. He is the priestly Son of God who ventured into the far country of sin and death that he might suffer their desolation in our place and bear it away. He is also, at the same time, the royal Son of man who is exalted to homecoming with God by virtue of his covenant faithfulness, his unbroken obedience, even to the point of embracing a shameful and violent death. Although the righteousness of the law is fulfilled in his person, both actively and passively, it is essentially his person and not the law, his compassion, not his vicarious punishment, that determines his saving significance. He completely embraces our destruction, carrying us to death in his death, that we might be raised in and with him to newness of life.

3. This dual, dialectical perspective extends, finally, into Barth's discussion of Christ's resurrection. Just as the cross represents the fulfillment of Jesus Christ's life history as the history of reconciliation, so his resurrection represents the fulfillment of that same life history as the history of God's self-revelation. Reconciliation and revelation (and therefore love and knowledge) are always deeply interconnected in Barth's theology, never dissociated.[20] "Revelation takes place in and with reconciliation. Indeed, the latter is also revelation. As God acts in it he also speaks. . . . Yet the relationship is indissoluble from the other side as well. Revelation takes place as the revelation of reconciliation."[21] In other words, revelation culminates in Christ's resurrection much as reconciliation culminates in his cross. The reconciliation fulfilled by Christ's death is the very substance manifested in the revelation at once fulfilled and yet inaugurated by his resurrection.

Because reconciliation can only be described dialectically as divine humiliation for the sake of human exaltation, revelation as the heart of the resurrection requires an equally dialectical mode of explication. From one perspective Christ's resurrection reveals reconciliation as the humiliation of God's Son in human flesh. From this standpoint the resurrection is "the great verdict of God." It fulfills and proclaims "God's decision concerning the cross." It shows that God accepts the cross as the self-abasing act of compassion in which God's Son, for the sake of the world, "fulfilled the divine wrath . . . in the service of di-

---

20. The discussion and evaluation of Barth in Alister E. McGrath's *Iustitia Dei: A History of the Christian Doctrine of Justification from 1500 to the Present Day* (Cambridge: Cambridge University Press, 1986) is impaired (among other reasons) by the unfortunate assumption that they are indeed dissociated (pp. 170-84). Barth establishes their interconnection unmistakably in I/1 and constantly reiterates it thereafter all the way through to the end of the *Church Dogmatics*. How could it be otherwise when both reconciliation and revelation find their identity in Jesus Christ, who is himself both of them in one? "Revelation in fact does not differ from the person of Jesus Christ nor from the reconciliation accomplished in him" (I/1, p. 119). A similar flaw mars the more recent analysis of Alan Torrance, who fails to appreciate the inseparability Barth establishes between "knowledge" *(Erkenntnis)* and "fellowship" or "communion" *(Gemeinschaft)* throughout his theology, not only centrally in II/1 but as early as I/1. See Torrance, *Persons in Communion: Trinitarian Description and Human Participation* (Edinburgh: T. & T. Clark, 1996). "In this fellowship in revelation which is created between God and humankind by the Holy Spirit there may be discerned the fellowship in God himself, the eternal love of God," which is identical with "the communion between the Father and the Son" in the Holy Spirit (I/1, p. 480, rev.). Knowledge of God and love for God, it might be noted, are as inseparable for Barth as they are for Calvin.

21. Karl Barth, *Church Dogmatics* IV/3, first half (Edinburgh: T. & T. Clark, 1961), p. 8; hereafter cited as IV/3.

vine grace" (IV/1, p. 309). From the other perspective, however, Christ's resurrection reveals that reconciliation must also be seen as the exaltation of the Son of man. "What is revealed is that in his identity with the Son of God this man was the Lord" (IV/2, p. 151). Faithful to God even unto the cross, this man is raised again, exalted and revealed as "the reconciliation of the world with God, and therefore the new humanity, the dawning of the new creation, the beginning of the new world" (IV/2, p. 145, rev.). In his resurrection this man is revealed as the Lord and Savior of the world.

While Barth accepts the full "historicity" of Christ's resurrection,[22] he puts the accent in another place. He does not allow the question of historicity (a peculiarly modern obsession) to obscure the resurrection's chief theological significance. Christ's resurrection means, above all, that the reconciliation Christ accomplished enjoys eternal reality and significance. That reconciliation itself, Barth holds, is "intrinsically perfect" and complete (IV/3, pp. 7, 327). "It does not need to be transcended or augmented by new qualities or further developments. The humiliation of God and the exaltation of humankind as they took place in him are the completed fulfillment of the covenant, the completed reconciliation of the world with God" (IV/2, p. 132, rev.). Reconciliation is eternally valid as a living, indivisible whole, because Christ is risen from the dead.

What needs to happen — and in Christ's resurrection and ascension what does happen — is for this reconciliation to be made contemporaneous with the rest of history. Easter involves Christ's "transition to a presence which is eternal and therefore embraces all times" (IV/1, p. 318). "His history did not become dead history. It was history in his time to become as such eternal history — the history of God with the human beings of all times, and therefore taking place here and now as it did then" (IV/1, pp. 313-14, rev.). "He is present here and now for us in the full efficacy of what . . . he was and did then and there" (IV/1, p. 291). The resurrection means Christ's "real presence" to us now, and "our

22. "The statement that Christ is risen necessarily implies that a dead man is alive again and that his grave is empty" (IV/2, p. 149). "The Resurrected is the man Jesus, who now came and went among them as such, whom they saw and touched and heard, who ate and drank with them" (III/2, p. 448). Like the creation of the world *ex nihilo*, however, this event transcends and exceeds the "historical" even as it includes it, for it has neither an ordinary historical cause nor an ordinary historical effect. Barth resorts to the term *Geschichte* rather than the term *Historie*, not because he denies the resurrection's historicity, but because in this event "history" in the modern, Troeltschean sense reaches its categorical limit (III/2, pp. 446-47). The distinction between *Historie* and *Geschichte* has, it might be noted, regularly flummoxed Barth's evangelical-conservative Protestant interpreters, thereby exposing the extent of their unbaptized modernism.

contemporaneity to him" in what he so perfectly accomplished then in our stead (IV/1, p. 348). It means "the contemporaneity of Jesus Christ with us and of us with him" (IV/2, p. 291). It makes him "the Contemporary of all human beings" (III/2, p. 440, rev.). Because Christ is risen from the dead, no time or place, no human life, is bereft of the presence (whether manifest or hidden, incognito for the time being or openly known) of the only Mediator and true Advocate between heaven and earth.

In closing, one last point should be noted about the Christology Barth constructed within the premises of Chalcedon. The saving work of Christ, as Barth explicated it, could not possibly have occurred unless in his person he had been both complete in deity and complete in humanity. His incarnational history could not otherwise have been at once the history of our reconciliation with God and of God's self-revelation to us. Unless two natures had met in Christ "without separation or division," yet also "without confusion or change," neither reconciliation nor revelation, as Barth explained them, could have taken place.

Yet Barth discerned one further element in Chalcedon. No symmetry between the two natures that met in Christ was possible. Christ's deity after all was deity, whereas his humanity was merely humanity. The precedence, initiative, and impartation were always necessarily with his deity even as the subsequence, absolute dependence, and pure if active reception were always necessarily with his humanity (IV/2, p. 116). In this light, from a Chalcedonian viewpoint, the relative superiority of Alexandrian over Antiochian Christologies emerges. For whereas Alexandrian Christology is typically correct on at least two out of three essentials, Antiochian Christology is typically correct on only one. Chalcedon, it will be recalled, sets forth two terms and a relationship. Alexandria is typically correct on one of the terms ("complete in deity") and also about the relationship (deity intrinsic to Christ's person with asymmetrical precedence over his humanity), but Antioch is typically correct about only one of the terms ("complete in humanity"), though its participatory notion of divinity can also allow for a kind of extrinsic asymmetry.[23] That Barth's Chris-

---

23. When Chalcedon asserts that the two natures which met in Christ are related "without confusion or change," it is rejecting a blatant or subtle Alexandrian tendency. When, on the other hand, it asserts that they are related "without separation or division," it is doing the same thing with respect to Antioch. What gives Alexandria the edge as far as Chalcedon is concerned, however, is that Antioch typically does not see Jesus' deity as intrinsic to his "person" (hypostasis). Alexandria and Chalcedon agree, implicitly or explicitly, that the unity of Christ's two natures is grounded in his "person" as the eternal Logos. However, for an Antiochian Christology that appears to meet the strictures of Chalcedon in this respect, see the discussion of Theodoret in Aloys Grillmeier, *Christ in the Christian Tradition*, vol. 1 (Atlanta: John Knox,

tology of dialectical juxtaposition makes this kind of discrimination possible even as it attempts so ingeniously to do justice to all three of the essentials is yet another tribute to its basic Chalcedonian character.

1975), pp. 488-95. For a strong defense of Chalcedon as a victory for Cyril, see John A. McGuckin, *St. Cyril of Alexandria: The Christological Controversy* (Leiden: Brill, 1994), and the literature there cited. Although "in the East, hardly anyone was happy," writes McGuckin, "the Chalcedonian symbol was more in the manner of a corrective of Leo than a substantiation of him" (pp. 241, 240). Appealing to careful, recent scholarship, McGuckin concludes that "in the main" Chalcedon defends "a Cyrilline prespective" (p. 236). In this light, what makes Barth specifically Chalcedonian rather than strictly Alexandrian is, of course, the strong counteremphasis his strategy of juxtaposition places on the truth he saw in the vital concern of Antioch for Christ's true (or "royal") humanity.

CHAPTER 7

The Mediator of Communion:
Karl Barth's Doctrine of the Holy Spirit

(1999)

The doctrine of the Holy Spirit is, as Adolf von Harnack once observed, the "orphan doctrine" of Christian theology. Unlike the doctrine of the Trinity or the doctrine of the Christ's person, it has never been stabilized by a conciliar decision of the church, although it is as vexing, contested, and uncertain as any doctrine the church has ever known. An omen of things to come emerged as early as the Council of Nicaea (325). Diverted by dissension over other questions, the council produced a creditable statement of the church's belief in God the Father, and especially of its belief in the deity of God the Son (which was of course the chief point at issue), but then closed rather weakly by stating its belief "And in the Holy Spirit" — with no further elaboration at all.

The deficiency was partly remedied by the ensuing Council of Constantinople (381). Words were added to the Nicene Creed which have remained normative for the church ever since. The Holy Spirit in whom the church believes, the creed now stated, is "the Lord and Giver of life, who proceeds from the Father; who with the Father and the Son together is worshipped and glorified; who spoke by the prophets." This statement, however slight, acknowledged the Holy Spirit's full and unabridged deity, indicated something of the Spirit's place within the Holy Trinity, and affirmed that the Spirit communicates God's Word to us through select human intermediaries. Unaddressed, however, were many matters that would divide Christendom throughout its history right down to the present day. To speak only very generally, these were matters having to do with revelation and salvation; with ecclesiology, ministry, and sacraments; with eschatology and society; with justification, sanctification, and glorification; and above all, as perhaps the overarching issue, with the unity and distinction between the saving work of the Spirit and the saving work of Christ.

Although Karl Barth's views on these unresolved matters have been vigorously disputed, the discussion has not been very fruitful so far for the simple reason that the scope and intricacy of his thought have yet to be sufficiently grasped. One point, for example, that has been widely overlooked is that Barth saw "revelation," "reconciliation," and "redemption"[1] as standing in a set of relationships that were subtle, flexible, and complex. Revelation and reconciliation, for example, were regarded as inseparable.[2] Just as revelation without reconciliation could only have been empty, so reconciliation without revelation could only have been mute. Revelation in fact imparted the reality of reconciliation, even as reconciliation formed the vital truth that revelation made known. Neither could be had without the other, since both were identical with Jesus Christ. Above all, they embraced a complex temporality. Revelation and reconciliation each centered inalienably on what had taken place in the life history of Jesus Christ there and then, while yet involving receptive, eucharistic, and participatory moments, continually, here and now. The relationship between what had already taken place "there and then" and what continues to take place "here and now" was, in effect, the decisive issue at stake in Barth's doctrine of the Spirit's saving work, as seen from the standpoints of both revelation and reconciliation.

"Redemption," on the other hand, which Barth defined as the future of reconciliation, was his category for the saving work of the Holy Spirit in its own right. Everything about the Spirit as seen less directly from the standpoints of revelation and reconciliation was, from the standpoint of redemption, to have been placed center stage, redescribed teleologically as a whole, and thereby amplified and enriched. A twofold perspective would result. Whereas reconciliation was redemption's abiding ground and content, redemption was reconciliation's dynamic consequence and goal. Redemption as the peculiar and proper work of the Spirit represented the consummation of all things, the resurrection of the dead, and eternal life in communion with God. It was the absolute future which would at once reveal and impart Jesus Christ in his inexhaustible significance for the whole creation. Whereas from the standpoint of reconciliation the

---

1. Although these terms obviously need to be defined, only a rudimentary orientation can be offered here. For more on the interconnection between "revelation" and "reconciliation," see my "Karl Barth's Christology: Its Basic Chalcedonian Character," elsewhere in this volume, pp. 131-47.

2. E.g., Karl Barth, *Church Dogmatics* I/1 (Edinburgh: T. & T. Clark, 1936), pp. 409-10; hereafter cited as I/1.

work of the Spirit served the work of Christ, from the standpoint of redemption the work of Christ served the work of the Spirit.[3]

Since Barth thought reconciliation never occurred without revelation, nor revelation without reconciliation, no critique which presupposes their separation, or fails to see their connection, could possibly be of much interest, yet such critiques are commonplace. Similarly, since he thought reconciliation was to be fulfilled by redemption, no critique can be very illuminating which presupposes that he saw reconciliation as the whole story in and of itself. Very ambitiously, Barth intended to develop a doctrine of the Holy Spirit's saving work that would be rigorously christocentric yet without becoming deficient in its grasp of essential trinitarian relations. No subordinationism, whether implicit or explicit, could be tolerated. Christ's reconciling work was not to be devalued but rather upheld as "intrinsically perfect,"[4] yet no "subordinationist" displacement could be allowed of the Spirit's own special work of redemption. While the christocentric aspect dominated Barth's discussion of the Spirit as seen from the standpoint of reconciliation, the antisubordinationist aspect, for which programmatic hints are dropped regularly along the way,[5] was to have been established most fully from the standpoint of redemption. Not until such large-scale structural moves as these are more carefully pondered in Barth's dogmatics will the discussion of his views on the Holy Spirit begin to be more satisfying and worthwhile.[6]

An overview of Barth on the Holy Spirit can be gained by seeing that he regards the Spirit as "the mediator of communion." The "communion of the Holy Spirit" (II Cor. 13:14), in which believers become "individually members of one another" (Rom. 12:5), is established as the Holy Spirit unites them with Christ by faith. Furthermore, through their definitive union and communion with Christ, as mediated by the Spirit, they are also at the same time given an indirect share in the primordial communion that obtains between the Father and the Son to all eternity. It is finally because the mediation of the Spirit obtains at this primordial level, as the eternal bond of love within the Holy Trinity,

---

3. The volume on "redemption" in Barth's projected dogmatics was unfortunately never written, and the volume on "reconciliation," though massive, remained incomplete.

4. Karl Barth, *Church Dogmatics* IV/3 (Edinburgh: T. & T. Clark, 1961, 1962), p. 327; hereafter cited as IV/3.

5. E.g., Karl Barth, *Church Dogmatics* IV/2 (Edinburgh: T. & T. Clark, 1958), pp. 507-11; hereafter cited as IV/2.

6. For representative criticisms, see Philip J. Rosato, *The Spirit as Lord: The Pneumatology of Karl Barth* (Edinburgh: T. & T. Clark, 1981); Thomas Smail, "The Doctrine of the Holy Spirit," in *Theology beyond Christendom*, ed. John Thompson (Allison Park, Pa.: Pickwick, 1986); Colin Gunton, *The Promise of Trinitarian Theology* (Edinburgh: T. & T. Clark, 1991); Robert Jenson, "You Wonder Where the Spirit Went," *Pro Ecclesia* 28 (1993): 296-304; Wolfhart Pannenberg, *Systematic Theology*, 3 vols. (Grand Rapids: Eerdmans, 1988-98).

that the Spirit can also serve as the mediator of communion in other ways. The Spirit thus plays a role in originating and maintaining the incarnation, or the communion between Christ's deity and his humanity *(communio naturarum)*, as well as a role in sustaining through time the primordial communion between the incarnate Son and his heavenly Father. The loving bond between Christ and believers by which they are incorporated into him as a community, as the body of which he himself is the head, takes place by the Spirit on this trinitarian and incarnational basis. The mediation of the Spirit thus moves in two directions at once: from the eternal Trinity through Jesus Christ to humankind, and from humankind through Jesus Christ to the eternal Trinity. It is a mediation of communion — of love in knowledge, and of knowledge in love — as the origin and goal of all things, made possible by the saving work of Christ.

The following survey will develop these themes. The saving work of the Spirit, in Barth's theology, is trinitarian in ground, christocentric in focus, miraculous in operation, communal in content, eschatological in form, diversified in application, and universal in scope. Since Barth's doctrine of the Holy Spirit is enormously rich and complex, what follows can be no more than a sketch.

1. Trinitarian in Ground

The saving work of the Holy Spirit, as Barth understood it, is trinitarian in ground. Since all God's works in the world find their basis in the Trinity as it is in itself (e.g., IV/2, pp. 345-46), the same pertains of the Spirit. "What he is in revelation," writes Barth, "he is antecedently in himself. And what he is antecedently in himself he is in revelation. Within the deepest depths of deity, as the final thing to be said about him, God is the Spirit as he is God the Father and God the Son. The Spirit outpoured at Pentecost is the Lord, God himself, just as the Father and just as Jesus Christ is the Lord, God himself" (I/1, p. 466). The Spirit's person and work are trinitarian in ground because the Spirit reiterates and confirms in time his mode of operation in eternity. "He simply does in time," writes Barth, "what he does eternally in God" (I/1, p. 471).

A Basic Rule

Barth understands the Spirit's temporal manifestation according to a basic rule which governs his entire theology. The rule is that statements about the immanent Trinity can be reached only as "confirmations and underlinings" of the economic Trinity, and conversely that statements about the economic Trinity find their "indispensable premises" in the immanent Trinity (I/1, p. 479). Doctrinal construction thus moves initially from below to above. It proceeds from reflecting on the economic Trinity as attested in Scripture to the immanent Trinity that confirms and underlines it. The order of being, on the other hand (and therefore also basically the order of knowledge), involves a movement from above to below, from the immanent Trinity to the economic Trinity. For the economic Trinity reiterates in time God's reality as it is antecedently in itself. The logic of discovery can thus be distinguished from the logic of the concepts. In the logic of discovery *(ordo investigandi)* the economic Trinity has the precedence, whereas in the logic of the concepts *(ordo essendi* and *ordo cognoscendi)* it is the immanent Trinity which has the precedence. In any case, what is at stake are not two different Trinities, but two different forms (eternal and temporal) of one and the same Trinity.[7] Barth's rule presupposes that the temporal form of the Trinity is grounded by God's prior trinitarian reality, even as that prior reality is then reiterated by the temporal form.

Applied specifically to the Holy Spirit, the rule entails that when God turns to us in the Holy Spirit (as also when he does so in the Father and the Son), he manifests himself "as the One he is and not under a mask behind which he is really another" (IV/2, p. 343). The person *(hypostasis)* of the Spirit is no different — no different in being, essence, or identity — in relation to us than he is antecedently in himself, and what he is antecedently in himself he discloses and confirms in relation to us. His saving work in our midst reiterates in temporal form the prior mode of existence that is his to all eternity.

How, then, is the Spirit's prior operation to be understood, and what is the nature of his eternal reality? What is the Spirit's essential role within the transcendent life of the Godhead? Following Augustine, Barth views the Spirit as the eternal act of love, of communion and peace, obtaining within the immanent Trinity. "He is," writes Barth, "the common element, or, better, the fellowship, the act of communion, of the Father and the Son" (I/1, p. 470). He is the act in which the Father and the Son mutually love one another — their ineffable communion, their inseparable unity, their unbroken peace — to all eternity. The Holy Spirit is the love in which God dwells eternally in and for himself.

No Mere Neutral Relation

The Spirit cannot be understood, however, merely as a neutral relation or principle, for in God's act God's being is always at stake (II/1, pp. 257-72). "What

7. E.g., Karl Barth, *Church Dogmatics* II/1 (Edinburgh: T. & T. Clark, 1957), p. 346; hereafter cited as II/1.

proceeds from God," writes Barth, "can only be God once again" (I/1, p. 473). "What is between [the Father and the Son], what unites them," he explains, "is no mere relation" (I/1, p. 487). Just as fully as the Father and the Son, the Holy Spirit is "a mode of being of the one essence of God" (I/1, p. 473). In the eternal love of the Father for the Son, and of the Son for the Father, God is thus God a third time as the Holy Spirit. The person of the Spirit as a divine mode of being presupposes the distinction of the Father from the Son, and of the Son from the Father, within the Godhead. As the third "person" or *hypostasis* (i.e., concrete mode of existence) of the Trinity, he is the common factor of communion in love and knowledge between them. The Spirit is not only consubstantial with the Father and the Son, but also hypostatic in the same sense as they are. "He is what is common to them," writes Barth, "not insofar as they are the one God, but insofar as they are the Father and the Son" (I/1, p. 469). It is "the essence of the Holy Spirit" to exist hypostatically in no other way than as "the full consubstantial fellowship" between the Father and the Son (I/1, p. 482). As the blessed bond of peace in whom and by whom the two share their common unity, the Holy Spirit thus occupies a "mediating position between the Father and the Son" (I/1, p. 482). Through the person or *hypostasis* of the Spirit, their ineffable communion in love and knowledge is conveyed, confirmed, and fulfilled to all eternity.

Barth's Augustinian way of speaking about the Spirit's role in this primordial trinitarian communion is textured and complex. Agential and nonagential language are both seen as necessary. A kind of mysterious conceptual iridescence results. Following Barth's pattern of usage, we might say that the Spirit "mediates" the communion between the Father and the Son. We could then say that the Spirit is the "mediator" of this communion, but we might also want to say that the Spirit is equally its "mediation," or even that the Spirit just *is* this communion itself.[8] The Spirit is the *koinonia* between the Father and the Son, being at once both its mediator (agential) and yet also its mediation (nonagential, or perhaps better, only indirectly agential), but in any case a primordial, concrete form or *hypostasis* of the one being or *ousia* of God. The Spirit is fully God, equal in glory and excellency to

---

8. If this interpretation of how Barth understands the Spirit's role is correct — that the Spirit is at once the subject and the term of *koinonia* — then Barth's view is not incompatible with a beautiful statement formulated by Robert W. Jenson. "The Father and the Son," Jenson writes, "love each other, with a love that is identical with the Spirit's gift of himself to each of them." This statement, which views the Spirit as the term and the subject of love, suggests directions in which the Spirit's active role in the *koinonia* of the Trinity might be developed without leaving Barth's framework, but in ways that Barth did not pursue. See Jenson, *Systematic Theology*, vol. 1 (New York: Oxford University Press, 1997), p. 158.

the other two *hypostases,* even though very different from them in the order and manner of his subsistence within the dynamics of the eternal Trinity. The main point, however, is clear. The Holy Spirit is God insofar as God is eternally communion *(koinonia).*[9]

The Filioque Clause

Barth's endorsement of the controversial *filioque* clause — the Western addition to the creed that the Spirit proceeds from the Father "and the Son" — is not difficult to understand in this light. For in Barth's interpretation, the *filioque* clause conforms to the basic rule that God is no different in relation to us than he is antecedently in himself. "Even supporters of the Eastern view do not contest the fact," observes Barth, "that in the *opus ad extra* . . . the Holy Spirit is to be understood as the Spirit of both the Father and the Son" (I/1, p. 479). However, if this point is granted for the economic Trinity, then according to the rule ("as in the economic Trinity so in the immanent Trinity"), it can only mean that the Holy Spirit (being no different in himself than to us) is also the Spirit of the Father and the Son from all eternity. Within the immanent Trinity, in other words, the Holy Spirit must be conceived as the eternal act of communion between the Father *and* the Son, as the act of their mutual self-impartation, as the love and gift which proceeds between the two of them antecedently in the Godhead.

It is precisely this double procession in eternity which grounds and confirms what God the Holy Spirit undertakes in the form of his temporal activity. "We know him thus," writes Barth, "in his revelation. But he is not this because he is it in his revelation." Just the reverse: "because he is it antecedently in himself, he is it also in his revelation" (I/1, p. 471). The basic rule therefore presupposes the substantial truth of the form assumed by God's self-revelation in time. The substance of this truth cannot be surpassed merely because the form

---

9. Although Barth would say that God's being *(ousia)* is in communion *(koinonia),* he would not speak of God's being *as* communion. He would instead see God's *ousia* as a readiness for *koinonia. Koinonia,* he would say, logically presupposes the three divine "modes of being" *(hypostases).* Although there is no *ousia* without the *hypostases* and no *hypostases* without the *ousia,* the divine *ousia* is logically prior. Barth identifies the *ousia* itself as a single, self-identical divine subject, who is free and sovereign in trinitarian self-differentiation. The one divine *ousia* exists in and only in the three divine *hypostases. Koinonia* presupposes the three divine *hypostases,* just as the *hypostases* presuppose the one divine *ousia.* It is therefore in the Holy Spirit, and not directly in the divine *ousia* as such, that the eternal *koinonia* of the three *hypostases* is to be found. The relation between the one *ousia* and the three *hypostases* cannot be captured by a single, unified thought (I/1, pp. 368-69; cf. pp. 359, 382).

it has taken is temporal — "as though somewhere behind his revelation there stood another reality of God" (I/1, p. 479). On the contrary, the reality of the Holy Spirit as encountered in this form "is his reality in all the depths of eternity" (I/1, p. 479). As in time so also in eternity, the Spirit proceeds from both the Father and the Son.

A denial of the *filioque* clause, Barth suggests, has several unacceptable consequences. First, it implies a loss of mutuality in love between the Father and the Son, thus moving in the direction of subordinationism. For a Trinity in which the Spirit proceeded from the Father but not also from the Son, would be a Trinity in which the God of love was really the Father in some supreme or essential sense not matched by the Son (and thus still less by the Spirit). Furthermore, this denial also appears to imply a significant loss of consubstantiality in their fellowship, thereby moving in the direction of tritheism. For, again, a Trinity in which the Spirit did not proceed from the Son as well as from the Father, uniting each in co-equality with the other, would seem to be a Trinity whose unity was somehow dominated and grounded by the Father alone over and against the apparently separate (as well as lesser) *hypostases* of the Son and the Spirit (I/1, p. 483). Barth rejects as overly "separationist" the idea, associated with Basil of Caesarea, that the *hypostasis* of the Father functions as the source and ground for the other two *hypostases'* deity *(ousia)*. He sees the three *hypostases* as equiprimordial within the one *ousia* of God, regardless of their real relational distinctions as *hypostases.* The Spirit who proceeds from the Father and the Son, and by whom the Father and the Son are united eternally in the communion of mutual love, is equiprimordial with them in the one *ousia* of God.[10]

No Anthropological Ground

Finally, a denial of the *filioque* clause would, Barth believes, have unacceptable anthropological consequences. As Barth interprets it, the activity of the Holy

---

10. The *filioque,* as Barth saw it, does not denote a twofold origin of the Spirit from the *hypostases* of the Father and the Son, but rather a "common origin" from the *ousia,* Godness, or single sovereign subjectivity that the three of them embody (commonly yet distinctly) and presuppose (I/1, pp. 486-87). Along basically Athanasian lines, Barth held that each of the three divine *hypostases* perfectly instantiates this *ousia,* Godness, or indivisible subjectivity. Because the Spirit does not originate from an "impersonal nature" or, perhaps better, from a nonagential *ousia,* he too acts as subject. Father, Son, and Holy Spirit denote the three concrete modes of being *(hypostases)* of the one simple (noncomposite) divine subject *(ousia),* each of which is constituted by its relationship to the others, each of which subsists simultaneously with the others, and each of which just is this one divine subject indissolubly. Cf. II/1, pp. 57-60.

Spirit *ad extra* can in no sense be anthropological in ground. The *filioque* clause safeguards the fact that in ourselves we have "no possibility" of an opening, readiness, or capacity for God — unless it comes from the Holy Spirit who proceeds eternally from both the Father and the Son (I/1, p. 480). The two-sided communion in the inner being of God (which cannot be maintained properly where the *filioque* clause is denied) is a necessary condition for the two-sided communion between God and human beings. Without the *filioque* clause, says Barth, our fellowship with God would lose its "eternal basis" and "guarantee" (I/1, p. 481). "The love which meets us in revelation, and then retrospectively in creation, is real love, supreme law and ultimate reality, because God is antecedently love [i.e., two-sided love] in himself" (I/1, pp. 483-84). Through the person of the Holy Spirit as the mediator of communion, we become what we neither are nor can be of ourselves: persons "who belong to God, who are in real fellowship with him, who live before God and with God" (I/1, p. 450).

What is impossible for us by nature we receive through the operation of the Spirit. Expressed in terms of the *filioque* clause, it can be said that the Spirit who proceeds from the Father to the Son, and from the Son to the Father, is the very Spirit who unites us in communion with God. The Spirit proceeds to us from the Father in order to unite us with the Son (i.e., the incarnate Son). At the same time, the Spirit also proceeds to us from that Son, who thereby unites us with the Father. As we are so united by the Father with the Son, and by the Son with the Father, the Spirit's double procession in eternity is reiterated in temporal form. "The intra-divine two-sided fellowship of the Spirit, which proceeds from the Father and the Son, is the basis of the fact that there is in revelation a fellowship in which not only is God there for humankind but in very truth — this is the *donum Spiritus sancti* — humankind is also there for God" (I/1, p. 480, rev.). Once again it is confirmed that as *ad intra* so also *ad extra*, the Holy Spirit "is the Spirit of both the Father and the Son" (I/1, p. 479).

By grounding the possibility of our communion with God in the Spirit's double procession from all eternity, Barth reinforces an argument he had previously been developing. As the Holy Spirit draws us into himself, the argument runs, and thus into the ineffable communion of the eternal Godhead, he remains unconditioned by any human capacity. It is in just this sense that the Spirit is revealed as the Lord of the communion that occurs. In our communion with God — and thus in the supreme event whereby the Spirit exists for us as the Giver of Life — he is and remains "absolutely other, superior" as the living Lord (I/1, p. 454). Therefore, as Barth repeatedly emphasizes, under no circumstances may statements properly about the Holy Spirit be merged or confused with statements about human nature (e.g., I/1, p. 462). The ineffability of the eternal communion between the Father and the Son in the Godhead finds its parallel in the "incomprehensibly real way" by which we ourselves are drawn into that very same communion by the Spirit (I/1, pp. 450-51). Just as the eternal communion between the Father and the Son in the person of the Spirit is no less real for being ineffably grounded in divine freedom, so our own participation in that communion (through the Son in the Spirit) is also no less real for being grounded solely in the freedom of God — and hence in no way in ourselves. To participate in this communion is always a gift of grace exceeding the capabilities of human nature.

The strictness with which human participation in the eternal communion of the Trinity is grounded solely in the divine freedom and not at all in human capacities "has never," Barth remarks, "been understood in Catholicism (not even in Augustine) and only very partially even in post-Reformation Protestantism. Modernist Protestantism in its entirety has simply been a regression to pre-Nicene obscurities and ambiguities regarding the Spirit" (I/1, p. 468). For Barth Luther's confession from *The Small Catechism* remains definitive: "I believe that I cannot of my own reason or power believe in Jesus Christ my Lord or come to him" (quoted in I/1, p. 465). Everything depends on whether the basis for human communion with God "is sought in God alone and not anywhere else, not in ourselves" (I/1, p. 466). Fellowship with God — our participation in the eternal communion of the Trinity, as effected by the Holy Spirit — is thus conceived as entirely trinitarian, and in no sense anthropological, in ground.

2. Christocentric in Focus

The Holy Spirit's saving work is also conceived as christocentric in focus. Far from the Spirit-oriented Christology that some have suggested he presented, what Barth actually develops is a Christ-centered pneumatology. Indeed, this distinction points to an important difference between Barth and the modernist or liberal theologies he opposed. For in Barth's theology it is Jesus Christ who constitutes the saving significance of the Holy Spirit in a way that is not true in reverse. That is, the saving significance of Jesus Christ is not to impart and bear witness to the Holy Spirit so much as it is the saving significance of the Holy Spirit to impart and bear witness to Jesus Christ. "There is no special or second revelation of the Spirit," writes Barth, "alongside that of the Son" (I/1, p. 475). The Holy Spirit brings no "independent content" of his own, but instead a content which is determined "wholly and entirely" by Jesus Christ (I/1, p. 452).

The significance of the Holy Spirit is not found directly or independently in himself. The Spirit does not signify, as in so many Spirit-oriented

Christologies, that salvation consists exclusively or chiefly in effecting something *in nobis,* whether religious experiences, renewed dispositions, or a new mode of being in the world. On the contrary, the presence and power of the Spirit are understood to attest what the incarnate Word of God has done for our salvation apart from us *(extra nos)* (cf. IV/1, pp. 211-83) and to mediate our participation in it by faith *(participatio Christi)* (cf. IV/2, pp. 518, 526-33, 581-84). The Spirit who enabled Christ alone to accomplish our salvation as a finished work there and then is the very Spirit who enables us to participate in it and attest it here and now. Because the person of Jesus Christ has not only enacted but is and remains our salvation, he is and remains the enduring focus of the Spirit's work. This focus can be indicated through three points.

Testing for a Spirit-Oriented Christology

First, in an interesting excursus on the Trinity, Barth asks whether there might not be various reasons to think of the Son as proceeding eternally not only from the Father but also from the Spirit (I/1, pp. 485-86). If that were the case, then the Son would originate from the Spirit eternally, and the Spirit could then reasonably be regarded as the focus of the Son's work rather than the other way around. A trinitarian basis would thereby exist for the kind of Spirit-oriented Christology that Barth rejects as opposed to the kind of Christ-centered pneumatology he affirms. Two possible reasons — one systematic and the other exegetical — are entertained for thinking that the Son might somehow proceed from the Spirit.

The systematic reason pertains to the doctrine of the *perichoresis.* Being based as Barth sees it on a simple confusion, it is readily dismissed. The mutual indwelling or coinherence of the three modes of being in God, as posited by the doctrine of *perichoresis,* actually has nothing to do, as Barth points out, with a "circle of mutual origins" (I/1, p. 485). Although the *perichoresis* is "complete and mutual," the doctrine does not describe the origins of the three divine *hypostases* or modes of being. Its function is simply to offer "a further description of the *homoousia* of Father, Son, and Spirit." It signifies that by virtue of their common essence they fully interpenetrate one another in and with their hypostatic distinctions. Having no bearing on the question of their origins, it needs "no supplementation" in that direction (I/1, p. 485).

The exegetical reason, on the other hand, concerns certain well-known passages from the New Testament which seem to ascribe an originating role to the Spirit in Jesus' life history, especially in the circumstances surrounding his birth, baptism, and resurrection (e.g., Matt. 1:18; Luke 1:35; Mark 1:9ff. and par.; Mark

1:12; Rom. 1:3). Might not such passages seem to imply a Spirit-oriented Christology? Might they not suggest that Jesus' relationship to God was originated by the Spirit in much the same way as anyone else's might be? Don't they suggest that the distinction between Jesus and others, regardless of how significant, can never be more than a matter of degree? Most of all, don't they suggest that Jesus' relationship to God should be seen along the lines of an *unio mystica* as opposed to an *unio hypostatica* (cf. II/1, pp. 485-86)? Barth's strategy at this point is not to develop an extensive case so much as to indicate how such passages can be accommodated within the framework of the actual Christ-centered pneumatology that he takes to be predominant and normative in the New Testament. At a minimum Barth thereby demonstrates the nonnecessity of a Spirit-oriented Christology for an ecclesial reading of such passages.

Barth observes that the passages in question always pertain to Jesus as a human being and thus to "another essence" than that of the Spirit (I/1, p. 485). They neither require nor suggest that the Spirit makes it possible for the divine Son to be the Son.[11] From a Nicene and Chalcedonian point of view, one may infer that the Spirit's role is again one of mediation, uniting the entire life history of Jesus (once-for-all and then continually), through his virgin birth, his baptism, and his resurrection, uniquely with the eternal Son of God, and the eternal Son of God uniquely with the life history of Jesus. The Son does not owe his eternal Sonship to the Spirit. The passages as so read are consistent with the basic rule that what the Holy Spirit does *ad extra* is a reflection of what he does *ad intra* (I/1, p. 486). For whether *ad intra* (in uniting the eternal Son with the Father) or *ad extra* (in uniting Jesus with the eternal Son), the Spirit's mediating operation always presupposes (among other things) the existence of the eternal Son. At the same time, the crucial distinction between an *unio hypostatica* and an *unio mystica* is conceptually sustained (cf. IV/2, pp. 55-57). For on the basis of the *unio hypostatica* as effected by the Spirit (i.e., his uniting the history of the human Jesus uniquely with the *hypostasis* of the eternal Son), something is said of Jesus that "cannot be said of any other creature, even any prophet or apostle," namely, that "Jesus Christ alone is very God and very man" (II/1, p. 486).[12] Therefore, no basis for a Spirit-oriented Christology is found to exist along these lines.

---

11. Cf. Karl Barth, *Church Dogmatics* III/2 (Edinburgh: T. & T. Clark, 1960), pp. 333-34 (hereafter cited as III/2), and Karl Barth, *Church Dogmatics* IV/4 (Edinburgh: T. & T. Clark, 1969), p. 98 (hereafter cited as IV/4).

12. Cf. Karl Barth, *Church Dogmatics* IV/1 (Edinburgh: T. & T. Clark, 1956), p. 210; hereafter cited as IV/1.

The Spirit's Role in the Incarnation

In Barth's account of the incarnation, Jesus Christ is again set forth as the focus of the Spirit's work (IV/2, pp. 323-25). On the one hand, the incarnation points to Jesus' uniqueness in relation to the Spirit. As a human being who "came into being" through the Spirit, Jesus has never needed to receive the Spirit (IV/2, p. 324). The creedal affirmation that he was "conceived by the Holy Spirit and born of the Virgin Mary" signifies this "important basic connection." For it means that Jesus is not someone "who was subsequently gifted and impelled by the Spirit like others. . . . He has the Spirit at first hand and from the very first." Conceived by the Spirit, he himself gives life in and through the Spirit, "without reserve or limit — the fullness of the Spirit — so that his being as flesh is directly as such his being as Spirit also" (IV/2, p. 324).

On the other hand, this relationship also defines and orients the Spirit's work. "It is in this radical sense," writes Barth, "that the Holy Spirit is the Spirit of Jesus himself" (IV/2, p. 325). Through his hypostatic union with the eternal Son of God, as effected by the Spirit, Jesus is the one truly spiritual human being. "It is as such that he traverses the way which leads to the cross. But it is also as such that he is revealed and known when he is raised from the dead." The latter point is decisive for the Spirit's saving significance. "The Spirit is holy as the power in which the human Jesus is present and alive even after death as the one who was crucified for the world's salvation, and also as the power in which he continually acts as the human being he became and was and is, as the one who was crucified in the flesh" (IV/2, p. 325, rev.).

Once again it is clear that the human Jesus is not regarded as significant because he imparts some direct or independent work of the Spirit (as in Spirit-oriented Christologies). Instead the Spirit is regarded as significant for two reasons: first, because he equips Jesus Christ to accomplish the world's salvation through his incarnation, death, and resurrection; and second, because through proclamation and sacrament he unites believers with Christ, and brings them into communion, so that they may dwell in him and he in them eternally. Jesus Christ thus forms the substance of the Spirit's role in imparting salvation, even as the Spirit's role in that salvation always centers on Jesus Christ as a unique person (God incarnate) who has accomplished a unique work (reconciliation). The Spirit's abiding content and focus is therefore Jesus himself. The Spirit is not merely the Lord, but "the Spirit of the Lord Jesus" (IV/2, p. 323), who presupposes, attests, and imparts the centrality of the Lord Jesus Christ.

The Spirit Mediates the Christus Praesens

This point is deepened when Barth argues that the operation of the Holy Spirit and the presence of Christ coincide.[13] The Holy Spirit, he writes, "is no other than the presence and action of Jesus Christ himself: his outstretched arm; he himself in the power of his resurrection, i.e., the power of his revelation as it begins in and with the power of his resurrection and continues its work from this point" (IV/2, pp. 322-23). It is by the power of the Holy Spirit that Jesus enables human beings to see, hear, and accept him for who he is — "the Son of Man who in obedience to God went to death for the reconciliation of the world and was exalted in his humiliation as the Son of God" (IV/2, p. 323). The Holy Spirit is the power whereby Jesus as such attests and imparts himself as crucified and risen. "Thus the only content of the Holy Spirit is Jesus; his only work is his provisional revelation; his only effect the human knowledge which has [Jesus] as its object" (IV/2, p. 654). The Spirit establishes and mediates a communion of love and knowledge between Christ and faith.

As disclosed by the Spirit, in other words, the knowledge of Jesus is not something merely cognitive, for it claims those who are addressed by the gospel as whole persons. In the power of the Spirit through the proclamation of gospel, Jesus is present to believers and believers to him. "Where the human Jesus attests himself in the power of the Spirit of God, he makes himself present; and those whom he approaches in his self-attestation are able also to approach him and to be near him" (IV/2, p. 654). Mutual self-presence becomes the basis for mutual self-impartation. "More than that, where he makes himself present in this power, he imparts himself; and those to whom he wills to belong in virtue of this self-presentation are able to belong to him" (IV/2, p. 654). Just as Jesus gives himself by the Spirit to those who receive him, so also are those who receive him enabled to belong to him by the Spirit in return. The Spirit mediates the self-impartation of Jesus himself, through

13. In this respect Barth follows Calvin closely. See Werner Krusche, *Das Wirken des Heiligen Geistes nach Calvin* (Göttingen: Vandenhoeck & Ruprecht, 1957), pp. 146-51. "What is distinctive about the Holy Spirit is not that he becomes present in and for himself, but rather that he makes Christ present. Calvin can speak of this in two ways. He can say that *the Spirit* makes Christ and the salvation he effected present, or that *Christ* makes himself and the salvation he effected present *through the Spirit*" (p. 151). Although Barth employs the second of these idioms throughout vol. IV of his dogmatics, that should not be taken to imply that he holds a merely nonagential view of the Spirit. Barth's chosen idiom is appropriate to the doctrine of reconciliation, where he understands the accomplishment of reconciliation in a thoroughly christocentric way. One would expect the other, more agential idiom (which recurs throughout the dogmatics) to have reemerged prominently in the doctrine of redemption.

which believers are drawn into union with him in order to receive and return his love.

In short, the saving activity of the Holy Spirit, as understood by Barth, is always Christ-centered in focus. In various christocentric ways the Spirit functions as the mediator of communion. In the incarnation *(concepto de Spirito sancto)*, he effects the union of Christ's deity and humanity *(communio naturarum)*. In Christ's obedience as fulfilled in his death, he operates as the bond of peace between the Father and the Son. In the risen Christ's ongoing self-revelation and self-impartation, he creates communion between Christ and faith. In no sense that would be independent, supplemental, or superior does the Spirit's activity ever focus on itself, for in the one economy of salvation the Spirit serves the reconciliation accomplished by Christ from beginning to end.[14]

3. Miraculous in Operation

The work of the Holy Spirit, as Barth saw it, is miraculous in operation. Within the trinitarian and christocentric framework of his theology, this theme elaborates his point that the Spirit's work is never "anthropological in ground." The Holy Spirit is seen as the sole effective agent *(solus actor efficiens)* by which communion with God is made humanly possible. In their fallen condition *(status corruptionis)* human beings cannot recover a vital connection with God. Their minds are darkened, their wills are enslaved, and the desires of their hearts are debased. Through the proclamation of the gospel, however, the impossible is made possible, but only in the form of an ongoing miracle. This miracle is the operation of the Holy Spirit, not only to initiate conversion *(operatio initialis)*, but also to continue it throughout the believer's life *(operatio perpetua)*. The only condition (necessary and sufficient) for new life in communion with God is the Spirit's miraculous operation in the human heart *(operatio mirabilis)*. Faith in Christ, hope for the world, and consequent works of love have no other basis *in nobis* than this unceasing miracle of grace. Faith, hope, and love, in other words, do not depend on regenerated capacities, infused virtues, acquired habits, or strengthened dispositions in the soul. Those who are awakened to lifelong conversion by the Spirit never cease to be sinners

14. A good example of a contrary view can be found in Jenson, *Systematic Theology,* vol. 1, pp. 146-61. Jenson requires a supplemental saving work of the Spirit, since he explicitly denies what Barth takes to be the very heart of the New Testament, namely, that "Christ fully accomplished our salvation at Golgotha" (p. 179). Most of Jenson's censure of Barth's pneumatology can be traced back to this fundamental disagreement.

in themselves. Yet despite their continuing sinfulness, the miracle of grace never ceases in their hearts.[15]

Against Emanationism

What Barth is asserting can be explained against the foil of what he rules out. The familiar alternatives of either divine "determinism" or human "free will" are both categorically rejected. Only some of their subtler forms can be considered here.[16] One of these would be the kind of "emanationism" that emphasizes divine grace at the expense of human freedom. As being used here, "emanationism" would be the belief that God and only God is the acting subject in works of Christian love. Christian love would be the prolongation of divine love, and Christians would be the channel through which it flows. They would function merely as passive instruments that are used by God, possessing no relevant agency of their own. By contrast, Barth affirms that "it is not the work of the Holy Spirit to take from us our own proper capacity as human beings, or to make our capacity simply a function of his own overpowering control. Where he is present, there is no servitude but freedom" (IV/2, p. 785). No view of Christian love would be acceptable to Barth which did not allow for genuine human agency and freedom.[17]

Against Synergism

When human freedom is stressed at the expense of divine grace, on the other hand, the opposite error occurs. The belief, known as "synergism," that human

15. The commendable effort by Eugene F. Rogers, Jr., to bring Barth and Aquinas into convergence founders at this very point, for Rogers does not take Barth's conception of the Spirit's miraculous operation adequately into account. Stated in terms of Thomistic vocabulary, supernatural operations in the soul, as Barth understands them, do not require the actuation of habits, nor do they tend toward such actuation. Barth believes that Thomistic views to the contrary cannot (logically cannot) escape the problems of synergism. When Barth states that human freedom is *entirely* dependent on grace, he means without the subvention of infused habits, virtues, or principles in the soul. See Rogers, *Thomas Aquinas and Karl Barth: Sacred Doctrine and the Natural Knowledge of God* (Notre Dame, Ind.: University of Notre Dame Press, 1995), pp. 188-92; cf. pp. 76-79.

16. For more on Barth's rejection of determinism, see George Hunsinger, *How to Read Karl Barth: The Shape of His Theology* (New York: Oxford University Press, 1991), pp. 207-15; for his rejection of "Pelagian" and "semi-Pelagian" forms of autonomy, see pp. 215-18; cf. pp. 223-24.

17. Barth sees "emanationism" reflected in some statements of Nygren, who in turn draws upon Luther (IV/2, p. 752).

freedom "cooperates" with divine grace in effecting salvation would be an example. Roman Catholic and modern Protestant theologies, as Barth sees them, both exhibit this failing. In his pointed and famous essay "No!," for example, Barth rejects several options that he thinks resemble Brunner's unfortunate "point of contact." These include the "Augustinian" position in which divine and human activity are "indirectly identical" and the "Thomistic" position in which "the divine *causa materialis* and the human *causa instrumentalis*" cooperate in effecting salvation.[18] What is common to all such views, Barth objects, is "the systematic coordination of nature and grace" (IV/2, p. 96). Coordinations are properly "systematic" when the formal relations between their terms can be stated without resort to paradox, anomaly, or disjunction in describing the radically new. Systematic coordinations offer familiar, intelligible pictures based on such schemes as "causality" (superior and inferior), "growth" (gradual and partial), or some other form of "commensurability" (mutually limiting and complementary aspects of a larger unified whole).

No "synthesis" which systematically coordinates God and humankind (grace and nature), whether with respect to reason or volition, can, Barth argues, be valid (IV/2, p. 99). Grace is not a matter of repairing this or that human capacity, but of contradicting fallen human nature as a whole, with all its capacities or incapacities, so that it actually transcends itself despite its fallenness. The "formal relation" between grace and nature is that of "miracle," not superior and inferior "causality," or gradual and partial "restoration" (IV/2, p. 101). Grace and nature are not partial, mutually limiting components of a single reality. Not even dialectically can they be identified as one. Although coexisting together in a certain common history, and moving toward a common goal, they do not coexist in any "natural" or "commensurable" way. Grace is rather that miracle by which human reason in its radical fallenness is so contradicted, disrupted, and liberated that it provisionally grasps revelation. At the same time, human volition in its radical fallenness is likewise so contradicted, disrupted, and liberated that it provisionally fulfills the divine will (IV/2, p. 97). Barth writes:

> The doctrine of the point of contact . . . is incompatible with the third article of the creed. The Holy Spirit, who proceeds from the Father and the Son and is therefore revealed and believed to be God, does not stand in need of any point of contact but that which he himself creates. Only retrospectively is it possible to reflect on the way in which he "makes contact" with human

---

18. Barth, "No! Answer to Emil Brunner," in *Natural Theology,* introduction by John Baillie (London: Geoffrey Bles, 1946), pp. 65-128, on p. 85. Further citations are given directly in the text.

beings, and this retrospect will ever be a retrospect upon a *miracle*. (p. 121, rev.)

The root metaphor for this strange operation *in nobis* is not something analogous to ordinary processes but something unheard of, something that is not organic but disruptive, not gradual or cumulative but instantaneous and continual, not something partial but total. What the miraculous operation of the Holy Spirit brings about, that is, is not essentially restoration or healing but resurrection from the dead.

Human Cooperation Does Not Effect Salvation

Barth does not deny that human freedom "cooperates" with divine grace. He denies that this cooperation in any way effects salvation. Although grace makes human freedom possible as a mode of acting *(modus agendi)*, that freedom is always a gift. It is always imparted to faith in the mode of receiving salvation *(modus recipiendi)*, partaking of it *(modus participandi)*, and bearing witness to it *(modus testificandi)*, never in the mode of effecting it *(modus efficiendi)*. As imparted by the Spirit's miraculous operation, human freedom is always the consequence of salvation, never its cause, and therefore in its correspondence to grace always eucharistic *(modus gratandi et laudandi)*.[19] These distinctions apply both objectively and subjectively, that is, not only to salvation as it has taken place *extra nos,* but also as it occurs *in nobis.* Since to be a sinner means to be incapacitated, grace means capacitating the incapacitated despite their incapacitation. Sinners capacitated by grace remain helpless in themselves. Grace does not perfect and exceed human nature in its sorry plight so much as it contradicts and overrules it.

19. This way of formulating Barth's position brings out its implicit resolution of the sixteenth-century "synergist" controversy between Philippist- and Gnesio-Lutherans. Barth in effect takes something from both sides of the dispute while transcending each. Although he agrees with the Philippists in insisting on something like a *modus agendi,* he sides with Gnesio-Lutherans like Flacius on the question of human incapacity. (See his favorable and perceptive comments on Flacius and the surrounding controversy in III/2, pp. 27-29.) Barth transcends the overly restrictive "active/passive" polarity, around which the dispute bogged down, by allowing for a "mode of acting" that without being causal is at once receptive, participatory, witnessing, and eucharistic. His resolution differs from that taken by the Formula of Concord (and perhaps keeps him closer to Flacius and even Luther) in that it assimilates *renovatio, regeneratio,* and *conversio* into the paradigm of "resurrection" rather than into that of a gradual process like "healing." On the historical controversy, see Chr. Ernst Luthardt, *Die Lehre vom freien Willen und seinem Verhältnis zur Gnade* (Leipzig: Dörffling und Franke, 1863), pp. 191-278.

What happens is this: *in nobis,* in our heart, in the very center of our existence, a contradiction is lodged against our unfaithfulness. It is a contradiction that we cannot dodge, but have to validate. In confronting it we cannot cling to our unfaithfulness, for through it our unfaithfulness is not only forbidden but canceled and rendered impossible. Because Jesus Christ intervenes *pro nobis* and thus *in nobis,* unfaithfulness to God has been rendered basically an impossible possibility. It is a possibility disallowed and thus no longer to be realized . . . , one we recognize as eliminated and taken away by the omnipotent contradiction God lodges within us.[20]

In this miraculous and mysterious way, by grace alone — that is, through a continual contradiction of nature by grace resulting in a provisional "conjunction of opposites" *(coniunctio oppositorum)* — the blind see, the lame walk, and the dead are raised to new life (cf. Matt. 11:4).[21]

Descriptive Adequacy Defies Systematic Coordination

When this miraculous operation is described without resort to "synthesis," "system," or relativizing conceptual "coordination" — that unholy triumvirate against which Barth railed in theological construction — the results can only be counterintuitive. His account of the "awakening to conversion," which, he says, "has its analogy only in the resurrection of Jesus Christ from the dead" (IV/2, p. 556), is a good example. Conversion happens to and in the human person. "It involves the total and most intensive conscription and cooperation of all one's inner and outer forces, of one's whole heart and mind" (IV/2, p. 556, rev.). Not merely something inward, it includes the physical and social dimensions of one's life as well. Nevertheless, while showing that divine action "does not exclude but includes human action" (IV/2, p. 556), conversion belongs to "that order of action which is specifically divine" (IV/2, p. 557, rev.). Therefore, "on this aspect — its true and proper aspect — it is a miracle and a mystery." It is "not the work of one of the creaturely factors, coefficients and agencies which are also operating and perceptible" (IV/2, p. 557, rev.). Any awakening to conversion is rather solely the work of God, "who uses these factors and himself makes them coefficients and agencies for this purpose" (IV/2, p. 557).

20. Barth, "Extra Nos–Pro Nobis–In Nobis," *Thomist* 50 (1986): 497-511, on p. 510. (Cf. IV/4, pp. 13-23, on p. 22.)

21. Note that Barth speaks of sanctification "in direct analogy to the doctrine of justification" (IV/2, p. 515) as involving a provisional state of *"simul peccator et sanctus"* (IV/2, p. 575; cf. pp. 572-73).

In a pithy conclusion that typifies his antisystematic thought, Barth remarks:

> We are thus forced to say that this awakening is both wholly creaturely and wholly divine. Yet the initial shock comes from God. Thus there can be no question of coordination between two comparable elements, but only of the absolute primacy of the divine over the creaturely. The creaturely is made serviceable to the divine and does actually serve it. It is used by God as his organ or instrument. Its creatureliness is not impaired, but given by God a special function or character. Being qualified and claimed by God for cooperation, it cooperates in such a way that the whole is still an action which is specifically divine. (IV/2, p. 557)

Note that this awakening is seen from two different standpoints which are merely juxtaposed, not synthesized. For the occurrence is not said to be partially divine and partially creaturely, but "wholly divine" and "wholly creaturely." Emphasis falls strongly on the asymmetry that Barth posits between divine and human agency. The two factors repel all systematic coordination as "comparable elements," for divine agency as such retains "absolute primacy" as the sole effective factor in conversion. The human person is an "organ or instrument" of this divine work, yet not passively (as in "emanationism"). Rather, the human will actually "cooperates" with the divine work, and in its own way actually enacts it ("wholly human"), yet without becoming its secondary cause (as in "synergism"). Human freedom is not coerced, yet neither does it operate by its own strength. Divine grace is not conditioned by human freedom, yet uses it to achieve the divine ends. Human freedom depends on nothing but divine grace, yet ordinary human capacities are strangely actuated ("given a special function or character") despite their manifest inutility. Freedom is given only as it is actually received, and the gift is not intermittent but continual.

No familiar "system" of causality or growth, no unified conceptual scheme, can accommodate this set of anomalies or adequately describe it. As a miraculous operation, conversion conforms only to something like the "Chalcedonian pattern." Divine and human agency thus cooperate "without separation or division," "without confusion or change," and "without symmetry or systematic coordination" regarding efficacy.[22] This drastic alternative to conceptual closure expresses Barth's core belief that the saving work of the Holy Spirit is miraculous in operation.[23]

---

22. On the Chalcedonian pattern in Barth's thought, see Hunsinger, pp. 185-88, 201-18.

23. A fuller discussion would need to explore the place Barth might still allow for gradual or cumulative regeneration within the spiritual life of the believer. Although such a place can-

4. Communal in Content

The work of the Holy Spirit, as Barth saw it, is communal in content. Three distinct forms of communion — with Christ, with the Trinity, and with one another — all take place by the Holy Spirit. As the mediator of communion, the Spirit unites believers with Christ, through whom they participate in the eternal communion of the Holy Trinity while at the same time also finding communion with one another. "Communion" means love in knowledge, and knowledge in love, thus fellowship and mutual self-giving. It means sharing and participating in the being of another, without the loss of identity by either partner; for in true fellowship the identity of each is not effaced but enhanced; indeed, the identity of each is constituted not in isolation but only in encounter with another. The deepest form of communion, as depicted in the New Testament, is mutual indwelling, an I-Thou relation of ineffable spiritual intimacy (*koinonia*). The Spirit who proceeds from the Father and the Son, the Spirit of the Lord Jesus Christ, is at once the mediator of this indwelling and yet also the indwelling itself, the mediator, the mediation, and the very essence of what is mediated. The Holy Spirit is the Spirit of *koinonia*.

Koinonia with Christ: Uniting the Disparate

The mutual indwelling of Christ's two natures, established by the Spirit in the incarnation, serves as the backdrop for his uniting of Christ with the church. In both cases, Barth suggests, "the work of the Holy Spirit is to bring and to hold together that which is different" (IV/3, p. 761). If an analogy may be permitted, the Holy Spirit operates something like the "strong force" in modern physics, which holds disparate entities together within an atom's nucleus; for the Spirit serves as the incarnation's ultimate unifying ground, holding together the otherwise disparate realities of deity and humanity in Christ's person (IV/1, p. 148). Unlike the strong force, however, the unity effected by the Spirit can be described only as "a history," not as "a datum or a state" (IV/3, p. 761). In that sense the Spirit's unifying work is paradigmatic. It applies not only to the incarnation, but also to "that which would seem necessarily and inexorably disparate in the relationship of Jesus Christ to his community" (IV/3, p. 761, rev.; cf.

---

not be completely ruled out (e.g., IV/2, pp. 566, 794), it seems undeniable that in Barth's soteriology this aspect is underdeveloped and excessively diminished. A Barthian solution after Barth might try to move in a dialectical rather than a synthetic direction, alternating back and forth between a holistic scheme informed by "resurrection" ("again and again") and a gradualistic scheme informed by "regeneration" ("more and more").

IV/2, pp. 652-53). The miraculous operation of the Spirit joins disparate realities for the sake of communion.

By mediating Christ to the community and the community to Christ, the Spirit establishes "the unity of Jesus Christ in the heights and in the depths, in his transcendence and in his immanence" (IV/3, p. 760). He grounds "the unity in which Jesus Christ is at one and the same time the heavenly head with God and the earthly body with his community" (IV/3, p. 760). As in the incarnation, what happens is a linking of the divine and the human: "the divine working, being and action on the one side and the human on the other" (IV/3, p. 761). Two freedoms are mysteriously conjoined: "the creative freedom and act on the one side and the creaturely on the other." Disparate realities unite across the divine/human ontological divide: "the eternal reality and possibility on the one side and the temporal on the other" (IV/3, p. 761). The Spirit "brings and holds together Christ and his community, not to identify, intermingle or confound them, not to change the one into the other, or to merge the one into the other, but to coordinate them, to make them parallel, to bring them into harmony and therefore to bind them into a true unity" (IV/3, p. 761, rev.). The Holy Spirit "constitutes and guarantees the unity of the *totus Christus*" (IV/3, p. 760) through a mediation of *koinonia* in union, correspondence, and love.

Participating through Christ in the Koinonia of the Trinity

Communion with Christ in the Spirit involves participation in the communion of the Holy Trinity. Those joined to Christ by faith are granted a share through him in that communion where God is eternally God: the primordial communion of love and knowledge between the Father and the Son in the Holy Spirit. When he seeks and creates fellowship *(koinonia)* for its own sake (II/1, p. 276), God has no other end than this participation in view. "He receives us through his Son into his fellowship with himself" (II/1, p. 275). "He takes us up into his fellowship, i.e., the fellowship which he has and is in himself" (II/1, p. 276). "In his unique being with and for and in another," the triune God "does not exist in solitude but in fellowship" (II/1, p. 275). "His innermost self is his self-communication; and loving the world, he gives it a share in his completeness" (II/1, p. 277). Love means "not to wish any longer to be and have oneself without the beloved" (II/1, p. 33, rev.). In seeking and creating this communion, God "wills to be ours, and he wills that we should be his. He wills to belong to us and he wills that we should belong to him. He does not will to be without us, and he does not will that we should be without him" (II/1, p. 274). The very God who does not will to be and have himself without us, the God of love, is the God who through the Son in the Spirit takes us up into his communion with himself. "God brings us to participate in the love in which as the Father he loves the Son, and as the Son the Father" (IV/2, pp. 778-79). Through this participation God makes our action "a reflection of his eternal love," and makes us "into those who may and will love" in return (IV/2, p. 779).

Our participation in the love of the Holy Trinity is grounded, it may again be noted, solely in the freedom of God. God is free to be present with the creature, despite the indissoluble divine/human ontological divide, in order to establish this participation. Divine freedom for *koinonia* with the other is what Barth means by "the absoluteness of God." "The absoluteness of God . . . means that God has the freedom to be present with that which is not God, to communicate himself and unite himself with the other, and the other with himself" (II/1, p. 313). This divine/human union and self-communication "utterly surpasses all that can be effected in regard to reciprocal presence, communion and fellowship between other beings" (II/1, p. 313). Divine freedom for *koinonia* is another name for the Holy Spirit, who unites us with Christ, and through him with the eternal Trinity, in unsurpassable communion.

We do not participate in God's eternal love without participating in the truth of God's self-knowledge. "Revelation" is the effecting of this participation.[24] No knowledge of God occurs apart from fellowship with God (II/1, p. 182), so that knowing and loving God are inseparable (II/1, pp. 32-33). Knowledge of God, in Barth's theology, is essentially a form of *koinonia*.[25] The key word is again "participation." Our knowledge of God through the gospel is true, Barth urges, because it participates in the truth of God's self-knowledge. "God knows himself: the Father knows the Son and the Son the Father in the unity of the Holy Spirit. This occurrence in God himself is the essence and strength of our knowledge of God" (II/1, p. 49). "Through God's revelation" we become "participants" in this occurrence (II/1, p. 49), receiving and having a part in God's eternal self-knowledge (II/1, p. 68). For as "God gives himself to

24. The Holy Spirit, as Barth develops at great length, is both the subjective reality and the subjective possibility of revelation (Karl Barth, *Church Dogmatics* I/2 [Edinburgh: T. & T. Clark, 1956], pp. 203-79; hereafter cited as I/2). The Spirit, in other words, is the means by which we come to enjoy "the communion with God which is realized in the revelation of God" (I/2, p. 257). God's revelation in Jesus Christ cannot be known apart from our reception of it and participation in it through the miraculous operation of the Holy Spirit.

25. The important work by Alan J. Torrance, *Persons in Communion: Trinitarian Description and Human Participation* (Edinburgh: T. & T. Clark, 1996), curiously overlooks this point. Only by driving a wedge between "revelation" and "communion" in Barth, as though they were not mutually coinherent, can Torrance reproach Barth for focusing on revelation at the expense of communion.

us to be known in the truth of his self-knowledge" (II/1, p. 53), "we receive a share in the truth of his knowledge of himself" (II/1, p. 51).

While our participation in God's self-knowledge is "true and real," it is always an "indirect participation" (II/1, p. 59). It is indirect because it is mediated in and through Jesus Christ. Through the true humanity of Jesus (with whom we are united in *koinonia* by faith), we come to share, indirectly, in God's own trinitarian self-knowledge. In the humanity of Jesus Christ, God has lowered himself to us in order to raise us to himself (II/1, p. 55). As God's one true covenant partner, Jesus is "the first and proper [human] subject of the knowledge of God" (II/1, p. 252). Through our union with Christ effected by the Spirit, God gives us "a part in the truth of his knowing" and, through his knowing, in the divine self-knowledge. "The eternal Father knows the eternal Son, and the eternal Son knows the eternal Father. But the eternal Son is not only the eternal God. In the unity fulfilled by the grace of the incarnation, he is also this man Jesus of Nazareth." Everything depends on the particular "knowledge that is and will be present in this man, Jesus," for his human knowing of God is, by its coinherence with the eternal Son, the appointed vehicle of mediation through which we come to take part in the truth of God's self-knowledge (II/1, p. 252). As we are "taken up into fellowship with the life of the Son of God" (II/1, p. 162), we are given "fellowship in his knowledge of God" (II/1, p. 252).

Koinonia with One Another in Christ

As the Spirit incorporates us into Christ, and so into communion with the Holy Trinity, we also become members one of another. Between the first and second comings of Christ, the principal work of the Spirit is to form the community of Christ. The Spirit gathers the community in faith (IV/1, pp. 643-739), builds it up in love (IV/2, pp. 614-726), and sends it out into the world in hope (IV/3, pp. 681-901). "The Holy Spirit," writes Barth, "is not a private spirit"; the community that he gathers is not "a pile of grains of sand or an aggregate of cells" (IV/1, p. 149). In Christ the individual presupposes the community, even as the community comes to fruition in each member. "There cannot be one without the other." Scripture ascribes salvation to the individual, Barth observes, only "in the existence of the community," and salvation is appropriated by the community only "in the existence of the individuals of which it is composed" (IV/1, p. 149). In principle, therefore, "there can be no possible tension between the 'individual' and the 'community'" (II/2, p. 313). No compromise needs to be made between them, and "no continual reacting" needs to occur "on the one side or the other" — i.e., no individualism at the expense of the community, no collectivism at the expense of the individual. Nevertheless, the Holy Spirit works "first in the community of God and only then . . . in individual Christians" (IV/1, p. 154). While "we must not cease to stress the individual" (IV/1, p. 150), we must not fail to see that "the being of the Christian . . . is a being in relation" (IV/1, p. 153). It is primarily in the *koinonia* of the community, therefore, not in the individual as such, that the work of the Holy Spirit is fulfilled (IV/1, pp. 150-51).

The precedence of the community in Barth's pneumatology is distinguished from an abstract collectivism. The community "does not lead to any independent life in relation to its members. It lives in them."[26] The community gathered by the Spirit is a true fellowship, not "a collective in whose existence . . . the individual is not required as such," and for which the individual's "particularity is a *pudendum*" (IV/2, p. 635). The union of believers is firm, "but it is a union in freedom, in which the individual does not cease to be this particular individual," so that each member is united to the other in all his or her particularity (IV/2, p. 635). The individual, Barth writes, "does not stand merely in or under the whole, but in his own place he is himself the whole. And whatever proceeds from the whole proceeds from himself. As each is for all, so all are for each" (II/2, p. 312). The community as a whole thus "reaches its consummation" as the Holy Spirit works in the lives of its individual members (II/2, p. 314). "The *particula veri* of 'individualism'" (II/2, p. 311) is not lost; that is, the Spirit actually exercises authority and operates "in their hearts and in their free personal responses" (II/2, p. 314). The primacy of the community, therefore, does not exclude but includes the significance of the individual as a locus of the Spirit's communal work.

What makes this community distinctive is that its members uphold one another in fellowship instead of causing one another to fall (IV/2, pp. 816-17). It is a community that lives by the forgiveness of sins, where one sinner may love another, because the sins of each and all have been taken away (IV/2, p. 818). It is also a community whose members bear faithful and joyful witness to Christ for the sake of each other and the world. "Only by the Holy Spirit do they become free for this action. But by the Holy Spirit they do become free for it. By the Holy Spirit the individual becomes free for existence in an active relationship with the other in which he is loved and finds that he may love in return" (IV/2, p. 818). Finally, it may be mentioned that the *koinonia* established

---

26. Karl Barth, *Church Dogmatics* II/2 (Edinburgh: T. & T. Clark, 1957), p. 311; hereafter cited as II/2.

by the Spirit also equips the community in freedom for solidarity (though not conformity) with the world (IV/3, pp. 762-95).

The saving activity of the Holy Spirit, as understood by Barth, is therefore communal in content. The Spirit is the presence and power of *koinonia* joining believers to Christ and through him to God and one another. "In the Holy Spirit," writes Barth, "they thus know themselves in and with him [Christ]; themselves in their union with him, and also with one another, in the fellowship of faith and hope and love in which they express themselves as his and find self-awareness as this people which has a common descent" (IV/2, p. 651). *Koinonia* with Christ in the Spirit means *koinonia* with the Trinity and with one another, including solidarity with the world.

5. Eschatological in Form

The work of the Holy Spirit, as Barth saw it, is eschatological in form. Contrary to what is sometimes said, Barth does not see the Spirit merely as the epiphany of an eternal present. Through the proclamation of God's Word, the Spirit acts to make contemporary, to reveal, and to impart the reconciliation wrought and embodied by Jesus Christ — a living salvation that is all-encompassing, differentiated, and unified in itself. This "intrinsically perfect work," writes Barth, "is still moving toward its consummation" (IV/3, p. 327). But in this consummation it will not be another work than it was as the finished work of Jesus Christ for our sakes on the cross, nor will it be another work than it is in our reception of it here and now by the Spirit, nor again will it be another work than it already has been from before the foundation of the world in God's pretemporal decision of election. The final consummation toward which this work is moving; the cross on which it was accomplished; the sending of the Spirit through which it is contemporized, revealed, and imparted here and now; the primordial decision of election by which it is grounded in eternity — all these are not to be set alongside one another, Barth proposes, as though they were separate events that are only externally or narratively connected. They are rather to be seen as distinctive and irreplaceable variations of one and the same event.

Barth reflects on the mystery of Christ's saving work from two different temporal perspectives. The one might be called a "single-act" perspective, and the other a "narrative" perspective. The two cannot be integrated or synthesized; they can only be juxtaposed and ordered in relation to one another. Although both are necessary, they cannot be expressed together by a unified thought. The only option is to alternate back and forth without closure. When speaking in the idiom of the single-act perspective, the narrative perspective must be tacitly presupposed, and vice versa. For longer or shorter stretches, Barth speaks in the idiom of the one before switching over to the other and then back again. Here, too, faith means perceiving what is not said.

The perspectives are not of equal status in their antithesis. The single-act perspective takes precedence, because it expresses the ontological priority of eternity. This priority is what determines Barth's eschatology. "The New Testament speaks eschatologically when it speaks of humanity's being called, reconciled, justified, sanctified and redeemed. In speaking thus it speaks really and properly. One has to realize that God is the measure of all that is real and proper, that eternity comes first and then time, and therefore the future comes first and then the present" (I/1, p. 464). The significance of this statement would be difficult to overestimate.

Barth thinks of the saving work of Jesus Christ as a single divine action. In its perfection this action is infinitely rich and manifests itself in an ordered multiplicity of forms. The Holy Spirit's mission, as seen from the standpoint of reconciliation, occurs within this all-embracing context. It is one form of the being of Jesus Christ in his work. Along with other forms, it is conceived in terms of the pattern of dialectical inclusion — which is to say that in each form, and therefore also in this form, the divine action manifests itself as a whole, without either exhausting itself as an action or rendering the other forms superfluous. Each form plays a role in the fulfillment of God's purposes in history, and in each one the being of Jesus Christ in his work is uniquely present in its unity and entirety. Within this broad conceptual framework, the Spirit's sending is conceived as the eschatological manifestation of Christ's presence prior to the final consummation.

In this work the being of Jesus Christ coincides with that of God. But God's being is perfect as a qualitative and indivisible whole. Therefore, in his saving work the being of Jesus Christ is also perfect in that same distinctive sense. "The being of Jesus Christ was and is perfect and complete in itself in his history as the true Son of God and Son of Man" (IV/2, p. 132). In this history, and especially in his saving death, "he has made a perfect sacrifice" (IV/1, p. 281) — that is, one that is "significant in and by itself" (IV/1, p. 227), that is "entire and perfect" (IV/1, p. 281), that "cannot and need not be continued or repeated or added to or superseded" (IV/1, p. 281). Since "God in Christ was its subject," this work constitutes "a unique history" (IV/1, p. 76), defined as "a perfect happening" (IV/1, p. 283), a "self-contained and completed event" (IV/1, p. 76), whose content is "new and eternal" (IV/1, p. 281).

By virtue of its uniqueness as a "perfect" and "completed" occurrence — and here is Barth's leading idea — Christ's saving work as it confronts us today is "not a process" (IV/1, p. 76), not something quantitative that grows by accretion or admits of degrees. Nor is it an event whose activity has ceased as if it needed to be perpetuated or re-presented by something outside itself. Nor does it lack anything in itself, as if it were in some sense still merely a potentiality waiting to be actualized or completed by something beyond itself. This work "needs no completion or re-presentation. It would encroach on its perfection and glory if we were to place alongside it events which complete or represent or actualize it" (IV/1, pp. 295-96). There is nothing beyond or above this event. It is "final and absolute" (IV/1, p. 297). In a word, the saving work of Jesus Christ cannot be superseded, completed, continued, supplemented, repeated, or actualized by anything outside itself. Although it indeed continues, it does not go on as a cumulative process that admits of degrees or that can be divided or subdivided into quantitative parts. As a work that is intrinsically perfect, it is (and can only be) a work that continues as a qualitative and indivisible whole.

"He himself is the whole" (IV/1, p. 20). What is at stake is not just a work that is intrinsically perfect, but the being of Jesus Christ in this work. It is only because he himself is in this work, and essentially inseparable from it, that it can be what it is in its indivisible wholeness. He himself as such is the unity and content of this work. What the Christian message "says at its heart as the doctrine of the atonement is that he himself is and lives and rules and acts, very God and very man, and that he is peace and salvation" (IV/1, p. 20). He himself is the one whom this message serves at all points, "the truth of all it attests and proclaims as true, the actuality of all it attests and proclaims as actual" (IV/1, p. 20, rev.). His saving work is indivisible, because he himself is indivisible. His being is inseparable from his work even as his work is inseparable from his being. Where he is present, it is present. Where it is present, he is present. He himself, in the intrinsic perfection of his work, is an indivisible whole.

Although he is "single, unitary, consistent and free from contradiction, yet for all his singularity and unity his form is inexhaustibly rich" (IV/1, p. 763). He must continually be seen and appreciated in new lights and new aspects. "For he does not present himself in one form but in many — indeed, he is not in himself uniform but multiform. How can it be otherwise when he is the true Son of God who is eternally rich?" (IV/1, p. 763). It belongs to the perfection of his being (and this idea is pivotal) that his form should be as inexhaustible as his content is indivisible. In his saving work the being of Jesus Christ is eternally resourceful in its self-demonstration and self-manifestation. The indivisible wholeness of his work, and in this work his being, is not uniform but multiform in itself.

"The reconciliation of the world with God as it has taken place in Jesus Christ," writes Barth, must be seen in its multiplicity as "one mighty truth"

(IV/2, p. 5). The unifying power of this truth is shown as it assumes an astonishing diversity of forms without dissolving into quantitative parts. "It is indivisible. It would not be the truth in any of its forms if it were not the whole truth in each of them." "As the action and work of God," this unified and powerful truth — "the truth of the atonement" — is a "divinely living truth," a truth that is "rich and varied in its unity." It can therefore be known and respected only in its freedom to disclose itself anew. "It is the friend only of those who respect its freedom and are therefore free to follow it, to know it afresh . . . in a new aspect" (IV/2, p. 5). But whatever the various aspects or forms, it always occurs in its perfection as a qualitative whole. "It is not more in one case or less in another. It is the one thing taking place in different ways, in a difference of form corresponding to the willing and fulfillment of the action of its one Subject, the living Jesus Christ" (IV/3, p. 293).

The structure of Barth's christocentric eschatology involves not only an original form (resurrection) and a final form (redemption), but also a form intervening between the two. What Jesus disclosed initially to his disciples in his resurrection appearances, and what he will disclose universally on the last day, he also discloses to faith here and now — through the sending of his Holy Spirit. Like the other two forms, the sending of the Spirit means the arrival of the eschaton. Occurring "between the times" of resurrection and redemption, it composes the "second and intermediate form" (IV/3, p. 349), or the "middle form" (IV/3, p. 350), of the promised future in which Jesus manifests himself in his saving significance for all things. Taken together, therefore, his resurrection appearances, his apocalypse on the day of redemption, and his coming here and now in the Spirit are not three separate events. They are three different forms of one and the same event — the eschatological event of "his one new coming" or parousia after his being crucified, dead, and buried (IV/3, p. 295). In its own distinctive way, therefore, the middle form of this eschatological event — the sending of the Spirit — functions just like the other two. It, too, manifests the being of Jesus Christ in his work. It manifests him, that is, as a qualitative and indivisible whole.

This wholeness can again be described from two standpoints, the one more nearly substantive, the other more nearly personal. Seen from the standpoint of its content, the eschatological differentiation of the times, though real, is essentially formal. Through the sending of the Spirit, the "great alteration" of all things in Jesus Christ becomes present "in provisional form." "It is only the manifestation of the alteration that is different" (IV/1, p. 328). The alteration is no less real and complete in the Spirit than it will be at last in redemption. "There can be no question . . . of understanding the alteration as more real and complete in its final form and less real and complete in its provisional" (IV/1, p. 328). Salvation is as real and complete in the sending of the Spirit as it was on the day of resurrection and as it will be at the end in redemption. As something perfect in itself, it does not come now in any lesser degree, though this form of its manifestation is clearly provisional. "It is all provisional: not our new creation and regeneration as accomplished on the cross and resurrection of Jesus Christ, but its present manifestation; not our justification, but its present form; not the being of Jesus Christ in us and our being in him, but the form in which we are now with him, raised and quickened and resurrected with him" (IV/1, p. 330). Through the sending of the Holy Spirit, the content of salvation becomes present, in provisional form, as a qualitative and indivisible whole.

"Alive in the Spirit," Jesus is the Lord who is present to all times though bound to none (IV/4, p. 211). Yet his life as lived in the Spirit cannot be separated from his earthly history. "His history has been, but it has not passed" (IV/3, p. 224). By virtue of his resurrection, it is the history which "overlaps all others," being "the promise given also to our histories that one day they will have been but will not have passed." As the one who so lives in the Spirit, the risen Lord imparts himself to ourselves — and thus his history to our histories. (He does not impart himself without his earthly history, for his history is inseparable from his being even as his being is inseparable from his history.) Through the sending of the Spirit — and here is another pivotal idea — his one saving history, having taken place "primarily" there and then, takes place also "secondarily" here and now (IV/3, p. 224).

What occurs, that is to say, as he imparts himself to faith is not another history than that which took place there and then. It is one and the same history made present in new form, occurring in fulfillment of that which took place there and then. Through the sending of the Holy Spirit, Jesus Christ continues the completed action of his history and brings it to its interim fulfillment. It is the fulfillment in which "this action hastens from his resurrection as its first revelation to a few, to its final and general revelation to all" (IV/1, p. 648). It is the fulfillment in which he imparts and confirms to faith "his life as the theme of that action" (IV/1, p. 648). "This is not a different work, a second work alongside, behind and after the work of . . . reconciliation. It is the one divine work in its movement, its concrete reference, to specific human beings, wherein for the first time it reaches its goal" (IV/4, p. 29, rev.).

Through the sending of the Spirit, Jesus Christ makes those who receive him by faith into "contemporaries" of his completed history so that they actually "participate" in it here and now (IV/1, p. 648). At the same time, he also makes his history contemporary to them so that it enters into their own life histories. The history which took place there and then "does not remain external" to them but "becomes internal" here and now to their hearts and minds and lives (IV/4, p. 29). Contemporaneity in the Spirit is what makes it possible for their histories to participate in his, even as his history participates in theirs. It is the means by which the reality of who he is and what he has accomplished is made present to them and they to it. It is "the true and direct bridge from once to always, from himself in his time to us in our time" (IV/1, p. 315).

Contemporaneity with Christ in the Spirit embraces the full range of eschatological complexity. Since those to whom the Lord comes have died and risen with him, what this contemporaneity imparts is something accomplished and fulfilled. Since their new reality in him is still hidden, what it imparts is yet to come. Since they actively partake of it by faith, what it imparts is present even now. In effect, their contemporaneity with Christ occurs within an eschatological horizon that bears a decided orientation toward the future, for the sending of the Spirit is, supremely, "the present irruption" of their "eternal future," the "advent" of that new humanity before God which is already theirs in Jesus Christ (IV/3, p. 249). It is the provisional and prospective irruption of their coming salvation as an indivisible and qualitative whole.

The Holy Spirit is sent as the "awakening power" by which that goal is attained provisionally here and now (IV/1, p. 643). He is the power "in which it takes place that there are human beings who can and must find and see that [Jesus Christ] is theirs and they are his, that their history is genuinely enclosed in his and his history is equally genuinely enclosed in theirs" (IV/1, p. 648, rev.). He is the power which gives them the freedom to receive the crucified Lord and to acknowledge his history for what it is (IV/1, p. 648). By his awakening power the cross at the center of this history is revealed in its mystery as "the one total and final truth" (IV/3, p. 903). He is thus the power of the promised future in which the cross of Christ will at last be unveiled as the end (and beginning) of all things. "Fundamentally and generally," nothing more can be said of the Holy Spirit than that he liberates people for this truth (IV/1, p. 648; IV/4, p. 29).

"Eschatological" means "looking into the furthest and final future, and from there back again into the present" (IV/1, p. 608). When considered from this perspective, the present appears in its unfinished aspect of becoming. It can thus be said of the same Jesus Christ elevated in eternity to perfection that "he himself is only on the way to the end included in this beginning" (IV/3, p. 328). It can also be said that the world, though reconciled in him, has not yet been "perfected and redeemed" (IV/3, p. 328). Although in Christ believers have already come into being (IV/2, p. 307), "it is true that they are not for him that which corresponds to what he is for them" (IV/3, p. 364). In short, when looking back into the present from the future, "what is true in itself has yet to become true" (IV/3, p. 917). "It is not yet the perfect life which it is properly and finally destined to be" (IV/4, p. 40). The "absolute future" of Christ's one parousia (IV/4, p. 40) has yet to be revealed in the dignity of its final form.

6. Diversified in Application

The work of the Holy Spirit, as Barth saw it, is also diversified in application. Divine activity is so richly diverse that it cannot be captured by any law, but must continually be sought afresh from one new situation to the next. Although God "is always wholly the One he is," writes Barth, "the mode of his action varies" (II/1, p. 315). Diversity in the divine activity might be said to have both a general and a particular aspect, for God is thought to speak and act variously, not only on the larger scale of the *magnalia dei* in creation, reconciliation, and redemption, but also on the smaller scale of his particular relationship with every creature. In large things and in small, one and the same God speaks and acts "differently yesterday, differently today, and differently tomorrow. . . . He is always infinitely diverse in his communion with each individual angel, thing, human being, or believer, as compared with all the rest" (II/1, p. 316, rev.). If the diversity of God's activity does not destroy but confirms God's oneness, that can only mean "the triumph of God's freedom in immanence" (II/1, p. 316).

> God is sufficiently free to indwell the creature in the most varied ways according to its varying characteristics. . . . Of course, God too in his relationship to the world can react only in a certain way and not otherwise — that is, according to his own standpoint, in correspondence with his divine being, as he determines and wills in his freedom. . . . But . . . he remains unbound from the point of view of the world and its specific determinations. His presence in the life and being of the world is his personal and therefore actual presence expressed in continually new forms according to his sovereign decisions. (II/1, p. 314)

> We must go further still. God is sufficiently free to differentiate his presence infinitely, and decisively, not merely with respect to the variations of the creature, but also in himself, that is, according to the demands of his own intention with regard to the creature. The relationship and fellowship of God with the world is not bound to a definite scheme, to the quantum and quale of a certain mode of action uniformly proceeding from him. (II/1, p. 315)

But it does so as the one work of one unvarying wisdom, which excludes

the fortuitous and the contradictory, which does not will at random or jux-
tapose incompatible elements, but which in the abundance of its effects
wills only one thing, namely itself, and which orders all things to its own
glory but also to the life and healing of the other which has its being by it
and in it. (II/1, p. 318)

In short, God is "ever diversely manifested in his freedom, yet ever the same,
never and nowhere a different God" (II/1, p. 318). For "the abundant variety of
the divine presence [is] grounded in the divine freedom" (II/1, p. 319).

The divine freedom for diversity allows God to attend to each human being in particular. God does not merely act to save the world in general. God addresses each one within the context of the whole.

When a man can and must believe, it is not merely a matter of "also," of his
attachment as an individual to the general being and activity of the race
and community as determined by Jesus Christ. In all the common life of
that outer and inner circle he is still himself. He is uniquely this man and no
other. He cannot be repeated or represented. He is incomparable. He is this
in body, existing in the span of this time of his. He is this sinful man with
his own particular pride and in his own special case. For all his common life
he is alone in this particularity. It is not simply that he also can and must
believe, but that just he can and must believe. (IV/1, p. 754)

No one comes to believe in Christ without encountering him directly. All that
Christ is and has done is brought to bear on one's own particular human existence: "In this event it takes place that Jesus Christ lives not only 'also' but
'just' as his Mediator and Savior and Lord, and that he shows himself just to
him as this living one. He became a servant just for him. It was just his place
that he took, the place which is not the place of any other. In this place he
died just for him, for his sin. And, again, in his place he was raised again from
the dead" (IV/1, p. 754). The person encountered by Christ in the Holy Spirit
is removed from the great crowd and addressed as if no one else existed, as if
no one else had needed God's saving act of love, as if no one else had been
blessed by Christ's death.

Therefore the Yes which God the Father spoke to him as His Son in the resurrection is spoken not only also but just to him, this man. In Him, it was
just his pride, his fall which was overcome. In Him it is just his new right
which has been set up, his new life which has appeared. And in Him it is
just he who is called to new responsibility, who is newly claimed. It is just he
who is not forgotten by Him, not passed over, not allowed to fall, not set

aside or abandoned. It is just he — and this is the work of the Holy Spirit — who has been sought out, and reached, and found by Him, just he whom He has associated with Himself and Himself with him. God did not will to be God without being just his God. Jesus did not will to be Jesus without being just his Jesus. The world was not to be reconciled with God without just this man as an isolated individual being a man — this man — reconciled with God. The community was not to be the living body of Christ without just this man being a living member of it. The whole occurrence of salvation was not to take place but just for him, the grace addressed in this judgment just to him, just his justification, just his conversion to God. The gift and commission of the community of Jesus Christ is personally just his gift and commission. And all this not merely incidentally, among other things, or only in part for him, but altogether, in its whole length and breadth and height and depth just for him, because Jesus Christ, in whom all this is given to the world and the community, in whom God has sacrificed Himself for it, is Jesus, the Christ, just for him. That this shines out in a sinful man is the mystery, the creative fact, in the event of faith in which he becomes and is a Christian, so that he can and must acknowledge and recognize and confess as such what is proper to him as this subject. (IV/1, pp. 754-55)

Of course, the personal address of the gospel to each person in particular cannot be detached from the universal significance of Christ's work and concern. "It can never be a *pro me* in the abstract, but includes in itself and is enclosed by the communal *pro nobis* and the even wider *propter nos homines*" (IV/1, p. 775). The particularity by which each one is claimed must be kept in its proper connection with the gospel's relevance to the sociality of humankind. "We can and should give it all its own weight as *pro me*. It carries the *pro nobis* and the *propter nos homines,* just as it is carried by them. There is no *pro nobis* or *propter nos homines* which does not include within itself and is not enclosed by the *pro me*. In its connection, its unity with this, it has its own dignity and truth and actuality, which, if it is not greater, is certainly not less — the dignity, truth and actuality which is proper to the individual Christian subject, just to me and to thee, to this one and that one, who are believers in Jesus Christ" (IV/1, p. 755). No particular address and significance exists without a larger universal significance, but no universal significance effaces the gospel's relevance for each one in particular, just as he or she is. "Without the *pro me* of the individual Christian there is no legitimate *pro nobis* of the faith of the Christian community and no legitimate *propter nos homines* of its representative faith for the non-believing world. The being and activity of Jesus Christ has essentially and necessarily the form in which He addresses Himself, not only also, but just

181

to the individual man, to thee and to me, to this man and that man, in which He makes common cause with the individual in his very isolation, in which His Holy Spirit speaks to his spirit" (IV/1, p. 755). "When this is observed, the *pro nobis* and the even more comprehensive *propter nos homines* will not be submerged and disappear in the *pro me*, but in and with the *pro me* they will necessarily be given the same degree of honor" (IV/1, p. 756).

In a similar manner, the diversity and gifts of each individual are honored and validated in the formation of the Christian community by the Spirit. "The gifts of the grace granted to this community *(charismata)* may be many and varied (I Cor. 12:4-11), but they all have one thing in common which guarantees their cooperation and the unity of the church. . . . They are all gifts of the same Spirit, who divides to every man severally as he will — for he is not a spirit of the community who exercises a neutral rule, but One who has as such his particular will for each Christian. All differences *(diaireseis)* in the community rest on the variety of his distribution *(diairein)*" (IV/2, p. 321). The recurring pattern of *koinonia* — of unity-in-diversity and of diversity-in-unity — is again manifested at this level of the Spirit's mediating work.

> The Holy Spirit is the Spirit of the Lord, and himself the Lord. Therefore his instruction does not consist merely in the fact that he advances considerations, or provides the material for them. It is certainly part of his instruction to cause or summon us to test ourselves and our situation, to consider most carefully our possibilities and choices. This is the task of theological ethics, which shows itself to be such by the fact that it leads us, in face of the many possibilities with which we are confronted, to ask what God wills of us, what is the command of God here and now by which we are to direct our life and conduct. But the Holy Spirit is rather more than a professor of theological ethics. He is the One — and this is his instruction — who actually reveals and makes known and imparts and writes on our heart and conscience the will of God as it applies to us concretely here and now, the command of God in the individual and specific form in which we have to respect it in our own situation. . . . What we are given in [his instruction] is not merely general principles and lines of action which leave plenty of room for selection in detailed interpretation — as if it were not the details that really matter! On the contrary, he shows us the only good possibility which is there for us here and now in the freedom of our point of departure and which we not only may but must select and grasp in all circumstances. (IV/2, p. 372)

In the face of the many possibilities for action which confront us, Barth proposes, the Holy Spirit is known in our lives as the One who, when sought and invoked by faith, "actually reveals and makes known and imparts and writes on our heart and conscience the will of God as it applies to us concretely here and now, the command of God in the specific form in which we have to respect it in our own situation" (IV/2, p. 372). The spiritual impartation of this instruction is said to be as authoritative and precise as it is beyond all prior anticipation. Therefore, although this work of the Spirit cannot be captured in advance by any law, "he shows us the only good possibility which is there for us here and now in the freedom of our point of departure and which we not only may but must grasp in all circumstances" (IV/2, p. 372). The Spirit's diversified application of God's will to our lives is thereby conceived as being differentiated just for us in a way that is incomparably singular, apt, and concrete.

Although Barth believes that this form of specific spiritual guidance and direction is imparted to the community as well as the individual Christian (IV/2, p. 373), the diversity of the Spirit's workings is also thought to have a number of different implications for the life of the community in the world. When discussing the upbuilding of the community by the Spirit, for example, Barth stresses that in the ordering of its own specific functions and tasks, the community must ever seek a differentiated internal ordering that is flexible rather than rigid. This flexibility, he suggests, will correspond "to the directness with which each [member of the community] receives orders from the Lord himself" (IV/2, p. 631). Hence in this community, Barth writes, "new dispositions may be made at any time by which (without any question of degradation on the one side or decoration on the other) the last become first and the first last: a leading worker or overseer again dropping back into the ranks and having an important contribution to make as a laborer; and a laborer or apprentice, without any long training or experience, having the opportunity to work at a higher or even the very highest job" (IV/2, p. 631). Therefore, with respect to the community as well as to the individual, the work of the Holy Spirit is conceived as differentiated in application in such a way that all fruitless legalism, all willful self-reliance, and all rigid hierarchicalism will be forestalled for those who do not fail to call upon the Spirit by faith.

7. Universal in Scope

Finally, the work of the Holy Spirit in Barth's theology is universal in scope. In the case of those to whom the Spirit is given, writes Barth, the knowledge of "Jesus Christ as Reconciler, Mediator, Lord, Head, and Savior" becomes "the decisive and controlling factor in their own existence" (IV/2, p. 327). But "by this knowledge human beings are divided, not into the good and bad, the elect and reprobate, the saved and lost, but into Christians and non-Christians. They are divided, we may add, in the relative and provisional way in which they can be divided in the relative and provisional state of human history, where sin and death are still powerful, this side of this aeon" (IV/2, pp. 327-28). This relative and provisional division remains entirely "subject to the judgment of Jesus Christ" regarding its final validity, and those who are Christians are asked each day anew whether they are still Christians, and each day anew they need the Holy Spirit to remain so (IV/2, p. 328).

Non-Christians, however, are not to be regarded, Barth proposes, as outside the scope and promise of the Holy Spirit. "For the Holy Spirit," he writes, "as Jesus Christ is risen, is promised to them too," with a pledge that extends from time to eternity. "They are not condemned," Barth continues, "to the unspiritual life in which they exist as non-Christians. Or if so, it is they who do it. And they themselves are not the final court" (IV/3, p. 354). For Jesus Christ, Barth writes, "is the hope of these others too. And supposing more importance is attached to those who are not yet Christians? Supposing they are more interesting to him than Christians in his will and action? Supposing the greater weight of his will and action falls in this sphere? Supposing his light shines brighter here, and his Word is more living and active? . . . Supposing the Christian is deceived in judging another to be a non-Christian, because the knowledge of Jesus Christ has already found a lodging in that other person in a form which the Christian and perhaps the other as well does not recognize?" (IV/3, p. 365, rev.). One thing, however, is sure. The universal scope of Christ's saving work, and therefore of the work of the Spirit which accompanies it, means that "the promise of the Spirit already avails for [that person] and applies to [that person]" (IV/3, p. 355) — and therefore to all such persons — as a pledge for both time and eternity. The work of the Spirit is thereby understood as universal in scope in such a way that the church's distinction from the world is rendered entirely tentative and provisional, for the promise of the Holy Spirit avails and applies not just to some but to all.

8. Conclusion

The following contours have emerged. The Holy Spirit's mediation of communion, as Barth saw it, is trinitarian in ground (not anthropological), christocentric in focus (not pneumatocentric), miraculous in operation (not "natural"), communal in content (not individualistic or collectivist), eschatological in form (neither epiphanist nor triumphalist), diversified in application (not unvarying or undifferentiated), and universal in scope (not simply ecclesial).

Within these contours Barth's theology of the Holy Spirit is a theology of *koinonia*, and *koinonia* is the essence of the Spirit's work.

More specifically, therefore, the results are these. The Holy Spirit mediates the communion between the Father and the Son within the Holy Trinity. This mediating activity is then paradigmatic for every aspect of the Spirit's work in relation to the world. In various ways the Spirit's operation in time reiterates his operation in eternity.

Unlike soteriologies in which the Spirit represents a new and supplemental saving intervention alongside that of the Son, the Spirit does not adopt the faithful directly into the communion of the Holy Trinity. The Son is not merely the prototype of the faithful's relationship to the Father.[27] The incarnate Son is the one who has enacted their salvation in his own person. He is the one who perpetually embodies their salvation and principally mediates it. The flesh of the Son, his body and blood, is the indispensable means through which the faithful receive righteousness and life. His flesh is also the indispensable means through which they come to participate indirectly in the life of the Holy Trinity. Therefore, the adoption of the faithful occurs only as the Spirit incorporates them into the humanity of the Son, and conforms them to it, making them by grace through faith into the body of Christ. The Spirit establishes the incarnation *(concepto de Spirito sancto)*, the hypostatic union of Christ's deity and humanity *(communio naturarum)*, for the very purpose of realizing this salvation.

Like Lombard, who held that the Holy Spirit moves us to love God "without any intervening habit" (I *Sentences* 17),[28] Barth argued that the work of the Holy Spirit is always miraculous in operation. The mediation of communion to godless sinners by the Spirit, in other words, finds a true analogy only in the creation of the world *ex nihilo* and the resurrection of our Lord from the dead. The *koinonia* that is mediated in the Spirit between Christ and the church then finds its necessary counterpart in the *koinonia* the church enjoys among its members. This *koinonia* is still eschatological in form. It is enjoyed only provisionally, pointing beyond itself to a future consummation. The Spirit's joining of Christ and his community here and now is only a foretaste of that great *koinonia* in and with Christ toward which the Spirit is secretly driving all things and which he will finally reveal (and in revealing impart) to the whole creation. All things, and each in its own way, will be gathered up by the Spirit into Christ and just so given a share in the eternal *koinonia* of the Holy Trinity.

---

27. Cf. Bruce D. Marshall, "Action and Person: Do Palamas and Aquinas Agree About the Spirit?" *St. Vladimir's Theological Quarterly* 39 (1995): 379-408.

28. Quoted by Marshall, "Palamas and Aquinas," p. 389.

CHAPTER 8

Mysterium Trinitatis:
Karl Barth's Conception of Eternity

(1999)

"What, then, is time?" asked Saint Augustine. "I know well enough what it is pro-vided that nobody asks me; but if I am asked what it is and try to explain, I am baffled."[1] Among the familiar puzzles involved in trying to explain time is the paradoxical nature of what we call the present. On the one hand, the present seems to be nothing but a fleeting moment. "The present is time," Augustine ob-served, "only by reason of the fact that it moves on to become the past" (p. 264). If so, "how can we say that even the present *is*, when the reason why it *is* is that it is *not to be?* In other words, we cannot rightly say that time *is*, except by reason of its impending state of *not being*" (p. 264). From this point of view, the present is an elusive instant. It cannot be divided into parts, because it has no duration. A mathematical point would seem to be an apt analogy for this "flowing now" *(nunc fluens)*, since each present instant is indivisible; yet because the present flows, it would also seem analogous to a river or, perhaps more precisely, to a straight line constituted by a steady succession of contiguous indivisible points.

On the other hand, the present also seems to be a real duration that per-sists without interruption, indeed the only moment that actually endures. Since the future is not yet and the past is no longer, it seems that past and future do not strictly exist, and that what actually exists is the present alone. Only the present is what we directly experience, and only the present abides. Since nei-ther the past nor the future can be said to exist, "it might be correct," stated Au-gustine, "to say that there are three times, a present of past things, a present of

---

1. Augustine, *Confessions* 11.14, in Augustine, *Confessions*, trans. R. S. Pine-Coffin (Lon-don: Penguin Books, 1961), p. 264. (Hereafter page numbers are cited in text.)

present things, and a present of future things" (p. 269). If past and future exist, in other words, it is only as functions of present consciousness. The past is a function of memory, the present a function of attention, and the future a function of expectation. "Some such different times do exist in the mind," Augustine concluded, "but nowhere else that I can see" (p. 269). From this point of view, the present is not a fleeting instant, but a persisting duration. A circle or a sphere might offer a possible analogy for this abiding present *(nunc stans)*, since the present of our consciousness is continuous and encompassing, like the periphery of these mathematical objects.

Broadly speaking, there are two main views of eternity, and they correspond, more or less, to these two different facets of the present. One view resembles the abiding present of unitary consciousness *(nunc stans)*, while the other aligns itself with the flowing present of successive instants *(nunc fluens)*. Until modern times, the former view has been most familiar in Christian theology. Associated with Augustine, Boethius, and Anselm, it posits eternity as an abiding present but with a difference. What is present to human consciousness as a sequence of moments, one after another, is present to divine consciousness simultaneously. Past, present, and future are not successive for God as they are for us. The divine eternity is an "eternal now" *(nunc aeternitatis)* that embraces our temporal past, present, and future comprehensively *(totus)*, holding them together in God's consciousness or knowledge all at once *(simul)*. God's eternal now is in one sense more like a mathematical point than a straight line, since it cannot be divided into parts; yet it also seems analogous to a circle or a sphere, since it encompasses all temporal moments simultaneously within itself.

The eternal now as traditionally conceived gives rise to many conundrums. If God knows the future before it happens, for example, doesn't that entail fate or determinism? Under these circumstances, how can human freedom and temporal contingency really exist? If all temporal moments are encompassed simultaneously in eternity, furthermore, doesn't that finally make temporal sequence itself into an illusion? How can past, present, and future be real in themselves, or else how can their sequence be real in eternity for God? Questions can also be raised from the standpoint of Scripture. Is the biblical God really eternal in the sense of this "eternal now"? According to the Bible, Oscar Cullmann has argued, God's time is something more like "everlastingness." It is much like our time, only indefinitely extended. The real contrast is not between time and timelessness, but between limited time and endless time.[2]

---

2. Oscar Cullmann, *Christ and Time* (Philadelphia: Westminster, 1951), p. 46. For this and other references I am indebted to William C. Placher's fine essay, "The Eternal God," in *Narratives of a Vulnerable God* (Louisville: Westminster/John Knox, 1994), pp. 27-52.

In the modern period considerations like these have led to the exploration of another model for eternity. Eternity, it is proposed, is distinct from time but not separate from it. Eternity is a transcendent, transhistorical dimension that runs along in tandem with time while yet being immanent within it. Eternity is not a stationary present over against time that incorporates all time simultaneously, but a flowing present that accompanies the succession of time as it occurs. Eternity shapes or directs the temporal process largely by virtue of possessing the plenitude of a larger essence and a greater amplitude for the future. This processional view of eternity has its philosophical forebears in Whitehead and Hegel, and its theological descendants in recent interpreters like Ogden and Tracy on the Whiteheadian side, and Pannenberg, Moltmann, and Jenson on the Hegelian. In either case eternity, like time, is a flowing now, a *nunc fluens,* that not only moves along with time but also requires time for its own self-actualization.

From the standpoint of the more traditional view, this later point is damaging. A God who needs the world for the purpose of self-actualization is not the biblical God. A Creator whose being is conditioned and restricted by the creation is not Israel's Lord. An eternity dependent upon and limited by its interaction with time is not compatible with the God of free and sovereign grace. The processional view of eternity evacuates God of his deity, it is thought, and makes eternity dwindle into some sort of finite infinity. For God's eternal being is seen as inextricable from the temporal being of the world. Both are essentially implicated in one and the same process of becoming. Although Whitehead and Hegel differ on whether the process is organic or dialectical and on just why God needs the world, both agree that God's being is in the process of becoming along with the world, that God's being is composite, that God is more fully actualized at the end of this process than at the beginning, and that without this or some such process God would not and could not be fully actual as God.[3] God needs the world, or at least some world, in order to achieve self-actualization.

Karl Barth's conception of eternity does not fit neatly into either of these standard views. His conception overlaps elements of each while transcending both. More precisely, although Barth stands mainly in the tradition of Augustine, Boethius, and Anselm, he modifies this tradition in order to appropriate what is valid in Hegel. His primary motivation, however, is not to reconcile these divergent traditions. It is rather to think through the conception of eter-

---

3. For an excellent technical discussion, see Brian Leftow, "God and the World in Hegel and Whitehead," in *Hegel and Whitehead,* ed. G. Lucas, Jr. (Albany: SUNY Press, 1986), pp. 257-67.

nity in thoroughly trinitarian terms. Eternity for Barth is not the container in which God lives. It is a predicate of God's triune being. For that reason eternity exemplifies and guarantees God's full and sovereign freedom. Nowhere is Barth's focus on God's freedom as the Lord more significant than in his trinitarian conception of eternity. By granting primacy to the divine freedom at the heart of God's trinitarian life, Barth can side with the traditional view on eternity's radical otherness and perfect transcendence while also incorporating themes of dynamism, teleology, and immanence that characterize the more modern view.

A terminological headache may be noted at the outset. When discussing eternity, Barth's use of the word "time" can be quite ambiguous. The word's meaning sometimes shifts, it seems, from one sentence to the next. A more vexing case would be difficult to recall unless it were Paul's slippery use of the word *nomos* in Romans 7–8. Barth can say in one place, for example, that "Time has nothing to do with God"[4] while also asserting that "God . . . is supremely temporal."[5] A careful reading shows, however, that Barth intends at least three points. First, in some strong sense eternity is timeless. Second, eternity is a mode of time that is peculiarly God's own. Finally, the eternal temporality of God is the condition for the possibility not only of our having time at all, but also for time's redemption. The vagaries of the word "time" reflect, perhaps, the agony and the ecstasy of theological language as Barth used it in general. "God is light," Irenaeus once remarked, "and yet God is unlike any light that we know" (*Adversus haereses* 2.13.4). Barth knew this dictum and cited it (II/1, p. 190). It offers a possible paradigm for his use of the word "time." It is as though he were saying: "God is temporal, and yet God's temporality is unlike any time that we know." The time peculiar to God is at once the presupposition of creaturely time, and yet so utterly different as to be ineffable.

Barth's Conception of Eternity: Its Trinitarian Background

God's time is as ineffable for Barth as the doctrine of the Trinity that gives it form. Barth makes perhaps the first sustained attempt in history to reformulate eternity's mystery in fully trinitarian terms. The mystery of eternity becomes in effect a subtopic in the mystery of the Trinity. Eternity holds no perplexities

---

4. Karl Barth, *Church Dogmatics* II/1 (Edinburgh: T. & T. Clark, 1957), p. 608; hereafter cited as II/1.

5. Karl Barth, *Church Dogmatics* III/2 (Edinburgh: T. & T. Clark, 1960), p. 437; hereafter cited as III/2.

that cannot be stated in trinitarian terms, and the Trinity has no formal aspects irrelevant to the question of eternity, so that the form of the Trinity and the form of eternity coincide. Barth unfolds the mystery of God's eternal time within a fully trinitarian framework.

How to relate God's oneness to God's threeness and vice versa is, needless to say, at the heart of trinitarian doctrine. Three aspects of this question are relevant in Barth's reformulation of eternity. The Trinity as Barth understands it means that God is self-identical, self-differentiated, and self-unified. God is self-identical in being *(ousia)*, self-differentiated in modes of being *(hypostases)*, and self-unified in eternal life *(perichoresis)*. The *perichoresis* presupposes God's self-differentiation as Father, Son, and Holy Spirit, even as those three *hypostases* in turn presuppose God's self-identity as the Lord. To oversimplify for a moment, we may say that the one divine being correlates with God's freedom, that the three divine modes of being correlate with God's love, and that their perpetual unification correlates with God's eternal life. The trinitarian God is thus the living God who loves in freedom, or more technically, the Trinity is the *perichoresis* of the three *hypostases* in the one *ousia*.

The depth of the divine *ousia* is, for Barth, a single, self-identical subject, an acting I, the Lord, who is free and sovereign in trinitarian self-differentiation. The Lord does not exist in abstraction, for the one divine *ousia* exists in and only in the three divine *hypostases*. The three *hypostases* are, in turn, God's free subjectivity as the one Lord. The acting divine subject differentiates himself into three while yet remaining indivisibly one. He also unifies himself as three in the communion of his eternal life. This communion takes the form of mutual indwelling. *Perichoresis* means that the Father is in the Son, and the Son in the Father, in the communion of the Holy Spirit, to all eternity. It means that each *hypostasis* participates in the other *hypostases* completely. It means that they dwell in one another more closely, if possible, than a mathematical point, while yet retaining their essential identifying distinctions. In the trinitarian communion of God's love, the otherness of the other is not lost but enhanced. The Father remains the Father, the Son remains the Son, and the Spirit remains the Spirit in the midst of their mutual indwelling. Note that Barth does not see the divine *ousia* as a function of the *perichoresis*, as do some recent theologies, but rather the reverse. The *perichoresis*, states Barth, is "a further description of the *homoousia* of Father, Son, and Spirit."[6] Although there is no *ousia* without the *hypostases*, and no

---

6. Karl Barth, *Church Dogmatics* I/1 (Edinburgh: T. & T. Clark, 1936), p. 485; hereafter cited as I/1.

hypostases without the *perichoresis,* the divine *ousia* is, in Barth's judgment, logically prior and determinative (I/1, p. 351).[7]

The relation between the one *ousia* and the three *hypostases* cannot, Barth contends, be captured by a single, unified thought. This contention, which separates Barth from all standard philosophical theologies and all theologies that seek ordinary coherence, is of far-reaching significance. Barth frankly acknowledges the "great difficulties" at this point that have typically beset trinitarian doctrine. "We, too," he states, "are unable to say how in this case 3 can really be 1 and 1 can really be 3. We, too, can only state that in this case it all has to be thus, and we can state it only in interpretation of the revelation attested in the Bible and with reference to this object" (I/1, p. 367). All our concepts are inadequate in the face of this trinitarian mystery. They are "radically ill-suited to this object" (I/1, p. 368). They can only point beyond themselves to a truth they cannot properly express (I/1, p. 429). The unity of God's oneness-in-threeness and threeness-in-oneness is, states Barth, a unity for which "we have no formula, but which we can know only as the incomprehensible truth of the object itself" (I/1, p. 368).

Any attempt at conceptual closure at this point will, Barth argues, be profoundly unsuitable. Either God's oneness will be stressed at the expense of God's threeness, or God's threeness at the expense of God's oneness. Barth's drastic alternative is a strategy of juxtaposition. The Lord God, he asserts, is at once a single, indivisible subject, and yet also Father, Son, and Holy Spirit. No harmonization of these predications is either possible or appropriate. No sys-

---

7. Although Barth has sometimes been labeled a "modalist," the charge is mistaken. Two reasons seem to lie behind the mistake. First, Barth uses the term "mode of being" to translate *hypostasis.* He seems to prefer "mode of being" to "mode of existence," partly because "existence" is a term he usually reserves for human existence, and partly because he sees the *hypostases* as essential determinations of God's eternal *being (ousia).* "Mode of being" in this sense obviously has nothing to do with "modalism." The second reason relates to the way Barth connects God's Lordship and free subjectivity ("I am the Lord") with the divine *ousia* itself, to which he seems to grant logical and perhaps ontological precedence (though he sees both the *hypostases* and the *ousia* as primordial and ontologically basic). Modalism, however, means that the trinitarian *hypostases* are merely manifestations of God in history, but not essential distinctions within the eternal Godhead itself. For Barth, however, the trinitarian *hypostases,* each of which is fully God, coexist in, with, and for one another eternally and essentially. Barth repeatedly states that the living God would have been an eternal communion of love and freedom between the Father and the Son in the unity of the Holy Spirit, whether the world had been created or not. Nothing could be farther from modalism. "Social trinitarians," on the other hand, who are usually the ones making this charge, might ask themselves whether they can do as much justice as Barth can to the clear biblical witness to God as a single acting subject who is the Lord. In any case, modalism can be charged against Barth only out of ignorance, incompetence, or (willful) misunderstanding.

tematic unity or principle that resolves the antithesis between them can be descriptively adequate. Adequacy at this point is a higher virtue than consistency. By switching back and forth dialectically between statements about God as one and statements about God as three, Barth proposes to provide as descriptively adequate an account as might be possible of a reality that is, by definition, inherently ineffable. "Theology," he writes, "means rational wrestling with the mystery. But all rational wrestling with this mystery, the more serious it is, can lead only to its fresh and authentic interpretation and manifestation as a mystery" (I/1, p. 368). On all sides good care must be taken to see "that the *mysterium trinitatis* remains a mystery" (I/1, p. 368). Since the reality of God's oneness and God's threeness cannot be reconciled in thought, a "trinitarian dialectic" must be devised in which statements to the one side are continually "counterbalanced" by statements to the other (I/1, p. 369). When the one is in the foreground, the other can only be tacitly presupposed, and vice versa. In practice, therefore, the concept of God's triunity, states Barth, "can never be more than the dialectical union and distinction in the mutual relation between two formulae that are one-sided and inadequate in themselves" (I/1, p. 369).

Barth carries this basic dialectical strategy into many theological questions. Two will be of special interest when we return to consider his conception of eternity more directly. One concerns his understanding of God's eternal life, and the other his understanding of God's perfection. "Life," Barth writes, "is the fundamental element in the divine being" (II/1, p. 322). To describe God as "the living God" is "no mere metaphor" (II/1, p. 263). Nor does it merely describe God's relation to the world. It describes "God himself as the One he is" (II/1, p. 263). God lives first of all in and for himself. He would still be the living God even if he had never created the world and even if he had not acted to redeem it. In either case, Barth stresses, "nothing would be lacking in his inward being as God in glory, as the Father, Son and Holy Spirit, as the One who loves in freedom."[8] God in no way needs the world in order to be who he is: the living God who loves in freedom. "God seeks and creates fellowship between himself and us, and therefore he loves us," writes Barth. "But he is this loving God without us as Father, Son and Holy Spirit, in the freedom of the Lord, who has his life from himself" (II/1, p. 257).

God's life takes a particular form. It resides, says Barth, in the "process of generation" whereby God "posits himself as the living and loving God" (II/1, pp. 305, 302). That is, God's life is the process by which he posits himself as the Holy Trinity. His life is a life of free distinction and communion in the *perichoresis* of the Father, the Son, and the Holy Spirit. In the freedom of his

8. Karl Barth, *Church Dogmatics* IV/1 (Edinburgh: T. & T. Clark, 1956), p. 213.

eternal love, "God lives as he who is" (II/1, p. 307). God is the One who lives in the *perichoresis* of the three *hypostases,* "in their being with each other and for each other and in each other, in their succession one to another" (II/1, p. 297). Therefore, God's being, Barth concludes, does not exclude but includes becoming. If it is possible to speak of "an eternal self-realization" in God (II/1, p. 306), it can only be in the sense of a perpetual movement from perfection to perfection. The unity of the triune God, Barth states, is "the unity of a being one which is always also a becoming one" (I/1, p. 369). It is a unity always becoming one because it is perpetually positing itself as three. With respect to the Trinity Barth writes: "What is real in God must constantly become real precisely because it is real in God (not after the manner of created being). But this becoming (because it is this becoming) rules out every need of this being for completion. Indeed, this becoming simply confirms the perfection of this being" (I/1, p. 427). God's life in and for himself, his inner life in love and freedom, his being in the process of becoming, his one *ousia* in three *hypostases* in the process of *perichoresis,* is a perfect work *(opus perfectum)* that occurs in perpetual operation *(in operatione perpetuus)* (I/1, p. 427). In the dynamism of his one eternal life, God, who is his own basis, his own goal, and his own way from the one to the other, continually becomes who he is.

When speaking about God's perfections, Barth adopts the same dialectical method. Again, the unity of God's being is seen as so ineffable that it cannot be properly expressed by the concepts at our disposal. Instead of closure or a unified conception, Barth resorts once more to the strategy of dialectical interconnection and juxtaposition. Instead of a conceptual synthesis, he leaves us with an unresolved antithesis. What the antithesis describes is an ineffable unity-in-distinction. Theological description moves back and forth, repeatedly, from unity to distinction and back again, the one counterbalancing the other. Both the unity and the distinction describe God's being as a whole, not two separate parts that constitute the whole. Note that Barth does not think God's being is dialectical or antithetical in itself, only that our minds are incapable of grasping its unity through a single principle or system. Although the divine reality is unified, constant, and stable in itself, it is also endlessly vibrant in its life. The best theological grammar available to describe it is dialectical and full of reversals.

Where other theologies speak of God's properties or attributes, Barth prefers to speak of God's perfections. "We choose the latter," he explains, "because it points at once to the thing itself instead of merely to its formal aspect, and because instead of something general it expresses at once that which is clearly distinctive" (II/1, p. 322). Other realities may have attributes, but only God has perfections. Note that his perfections are perfections of the Holy Trinity. God is the one Lord who distinguishes himself eternally as Father, Son, and Holy Spirit, and God is also the three divine "persons" who perpetually become one in the communion of their eternal life. God is, that is to say, the One who loves in freedom. "In this," says Barth, "he is the perfect being: the being which is itself perfection and so the standard of all perfection; the being, that is, which is self-sufficient and thus adequate to meet every real need; the being which suffers no lack in itself and by its very essence fills every real lack" (II/1, p. 322). The one true perfection of God, states Barth, is his loving in freedom as such, but this perfection is really lived out by him "and therefore identical with a multitude of various and distinct types of perfection." The one being of this God is "eternally rich." "To know him means to know him again and again, in ever new ways — to know only him, but to know him as the perfect God, in the abundance, distinctness and variety of his perfections" (II/1, p. 322).[9]

The one God who posits himself as three is also the same God who posits himself as many. The three are his *hypostases* or concrete modes of existence; the many are his perfections. The many perfections of God confirm and glorify his oneness. "He is who he is and what he is," writes Barth, "in both unity and multiplicity. He is the one who is this many, and the many who are this one. The one is he who loves in freedom. The many are his perfections — the perfections of his life" (II/1, p. 323). At this point Barth sees "an exact parallel" to the doctrine of the Trinity (II/1, p. 326).

> As it is of decisive importance not to dissolve the unity of the Godhead [*ousia*] tritheistically into three gods, but to understand the three modes of being [*hypostases*] strictly as the modes of being of the one God with whom we have to do in all his works, so it is of equal importance to interpret God's glory and perfections, not in and for themselves, but as the glory of the Lord who alone is able to establish, disclose and confirm them as real glory. (II/1, p. 327)

Like the doctrine of God's *hypostases,* "the doctrine of God's perfections consists at every point only in the development and confirmation of the doctrine of his being [*ousia*]" (II/1, p. 327).

In drawing this trinitarian parallel, Barth separates himself from the venerable theological tradition that regards simplicity as more basic in God than multiplicity. Traditionally, it has typically been held that because God's simplic-

---

9. Barth specifies "the perfections of the divine loving" as grace, mercy, and patience (paired respectively with holiness, righteousness, and wisdom in correlation with God's freedom), and "the perfections of the divine freedom" as unity, constancy, and eternity (paired respectively with omnipresence, omnipotence, and glory in correlation with God's love).

ity is proper to his being, multiplicity can only be ascribed to his being improperly. "The life of God was identified with the notion of pure being," but this identification, says Barth, only shows that at this point "the idea of God was not determined by the doctrine of the Trinity" (II/1, p. 329). "The fundamental error of the whole earlier doctrine of God is reflected in this arrangement: first God's being in general, then his triune nature — with all the ambiguities and sources of error which must result from this sequence" (II/1, pp. 348-49). Barth agrees with this tradition about simplicity, but disagrees about its exclusion of multiplicity as supposedly improper to God. God's "simplicity" means that God's being is both singular and indivisible (II/1, pp. 442-45). The singularity and indivisibility of God are not denied, however, but upheld in traditional trinitarian doctrine. "The name Father, Son and Spirit," writes Barth, "means that God is the one God in threefold repetition. . . . He is God in this repetition, but for that very reason he is the one God in each repetition. . . . Identity of substance implies the equality of substance of the 'persons'" (I/1, pp. 350-51). The mystery of the Trinity at this point is precisely this, that because God's being in its simplicity admits of no parts or degrees, each of the three divine *hypostases,* in simultaneity with the other two, is fully and perfectly God.[10]

By carrying the trinitarian pattern over into his discussion of how simplicity and multiplicity are related in God's inner being, Barth again exemplifies the dialectical logic of his theology. "In God," he writes, "multiplicity, individuality and diversity do not stand in any contradiction to unity" (II/1, p. 332). Just because God's inner being is that of the Trinity, "God's being transcends the contrast of *simplicitas* and *multiplicitas,* including and reconciling both" (II/1, p. 333). Barth concludes:

> If God is the God who is rich in himself, and if he is the one true God even in his works *ad extra,* we cannot emphasize either his *simplicitas* or his *multiplicitas* as though the one or the other *in abstracto* were the very being of God, as though the one inevitably excluded the other. We can only accept and interpret God's *simplicitas* and *multiplicitas* in such a way as to imply that they are not mutually exclusive but inclusive, or rather that they are both included in God himself. (II/1, p. 333)

Moreover, just because God's inner being is that of the Trinity, the multiplicity of God's perfections must also be thought through in terms of the *perichoresis.*

---

10. It was essentially this insight into the divine mystery which enabled Athanasius to resolve the Arian crisis. See T. F. Torrance, "The Doctrine of the Holy Trinity according to St. Athanasius," in *Trinitarian Perspectives: Toward Doctrinal Agreement* (Edinburgh: T. & T. Clark, 1994), pp. 7-20.

From this standpoint the unity of the divine perfections is not static but dynamic. The multiple perfections of God maintain their distinctive identity — not only for us but for God[11] — even as they perpetually become one (II/1, p. 333). What Barth says in a slightly different connection would apply also to the divine perfections: God's reality is of such a character that any one perfection exists with all the others, in the others, alongside of and after the others, in "an eternal simultaneity and successiveness" (II/1, p. 343). From this point of view once again, the unity of God — the unity of the one *ousia* in three *hypostases,* the unity of his freedom in love, the unity of his *simplicitas* in *multiplicitas* — "is dynamic and to that extent, diverse" (II/1, p. 343). Barth summarizes the dialectical logic: "What we have here is, then, a complete reciprocity in the characterization of the one [divine] Subject. Always in this reciprocity each of the opposing ideas not only augments but absolutely fulfills the other, yet it does not render it superfluous or supplant it. On the contrary, it is only in conjunction with the other — and together with it affirming the same thing — that each can describe the [one divine] Subject, God" (II/1, p. 343).

A long and difficult tract of theology lies behind us. From it we may extract especially the following points. Barth is attempting to think through the reality of God in thoroughly trinitarian terms. Three main concepts therefore need to be taken into account and coordinated: God's being *(ousia),* God's modes of being *(hypostases),* and God's becoming *(perichoresis).* God's being correlates with God's Lordship. As the Lord, God is one acting subject — indivisible, sovereign, and singular — the God who is supremely free. God's modes of being correlate with God's internal concrete relatedness. As Father, Son, and Holy Spirit, God is an eternal communion of love. The three divine "persons," each of whom is fully God, coexist simultaneously in mutual self-giving. Finally, God's becoming correlates with God's vitality. As the living God, God's being is in the process of becoming. This life process occurs independently of any relationship that God may have with the world. The triune God does not need the world for the sake of self-actualization, for this God is always already totally actual in the *hypostases* and perfections of his eternal life. Although God's being is simple and not composite, it not only includes various distinctions within itself, but these distinctions coinhere at once simultaneously and dynamically. Each distinction exemplifies the divine being as a whole without

---

11. Parallel to the distinctions among the *hypostases,* Barth sees the distinctions among God's perfections as real for God and not merely for us. In scholastic terminology, they are therefore *distinctionae formales* and not merely *distinctionae rationis ratiocinatae.* In other words, these distinctions are not merely mental conveniences, but inherent in the being of God. See Richard A. Muller, *Dictionary of Latin and Greek Theological Terms* (Grand Rapids: Baker, 1985), p. 94.

losing its particular distinctiveness.[12] No earthly analogy can capture the singularity of this God, whose mystery is best attested in theology by the adoption of a dialectical logic. With these points in mind, we are ready for Barth's conception of eternity.[13]

Barth's Conception of Eternity:
Its Trinitarian Form and Content

God is eternal, Barth states, both "in himself" and "in all his works" (II/1, p. 608). God's being eternal in and for himself is independent of all his works, and yet also the basis of all his works. The distinction between God's being in and for itself and God's being in relation to the world will be of great importance in understanding Barth's conception of eternity. Unfortunately, Barth does not always keep this distinction clear as his exposition unfolds. Although certain ambiguities and difficulties arise as a result, I do not think they are finally insuperable.

Barth opens his discussion of eternity with a threefold distinction. He distinguishes between "pure duration," "beginning, middle and end," and "simultaneity." Roughly speaking, this distinction corresponds to the trinitarian distinction between being, modes of being, and becoming, or between *ousia,* *hypostases,* and *perichoresis,* or between freedom, love, and life. This distinction signals that Barth's discussion of eternity will be one long variation on a theme. The theme is the doctrine of the Trinity, now transposed into the key of temporality but patterned to echo the same intricate trinitarian score.[14] Barth opens with a basic definition: "The being is eternal," he states, "in whose duration beginning, middle and end are not three but one, not separate as a first, a second and a third occasion, but one simultaneous occasion as beginning, middle and

---

12. My use of the word "exemplify" needs to be taken in context. I use it in the sense of "hypostatize," that is, to render substantially and concretely existent. Here as elsewhere in dogmatic theology Hilary's dictum holds true: *Non sermoni res, sed rei sermo subiectus est* (*De Trinitate* 4). It is not the reality that is subject to the word, but the word to the reality. In other words, the object interprets the terminology, not the terminology the object (cf. I/1, p. 354).

13. Barth discusses eternity and time at regular intervals throughout the *Church Dogmatics.* What follows is a critical exposition only of the material on "the eternity of God" found in II/1, pp. 608-40.

14. In his severe criticism of Barth's conception, Richard H. Roberts fails almost entirely to take its trinitarian structure into account. "The relative worth of Barth's doctrine of the Trinity . . . is not of prime importance here . . ." (Roberts, "Karl Barth's Doctrine of Time," in *A Theology on Its Way? Essays on Karl Barth* [Edinburgh: T. & T. Clark, 1991], p. 19). Much of Roberts's exasperation can perhaps be traced back to this oversight.

end. Eternity is the simultaneity of beginning, middle and end, and to that extent it is pure duration" (II/1, p. 608). Eternity, that is to say, is the mutual coinherence of three concrete temporal forms, distinct but not separate, that exemplify one undivided duration, identical with the *ousia* of God. Note that Barth does not mean to imply, by the way, that beginning, middle, and end can be simply equated with Father, Son, and Holy Spirit. Although there may be a loose correlation here, it is not strict.[15] The trinitarian parallel is much more nearly formal than substantive. The same theological grammar that governs Barth's doctrine of the Trinity is being applied with suitable modifications to his conception of eternity — no more, no less.

The initial definition allows Barth to draw a categorical distinction between eternity and time. The three temporal forms of eternity — beginning, middle, and end — coexist simultaneously "without separation, distance or contradiction" (II/1, p. 608). Their mutual unity-in-distinction and distinction-in-unity signifies their divine perfection. It is just this perfection that is lacking to time in its created form. "Eternity has and is the duration that is lacking to time," states Barth. "It has and is simultaneity" (II/1, p. 608). Eternity for Barth thus correlates with perfection, and created time with imperfection. Eternity is the perfect archetype and prototype of time, but time is merely the imperfect copy of eternity. Time's imperfection is its lack of unity, constancy, and simplicity, therefore its separation, division, or contradiction in its modes of beginning, middle, and end, its tendency toward dissolution and nonbeing. In this sense, for Barth, "time can have nothing to do with God" (II/1, p. 608). God's eternal being is not implicated in time's imperfection. "Eternity is not, then, an infinite extension of time both backwards or forwards" (II/1, p. 608). Nor is it ensnared in one and the same process of becoming along with the world. Its own unique process of becoming moves from perfection to perfection, from pure duration to pure duration, in the simultaneity of its own eternal forms. Eternity has no tendency toward dissolution and nonbeing just because it is pure duration.

Eternity and freedom, Barth observes, are linked in the scriptural depiction of God. "Whenever Holy Scripture speaks of God as eternal, it stresses his freedom" (II/1, p. 609). Eternity and sovereignty mark the ontological divide that distinguishes God from the world. Scripture sets God at the beginning and end of all things. It sets him high above and unfathomably beneath all that is not God. But it does so, states Barth, only to understand God as the one who is "utterly present" to humankind, and who "in his own person" has "complete

---

15. Each member of the Trinity, Barth states, is "all at once in his own essence undividedly beginning, succession, and end" (II/1, p. 615).

power" over humankind (II/1, p. 609). The ontological otherness of God does not — as is often mistakenly concluded from Barth's famous use of the term "wholly other" — prevent God's immanence in the world. On the contrary, argues Barth, God's presence to the world is so pervasive, multiform, and rich that it represents "the triumph of God's freedom in immanence" (II/1, p. 316). "God can be present to another," Barth writes. "This is his freedom. For he is present to himself. This is his love in its internal and external range. God in himself is not only existent. He is co-existent. And so he can co-exist with another" (II/1, p. 463). By contrast to modern processional views of eternity, God's immanence in the world is not an order of ontological necessity, but a decision of free and sovereign grace. God's immanence neither contradicts nor compromises his freedom, but rather exemplifies and expresses it. "To grant co-existence with himself to another," writes Barth, "is no contradiction to his essence. On the contrary it corresponds to it" (II/1, p. 463). Eternity thus correlates with the divine freedom to act and prevail in love. "Eternity is the source of deity in God," Barth concludes, "in so far as this consists in his freedom, independence and lordship" (II/1, p. 610). The eternal otherness of God is and guarantees this freedom. God is free to be constant in love, just because, being eternal, time has no power over him (II/1, p. 609).

Because eternity is the pure duration of God's being in and for himself, and therefore also of his being for the world, it cannot be defined merely as the negation of time. Eternity is rather the unique time of the triune God. It is the time of God's self-identity, self-differentiation, and self-unification, the time of the *perichoresis* of the three *hypostases* in the undivided divine *ousia*, the time of the divine life of divine love in divine freedom. In this sense eternity is not merely "timelessness." It does not merely exist as time's negative in the form of a bipolar opposition. Eternity is rather the positive mode of time unique to the Trinity. The classic definition of Boethius meets with Barth's strong approval, because it so aptly brings out that eternity is a positive rather than negative quality. "Aeternitatis est interminabilis vitae tota simul et perfecta possessio," wrote Boethius (*De consolatione philosophiae* 5.6). "Eternity is the total, simultaneous and perfect possession of interminable life."

What Barth does with this definition, in effect, is simply to relocate it within an explicit doctrine of the Trinity. Life and simultaneity are, as we have seen, ideas that Barth associates with the trinitarian *perichoresis*. Totality, perfection, and possession are, in turn, ideas that correlate with the simplicity, singularity, and sovereignty of the trinitarian *ousia*. From this standpoint, the one strikingly new element in the definition is "interminability." The definition states not merely that the divine life is endless or unlimited, but that it cannot possibly terminate, that it knows no possible dissolution, not only no tendency but no possible tendency toward nonbeing. Therefore, the definition of eternity does not depend on the negation of time. "We know eternity primarily and properly," writes Barth, "not by the negation of the concept of time, but by the knowledge of God as the *possessor interminabilis vitae.* It is he who is the *nunc,* the pure present. He would be this even if there were no such thing as time" (II/1, p. 611). God is the sovereign possessor of pure self-presence, of interminable trinitarian life, of perfect love in perfect freedom, "before and beyond all time and equally before and beyond all non-temporality" (II/1, p. 611).

The ideas of simultaneity and totality, however, seem to imply certain distinctions not found in the Boethian definition. From a trinitarian standpoint, at least as Barth carries it through, they can be taken to imply temporal distinctions that correlate with the trinitarian *hypostases.* They are taken to imply, in other words, the distinctions of beginning, succession, and end. It is beginning, succession, and end that God possesses perfectly, simultaneously, and totally in his interminable trinitarian life. Note, however, that here is where Barth's account, as mentioned earlier, starts to become slippery and ambiguous. Although Barth fails to keep the distinction clearly before us, God's being as it is in itself needs to be more carefully distinguished, though not separated, from God's being in relation to the world than his account quite manages in practice, though it is surely what he intends. More precisely, Barth presupposes, but does not always make sufficiently clear, that God's trinitarian life includes a form of beginning, middle, and end peculiar to itself. The beginning, middle, and end that God possesses simultaneously and totally are, first of all, peculiar to the trinitarian *perichoresis,* to the eternal process of becoming, in which God moves from perfection to perfection in and for himself. This eternal becoming, in which his own absolute beginning, succession, and end are all present to God simultaneously — that is, his own eternal self-positing of himself as Father, Son, and Holy Spirit — in turn serves as the basis on which all creaturely time can be and is taken up by God and made present to himself in its totality simultaneously. In short, God also makes all creaturely time present to himself in the mode of simultaneity, and this simultaneity does not obliterate but upholds creaturely temporal distinctions. What makes the simultaneity of all creaturely time in God both possible and intelligible, however, is the prior simultaneity of God's own unique time in and for himself.

Barth writes:

> God's eternity is itself beginning, succession and end. To this extent it also has them, not conditioned by them but itself conditioning [them] as beginning, succession and end. It has them actively, not passively, not from another being or from time, but from itself and therefore in itself. God is both

the prototype and foreordination of all being, and therefore also the prototype and foreordination of time. God has time because and as he has eternity. (II/1, p. 611)

When Barth states here that eternity is beginning, succession, and end, he cannot be equating eternity with creaturely time. "Beginning, succession and end"
can only mean those forms that are peculiar to God's trinitarian life in and for
itself. Barth thus goes on to say that eternity has these temporal forms "not
from another being or from time, but from itself." Just as God's *ousia* is presumably not conditioned by his *hypostases* but conditions them, so also God's eternity is not conditioned by the temporal forms it possesses but rather conditions
them. It conditions them by possessing them simultaneously without losing
their distinctions. These temporal forms in eternity are, in turn, the archetypes
that serve as prototypes for the creaturely forms of beginning, succession, and
end. They are the prototypes through which creaturely time, with its own peculiarities and limitations, is foreordained.

If this interpretation is reasonably correct so far, then it may help us when
Barth delivers his zinger: "God has time because and as he has eternity" (II/1,
p. 611). Recall Barth's previous statement that "time can have nothing to do
with God" (II/1, p. 608). That one meant that God is not implicated in the imperfections of creaturely time. Taken in context, the new sentence can only
mean that God nonetheless has *creaturely* time because and as he has eternity.
Whereas the previous statement emphasized God's otherness from time, the
new one highlights God's readiness for time. Eternity does not exclude but includes a certain peculiar mode of temporality, its own peculiar forms of beginning, middle, and end. In this mode they lack the instability that belongs to
creaturely time as such. On the other hand, these forms are not merely static or
frozen, for they coexist in a mode of dynamic simultaneity (II/1, p. 611). Because and as eternity has its own forms of beginning, succession, and end, it can
and also does have a relationship to the creaturely forms of the same. The
creaturely forms "are grounded and made possible and limited" by the eternal
forms (II/1, p. 610). Eternity decides, conditions, and controls them. Barth can
therefore conclude that eternity "is itself that which begins in all beginnings,
continues in all successions and ends in all endings" (II/1, p. 610). Eternity
grounds time in its basic forms and surrounds it on every side.

In himself as pure eternity, God really has "time," that is, his own special
mode of temporality, his own unique forms of beginning, succession, and end.
Therefore, he can and does have time for us, not just apparently or figuratively.
That is, he has a basis in himself for a positive relation to creaturely time, a basis
on which he can and does freely enter into time and take time for us. God has

time, writes Barth, "and therefore time for us, in virtue of his eternity" (II/1, p. 612). The time that God has for us is Jesus Christ. He himself is God's time for us. The time God has for us in Jesus Christ, says Barth, is "the time of his patience, our life-time, time for repentance and faith" (II/1, p. 612). It is a time uniquely grounded in eternity.

As the Mediator between God and humankind, between heaven and earth, Jesus Christ is also the Mediator between eternity and time. Eternity and time find their unity and their distinction in him. In him they are one while remaining distinct, and distinct while remaining one. In him eternity and time really have "fellowship" with one another (II/1, p. 616). In him, that is, they really coexist in the mode of mutual indwelling, of complete mutual participation and interpenetration, of *koinonia.* This fellowship or mutual indwelling has two vectors, as it were, one from above to below, and the other from below to above. Although the two vectors coexist simultaneously, each one, as Barth understands it, describes this fellowship as a whole. Recall Athanasius's famous statement that "God became human in order that humans might become God" (*De incarnatione* 54). God's becoming human without ceasing to be God represents, so to speak, the downward vector, while humankind's elevation to God without ceasing to be human represents the upward vector. Transposing into a temporal key, we may say that eternity thus becomes time without ceasing to be eternal, and that time, in turn, becomes eternal without ceasing to be temporal.

At this point in the exposition, in other words, the logic of the doctrine of the Trinity intersects with the logic of the doctrine of the incarnation. As if each of these logics were not difficult enough on its own, the difficulties are now compounded. It may help if we think in terms of two different grammatical patterns. The trinitarian pattern, as we have seen, is a pattern of dialectical inclusion. It is a pattern in which three different forms of one indivisible being are perpetually generated and unified. The three forms, each of which represents the one being in its totality, eternally coexist in, with, and for one another simultaneously. They include one another in unity and distinction. The incarnational pattern, in turn, derives from the historic Chalcedonian Definition. Formally speaking, it involves two terms and a relationship. The two terms, Christ's deity and his humanity, are related by a pattern of unity, distinction, and asymmetry. They are related, that is, "without separation or division" (unity), "without confusion or change" (distinction), and with a precedence allotted to Christ's deity and a subsequence to his humanity. What this Chalcedonian pattern governs is the fellowship between Christ's deity and his humanity.[16] It governs that fellowship in both its

---

16. Note that the pattern is merely a formal device, but that the fellowship is a concrete, substantive reality.

downward vector and its upward vector. It is from the standpoint especially of the upward vector that the point of intersection with the trinitarian pattern emerges most clearly into view.

From this point forward, Barth's exposition may be divided into three parts. First, he looks at the downward vector, then at the upward vector, then at the intersection of the incarnational pattern with the trinitarian pattern. The downward vector concerns the entry of eternity into time; the upward vector concerns the elevation of time into eternity; and the intersection concerns the conjunction of simultaneity and sequence in the union of eternity with time.

The Downward Vector: The Entry of Eternity into Time

Along with the Trinity, the incarnation is the basis on which Barth understands the nature of eternity, the nature of time, and the nature of their relationship. He begins with the downward vector in order to show its implications for the nature of eternity. He writes:

> The fact that the Word became flesh undoubtedly means that, without ceasing to be eternity, in its very power as eternity, eternity became time. Yes, it became time. What happens in Jesus Christ is not simply that God gives us time, our created time, as the form of our own existence in the world. . . . In Jesus Christ it comes about that God takes time to himself, that he himself, the eternal One, becomes temporal, that he is present for us in the form of our own existence and our own world, not simply embracing our time and ruling it, but submitting himself to it, and permitting created time to become and be the form of his eternity. (II/1, p. 616)

The entry of eternity into time carries implications for the nature of eternity itself. It means that God has fashioned the shape of eternity so that, without ceasing to be eternity, it conforms with the shape of time. From this standpoint, the incarnation is the fulfillment of creation. When God humbles himself in Jesus Christ by entering time, he becomes one of us, like us in all things. "In Jesus Christ," writes Barth, "God actually takes time to himself. He raises time to a form of his own eternal being." By conforming the shape of eternity to the shape of time, God does not contradict or diminish his deity. On the contrary, states Barth, "the true and fullest power of deity is displayed in the fact that it has such power over itself and its creature that it can become one with it without detriment to itself." God is and remains "timeless" in the sense that God does not share in time's imperfections. Yet God is not merely temporal in the sense of being ready for time by virtue of his own special mode of temporality.

By entering into time, God actually takes time, created time, into himself. He makes it into "his own garment and even his own body." This appropriation of time by eternity is what happens in the downward vector. "This is just what takes place," says Barth, "in Jesus Christ. His name is the refutation of the idea of a God who is only timeless" (II/1, p. 616). From this standpoint, eternity cannot be understood as "pure timelessness." For when the Word became flesh, eternity became time. "Without ceasing to be the eternal God," Barth writes, "God himself took time and made it his own" (II/1, p. 617, rev.).

The Upward Vector: The Elevation of Time into Eternity

The entry of eternity into time also carries implications for the nature of time. When eternity enters into time, time does not remain untouched by eternity. Generally speaking, the creation is fulfilled and surpassed. The "positive relation of God to the world established by the creation" is fulfilled by the incarnation (II/1, p. 616). For time in particular, this fulfillment means healing. It means that time's imperfection is transcended and overcome. In Jesus Christ, Barth writes, and in every act of faith in him, "real created time . . . acquires the character and stamp of eternity, and life in it acquires the special characteristics of eternal life" (II/1, p. 617). The imperfections of time are healed by their contact with the perfection of eternity. When God enters time in Christ, he does not succumb to it, notes Barth. "He always maintains his superiority to it. When he subjects himself to time, he does freely what he does not have to do. He masters time. He re-creates it and heals its wounds, the fleetingness of the present, the separation of the past and the future from one another, as well as their separation from the present" (II/1, p. 617, rev.). When God takes our time up into himself, he heals it by contact with the perfection of his love, "lifting it up to be the time of eternal life" (II/1, p. 618).

Note that time's healing is distinct from salvation from sin. Time's wounds, as here set forth, are inherent in the good creation. They may be exacerbated and corrupted by sin, but they are not identical with it, nor are they hostile to God. When measured by eternity, they are merely imperfections, not corruptions. Whether God would have become incarnate even if the world had not fallen into sin was, as we know, a question that Aquinas denied and Duns Scotus affirmed. Barth, however, regarded it as speculative and unanswerable when stated in that form. Nevertheless, Barth here approaches the position of Scotus. He affirms that, among other things, the incarnation resolves a plight logically independent of sin, namely, the plight of transitoriness and dissolution into nonbeing. He does so, however, in a remarkably Thomistic way. Although Barth disagreed with the standard Thomistic understanding of nature and grace as applied to sin, he agreed with it as applied to transitoriness. Barth agreed with Aquinas, in other words, that in the work of healing time, grace does not destroy nature, but rather perfects and exceeds it.[17]

Note also that the upward vector depends entirely on the downward vector. The fact, in other words, that eternity includes a potentiality for time does not mean that time includes a potentiality for eternity. Time is not coeternal with God. In itself and as such it does not share at all in the predicates of eternity (II/1, p. 614). Nor does time cease to be time even in its healing. Although the creature tastes eternity through its fellowship with God, "it does not on that account itself become God and therefore eternal" (II/1, p. 609). Time remains time, only in a healed and eternal form, a form that for now can only surpass our understanding. Time's healing, in any case, comes to time strictly from without as the gift and miracle of grace.

The Conjunction of Simultaneity and Sequence: The Union of Eternity with Time

Time does not exist, Barth concludes, apart from eternity's embrace. Eternity embraces time on all sides, preceding, accompanying, and fulfilling it. To say that God is eternal means that God is "the One who is and rules before time, in time, and again after time, the One who is not conditioned by time, but conditions it absolutely in his freedom" (II/1, p. 619). God does this in three ways. "He precedes [time's] beginning, he accompanies its duration, and he exists after its end." This threefold relation, states Barth, is "the concrete form of eternity as readiness for time" (II/1, p. 619). The temporality of eternity is thus distinguished into pretemporality, supratemporality, and posttemporality. These are the three forms of eternity in its relation to time. Like the three divine *hypostases* of the Trinity, each of them embodies eternity as a whole, and like them each exists in simultaneous coexistence with the others. Finally, in analogy to the trinitarian *perichoresis*, each coinheres with the others dynamically, moving in its own inherent teleology from perfection to perfection, always the same yet ever new.

Each form of eternity's readiness for time will now be taken up in order.

---

17. For an analysis of the disagreement between Barth and Aquinas on nature and grace with respect to sin, see my essay "Baptized into Christ's Death: Karl Barth and the Future of Roman Catholic Theology" in this volume (pp. 251-76). Briefly, with respect to sin Barth held that grace is the *Aufhebung* of nature, thereby incorporating a strong element of negation (the cross) overcome in turn by the negation of the negation (the resurrection).

1. God is pretemporal. God's existence precedes human existence and that of all things. Barth writes: "God was in the beginning which precedes all other beginnings. He was in the beginning in which we and all things did not yet exist. He was in the beginning which does not look back on any other beginning presupposed by this beginning itself. God was in himself. He was no less himself, no less perfect, not subject to any lack, superabounding from the very first even without us and the world" (II/1, p. 621). God is who he is perfectly in his pretemporal mode of existence. For he is who he is before the world and without it. He is, that is to say, the Holy Trinity. "This pre-time is the pure time of the Father and the Son in the fellowship of the Holy Spirit" (II/1, p. 622). God's eternal existence as the Holy Trinity precedes his relationship to the world, and everything in his relationship to the world presupposes his eternal existence as the Trinity. The Trinity is therefore the presupposition of creation, reconciliation, and redemption. It is also the presupposition of God's pretemporal decision of election. In this "pure divine time" of perfect trinitarian existence, "there took place," writes Barth, "the appointment of the eternal Son for the temporal world, there occurred the readiness of the Son to do the will of the eternal Father, and there ruled the peace of the eternal Spirit — the very thing later revealed at the heart of created time in Jesus Christ" (II/1, p. 622).

The mysterious coinherence of eternity with time in the incarnation, together with the equally mysterious coinherence of God's pretemporality with God's supratemporality, means, as the New Testament regularly attests, that Jesus Christ existed "before the foundation of the world." "For Jesus Christ is before all time, and therefore eternally the Son and the Word of God, God himself in his turning to the world, the sum and substance of God insofar as God chose to create and give time, to take time to himself, and finally to fix for time its end and goal in his eternal hereafter" (II/1, p. 622). Everything temporal is predestined in Jesus Christ. Everything temporal comes from God's free eternal love. Everything temporal is penetrated and ruled by this free love from all eternity. In his pretemporal turning to the world, Barth states, "and with it to a time distinct from his eternity, this God, Yahweh Sabaoth, is identical with Jesus Christ" (II/1, p. 622).

2. God is supratemporal. This term is adopted for lack of a better alternative. It means not only that God is over time, but that God also exists with time and even in time. God not only embraces time on all sides, accompanying it at all points, but also pervades time from within, radiating out in all directions from a center within time itself, namely, from the event of the incarnation. The incarnation is "the concrete form" of eternity in its supratemporal significance.

God's eternity is so to speak the companion of time, or rather it is itself accompanied by time in such a way that in this occurrence time acquires its hidden center, and therefore both backwards and forwards its significance, its content, its source and its goal, but also continually its significant present. Because, in this occurrence, eternity assumes the form of a temporal present, all time, without ceasing to be time, is no more empty time, or without eternity. It has become new. This means that in and with this present, eternity creates in time real past and real future, distinguishes between them, and is itself the bridge and way from the one to the other. Jesus Christ is this way. (II/1, p. 627)

The real future that eternity creates in time is the future of eternal life in communion with God. The real past, in turn, is the past of sin and death as abolished in the cross of Christ. This old reality of sin and death is "continually opposed" by the new reality of eternal life, even as the new reality "comes breaking in triumphantly" again and again (II/1, p. 627). Jesus Christ stands between the old reality and the new. "In him the equilibrium between them has been upset and ended. He is the way from the one to the other and the way is irreversible. He is the turning" (II/1, p. 628). Therefore, "the past is that from which we are set free by him, and the future that for which we are set free by him" (II/1, p. 628). "To have time and to live in time means to live in this turning. In this turning we live — not in eternity, but in the real time healed by God, the time whose meaning is immediate to God" (II/1, p. 629). Time is not therefore essentially a process of dissolution leading only to nonbeing and death. For "time has acquired its middle point in Jesus Christ, and has therefore been made new" (II/1, p. 629).

3. God is posttemporal. This statement completes the idea of eternity as that which embraces time. God is after all time and after each time. Barth writes:

We move to him as we come from him and may accompany him. We move towards him. . . . He is when time will be no more. For then creation itself, the world as a reality distinct from God, will be no more in its present condition, in everything which now constitutes its existence and being. . . . For everything will have reached its goal and end. Man here and now reconciled to God will be redeemed. . . . The meaning and necessity of all ways and movement are fulfilled and exhausted in it. It is the perfection which remains, so that over and beyond it there is no new horizon. This perfection is God himself in his post-temporality. (II/1, p. 629)

God is not only the beginning of all beginnings, but the end of all endings. He is "the Last as he was the First. He is, therefore, the absolute, unsurpassable future of all time and of all that is in time" (II/1, p. 630). The end of all things will mean final judgment. God will look back and judge everything, deciding "what it has been and how far it has really been, just as he had already decided when it did not exist." Everything will be gathered up and sifted through. "Corresponding to this judgment, all that has been will be before him what it must be, accepted or rejected, acquitted or condemned, destined for eternal life or eternal death" (II/1, p. 630). God will be the fulfillment or the demise of each one.

The end of all things will also mean the final revelation. God's kingdom is real in some strong sense even now, Barth contends, although its reality is concealed from us. "It is only in its revelation that the kingdom of God is post-temporal and therefore lies in the future. . . . God's revelation stands before us as the goal and end of time." At the end of all things we shall no longer believe in God's kingdom. We shall see it. "It will be without the concealment which surrounds it in time and as long as time continues" (II/1, p. 630). "We shall then have that for which we must now pray, and which we do really receive in its fullness, but in the veil of hope, so that we must continually pray for it again" (II/1, p. 631).

In short, God himself in his posttemporal form is the eternity toward which we move. "To this extent he is the God of hope, the imminent peace which is prepared and promised to his people, into which it has not yet entered but will enter." He is the fulfillment which we await and for which we hope and pray. "God has and is also that which so far we do not have and are not" (II/1, p. 631). What God is yet to be at the end, he is already in himself, and has been from the beginning; and what he is yet to disclose to his creatures, he will also finally impart; and what he will finally impart to them will be a share in his own unsurpassable, irreversible, and interminable glory and life.

Barth stresses, finally, that, in analogy to the trinitarian *hypostases* (II/1, p. 639), no rivalry can exist between the three forms of eternity (II/1, p. 631). Each form needs to be emphasized in its own way. They are not to be played off against one another, as has too often occurred in the history of theology. They coexist together in union with time in a real simultaneity that is also a real sequence. In the beginning, middle, and end, in equal divinity — in the same love and freedom — God is the one and all. "So then," Barth writes, "if we are to love him and know him, we must give him equal attention and seriousness in all three dimensions. . . . We must emphasize this, because when our thinking is by nature systematic, it is so easy to be guilty of some kind of preference, selection or favoritism in this matter, and therefore of the corresponding omissions" (II/1, p. 631).

The internal distinctions of eternity reflect the life of the triune God. "Eternity is really beginning, really middle, and really end, because it is really the living God. There really is in it, then, direction, and a direction that is irreversible. . . . There is no uniformity in it. Its forms are not to be exchanged or confused" (II/1, p. 639). They coexist simultaneously in a perichoretic unity-in-distinction and distinction-in-unity, moving dynamically in perfection from perfection to perfection, and therefore from their pretemporal beginning through their supratemporal middle to their posttemporal end (II/1, p. 640).

Although eternity is surely "a complete mystery," Barth states that it is also "completely simple" (II/1, p. 639). It is as mysterious and as simple as the Trinity itself. But in any case it is the pure temporal essence of the living God. Barth concludes:

> In the last resort when we think of eternity, we do not have to think in terms of either the point or the line, the surface or space. We have simply to think of God himself, recognizing and adoring and loving the Father, the Son and the Holy Spirit. It is only in this way that we know eternity. For eternity is his essence. He, the living God, is eternity. And it is as well at this point, in relation to the threefold form of eternity, to emphasize the fact that he is the living God. (II/1, p. 639)

CHAPTER 9

Beyond Literalism and Expressivism: Karl Barth's Hermeneutical Realism

(1987)

TO HANS W. FREI ON THE OCCASION OF
HIS SIXTY-FIFTH BIRTHDAY

Karl Barth's approach to the interpretation of biblical texts might be called "hermeneutical realism." The realism of this approach can be understood by contrasting it with two competing options which Barth transcends while incorporating elements of each. For the sake of convenience I will call these competing options "literalism" and "expressivism." The question to be considered in distinguishing these options is how text and referent are related. Three issues in particular are involved in this relationship: the mode of textual reference, the mode of textual address, and the mode of referential certainty. I will call the mode of textual reference the "semantic force," the mode of textual address the "logical force," and the mode of referential certainty the "assertive force." Each of these issues depends largely on what one identifies as the textual referent itself. On all these matters Barth differed from literalism and expressivism.

Barth consistently rejected the kind of scriptural interpretation which saw no discrepancy between text and referent. Regardless of what that referent might be, whether God, Jesus Christ, some historical event, some human experience, or anything else, the relation between text and referent was never, as Barth saw it, one of perfect coincidence. The "assertive force" of Scripture, while strong where it mattered, was not absolute. Nor was the "logical force" of Scripture exclusively or even primarily cognitive or informational, as though even figurative language could be translated without remainder into informative propositions to be rationally appropriated. Nor, finally, was the "semantic force" of scriptural language about God to be construed as univocal, as though a word had exactly the same meaning when used of the Creator as it did when used of the creature. In each of these ways Barth diverged from hermeneutical literalism.

A good example of Barth's nonliteralistic scriptural interpretation can be seen in his discussion of the motif from the resurrection accounts of Jesus' empty tomb. In Barth's interpretation the empty tomb is assessed for what I will call both its "intratextual" and its "extratextual" status. On the hermeneutical question of the empty tomb, Barth wrote:

> Christians do not believe in the empty tomb, but in the living Christ. This does not mean, however, that we can believe in the living Christ without believing in the empty tomb. Is it just a "legend"? What matter? It still refers to the phenomenon ensuing the resurrection, to the presupposition of the appearance of Jesus. It is the sign which obviates all possible misunderstanding. It cannot, therefore, but demand our assent, even as a legend. Rejection of the legend of the empty tomb has always been accompanied by the rejection of the saga of the living Jesus, and necessarily so. Far better, then, to admit that the empty tomb belongs to the Easter event as its sign.[1]

Unlike hermeneutical literalism, Barth does not accord an objective, extratextual status to the empty tomb. The empty tomb mentioned in the text need not coincide with a factual, extratextual referent. The empty tomb may well, as far as its extratextual status is concerned, be nothing more than legendary. There would be no point, from Barth's point of view, to any attempt at going behind the text, whether from apologetical or skeptical interests, in order to establish one way or the other the status of the empty tomb as an extratextual fact.

When the true referent of the resurrection accounts is properly recognized, the significance of the empty tomb falls into place as well. The true referent of the resurrection accounts is the living Jesus Christ. The objective, extratextual status of the living Jesus Christ is, as Barth reads the accounts, something quite inscrutable, involving a deeply mysterious conjunction of historical and suprahistorical, temporal and eternal, objectifiable and nonobjectifiable elements. The very same Jesus who had died on the cross and been laid in the tomb was present again to his disciples as a mystery which could only be adored. What had previously been inapprehensible — that Jesus was the incarnate Word of God — was now apprehensible. Jesus was now manifest to his disciples in the real and objective but mys-

---

1. Karl Barth, *Church Dogmatics* III/2 (Edinburgh: T. & T. Clark, 1960), p. 453; hereafter cited as III/2.

terious modality of God. He was now manifest as what in him had previously been hidden, that is, as the very being and presence of God, sovereign over life and death, strong and gracious to save.

But the Risen One, manifest in the mysterious modality of God, would not also have been manifest in his humanity without his "real and therefore physical resurrection from the dead." The whole humanity of Jesus, including his body, had to have a part in this event. As something less than physical, as something purely spiritual or disembodied, the event of his appearance would not have involved his whole identity as a human being. In the physicality of his resurrection, moreover, not only his real humanity but also his real deity was at stake. "It was because God Himself, the Creator, who was first hidden in the lowliness of this creature, in the death of this man, was now manifested in His resurrection, that it was absolutely necessary for this genuinely and apprehensibly to include nature, and therefore to be physical." For God, after all, was the Creator not only of heaven but also of earth, not only of the soul but also of the body, and was fully sovereign over each, as the resurrection stories themselves were meant to attest (III/2, p. 451).

Given this understanding of the risen Christ as the extratextual referent of the accounts, Barth's interpretation of the empty tomb as a "sign" becomes clear. "Sign" is essentially an intratextual category whose extratextual force is that of analogy. As an intratextual category, the sign of the empty tomb calls for explication in terms of related intratextual "signs," such as the "ascension" (a sign of the end to the Easter appearances) and the "virgin birth" (a sign of the earthly nativity of the eternal Word of God). As though in good literary-critical fashion, Barth proceeds to carry through just such an explication, yet all the while pressing for its theological point (III/2, pp. 452-53). The point of the empty tomb as an intratextual sign is, Barth concludes, to eliminate all possible misunderstanding about what kind of resurrection is being attested: real and therefore physical.

The extratextual referent of the "empty tomb" is therefore not a factual empty tomb, as hermeneutical literalism would suppose, but rather the risen Christ himself. However, since the risen Christ did not, according to Barth's interpretation, rise without his body, it would appear as if some further, though secondary, extratextual referent were implied. For although Barth never developed the point, would not his interpretation seem to entail as a referent, if not a factual empty tomb (whose story might well be a legend), at least something analogous to it, in effect its virtual equivalent?[2] Otherwise, would it not be hard

---

2. For example, if Jesus' body had been thrown into a common grave, presumably it would no longer be there.

to see how Barth's insistence on the physicality of Christ's resurrection could remain intelligible? This point is worth exploring for two reasons.

First, it helps to clarify Barth's relation to hermeneutical literalism. The relationship between scriptural text and historical referent has been a vexing problem for interpreters of Barth's theology, and his position has regularly been taken to task by conservative and liberal theologians alike (e.g., Carl F. Henry and Rudolf Bultmann). Quite possibly, Barth's reticence to specify the historical referent of the scriptural text as clearly in any given instance as his critics would demand may have had something to do with a lingering transcendentalism in his theology, of which he himself was at least partially cognizant.[3] It is more likely, however, that Barth's reticence had material theological grounds. The events surrounding Jesus Christ, as Barth understood them through their scriptural attestation, were infused from beginning to end with a deeply ineffable quality, yet their ineffability was not something accessible to naked observation, but apprehensible only by faith. Even the physicality of the risen Christ was ineffable, as was its exact relation to the corpse of the crucified Jesus and therefore to a factual empty tomb or its equivalent. Such matters, Barth seemed to feel, were better passed over in silence than specified too clearly one way or the other. The essential ineffability of these events did not make them any less real, Barth proposed, but it did make them essentially inaccessible to reductive forms of apprehension and analysis such as historical-critical method.[4] Barth was perhaps not as interested as he might have been in the theoretical question of what would count as disconfirmation for Christian claims about Jesus, but his position against hermeneutical literalists, whether liberal or conservative, was at least defensible. For it is by no means certain that Barth was wrong to insist that the scriptural texts about Jesus do not imply such ordinary historical referents as his literalist critics would suppose.[5]

The question about a factual referent to the scriptural texts on the empty tomb, secondly, can help to clarify Barth's more general hermeneutical posi-

---

3. Karl Barth, *Church Dogmatics* I/2 (Edinburgh: T. & T. Clark, 1956), p. 50; hereafter cited as I/2.

4. Karl Barth, *Church Dogmatics* III/2 (Edinburgh: T. & T. Clark, 1958), pp. 446, 451.

5. This is not, of course, the same thing as saying that they imply no ordinary historical referents at all, or no suprahistorical referent with ordinary historical entailments. By the way, I speak of "liberal" as well as "conservative" hermeneutical literalists here, because in their polemical moments liberals regularly provide literalist readings as examples of what they want to reject. Rudolf Bultmann, for example, in effect provides three readings of the resurrection stories: one crudely literal, one mythological (justified by eliminating the crudely literal elements), and one existentialist (as a way of interpreting the mythological reading in its contemporary relevance).

tion. The "empty tomb" can be read, Barth seemed to imply, as an imaginative response ("legend") bearing analogical force ("sign") to an essentially ineffable referent (the risen Christ). It was the ineffability of the referent itself which worked against literalism and pressed instead toward "analogy" as the proper category for describing how text and referent were semantically related. "Analogy" allowed the equally indispensable elements of reticence and predication to emerge in proper proportion with respect to such a referent. Reticence was required by the mystery, predication by the reality, of the event; and imaginative response was an eminently appropriate and well-nigh unavoidable scriptural strategy for depicting a referent which, though real, was largely incomprehensible.

Given this understanding of legendary text ("imaginative response"), referent ("real though incomprehensible, incomprehensible though real"), and their semantic relation ("analogy combining reticence and predication"), Barth felt justified in simply concentrating on the text itself. In the case of the biblical stories about Jesus, for example, Barth felt free to concentrate on intratextual matters such as typological exegesis (which is, in part, a question of intratextual analogies) or on the narrative patterns by which the identity of Jesus is cumulatively depicted through the interaction of character and circumstance. It was precisely the intratextual analogies and patterns (not the literal details) which interested him. He could admit the imaginative character of the stories by calling them "sagas," without being beset by tiresome literalist anxieties, not only because he considered these intratextual analogies and patterns to be an appropriate response to the subject matter, but also because he thought that it was these analogies and patterns themselves which carried the referential or extratextual force. That force, as we have seen, was itself analogical, so that for Barth the relation between text and referent, far from being literal, was essentially a relation between a network of intratextual patterns and a real but ineffable (extratextual) subject matter, mediated by analogical predication.[6]

The truth of the analogical predication, of course, depended on its having ultimately been guided and inspired by God. In, with, and under the human imaginative response to the biblical narratives, divine self-predication was believed to have been at work; and this belief itself could arise not as a rational in-

6. In his actual exegetical or hermeneutical practice, Barth sought to be guided by the *sensus literalis* in the sense that he did not find the meaning of the text in a subject matter accessible independently of the text. His reading of Scripture led him to assume a fittingness in the relationship between signifier and signified, that is, between textual depiction and intratextual as well as extratextual subject matter. However, intratextuality was, for Barth, never an end in itself, but was rather the bearer of extratextual semantic force. Intratextuality without extratextuality would merely aestheticize the subject matter.

ference about the text, but only as a response to the grace mediated through the text by the self-revealing God. It was this twofold conviction — that divine guidance lay behind the formulation of the textual predications, and that their truth was to be accepted only on the basis of divine grace mediated through the text — which separated Barth most sharply from all versions of "expressivist" biblical interpretation.

If against literalist interpretation Barth had to emphasize the humanity of the texts and the mystery of their referent, against expressivist interpretation he had to stress the otherness of the texts and the perspicuity of their referent. Barth rejected the kind of scriptural interpretation which construed the texts primarily in "expressivist" terms. The biblical texts were not essentially metaphorical or symbolic objectifications of the emotive responses, however profound, which sacred objects or events had aroused in the religious subjects by whom those texts were produced. The "logical force" of Scripture was not primarily noncognitive, noninformative, and nondiscursive. Because the texts were not essentially metaphorical in this sense, they did not require "correlation" with external material in order to make up their deficit — neither with philosophical speculation to interpret their implicit cognitive content, nor with cultural analysis to counteract their otherwise privatizing effect. Nor were they to be judged primarily as useful or not useful (rather than true or false) according to how well they expressed the range and richness of religious experience, or how well they suggested a contemporary way of being in the world. Moreover, the reliability or "assertive force" of scriptural language about God was not significantly compromised either by the cultural relativity of the texts or by their putatively expressivist character, on the basis of which all direct and descriptive reference of God could only be regarded as a tentative conceptual abstraction from the essentially emotive symbol. Finally, the "semantic force" of scriptural language about God was not basically equivocal. Although undeniably anthropomorphic, this language did not mean something completely different when applied to the Creator than when applied to the creature, nor was it more adequately translated into abstract, impersonal terms. In each of these ways Barth differed from hermeneutical expressivism.

At the heart of these differences from expressivism lay Barth's rejection of the premise that images and metaphors when applied to God cannot strictly and properly be true. On the contrary, Barth contended that the images and metaphors applied to God by Scripture were truthful without equivocation. When Scripture speaks not only of such matters as God's wrath or God's mercy, but also very vividly of God's face, God's eyes, God's arm, and so on, the semantic force of these metaphors was not to be construed equivocally, "as if" God felt wrath or mercy or "as if" God had such physical characteristics, whereas in truth God was a nonanthropomorphic reality who supposedly completely transcended such naive depictions. Barth proposed, by contrast, that though such depictions were not to be taken literally, neither were they to be interpreted by translating them into abstract, amorphous terms. Barth understood even the most anthropomorphic images in Scripture to mean that God's being not only transcended, but also overlapped and comprehended, both spirit and nature. The natural component of the anthropomorphic images was not to be interpreted away, because otherwise God's being would be reduced to the "formless, motionless being of a spirit." Such an abstract, absolute spirit — a spirit without nature — would be incapable of action, for "acts happen only in the unity of spirit and nature." A divine being incapable of action, a God who did not and could not act, would not be the God attested in Scripture, whose works of creation, redemption, and revelation were nothing if not real and proper deeds of love and freedom.[7]

Not only some, Barth argued, but all our images and concepts as applied to God are anthropomorphic. The distinction between the divine and the human did not, as is often assumed, coincide with that between spirit and nature, formlessness and form, abstract and concrete, impersonal and personal. The latter distinctions all exist and can be overcome within the world. They are all forms of human discourse and perception. In and of themselves they all in one way or another correspond to the human or creaturely sphere, and therefore in none of the distinctions does one term better correspond than the other to God. Consequently, "spiritual — i.e., abstract — concepts are just as anthropomorphic as those which indicate concrete perceptions" (II/1, p. 222). In other words, concepts applied to God on the basis of a *via eminentiae* or a *via negativa* are in principle no less anthropomorphic than metaphors and stories which convey God as acting.

Since all our language inevitably arises from and is formed by the human and creaturely sphere, the question in speaking about God was not whether but how to be "anthropomorphic." On what basis could a selection be made of which metaphors and concepts to use in speaking of God? The selection for expressivism was to be made on the basis of emotive experience; for Barth on the basis of divine revelation. For expressivism the selection was essentially flexible; for Barth it was essentially fixed. Expressivism thought of God's attributes as something to be postulated; Barth as something to be acknowledged. Anthropomorphic metaphors applied to God by Scripture were for expressivism objectifications of emotive experience; for Barth they were depic-

---

7. Karl Barth, *Church Dogmatics* II/1 (Edinburgh: T. & T. Clark, 1957), p. 267; hereafter cited as II/1.

tions of an agent. The semantic relation between metaphorical text and divine referent for expressivism was equivocal; for Barth it was analogical. For expressivism the divine referent was essentially other than metaphorically depicted; for Barth it was essentially similar. Conceptual redescription of the divine referent underscored, for expressivism, its disparity from the metaphorical text; for Barth it underscored their correspondence. In short, for expressivism, which metaphors and concepts to use was largely discretionary, emotively based, and fraught with the corresponding uncertainty; for Barth, which to use was largely obligatory, scripturally based, and secured with the corresponding confidence. "God's true revelation," Barth wrote, "comes from out of itself to meet what we can say with our human words and makes a selection from among them to which we have to attach ourselves in obedience" (II/1, p. 227).

Revelation meant, by definition, that God had provided for us what we could not provide for ourselves, what only God could give us and what God did give, namely, the terms of God's self-identification. It meant that God took definite form for us within the conditions of our human, creaturely sphere. It meant that God became truly and concretely accessible to us so that we could say Thou to God and pray to God without fiction or equivocation. It meant that our images, concepts, and words, grounded on God's revelation, could be "legitimately applied to God, and genuinely describe God even in this sphere of ours and within its limits" (II/1, p. 227).[8] God's self-revelation meant that God's being had made itself perspicuous.

Analogy was the decisive category by which Barth's view of metaphor was separated from that of expressivism. Scriptural metaphors for God, no matter how "anthropomorphic," really corresponded, in Barth's view, to the being of God itself. They did so, of course, by no power of their own, but solely by virtue of divine grace. The work of grace was essentially twofold: first, it provided the terms of God's self-analogization; then it imparted, verified, and actualized them to the recipient in the mode of personal encounter, according to the openness of the recipient and the divine good pleasure (the former ultimately depending on the latter). Yet in selecting anthropomorphic metaphors and allowing them to correspond to the divine being, God was not doing something inappropriate. God's truth was not at our disposal, Barth urged, but our truth was at God's disposal. In God, who was the truth, all truth found its unity. When God selected certain metaphors, concepts, and words from our sphere and allowed them to correspond to the divine being, there was a sense in which God was not selecting something alien, but something which belonged origi-

---

8. Cf. Karl Barth, *Church Dogmatics* I/1, 2nd ed. (Edinburgh: T. & T. Clark, 1975), pp. 315-16; hereafter cited as I/1.

nally and properly to God as the Creator. Certainly the truth in which we were to know God through this selection of metaphors, concepts, and words was God's truth in a very different way than it was ours. Yet it was nonetheless God's truth — "originally, primarily, independently and properly" — because it was the truth of the Creator in whom all truth was one (II/1, p. 228).

Contrary to hermeneutical expressivism, therefore, Barth argued that we are bound to the orientation and direction established by the metaphors God had selected (in, with, and under their human, culturally conditioned origination), and that these metaphors are used to describe God's essential identity, not improperly but properly, not equivocally but analogically, and therefore in reality and truth. Indeed, as already noted, Barth goes so far as to argue that anthropomorphic metaphors, as applied to God by Scripture, convey not a derivative but the original truth of the terms they employ. This point receives a number of striking illustrations.

"Arm" and "mouth," for example, are said to find their original and proper use when God makes the divine being to be their object, so that they refer (by way of analogy) primarily to God's acting and speaking and only secondarily to human realities. This is Barth's counterintuitive "analogy of truth," an analogy of extrinsic attribution, in which the divine side is the *analogans* and the human side is the *analogate* (II/1, p. 230; cf. pp. 238-39). A similar and even more emphatic point is made about the words "father" and "son." They do not, Barth contends, first and properly have their truth in the creaturely sphere.

> They have it first and properly at a point to which, as our words, they cannot refer at all, but to which, on the basis of the grace of the revelation of God, they may refer, and on the basis of the lawful claim of God and Creator they even must refer, and therefore, on the basis of this permission and compulsion, they can actually refer — in their application to God, in the doctrine of the Trinity. In a way which is incomprehensible and concealed from us, but in the incontestable priority of the Creator over the creature, God Himself is *the* Father and *the* Son. (II/1, p. 229)[9]

9. Whether the orientation and direction established by the logic of Barth's position on the divine selection of metaphors would require the regular, public use of male theological language in a church and culture in which such language was consistently abused to legitimate oppressive male-female relations is by no means a settled question. In general, the logic of Barth's analogical position would not require identical but only corresponding language to that of Scripture, so long as the language of Scripture was not substantially contradicted, but consonantly paralleled, supplemented, or illuminated. The deepest difficulty for the logic of this position would arise not about metaphor, but about whether the word "Father" is not also a proper name. In the case of God's names Barth tends, on exegetical grounds, to work with a scheme not of analogy, but of "identity" and "difference." See I/1, pp. 316-19; II/1, pp. 59f.

The veracity of the semantic relation between metaphorical text and divine referent, as conceived by Barth, rested on three main convictions: that God had engaged in self-revelation, that this self-revelation was attested in Scripture, and that this attestation was essentially reliable. The reliability of the textual reference to God was in part a question of linguistic possibility. Although scriptural metaphors, concepts, and words as such were, like all human language, "wholly and utterly insufficient," they were in all their human frailty, by the grace of divine revelation, "sufficient to apprehend God's being (the one, entire, indivisible being of God), and therefore to be true, to express and establish true knowledge of God."[10] The veracity of the semantic relation between text and referent could therefore not be impugned by appealing to the general insufficiency of human language to refer to God.

Nor could it be impugned on the grounds that the relation in question was admittedly incomprehensible. Confidence in the scriptural attestation of God's self-revelation, Barth argued, meant confidence that analogy held sway without our being able (or needing) to specify how. For the analogy spanned two utterly different modes of being, God's and ours, in themselves having no terms (or no comprehensible terms) in common, mediated strictly by the gracious and miraculous self-communication of God. The analogy of revelation between text and referent disclosed the identifying terms of a "wholly other" God.

This point requires closer explication. The key passage from Barth runs as follows: "But the truth is that human beings with their human word 'similarity' come to take part in the (as such) incomprehensible similarity that is established in God's veracious revelation, when in it God comes to take part in human existence and its human word."[11] The point on which everything turns is "incomprehensible similarity." The decisive question concerns what separates "incomprehensible similarity" from mere "equivocity." At first the answer would seem to be fairly straightforward. "Equivocity" denies that there is genuine similarity; "incomprehensible similarity" affirms that there is similarity but denies that we can specify just how it obtains. However, the concept of God as "wholly other" would logically seem to require the concept of equivocity rather than that of incomprehensible similarity. For it would seem that an ordinary word predicated of a "wholly other" referent could only have a sense (if any

10. Karl Barth, *Church Dogmatics* II/1 (Edinburgh: T. & T. Clark, 1956), p. 235.
11. My translation. "Sondern die Wahrheit ist die, dass der Mensch mit seinem menschlichen Wort 'Ähnlichkeit' Anteil bekommt an der als solcher unbegreiflichen Ähnlichkeit, die in Gottes wahrhaftiger Offenbarung damit gesetzt ist, dass Gott in ihr am Menschen und seinem menschlichen Wort Anteil nimmt" (Barth, *Kirchliche Dogmatik,* Band II, Teil 1 [Zürich: Theologischer Verlag, 1940], p. 256). Cf. II/1, pp. 226f.

sense at all) wholly other than the ordinary sense. The word would thus be used equivocally rather than analogically.

One way to escape this dilemma would be to shift from an ontic to a perceptual frame of reference. The concept "wholly other" would then turn out to mean "wholly inapprehensible in any ordinary sense." A referent "wholly inapprehensible," except under extraordinary conditions, might be conceived as possessing in itself enough real ontic similarity with the ordinary so as to make possible an analogical relation between ordinary word and extraordinary referent. Ontically, this referent might be "extremely different" but would not be "wholly other," yet the terms of its ontic similarity would be wholly inapprehensible except on the condition of a special disclosure such as self-revelation.

This solution to the dilemma, however, would be comprehensible, whereas the analogical relation Barth wants to posit is said to be "incomprehensible." Therefore, Barth's own (implicit) alternative would seem to go something like this. God is "wholly other" in the sense of being so incomprehensible that the logic of equivocity, which would otherwise seem to obtain, in this case does not apply. Rather than speculate on this matter in the abstract, we must keep to the logic of the events. The God who is wholly other and therefore wholly incomprehensible posits, in the event of self-revelation, an incomprehensible analogical relation between human word and divine referent. The very incomprehensibility of this relation consists in part in its being analogical precisely where we should logically expect it to be equivocal. We cannot fathom how the being of a wholly other God makes itself apprehensible to us. We cannot fathom how our words are made to take part in a similarity established by the event of divine self-revelation, nor how God's wholly other being makes itself to take part in those words. We can only point to the event wherein this twofold participation happens, appeal to the veracity of God, and speak of the miracle and mystery of divine grace. Yet we can speak of a real analogical relation with confidence, because it rests on the truthfulness of God. The analogical relation cannot be denied in favor of one that is equivocal without denying the veracity of God's self-revelation itself.[12]

12. It might be useful at this point to suggest something of the differences between Barth and Thomas Aquinas on the status of analogy in theological discourse. Although both regard the "semantic force" of such discourse to be analogical, Aquinas, at least on one reading of his work, construes that force as being more equivocal than does Barth. Barth holds that, by virtue of God's gracious activity, our scripturally based analogies do apply to God's being in itself, even if we can't specify how. By contrast, Aquinas seems to hold that such analogies do not apply to God's being in itself, even though it is as if the analogies did apply. The emphasis in Barth is on God as known, in Aquinas on God as unknown. Although these differences are subtle, even vex-

How to construe the semantic relation between text and referent was, Barth believed, "not a systematic but an exegetical decision" (II/1, p. 227). Barth's decision to construe the relation as analogical rather than univocal or equivocal depended not on general considerations but on his reading of the texts as a modern human being within the community of faith. If one asked about the "semantic force" — that is, about the mode of reference — of the biblical texts, then the referent itself was the decisive factor, Barth reasoned, which ruled out both the "literalist" and the "expressivist" solutions. The "univocal" solution proposed by the literalists was ruled out because it could not do justice to the referent's abiding mystery. It failed to honor the mysterious divine hiddenness in the midst of the divine revelation. Likewise, the "equivocal" solution proposed by the expressivists was ruled out because it could not do justice to the referent — this time to its self-predication. It failed to honor the perspicuous divine self-unveiling in the midst of the divine hiddenness. The alternative was therefore to construe the mode of reference "analogically." The reticence of analogy honored the mystery, the predication of analogy the perspicuity, of God's self-revelation as attested in Scripture.

If one were to ask, furthermore, about the "logical force" of the textual mode of reference — that is, about its mode of address — then again, Barth reasoned, the referent itself was such as to rule out both literalist and expressivist solutions. The primarily cognitive solution proposed by the literalists was ruled out because it could not do justice to the personal activity of the referent. It viewed the mode of address in abstraction from the One who

---

ing, much seems to hinge on the respective assessments of God's incomprehensibility. Divine incomprehensibility seems to place God beyond our knowledge for Aquinas, whereas for Barth it does not. (For Barth the divine incomprehensibility is given in and with, not beyond, our knowledge of God.) Perhaps it might be said that the problem of divine incomprehensibility prompts Aquinas to conceive of God as overcoming the soteriological distance between God and the sinful creature without as fully overcoming the linguistic distance (in this life). For Barth, however, overcoming the linguistic distance (so that our analogies impart real knowledge) is part and parcel of God's overcoming the soteriological distance. Hence for Aquinas the status of analogy in theological discourse leads to an emphasis on the "performative" aspects of theological truth, whereas for Barth the emphasis is more nearly "realistic," even though the "performative" implications are not to be denied. That is, Aquinas finally seems to stress that we are to respond as if the analogies held true, whereas Barth stresses that because the analogies hold true we are to respond accordingly. My understanding of Aquinas on this point has been shaped by the following works: George A. Lindbeck, *The Nature of Doctrine: Religion and Theology in a Postliberal Age* (Philadelphia: Westminster, 1984), pp. 66-67; David B. Burrell, *Aquinas: God and Action* (Notre Dame, Ind.: University of Notre Dame Press, 1979), pp. 3-11, 55-77, 162-75; Victor Preller, *Divine Science and the Science of God* (Princeton: Princeton University Press, 1967), pp. 179-271.

did the addressing. It turned the mode of address into a cognitive proposition to be considered in detachment and assessed in neutral terms. It failed to honor the active self-involvement of the Addressor in, with, and under the text. It thus failed to honor the corresponding self-involvement, whether acknowledged or not, of the addressee. The primarily emotive solution proposed by the expressivists was ruled out, on the other hand, because it could not do justice to the sovereignty of the referent. It viewed the mode of address in abstraction from the constraints established by the self-identification of the Sovereign who did the addressing. It turned the mode of address into an emotive symbol to be affectively appropriated and to be assessed in merely functional terms. It failed to honor the authoritative self-predication of the Addressor and therefore the corresponding acknowledgment required of the addressee. Barth's alternative was again a "realist" proposal which corrected, combined, and transcended the other two. The biblical texts' primary mode of address, Barth proposed, was neither cognitive nor emotive but kerygmatic — and therefore self-involving — on the part of Addressor and addressee. The cognitive and emotive proposals were not wrong so much as they were examples of misplaced concreteness with very misleading implications. Viewed concretely rather than abstractly, however, the cognitive and emotive elements in the address were both subordinate to the element of personal encounter. This encounter was, for both parties, fully self-involving. On the human side it required a decision from the whole person, not just from the head or the heart, though of course including both. It was to be a decision of complete reorientation, of gratitude and obedience, of conversion, of death and resurrection for the addressee, even as it had once meant death and resurrection for the Addressor.

If one were to ask, finally, about the "assertive force" of this textual mode of reference — that is, about the mode of certainty it allowed — then perhaps the best way to answer would be through a shift in analytical categories. Although the literalists would propose the "absolute" certainty associated with rational propositions, and the expressivists the "relative" certainty or uncertainty associated with emotive symbols, Barth's alternative can perhaps best be made clear by contrasting it with "foundationalism" and "relativism." This distinction does not coincide with that between "literalism" and "expressivism." For although literalists tend to be foundationalists, expressivists sometimes try to avoid outright emotive relativism by establishing some kind of "correlation" with foundationalist ideas. However, Barth's hermeneutical realism can be read as transcending both "foundationalism" and "relativism," while retaining elements of each.

Barth made no attempt to justify the truth claims of Christian theology by appealing to any kind of neutral, self-evident, and universally accessible assertions, whether historical, transcendental, existential, or some other species. Nor did he make theology somehow depend for its meaning and truth on such "foundational" assertions. On the contrary, he argued that the meaning and truth of theological assertions was not neutral but self-involving, not self-evident but revealed, and not universally accessible but context-dependent. Theological assertions could not be tested apart from the revelation they sought to articulate. In these ways Barth differed from foundationalism.[13]

Nor, on the other hand, did Barth attempt to justify theological assertions by making the criterion of meaning and truth their anthropological relevance. On the contrary, he argued that relevance could never be a sufficient and independent criterion in theology. When mere relevance or utility was made the overriding criterion, theological assertions could only fluctuate according to the vagaries of human self-exposition. Relevance as the sole or chief criterion made "God" a predicate of human needs, abandoned the objective constraints of divine self-revelation, and ended fatally in relativism.[14]

More positively, therefore, Barth contended that within the context of Christian theology, assertions could be justified only by virtue of their correspondence with the Word of God as attested in Holy Scripture. This correspondence was at once, be it noted, a divine gift and human work. As such, it was always an event of personal encounter which held the two (divine gift and human work) together in an active unity that preserved their proper order and distinction. In one way or another mediating this personal encounter (which by no means necessarily entailed a "peak experience") was Holy Scripture itself. As the indirect but concrete form of God's Word, Scripture established an objective standard by which the human work of theological formulation could be humanly (and only humanly) assessed. Human formulations and assessments ultimately depended for their power and authority on the divine gift which alone overcame all human impotence. Correspondence was thus an event in-

---

13. For a useful definition of "foundationalism," see Francis Schüssler Fiorenza, *Foundational Theology* (New York: Crossroad, 1984), pp. 285-89. See also Ronald F. Thiemann, *Revelation and Theology* (Notre Dame, Ind.: University of Notre Dame Press, 1985), chap. 14. Thiemann's valuable work has, of course, done much to bring the question of foundationalism into contemporary theological discussion.

14. When proclamation rests on the analogies chosen by God, Barth writes, "It will then have something definite to say, and that with a good conscience, with the promise of relevance, i.e., of standing in a real relationship to the reality proclaimed by it, and with the justified claim and well grounded prospect of obtaining a hearing" (II/1, p. 233). For a discussion of the place of functional criteria in Barth's theology, see George Hunsinger, "Karl Barth and Liberation Theology" and "Barth, Barmen, and the Confessing Church Today," chaps. 2 and 3 in this volume.

volving complex interaction among objectifiable and nonobjectifiable, absolute and relative, divine and human elements.

Insofar as Barth's realism emphasized the divine gift, it had certain features in common with foundationalism. For it justified theological assertions by virtue of their correspondence with an objective divine reality, indeed, with the "authentic information about God" received through divine revelation, with the Bible as "the authentic and supreme criterion" of theological formulation.[15] Insofar as Barth's realism emphasized the human work, on the other hand, it shared certain features with relativism. For human assertions about God were never to be mistaken this side of the eschaton for the truth of revelation itself. Human assertions here and now were never definitive, never more than provisional, always aiming at a truth they could never fully grasp, therefore always in need of revision. In practice the relativity of human assertion meant that we could never escape a measure of uncertainty. More precisely, it meant that we could never escape "the dialectic of certainty and uncertainty which is our part in this event . . . yet not in such a way that we are still in the grip of that dialectic; rather in such a way that the dialectic is directed and controlled from the side of the event which is God's part" (II/1, pp. 74-75). The "assertive force" of Scripture, as Barth interpreted it, would thus seem to involve a form of "realism" which construed the reality of God as being theory-independent in principle though not in practice, which allowed human assertions about God to be referential though without absolute certainty, and which overlooked neither divine nor human activity in the event of correspondence between divine and human utterance.[16]

To sum up: Barth's hermeneutical realism construed the "semantic force" of Scripture as analogical rather than univocal or equivocal, the "logical force" as wholly self-involving rather than merely cognitive or emotive, and the "assertive force" as provisionally sufficient rather than implausibly absolute or fatally relative. "Analogy" was required by a reading of Scripture which understood the referent to be at once ineffable and perspicuous, "self-involvement" by a referent itself involved in personal address, and "provisional sufficiency" by a referent who was sovereign, veracious, and on the way to realizing a goal.

---

15. For these quotations, see II/1, p. 210, and I/1, p. 264.

16. It is sometimes argued that in the earlier volumes of the *Church Dogmatics* Barth did not take explicitly into account the place of human reception in the event of revelation, or in the event of correspondence between divine and human utterance. Yet if Barth's doctrine of revelation is "incoherent," it cannot be for that reason. Barth knew well enough early on, and often stated explicitly, that "man is the subject of faith" (I/1, p. 245), and that in the human work of receiving and articulating revelation, "we are not passive but active" (II/1, p. 219).

APPENDIX

Three Views of Theological Language: A New Typology

	Literalism	Expressivism	Realism
Semantic Force	Univocal	Equivocal	Analogical (similarity despite dissimilarity)
Logical Force	Cognitive	Emotive	Self-involving (cognitive, emotive, practical)
Assertive Force	Absolute	Relative	Sufficient
Narrative Force	Factual Report	Mythological Expression	Legendary Witness
Metaphor/ Proposition	Subsumptive $P \to M$	Disjunctive $M \vee P$	Reciprocal $P \leftrightarrow M$

Semantic Force: The mode of textual reference
Logical Force: The mode of textual address
Assertive Force: The mode of referential certainty
Narrative Force: The mode of literary representation
Metaphor/Proposition: The mode of their relationship

Note: Each category is discussed in the essay except the last on how metaphor and proposition are related. *Literalism* regards metaphors as merely ornamental. They can be translated into propositions without loss, and this must done if they are to be understood properly. *Expressivism* regards metaphors as emotive. At the level of their manifest content they have no cognitive significance. At the level of their latent content, which is cognitive, they need to be interpreted by an external discipline like philosophy, psychology, or sociology. Religious metaphors have no cognitive content of their own. *Realism* regards religious metaphors as cognitively significant in their own right. They therefore stand in a reciprocal relationship with relevant propositions. Metaphors may, in certain cases, be the best way of articulating what is cognitively significant. Metaphors and propositions, therefore, neither ornament-and-subsume nor oppose-and-supplement but reciprocate-and-complement each other. Carl F. H. Henry is a good example of a literalist. Much academic liberal theology is expressivist (even when combined with pragmatism). Barth and Aquinas each, in various ways, exemplify the realist option (though contemporary realism must address modern questions Aquinas obviously did not have to face).

CHAPTER 10

Hellfire and Damnation: Four Ancient and Modern Views

(1998)

Introduction: The Uses of Hell

Hell is a doctrine that has always had its uses. The range of those uses can be conveniently traced by examining a passage from *Cold Comfort Farm*, the comic novel by Stella Gibbons, first published in 1932. The novel is set in rural England during the third decade of the twentieth century, a time when automobiles were not entirely unknown but not yet widely in use. The scene to be examined involves Flora Poste and Amos Starkadder. Flora is a young, sophisticated woman who has gone to visit her relatives in the country, and Amos is her gray-haired, grizzled cousin, a Scotsman who lives on the farm with other kinfolk and who serves as a lay preacher in town at the Church of the Quivering Brethren. Flora accompanies Amos to a preaching service one evening. They arrive by horse and buggy, enter the hall, and take their seats. Flora sits in the back near the exit, Amos by the platform up front.

> After the hymn, which was sung sitting down, everybody crossed their legs and arranged themselves more comfortably, while Amos rose from his seat with terrifying deliberation, mounted the little platform, and sat down.
>
> For some three minutes he slowly surveyed the Brethren, his face wearing an expression of the most profound loathing and contempt, mingled with a divine sorrow and pity. He did it quite well. . . .
>
> At last he spoke. His voice jarred the silence like a broken bell.
>
> "Ye miserable, crawling worms, are ye here again, then? Have ye come like Nimshi, son of Rehoboam, secretly out of yer doomed houses to hear

what's comin' to ye? Have ye come, old and young, sick and well, matrons and virgins (if there is any virgins among ye, which is not likely, the world bein' in the wicked state it is), old men and young lads, to hear me tellin' o' the great crimson lickin' flames o' hell fire?"

A long and effective pause. . . . The only sound . . . was the wickering hissing of the gas flares which lit the hall and cast sharp shadows from their noses across the faces of the Brethren.

Amos went on.

"Aye, ye've come." He laughed shortly and contemptuously. "Dozens of ye. Hundreds of ye. Like rats to a granary. Like field mice when there's harvest home. And what good will it do ye?"

Second pause. . . .

"Nowt. Not the flicker of a whisper of a bit o' good."

He paused and drew a long breath, then suddenly leaped from his seat and thundered at the top of his voice:

"Ye're all damned!"

An expression of lively interest and satisfaction passed over the faces of the Brethren, and there was a general rearranging of arms and legs, as though they wanted to sit as comfortably as possible while listening to the bad news.

"Damned," he repeated, his voice sinking to a thrilling and effective whisper. "Oh, do ye ever stop to think what that word means when ye use it every day, so lightly, o' yer wicked lives? No. Ye doan't. Ye never stop to think what anything means, do ye? Well, I'll tell ye. It means endless horrifyin' torment, with yer poor sinful bodies stretched out on hot gridirons in the nethermost fiery pit of hell, and demons mockin' ye while they waves cooling jellies in front of ye, and binds ye down tighter on yer dreadful bed. Aye, an' the air'll be full of the stench of burnt flesh and the screams of your nearest and dearest. . . ."

He took a gulp of water, which Flora thought he more than deserved. . . .

Amos's voice now took on a deceptively mild and conversational note. His protruding eyes ranged slowly over his audience.

"Ye know, doan't ye, what it feels like when ye burn yer hand in takin' a cake out of the oven or wi' a match when ye're lighten' one of they godless cigarettes? Aye. It stings wi' a fearful pain, doan't it? And ye run away to clap a bit o' butter on it to take the pain away. Ah, but" (an impressive pause) *"there'll be no butter in hell! . . ."*

It was at this point that Flora rose quietly and with an apology to the woman sitting next to her, passed rapidly across the narrow aisle to the door. She opened it, and went out.[1]

---

1. Stella Gibbons, *Cold Comfort Farm* (London: Penguin Books, 1938), pp. 97-99.

Among the uses of hell that emerge from this episode are the familiar ones of deterrence, motivation, entertainment, self-justification, and departure. The doctrine of hell has always been valued by its adherents as a moral deterrent. Even worldly philosophers who set no store by Christian belief have sometimes prized hell as a useful fiction for the masses, or else they have lamented that nothing comparable has replaced it in modern times. However, such optimistic assessments may show less wisdom than does Amos; he clearly expects that his hellfire preaching will have minimal moral effect. Again, Christians have commonly honored the doctrine for its power of motivation. Sinners are spurred to repentance and conversion; conscientious believers, to earnest endeavors of missionary outreach to the lost. It is obviously as easy to ridicule this motivation (like Flora) as it is to overplay it (like Amos). In any case, one may well wonder whether higher motivations might not actually exist. One may even wonder whether hell-avoidance as a motivation, with its inevitable self-seeking and high anxiety, is finally compatible with more commendable motivations such as joy, gratitude, loyalty, obedience, and the desire to share something exceedingly positive.

The entertainment value of hell, however, is not to be missed, both within and without the narrative. Within the narrative, hell functions for Amos and his congregation as something like the disaster movie of a bygone era; whereas for the author and her readers (as for Flora), the same function is not absent, though in ironic distance and at second hand. Both within the narrative and without, therefore, the live possibility of religious, or nonreligious, self-justification, as the case may be, can never be far behind: one all too knowingly places oneself outside the threatened and pitiful group on the basis of a supposedly superior position — a temptation facing Flora and the reader no less than Amos and his congregation. Finally, hell functions as a reason for departure. Whether rightly or wrongly or both, Flora stands for sophisticated modernity, inside and outside the church, when she exits before Amos draws his lurid, horrifying, and unwittingly comical sermon to a close.

As chronicled by D. P. Walker, hell has been in steady decline as a doctrine since the seventeenth century.[2] By 1985 Martin Marty, the church historian, could quip that "hell disappeared but nobody noticed."[3] In 1991, however, a national newsmagazine announced that in popular belief hell was making a "sober comeback."[4] Moreover, in a somewhat surprising development, a number

---

2. D. P. Walker, *The Decline of Hell* (London: Routledge & Kegan Paul, 1964).

3. Martin E. Marty, "Hell Disappeared. No One Noticed. A Civic Argument," *Harvard Theological Review* 78 (1985): 381-98.

4. "Hell's Sober Comeback," *U.S. News & World Report*, March 25, 1991, p. 56.

of strong defenders have recently arisen from among the ranks of the philosophers more than of the theologians.[5]

According to Wolfhart Pannenberg, the distinguished theologian, in the West the church history of the twenty-first century is likely to be written, not by so-called mainline Protestantism, but by Roman Catholicism and by the resurgent conservatism of the Protestant church.[6] The outlook for the more liberal churches is not bright. The mainline is fast becoming the sideline, and the sideline seems destined for oblivion. Interestingly, the more ascendant churches are precisely those in which a traditional belief in hell has always held a secure, if not completely undisputed, place. The time seems ripe for a survey of the traditional belief and of its competitors within historic Christianity.

Four different perspectives on hell will be examined by taking both ancient and modern authorities into account. Augustine will be paired with two recent writers who uphold the traditional belief, then Origen will be paired with J. A. T. Robinson, Arnobius with John R. W. Stott, and finally Maximus the Confessor with Karl Barth. These are among the most powerful advocates for the main options as taught and contested within historic Christian belief.

Eternal Punishment: The Catholic Faith

No one has had a stronger influence on Christian beliefs about hell than Augustine (354-430), the bishop of Hippo and great theologian of the church. The lines of biblical interpretation and rational argument that he developed have formed the basis of the catholic faith on this topic ever since he set them forth. Views such as those that he championed made their way into the so-called Athanasian Creed (ca. 381-428), which proclaimed: "At [Jesus Christ's] coming all human beings shall rise with their bodies and . . . those who have done evil will go into everlasting fire." Essentially the same position was officially adopted at the Fourth Lateran Council in 1215: "Those [the rejected] will receive a perpetual punishment with the devil." This belief has been normative not only for the Roman Catholic Church, but also for the confessional standards of the Protestant Reformation as instructed by Luther and Calvin. Today the contours of Augustine's position appear essentially unchanged in the arguments of Ro-

---

5. See, for example, Jerry L. Walls, *Hell: The Logic of Damnation* (Notre Dame, Ind.: University of Notre Dame Press, 1992), and Jonathan L. Kvanvig, *The Problem of Hell* (New York: Oxford University Press, 1993).

6. Wolfhart Pannenberg, "Christianity and the West: Ambiguous Past, Uncertain Future," *First Things* (December 1994): 18-23.

man Catholic theologians like Cardinal Joseph Ratzinger[7] and conservative-evangelical Protestant thinkers like J. I. Packer.[8] Modified versions of the Augustinian view are also present in contemporary discussion.

The definition that Augustine gave to the doctrine of hell can be analyzed into seven basic components. Although many of these components were of course present in Christian belief prior to his time, Augustine systematized and defended them in an unprecedented way. The result was what we may call "the strong view of hell."[9] Analyzing this view will provide us with a useful yardstick against which alternative or competing views within the Christian tradition can be measured and understood. The seven components of the strong, Augustinian view are as follows.

First, hell is actual. Not all human beings are saved. Those who are not saved are consigned to eternal damnation. "What true Christian," wrote Augustine, "does not believe in the punishment of the wicked?"[10] No other future for such people is open: "Their eternal damnation is a matter of certainty" (*Enchir.* 92). "For as a matter of fact," Augustine stated, "not all, nor even a majority, are saved" (*Enchir.* 97). Hell, as Augustine understood it, is no mere theoretical possibility. It is the eternal destiny that awaits the majority of the human race.

Second, hell is severe. No greater torment can be suffered than the anguish of those in hell. Their torment is a "supreme unhappiness,"[11] and a destiny that could not be more horrible. "It is the worst of all evils" (*CofG* 13.11). The "torments of the lost" will be "perpetual," said Augustine, and "unintermitted" (*Enchir.* 112). He explained: "To be lost out of the kingdom of God, to be an exile from the life of God, to have no share in that great goodness which God has laid up for those who fear him, and has wrought for those who trust in him, would be a punishment so great, that, supposing it to be eternal,

---

7. Joseph Ratzinger, *Eschatology: Death and Eternal Life* (Washington, D.C.: Catholic University of America Press, 1988), pp. 215-18. For a recent indication of official Roman Catholic teaching about hell, see *Catechism of the Catholic Church* (Collegeville, Minn.: Liturgical Press, 1994), p. 270 (#1035). The explicit affirmation that hell is actual (#1035) is implicitly held in tension with a hope that it is not (p. 275, #1058).

8. J. I. Packer, "Evangelicals and the Way of Salvation," in *Evangelical Affirmations*, ed. Kenneth Kantzer and Carl Henry (Grand Rapids: Zondervan, 1990). For a more extended argument, see Robert A. Peterson, *Hell on Trial: The Case for Eternal Punishment* (Phillipsburg, N.J.: Presbyterian and Reformed Publishing Co., 1995).

9. For a different definition of this term, see Kvanvig, chap. 1.

10. Augustine, *Enchiridion* 8, in Augustine, *The Enchiridion on Faith, Hope, and Love*, ed. Henry Paolucci (Chicago: Regnery Gateway, 1961); hereafter cited as *Enchir.*

11. Augustine, *City of God* 20.2, in Augustine, *City of God*, ed. David Knowles (Harmondsworth: Penguin Books, 1972); hereafter cited as *CofG*.

no torments that we know of, continued through as many ages as the human imagination can conceive, could be compared with it" (*Enchir.* 112). As Augustine noted, it is Jesus himself whom the Gospels depict as uttering the most severe warnings about eternal torment. "Who could fail to be appalled," Augustine exclaimed, by ". . . this vehement emphasis on that punishment, uttered from his divine lips?" (*CofG* 21.9).

Later tradition would come to distinguish between "negative pain" or the "pain of loss" (*poena damni*) and "positive pain" or the "pain of affliction" (*poena sensus*). This distinction was already implicit in Augustine. The pain of loss, he believed, arises from the loss of God. The damned have forfeited the great goodness for which they were created. They are forever alienated from life with God, having no communion with him. For this reason such persons also endure the second sort of pain at the same time, the pain of affliction. The intensity of their torment stands in direct proportion to the greatness of the good they have lost. Vivid biblical imagery of eternal fire, of weeping and gnashing of teeth, of the worm that does not die, and so on, conveyed the intensity of this loss.

Third, hell is endless. Those who endure it never perish, and their torment affords no escape. Because they are "not permitted to die," it can be said that for them "death itself dies not" (*Enchir.* 92). They persist in a kind of "second death" wherein "pain without intermission afflicts the soul and never comes to an end" (*Enchir.* 92). The soul "no longer derives its life from God" (*CofG* 13.3), and yet it survives in a death without death. It is a misery in which those who endure it "will never be living, never dead, but dying for all eternity" (*CofG* 13.11). It is a state of "everlasting wretchedness" with no possible exit (*CofG* 19.28). The lost are flung into an eternal fire "where they will be tortured for ever and ever" (*CofG* 21.23).

Fourth, hell is penal. It is the penalty for sin as appointed by God. Since the remedy for sin is faith in Jesus Christ, hell is the penalty for those who lack this faith. It is undoubtedly a form of retribution rather than a form of remedy. It is not meant to lead to repentance or amendment of life, because the time for repentance has passed. "Punishments are a means of purification only to those who are disciplined and corrected by them," Augustine noted (*CofG* 21.14). The penalty of eternal damnation, as meted out at the Last Judgment, obviously falls into a different category. It is not at all meant to improve the life of those on whom it is inflicted. As "eternal chastisement," it is inflicted exclusively "in retribution for sins" (*CofG* 21.14).

Fifth, hell is just. It is the punishment that corresponds to the offense. No other punishment would be adequate to the wickedness of sin against God. Who but a fool, wrote Augustine, would think otherwise? "Who but a fool would think that God was unrighteous, either in inflicting penal justice on those who had earned it, or in extending mercy to the unworthy?" (*Enchir.* 98). Being himself the very standard of justice, God could not possibly do something that is unjust (regardless of whether we can comprehend it or not). The human being "who does not obtain mercy finds, not iniquity, but justice, there being no iniquity with God" (*Enchir.* 98). Whoever is condemned has absolutely nothing to complain of "but his own demerit" (*Enchir.* 99). "Whatever the wicked freely do through blind and unbridled lust," explained Augustine, "and whatever they suffer against their will in the way of open punishment — this all clearly pertains to the just wrath of God" (*Enchir.* 27). Here as elsewhere "God commits no sin," and certainly not by inflicting the punishment on the wicked that they deserve (*CofG* 21.14). For "if not a single member of the race had been redeemed, no one could justly have questioned the justice of God" (*Enchir.* 99). Therefore, no one has grounds to complain when "the greater number who are unredeemed" are consigned "in their just condemnation to what the whole race deserved" (*Enchir.* 99).

Sixth, hell is ordained by God. It is not merely an impersonal consequence of sin. Nor is it merely something that sinners suffer as a consequence of misusing their freedom. It is God who consigns sinners to eternal death by denying them eternal salvation. "Assuredly there was no injustice in God's not willing that they should be saved," wrote Augustine, "though they could have been saved had he so willed it" (*Enchir.* 95). God always acts strictly according to his own good pleasure. He does not will anything that he does not carry out. Human obstinacy can never hinder God, who is omnipotent, "from doing what he pleased" (*Enchir.* 95). We must not suppose that hell represents a defeat for God "as if the will of God had been overcome by the will of human beings" (*Enchir.* 97). Indeed, it would be at once foolish and blasphemous to say "that God cannot change the evil wills of human beings, whichever, whenever, and wheresoever he chooses, and direct them to what is good" (*Enchir.* 98). "For it is grace alone that separates the redeemed from the lost" (*Enchir.* 99). If God chooses to convert evil persons, he demonstrates his mercy. If he chooses not to do so, he demonstrates his justice. For God is a God who has mercy on whom he will have mercy, and who hardens whomever he will harden (Rom. 9:15) (*Enchir.* 98). "No one is saved," Augustine explained, "unless God wills his salvation"; and if God so wills it, "it must necessarily be accomplished" (*Enchir.* 103). Conversely, no one is damned unless God so wills it according to his perfect justice.

Finally, hell is inscrutable. The inner logic of God's dealings with sinful human beings is beyond our capacity to fathom. How it can be fair for God to save some but not others when all are equally sinful is inscrutable. How the severity of endless torment from eternity to all eternity is commensurate with the actual offense of human sin is also beyond human ken. Our only recourse in such matters is to defer to the greater wisdom of God. "What we have neither had experience of through our bodily senses, nor have been able to reach through intellect," explained Augustine, "must undoubtedly be believed on the testimony of those witnesses by whom the Scriptures, justly called divine, were written" (*Enchir.* 4). It is on the basis of scriptural authority, not on that of rational intelligibility, that the catholic faith finally rests with respect to its teaching about eternal punishment. Many things that are obscure in this life will be made clear in the life to come. In particular, the fairness of God's not willing that the majority of the human race should be saved — "though they could have been saved had he so willed it" — is for now a matter of faith, but "then shall be seen in the clearest light of wisdom" (*Enchir.* 95; cf. *CofG* 20.2, 20). In the meantime, the important thing is not to doubt that God does well when he exercises his judgment, whether in mercy or in condemnation. "For if a man does not understand these matters, who is he that he should reply against God?" (Rom. 9:20) (*Enchir.* 99).

As already noted, Augustine's articulation here of the catholic faith has remained definitive to the present day. In this light, two more points are worthy of note. First, in its understanding of the New Testament witness, the Augustinian tradition always assigns pride of place to Matthew 25:31-46 (cf. *Enchir.* 69; 112; *CofG* 20.5, 9; etc.). This is the passage in which the Son of man returns in glory for the Last Judgment. All the nations are gathered before him and separated into the sheep at his right hand and the goats at his left. The former go away to eternal life and the latter to eternal punishment. The perfect parallelism of the two destinies — both being described as "eternal" in the same sense — presents a difficult crux of interpretation for any view that would depart from the Augustinian tradition. Whether the passage from Matthew 25 really deserves the hermeneutical primacy that tradition has assigned to it, however, remains a matter of dispute.[12]

Second, modern exponents of this tradition often depart from Augustine on a very interesting question. As Henri Blocher points out: "Among the modern, the most popular argument — the very soul for most apologies for the possibility of hell — refers to human *freedom*. Since the nineteenth century, one notices a systematic effort at *discharging* God from the responsibil-

---

12. For a full inventory and classification of the relevant passages, see John W. Wenham, "The Case for Conditional Immortality," in *Universalism and the Doctrine of Hell,* ed. Nigel M. de S. Cameron (Grand Rapids: Baker, 1992), pp. 169-74. Wenham finds 264 references in the New Testament to the fate of the lost.

ity of punishment."[13] Modern interpreters, in other words (including official or quasi-official representatives like Ratzinger and Packer), typically adopt an apologetic strategy that places them at significant variance with two of Augustine's main points: hell as divinely ordained and hell as inscrutable. In modern apologies hell is supposed to seem less inscrutable when human responsibility is nudged into the spotlight while divine judgment is quietly escorted to the shadows. Divine sovereignty is thus displaced by human "freedom"; and the frailty of human understanding, by would-be claims to "intelligibility." Rarely do Augustine's modern heirs pause to ask themselves whether the gains of this strategy really outweigh the losses, or indeed whether the strategy really works at all.

Universal Salvation: The Minority Report

If the official faith has its champion in Augustine, the best-known unauthorized alternative finds its ancient defender in Origen (ca. 185-254), the brilliant Alexandrian thinker who is aptly described, if not as the first "systematic theologian," then at least as "the first fully professional thinker" in the history of the church.[14] Origen developed a kind of "Christian Platonism" that sometimes seemed more Platonist than Christian, and this mixed outlook displayed itself nicely in his arguments for universal salvation. His views on this matter, of course, did not always find a welcome reception. *Apokatastasis,* or the final restoration of all things — a view associated with Origen's name — was explicitly condemned by a council at Constantinople in 543, and possibly also by the Fifth Ecumenical Council (553), though the latter condemnation remains uncertain and doubtful. Nevertheless, if we take the categories used to analyze Augustine and apply them to Origen, we obtain the following results. Origen and Augustine agree that hell is actual and just, but Origen denies that it is endless. This disagreement then modifies the other four points. The Origenist hell is less severe than the Augustinian. It is penal but not in the same sense. Although divinely ordained, it allots greater scope than Augustine did to human freedom. And it is finally less inscrutable than the Augustinian version would require.

For Origen, as for Augustine, hell is actual. Everyone must indeed pass

13. Henri Blocher, "Everlasting Punishment and the Problem of Evil," in *Universalism and the Doctrine of Hell,* p. 295. Note that although human freedom and responsibility have always been axiomatic for the Augustinian view, they have not always been assigned the apologetic function Blocher observes in the more recent arguments.

14. Brian E. Daley, *The Hope of the Early Church: A Handbook of Patristic Eschatology* (Cambridge: Cambridge University Press, 1991), p. 59.

through divine judgment as through a purifying fire or "flaming sword."[15] The purifying fire is God himself: "God, the Fire, consumes human sins. He crushes, devours, and purifies them."[16] Although the experience of purification is undoubtedly severe — consisting, Origen acknowledged, of "torments," "penalty," and "torture" for the soul[17] — and although the severity will vary greatly from one case to the next, its ultimate purpose is clearly not retributive, as in Augustine, but remedial. It is a form of "very unpleasant and bitter medicine" (*FP* 2.10). "God, our physician, in his desire to wash away the ills of our souls, which they have brought on themselves through a variety of sins and crimes, makes use of penal remedies . . . ," explained Origen, "even to the infliction of a punishment of fire on those who have lost their soul's health" (*FP* 2.10). God's wrath toward the sinner is thus by no means vindictive; "it has a corrective purpose."[18] God does not inflict punishment except as "the means by which certain souls are purified by torment" (*CC* 6.26).

Remedial punishment clearly implies, in many of Origen's remarks, that the torment will not last forever, and that all human beings will finally be saved. "There is a resurrection of the dead," wrote Origen, "and there is punishment, but not everlasting. For when the body is punished, the soul is gradually purified, and so is restored to its ancient rank" (*FP* 2.10). "All things" will finally be "restored — through God's goodness, through their subjection to Christ, and through their unity with the Holy Spirit — to one end, which is like the beginning" (*FP* 1.6). "The goodness of God through Christ will restore his entire creation to one end, even his enemies being conquered and subdued" (*FP* 1.6). However, until that time, declared Origen: "My Savior weeps for my sins. My Savior cannot rejoice while I remain in iniquity."[19] The very sorrow of the Savior shows that "God always wants to make good that which is wrong" (*CC* 4.69). "For the Almighty nothing is impossible, nor is anything beyond the reach of cure by its Maker" (*FP* 3.6). God will never cease his work for salvation until all resistance to his will is overcome.

In his account of salvation, Origen has to address the perennial question

---

15. Origen, *Hom., I Sam.* 28:10. Quoted by Lawrence R. Hennessy, "The Place of Saints and Sinners after Death," in *Origen of Alexandria,* ed. Charles Kannengiesser and William L. Peterson (Notre Dame, Ind.: University of Notre Dame Press, 1988), p. 300.

16. Origen, *Hom., Lv.* 5:3. Quoted by Hennessy, p. 305.

17. Origen, *On First Principles* 2.10, in Origen, *On First Principles,* ed. G. W. Butterworth (New York: Harper & Row, 1966); hereafter cited as *FP.*

18. Origen, *Contra Celsum* 4.72, in *Origen: Contra Celsum,* ed. Henry Chadwick (Cambridge: Cambridge University Press, 1953); hereafter cited as *CC.*

19. *Hom., Lv.* 7:2. Quoted by Henri Crouzel, *Origen* (San Francisco: Harper & Row, 1989), p. 247.

of how divine grace and human freedom are related. In his most typical remarks he does not seem to assign the same kind of sovereignty to divine grace
as did Augustine. The picture is complicated, however, and we need not resolve
it here beyond sketching out some broad outlines. Although Origen sees grace
as an indispensable aid, he seems to view it as significantly dependent upon the
work of human striving, even when it is finally decisive. At one point he imag-
ines a sail-ship that is navigated by sailors and driven by the wind. The naviga-
tion is like human freedom while the wind is like divine grace. Each "cooperates" with the other. If we use our freedom properly and well, God will always
assist us with benevolence. "Our perfection does not come to pass without our
doing anything, and yet it is not completed as a result of our efforts, but God
performs the greater part of it" (*FP* 3.1). Throughout the longer or shorter —
and sometimes perhaps incalculably long — period of purgation, purification,
and torment through which our souls must pass on the way to final salvation,
our efforts are fully summoned and engaged. "But we believe that at some time
the Logos will have overcome the entire rational nature, and will have remod-
elled every soul to his own perfection, when each individual, simply by the exercise of his freedom, will choose what the Logos wills, and will be in that state
which he has chosen" (*CC* 8.72). A balance seems to be struck, as Origen sees it,
between unflagging grace and recalcitrant freedom until the latter finally yields
to the former.

The end of all things, as Origen conceived it, is their return to the perfect
harmony of the beginning. This metaphysical return seems more nearly Pla-
tonic than Christian in inspiration. It involves a difficult scheme of preexistent
souls acquiring earthly bodies only as a result of the fall into sin and then living
in various states of disorder and disarray until finally rescued through trials of
purgation and grace after death. It is not always easy to determine how much
influence the great metaphysical parabola of descent and ascent is exercising on
Origen's thoughts. It is perhaps in the background of his allegorizing exegesis
of Scripture, however, which allows him to read New Testament passages about
eternal punishment in a much freer way than did Augustine, who worked so
unflinchingly with the literal sense. Allegorizing exegesis and metaphysical
scheme, however, do not fully explain what is perhaps finally Origen's most salient difference from Augustine on the question of eternal damnation: his
granting of unqualified primacy to the benevolence and mercy of God. Though
Origen's God is not without his own inscrutability, it is not the inscrutability of
an apparently malignant caprice.

A recent argument for universal salvation that owes something to Origen
— especially in his more evangelical voice — can be found in the writings of
J. A. T. Robinson, the New Testament scholar, popular Christian writer, and

bishop of Woolwich. If one is looking for an uninhibited proponent of universal salvation, Robinson leaves nothing to be desired. Yet his arguments are not always easy to decipher. Too often they seem to hesitate, if one may put it this way, between biblicism and existentialism with a fuzziness that defeats the willing reader. Apparently straightforward appeals to biblical texts are placed side by side with "existentialist" reinterpretations of biblical "myths." Why some texts are myths while others reveal objective states of affairs is never explained. As a working hypothesis, I will assume that Robinson feels secure in his belief in the old liberal triad of "God, freedom, and immortality." Beyond that, he holds (at least residually) beliefs about the saving work of Jesus Christ that appear to be more traditional than his espousals of myth would allow. Although in his more dispirited mood Robinson offers little more than existentialism spiked with the emotions of Christianity,[20] he also has a more confident mood as well. At least some of his arguments for universalism happily give evidence of the latter.

"Freedom" is a theme that Robinson assumes he can develop without any serious reference to the problem of sin. Freedom is just something that we have, an inviolable, sacred potency that even God had better respect exactly as it stands. It is as pristine a source of autonomy for Robinson as any Enlightenment philosopher could hope to conjure up. "God," Robinson assures us, "has as much interest in the preservation of our freedom as ever we have ourselves" (*IEG*, p. 121). Therefore, any solution to the problem of eternal destiny "which in any way compromises the fact of freedom stands self-condemned" (*IEG*, p. 120). The God so solicitous of our freedom will always work through "a gentle leading" (*IEG*, p. 122), a policy statement that might have surprised any number of biblical figures — like Jacob at Peniel, like Joseph at the hands of his brothers, like the money changers driven from the temple by Jesus, or like Paul blinded on the road to Damascus, to say nothing of whole armies like the Egyptians drowned at the Red Sea, or indeed of Jesus himself hanging from the cross. Nevertheless, if allowances are made for a certain unfortunate sentimentality, what Robinson seems to be aiming at is somehow reminiscent of Origen. "May we not imagine a love so strong that ultimately no one will be able to restrain himself from free and grateful surrender?" (*IEG*, p. 122). For Robinson, as for Origen, God will use his "infinite love" in such a way as finally to "conquer those last shreds of our pride and independence" (*IEG*, p. 124).

"Immortality" is not a word that Robinson greatly prefers, but he does affirm an afterlife. This he understands in terms of "resurrection," an idea that he

---

20. John A. T. Robinson, *In the End God* (New York: Harper & Row, 1968). See, for example, pp. 135-37. Hereafter cited as *IEG*.

develops in an admirably biblical sense insofar as he upholds a sophisticated, realist understanding of its "bodily" character (*IEG*, pp. 89-109). Unlike either Augustine or Origen, however, Robinson proposes a version of divine judgment that seems attenuated at best. The idea of hell as something actual is supposed to have existentialist significance (adding zest to our decisions), but none for the afterlife (*IEG*, pp. 128-29). The real severity of life without God is a theme that has vanished almost without a trace, involving neither the pain of loss nor the pain of affliction. Sin, as mentioned, is an idea that is conspicuous mostly by its absence; therefore, it can hardly be seen as the object of divine penalty, whether retributive or remedial. God himself, being nothing if not meek and mild, begins to take on the visage of a well-meaning and perhaps rather bumbling Anglican cleric. Too often Robinson leaves himself wide open to the withering assessment of H. Richard Niebuhr: "A God without wrath brought men without sin into a kingdom without judgment through the ministrations of a Christ without a cross."[21]

And yet Robinson would scarcely be worth considering if Niebuhr could have the last word. As a matter of fact, by what seems to be a happy inconsistency, Robinson by no means leaves us with "a Christ without a cross." Although the cross is not developed as a theme when Robinson discusses universal salvation, he clearly presupposes not only that it is the supreme manifestation of God's love, but also that it somehow involves Christ's having died for our sake and in our place (*IEG*, p. 133). It is the event of the cross that makes all the difference in Robinson's case for universal salvation. The cross, one notes with interest, is not allegorized through an existentialist slight of hand. It is presented as the definitive manifestation and the real enactment of a divine love in which the world has been reconciled to God (*IEG*, pp. 139-40).

Robinson's cross-centered case for universal salvation rests on three main points. First, there is an appeal to reality. "The New Testament asserts the final *apokatastasis*," writes Robinson, "the restoration of all things, not as a daring speculation, nor as a possibility, but as a reality — a reality that shall be and must be, because it already is. It already is, because it is grounded in what has been, the decisive act of God, once and for all, embracing every creature" (*IEG*, p. 110). The real person and work of Jesus Christ, as centered in his saving death, is the decisive act by which God has already reconciled all things to himself. Universal salvation will be the necessary consequence of the cross.

Second, there is an appeal to how God's justice is related to God's love. God's justice cannot be understood, Robinson urges, in the traditional, Augus-

---

21. H. Richard Niebuhr, *The Kingdom of God in America* (New York: Harper & Row, 1937), p. 193.

tinian sense. It cannot be understood as something over against and independent of God's love. "God's justice," Robinson explains, "is always the sternness of his *love*" (*IEG*, p. 117). "It is nothing other than love being itself, love in the face of evil, continuing to exercise its own peculiar power" (*IEG*, p. 116). Since God's justice works only through God's love, it is impossible that his justice should ever manifest itself in conflict with his love. But that very conflict, in effect, is precisely what the traditional, Augustinian view leaves us with when it affirms the justice of eternal torment in the face of the divine love.

Finally, there is an appeal to God's nature as revealed by the centrality of the cross. Robinson writes: "Christ, in Origen's old words, remains on the Cross so long as one sinner remains in hell. That is not speculation: it is a statement grounded in the very necessity of God's nature. In a universe of love there can be no chamber of horrors, no hell for any which does not at the same time make it hell for God. He cannot endure that, for that would be the final mockery of his nature. And he will not" (*IEG*, p. 133). The God we see in Christ could not be the willing supervisor of an eternal torment without entering into self-contradiction and thereby simply ceasing to be God (*IEG*, p. 118).

Robinson's cross-centered arguments help to clarify what is at stake between the Augustinian and Origenist traditions taken at their best. What is at stake, one might say, are two different views about how to interpret Scripture. The Augustinians hug close to the shoreline, so to speak, whereas the Origenists launch much farther out to sea. The Augustinians accuse the universalists of overlooking too much prominent timber when sighting the mainland, whereas the Origenists accuse the retributionists of not seeing the forest for the trees. The Augustinians would say that the forest is fraught with inscrutability; the Origenists, that any inscrutability is overridden by intelligible significance. The Augustinians would point to the rank undergrowth of sin in its great obduracy and abomination; the Origenists, to the towering peaks of divine love. The Augustinians would insist that faith must arise in this life as the necessary condition of deliverance; the Origenists would retort that the sufficient condition of deliverance is found in the assured persistence of divine grace. The debate, taken as a whole, arguably results in an impasse. Whether this impasse can be resolved is the theme to which we now turn.

Annihilationism: Retribution Tempered by Clemency

One effort to resolve the impasse is called annihilationism. This proposal is perhaps best understood as a cautious modification of the traditional Augustinian view. It agrees with the official tradition on every point but one. Hell is affirmed as actual, severe, penal, just, divinely ordained, and inscrutable, but it is not affirmed as endless. Like the Origenist tradition, this proposal suggests instead that the punishment of hell is limited. Unlike the Origenist tradition, however, the punishment is limited not by restoration but by annihilation. The wicked do not suffer eternal torment in the sense of suffering to all eternity after they are condemned. They are judged, terrified, and destroyed. Although this vision is not lacking in severity, it at least tempers severity with clemency. It is thus less inscrutable than the Augustinian view regarding how eternal punishment can be compatible with the nature of the divine compassion.

No distinguished theologian seems to have defended this proposal in the early church. Its only known proponent was Arnobius (fl. 304-10), an apologist who wrote a treatise attacking the errors of pagan worship and mythology. One of two fates, Arnobius argued, awaited human beings. If they have heeded God, they will be delivered from death; but if they have not known God, they will perish.[22] Those who die without God will undergo "annihilation," but it will not be sudden. Rather, it will be a "grievous and long-protracted punishment" (*AP* 2.61). Arnobius agreed with Plato that the wicked would be cast into flames, but he rejected Plato's belief in the immortality of the soul. Arnobius apparently made no use of the Christian belief in resurrection. He especially accentuated the pain of affliction experienced by the lost before they are allowed to perish.

Although annihilationism had no distinguished defenders, it is interesting to note that it did have some distinguished opponents. Both Tertullian and Augustine were familiar with the idea, and both put some effort into refuting it. It seems unlikely they would have done so had there not been at least some dissatisfaction among the Christian rank and file regarding the severity of the received tradition.[23]

Annihilationism has reappeared in recent times with some especially noteworthy defenders in the evangelical wing of the Protestant church. Prominent evangelicals like F. F. Bruce, Philip Hughes, John Wenham, and John Stott have all endorsed such a view. As was the case with Augustine, the arguments of these proponents are typically marked by careful attention to the literal sense of the biblical texts before any generalizations are ventured about the nature of God. An attempt is thus made to modify the traditional view on the basis of the very same texts by which it has always been defended.

---

22. Arnobius, *Against the Pagans* 2.14, in Arnobius, "Against the Pagans," in *The Ante-Nicene Fathers*, vol. 6, ed. Alexander Roberts and James Donaldson (Grand Rapids: Eerdmans, 1987); hereafter cited as *AP*.

23. See, for example, Tertullian, *On the Resurrection of the Flesh* 35; and Augustine, *Enchir.* 92; *CofG* 11.27; 19.28; 21.17.

A vigorous and concise case for annihilationism has been published by John Stott, the prolific Christian writer, evangelical elder statesman, and former rector of the All Souls Anglican Church in London. Hell is defined as a "banishment from God" that is "real, terrible and eternal."[24] Against the Origenist tradition, he sees no hint in the New Testament that a later reprieve or amnesty is possible. The point he wishes to explore is whether hell will involve, as the Augustinian tradition claims, the experience of everlasting suffering. "Will the final destiny of the impenitent," he asks, "be conscious torment, 'for ever and ever,' or will it be a total annihilation of their being?" (*EE*, p. 314). Scripture, he argues, does not point toward endless conscious torment, but rather toward final annihilation. If so, the Augustinian tradition will have to yield "to the supreme authority of Scripture" (*EE*, p. 315). Stott offers four arguments for his view.[25]

First, there is the argument from language. The typical vocabulary of the New Testament for the final state of perdition is, Stott suggests, the vocabulary of destruction. An extensive list of passages is adduced to back this observation. "It would seem strange," Stott concludes, "if people who are said to suffer destruction are in fact not destroyed" (*EE*, p. 316). Immortality is a gift of divine grace, not an irrevocable property of the soul. Although the impenitent will survive death and be raised up to judgment, they will finally be destroyed.

Second, there is the argument from imagery, and in particular that of fire. Fire is associated in our minds with "conscious torment," because of the acute pain we experience when burned. "But the main function of fire," observes Stott, "is not to cause pain, but to secure destruction, as all the world's incinerators bear witness" (*EE*, p. 316). Although in certain passages the fire itself is depicted as "eternal" and "unquenchable," "it would be very odd if what is thrown into it proves indestructible. Our expectation would be the opposite: it would be consumed for ever, not tormented for ever" (*EE*, p. 316). A number of objections are considered to this interpretation of fire imagery. It is argued that images like "unquenchable fire" are not incompatible with the annihilationist interpretation. Torment means that the impenitent will consciously experience both the pain of loss and the accompanying pain of affliction before they finally perish (*EE*, pp. 317-18). "The reality behind the imagery," Stott concludes, "is that all enmity and resistance to God will be destroyed" (*EE*, p. 318).

Third, there is the argument from God's justice. "I question," Stott states, "whether 'eternal conscious torment' is compatible with the biblical revelation

---

24. David L. Edwards and John Stott, *Evangelical Essentials: A Liberal-Evangelical Dialogue* (Downers Grove, Ill.: InterVarsity, 1988), pp. 312-20, on p. 314; hereafter cited as *EE*.

25. Note that Stott indicates that he holds this view "tentatively" (*EE*, p. 320).

of divine justice" (*EE*, p. 319). Although the immense gravity of sin is not to be minimized, nevertheless eternal conscious torment as a penalty does not seem proportionate to the offense. Stott in effect rejects the Augustinian appeal to inscrutability at this point.

Finally, there is the argument from New Testament texts which point toward some sort of universalism. These texts do not mean that all persons will be saved. Here Stott is firmly within the bounds of the Augustinian tradition. "The hope of a final salvation," he states, "is a false hope" (*EE*, p. 319). This conviction is based on the recorded warnings of Jesus that judgment will involve "a separation into two opposite but equally eternal destinies." Yet it is hard to see how the universalist passages could be true if the impenitent were eternally persisting in their impenitence. "It would be easier to hold together the awful reality of hell and the universal reign of God if hell means destruction and the impenitent are no more" (*EE*, p. 319).

These arguments, which are not weak, certainly deserve consideration as far as they go. Perhaps the strangest thing about them, however, is that they don't really go very far. They finally seem to be more nearly biblicist than evangelical in character. Jesus as a Teacher is afforded more prominence than Jesus as the Savior. Divine justice is considered from the standpoint of fairness, but not from the more deeply evangelical standpoint urged by Robinson when he asked about how God's justice was integrated with God's mercy. "I cherish the hope," writes Stott, "that the majority of the human race will be saved" (*EE*, p. 327). Although this seems a hope well worth cherishing, Stott articulates no real basis to make it convincing.

Reverent Agnosticism: None of the Above

When the question of universal salvation arose among the early Greek theologians, there sometimes emerged the theme of "holy silence." An initial instance of this theme may be found, for example, in Clement of Alexandria (ca. 155–ca. 220). When speaking about God's "work of saving righteousness," Clement developed a view of remedial punishment. Although this punishment took a different form for the virtuous than for the hardened, it led to repentance in either case. But that was not the whole story. "As to the rest," he wrote, "I keep silent, giving glory to God."[26] Clement did not abandon universal salvation as a hope,

---

26. Clement of Alexandria, *Stromateis* 7, 12.3–13.1. Quoted by Daley, "Apokatastasis and 'Honorable Silence' in the Eschatology of Maximus the Confessor," in *Maximus Confessor*, ed. Felix Heinzer and Christoph Schönborn (Fribourg: Editions universitaires, 1982), p. 321 n.

but he thought it best to be reticent in conclusion. A similar position may also have belonged to Origen. Although in my earlier remarks I have followed the standard interpretation, another possibility has recently been argued with some force. According to this newer outlook, Origen was more hesitant than has generally been appreciated. He did not attempt to reconcile all the statements of Scripture, because he did not really see how to do so. His views were more tentative than firm. He ventured different opinions in different places, but left the question of universal salvation open.[27] Another theologian who is generally thought to have defended universal salvation is Gregory of Nazianzus (330-89). Yet he too was a cautious supporter at best. He endorsed the universal hope of a final purgation from sins, but he could also state: "I know also a fire that is not cleansing, but avenging."[28] Finally, mention may be made of Maximus the Confessor (ca. 580-662). With him the note of holy silence openly reappears (although the contexts are often uncertain). God "loves all people equally," he wrote, and in the event of the cross God has effected "the complete salvation of the race."[29] Yet these matters are very difficult, he confessed, and there are certain problems of scriptural interpretation that it may be best to "honor by silence."[30]

Although Karl Barth is often labeled a "universalist," he is best understood as standing in the tradition of holy silence. If a forced option is urged between the proposition "All are saved" and the counterproposition "Not all are saved," Barth's answer in effect is: "None of the above." Barth deliberately leaves the question open, though not in a neutral fashion, but with a strong tilt toward universal hope. Like Origen, he finds it hard to see how God will not fully triumph in grace at the end. But like Augustine, he has a chastened sense that human sin is profoundly inscrutable. Like Origen more than Augustine, he does not find a fully clear picture emerging from Scripture. But like Augustine more than Origen, his final concern as a theologian is not so much to respect the compromised "freedom" of fallen humanity, but rather to respect above all the sovereign freedom of divine grace. The result is holy silence, or as it has sometimes also been called, "reverent agnosticism."

Barth is explicit in his rejection of the Origenist doctrine of *apokatastasis*. In its typical form, Barth observes, this doctrine argues for the restoration of all things by postulating "the infinite potentiality of the divine being" in relation

---

27. Crouzel, p. 264.

28. Gregory of Nazianzus, *On Holy Baptism* 40.36. Quoted by Daley, *Hope*, p. 84.

29. Maximus the Confessor, *Carit.* 1, 61 and *Amb. Th.* 4. Quoted by Daley, "Apokatastasis and 'Honorable Silence,'" p. 328.

30. Maximus, *Quae. Thal., Prol.* Quoted by Daley, "Apokatastasis and 'Honorable Silence,'" p. 316.

to "an optimistic estimate" of human freedom.[31] Not only are these two postulates improper, as Barth sees it, but the whole line of argument is really a groundless abstraction. The reasoning is abstract, because it posits theoretical possibilities or general principles rather than working directly from divine revelation so that the appropriate concrete particulars can be seen in relation to the relevant whole. When God is understood concretely, it is clear that he "does not owe eternal patience" to human beings who persist in the depravity of their sin, nor does he owe them final deliverance.[32] Sinners, according to biblical revelation, stand constantly under the threat of divine judgment and condemnation.

When sin is viewed concretely, moreover, it is clear that human freedom cannot be taken for granted as something that we just have. Freedom in the only relevant sense is at once the gift and requirement of God, and human beings have it only as they receive it and exercise it in obedience to God and by complete reliance on his grace. Freedom is not something that God merely "respects" in us, for it is not clear just what kind of freedom exists to be respected, unless it were the "freedom" to continue sinning. With respect to grace and freedom, Barth stands in the Pauline tradition as developed by Augustine and then especially as radicalized by Luther in works like *The Bondage of the Will*. The main characteristic of this tradition is perhaps that it heightens rather than resolves the conceptual tensions between divine sovereignty and human responsibility. These tensions can arguably not be resolved without distorting the actual encounters and renewed decisions at stake in an ongoing divine/human relationship situated in a living history.

If universal salvation should actually occur, writes Barth, "it can only be a matter of the unexpected work of grace" (IV/3, p. 477). It is not something we can calculate by a process of abstract reasoning which forgets that God is still God, and that sinners are still sinners. Not even the cross and resurrection of Jesus Christ can be used as the basis for such abstractions. In reply to christocentric universalists like Robinson, Barth writes: "Even though theological consistency might seem to lead our thoughts and utterances most clearly in this direction, we must not arrogate to ourselves that which can be given and received only as a free gift" (IV/3, p. 477). It is not for fallen sinners to deduce what God "must" do in consummating his work of salvation.

However, although there can be a danger of saying too much, there can

---

31. Karl Barth, *Church Dogmatics* II/2 (Edinburgh: T. & T. Clark, 1957), p. 295; hereafter cited as II/2.

32. Karl Barth, *Church Dogmatics* IV/3 (Edinburgh: T. & T. Clark, 1961 and 1962), p. 477; hereafter cited as IV/3.

also be a danger of saying too little. The need for "holy silence" does not annul the need for "holy speech." Although universal salvation cannot be deduced as a necessity, it cannot be excluded as a possibility. Neither the logical deduction nor the definite exclusion would properly respect the concrete freedom of God. When the reality of Jesus Christ is taken properly into account, "does it not point," asks Barth, "plainly in the direction of the work of a truly eternal divine patience and deliverance and therefore of an *apokatastasis* or universal reconciliation?" (IV/3, p. 478). This work would be "supremely the work of God" to which we as sinners have simply no claim; but although we cannot claim it as a right or a necessity, surely, writes Barth, "we are commanded to hope and pray for it" here and now. We hope and pray "cautiously and yet distinctly" that God's compassion should not fail, and that he will not cast us off forever (IV/3, p. 478).

Robinson asserted, it will be recalled, that God's justice could not be understood as something separated from God's mercy, for God's justice is in fact an expression of his mercy. Although no one has argued this point more forcefully or more extensively than Karl Barth, he still disagrees fundamentally with Robinson on a crucial point. He does not downplay the severity of God's justice, but if anything he amplifies it. The biblical God, Barth urges, is not merely a God who makes alive. Nor is he merely a God who slays and makes alive. He is a God who makes alive only by actually slaying, and who slays only to make actually alive. Again, this remark is not an abstract principle but, so to speak, a concrete narrative pattern derived from crucial elements in the biblical story, a pattern that keeps the final outcome at once oriented and yet also open. It is a remark that is concrete rather than abstract, because it is meant to be narratological rather than theoretical, and in that way theological rather than philosophical. The God of cross and resurrection whom Barth finds attested in Holy Scripture is not a God for the squeamish. But he is a God who encloses his No, however severe, within the amplitude of a much larger Yes; and yet who also hides his Yes, however luminous, deep within the abyss of his No.

No one, Barth teaches, will escape the wrath and judgment of God. "For we must all appear before the judgment seat of Christ" (II Cor. 5:10). In this judgment God does not pay obeisance to our freedom. On the contrary, he takes our freedom from us. He makes us so powerless that he hands us over to the power of our enemy, a power that is too great for us, that it may dominate us (II/2, p. 484). This enemy into whose hands we are delivered is our own sinful work. In judgment God abandons us to this work and therefore to our actual destruction. As indicated by the relevant New Testament passages, the punishment in each case is that we are handed over to the full consequences of the existence we have actually chosen for ourselves by our deeds. We do not withstand this judgment. We fall, but we fall only where we have put ourselves. We are not made alive; we are slain. "This is the work," writes Barth, "of the wrath of God. It is a stern, burning, destroying wrath. It is impossible . . . to make a single reservation or in any way to soften or diminish the severity of this event" (II/2, p. 485). Although the context for these remarks shows that Barth is thinking directly of those who have fallen away from their faith, or of those who have rejected their election, there is no reason to believe that he is not thinking indirectly of all others as well. For there is a solidarity in sin that will have similar dreadful consequences in punishment for all, regardless of any differences of degree, or of election, or of faith (cf. IV/3, p. 928).

The only question is not whether we will be judged according to our works, but whether there is somehow the possibility of hope for those who have no hope. Is there a possibility in and with the finality of our being destroyed that God may nonetheless still be enjoined to be our God? Is there a "final possibility — or, rather, an entirely new possibility beyond the completed judgment, beyond the payment of the last farthing" (II/2, p. 486)? Even for those who have rejected their election, "there is still the prospect of it," suggests Barth, "even if in endless remoteness and depth." God's punishment "is not an end in itself." God still offers something "by and beyond destruction." "What is meant," explains Barth, "is obviously the eschatological possibility, salvation on the day of the Lord. This does not remove or weaken the punishment, but it gives it a limit which encloses even that which is boundless in itself, eternal fire" (II/2, p. 486). Note that Barth does not separate the retributive and remedial elements in this punishment, nor does he diminish its severity. He looks only for the larger and hidden divine Yes that may yet surround, limit, and enclose the necessary No in all its terrible severity.

The wrath of God revealed from heaven (Rom. 1:18) is not split off from the rest of the divine life. It is a manifestation of God's saving righteousness. It is actually intrinsic, states Barth, to "the judicial sentence by which those Jews and Gentiles who believe in Jesus Christ are acquitted and justified. This sentence is itself annihilating in its action" (II/2, p. 487). Note that here Barth obviously accepts a form of annihilationism. Unlike Stott's version, it foresees not an annihilation for the few or for the many, but for all. It is an annihilation in which the only possible hope for anyone is the faith given and received by grace. This annihilation excludes all humankind, Barth comments, "from any freedom or justification except those that come by faith. It judges human beings absolutely. It utterly abandons them. It burns them right down to faith, as it were, that there it may promise and give them as believers both freedom and justification" (II/2, p. 487, rev.). God indeed annihilates us by his wrath when he hands us over to ourselves. "But what this involves," Barth writes, "is not foreign to the love of God. On the contrary, it is his love which burns in this way, burning away in human beings that which opposes and defies it, in order that they really live by faith in Jesus Christ" (II/2, p. 487, rev.), and at last be saved like a brand plucked out of the burning (Amos 4:11).

The judgment of God, the final redeeming act of God, and the return of Jesus Christ in the glory of his universal revelation are not so much three separate actions, suggests Barth, as one and the same action with three distinct aspects. This juridical, redemptive, and revelatory event will not occur only for believers. It will "not be particular but universal" (IV/3, p. 931). All human beings — each individual believer along with the whole Christian community and the entire human race — "will have to pass," states Barth, "into the burning, searching, purifying fire of the gracious judgment of the One who comes, and to pass through this fire no matter what the result may be" (IV/3, p. 931). Although the fire will be at once fearful yet also purifying and gracious, Barth deliberately ventures no suggestion about what the final result for unbelievers will be. He states only that everyone will somehow be released from "the contradiction in which they now exist," and that somehow every knee will bow, in heaven and on earth and under the earth, and every tongue confess that Jesus Christ is Lord (Phil. 2:10-11) (IV/3, pp. 931-32). The form that this confession and release will finally take for unbelievers is left open.

If one asks about the fate of those who never encountered the gospel, Barth retains his careful reticence. Like Augustine, he acknowledges that the majority of the human race actually falls into this category. Yet we may count upon it "quite unconditionally," he writes:

> that Jesus Christ has risen for each and every one of this majority too; that his Word as the Word of reconciliation enacted in him is spoken for them as it is spoken personally and undeservedly for [each individual believer], that in him all were and are objectively intended and addressed whether or not they have heard or will hear it in the course of history and prior to its end and goal; that the same Holy Spirit who has been incomprehensibly strong enough to enlighten his [the believer's] own dark heart will perhaps one day find a little less trouble with them; and decisively that when the day of the coming of Jesus Christ in consummating revelation does at last dawn it will quite definitely be that day when not [the believer] himself, but the One whom [the believer] expects as a Christian, will know how to reach them, so that the quick and the dead, those who came and went both *ante* and *post Christum,* will hear his voice, whatever its signification for them (John 5:25). (IV/3, p. 918)

The day of universal revelation, Barth suggests, as itself the day of judgment, will disclose that Jesus Christ himself has always somehow accompanied every member of the human race. If not directly through revelation by grace to faith, then he will have done so at least indirectly in some unknown and incognito form. That form will at last be divested of its hiddenness and revealed to each one for what it was and is and is to be, in its gracious significance and inevitable judgment, before the consuming fire of God.

If God's mercy were proclaimed without judgment, or if God's love were proclaimed without wrath, or if a myth of gentle leading were proclaimed in which none were slain to be made alive, and none were alive who had not been slain, then the cross of Christ would be unintelligible. God imposes no severity on others which, in the death of his Son on the cross, he has not already suffered himself to an incalculably greater degree. The punishment that we may suffer, writes Barth, "is surpassed even before it begins, and overshadowed at once, by that which the delivered Jesus Christ had to endure 'for the sake of our trespasses'" (II/2, p. 494). Barth elaborates:

> Before we are touched or can be touched by any pain which we have brought on ourselves by our sin and guilt, before we are sorry for or can be sorry for our sin, before death and hell can frighten us, and before we feel the greater terror that we are such sinners as have deserved death and hell, already in the One against whom we sin and are guilty and whose punishment threatens us we have to do with the God who himself suffers pain because of our sin and guilt, for whom it is not an alien thing but his own intimate concern. And as God is far greater than we his creatures, so much greater is his sorrow on our behalf than any sorrow which we can feel for ourselves.[33]

We know, states Barth, "only one certain triumph of hell" — the cross of Golgotha on which Jesus died for our sins — and "this triumph of hell took place in order that it would never again be able to triumph over anyone. . . . We know of only One who was abandoned in this way, and only of One who was lost. This One is Jesus Christ. And he was lost (and found again) in order that none should be lost apart from him" (II/2, p. 498). When we know this One by faith and see what he endured for the sake of the world, then no matter how desperate the situation may be, we will not abandon hope for anyone, not even for ourselves.

---

33. Karl Barth, *Church Dogmatics* II/1 (Edinburgh: T. & T. Clark, 1957), p. 373.

Conclusion: The Locus of Mystery

The strong view of hell as represented by Augustine would seem to be admirable at least for its unflinching consistency and for its steadfast appeal to the primacy and sovereignty of divine grace. If there is ever to be any larger hope within the bounds of traditional belief beyond the state of the question as Augustine left it, then that hope would seem necessarily to rest not on an appeal to unfettered human freedom (as in the weaker post-Augustinian apologies), but rather on an appeal to sovereign grace. For if it is indeed "grace alone," as Augustine argued, "that separates the redeemed from the lost" (*Enchir.* 99), and if, as he also urged, God can actually "change the evil wills of human beings, whichever, whenever, and wheresoever he chooses, and direct them to what is good" (*Enchir.* 98), then the church may finally have grounds for a larger hope than Augustine found it possible to affirm.

The New Testament texts as Augustine read them would have to be reconfigured into a very different hermeneutical whole. Although that whole may have been glimpsed by Origen, the hermeneutical tradition that he spawned has too often been encumbered by rationalizing and otherwise extraneous considerations. At its best, however, that tradition has focused concretely on the cross of Christ as the demonstration of God's love for the entire world. On that basis it has refused not only to separate God's justice so drastically from God's mercy, or indeed to leave the two standing in apparent, severe, and inscrutable contradiction. It has also refused to allow the important universalist passages in the New Testament to be so thoroughly marginalized by those that depict the ultimate consequences of divine wrath. If the mark of a good theology is that it knows how to honor the necessary mysteries, then there may be higher and reconfigured mysteries that the Augustinian tradition knows not of.

PART III

ECUMENICAL THEOLOGY

CHAPTER 11

Baptized into Christ's Death: Karl Barth
and the Future of Roman Catholic Theology

(1997)

A small but telling detail in the writings of Karl Barth is the theme of loneliness. Although he was a theologian of enormous scope and stature, or perhaps for that very reason, Barth often found himself in an isolated position when it came to the distinctive proposals of his work. Again and again he managed to set the terms for debate in a field where almost everyone seemed to disagree with him, even though they could not ignore him, and even though, as was also often the case, they had only just begun to understand him, if at all. With his uniquely innovative blend of modernism and traditionalism, he has continually baffled modernists and traditionalists alike. To this day even his most sympathetic interpreters (to say nothing of determined opponents) often end up distorting him, offering little more than a caricature to be either embraced or dismissed. Certainly one can only imagine Barth raising his eyebrows at the current crop of well-meaning enthusiasts who can think of no better way to promote his work than by extolling him as a "postmodernist" before his time. In any case, it seems safe to say that Barth's way of overlapping while also transcending the traditional categories of theological perception is at least one reason why the full measure of his achievement as a theologian has yet to be taken and assessed.

Barth's sense of theological isolation seems to have attuned him to the plight of others in comparable situations. He once opened an essay on Immanuel Kant with the remark: "The singularity of Kant's position can be seen already by the fact that . . . it is a solitary one." What Barth went on to say of Kant can be read as a piece of veiled autobiography: "He stands by himself . . . a

253

stumbling-block and rock of offence also in the new age, someone determinedly pursuing his own course, more feared than loved, a prophet almost everyone even among those who wanted to go forward with him had first to reinterpret before they could do anything with him."[1] Standing by oneself, doggedly pursuing one's own course, swimming against the stream — these were not merely the metaphors of solitary greatness, they were also imperatives to be lived out, if need be, in divergence from the rest of the Christian world. Barth could thus dramatize the responsibility of the individual Christian by remarking, again with autobiographical overtones: to the believer it is clear "that he can never regard himself as absolutely bound and controlled by others even if they are his best friends or the most eminent leaders of the community, but that in certain circumstances he may feel obliged to tread his lonely path without them or even in opposition to them, not singing with the choir, but singing solo in the hope that one day the choir will join him."[2] Nothing seems to have been more characteristic of Karl Barth than this readiness to risk everything, this astonishing venture of audacity and humility, in the hope that one day the choir might join him. The results, as he acknowledged in the final volume of the *Church Dogmatics*, were not always auspicious: "I foresee that this book," he observed with some poignancy, "which by human judgment will be my last major publication, will leave me in the theological and ecclesiastical isolation which has been my lot for almost fifty years."[3]

Barth's readiness to go it alone, to break with current fashions and venerated traditions, if necessary, whether inside or outside the church, was not without some startling consequences. It meant, as David Ford has pointed out, that he took up "an exposed position minimally supported by the prevailing culture and maximally in agreement with mainstream Christianity,"[4] regardless of how drastically that mainstream may also have been rechanneled along the way. It also meant, as Jewish theologian Michael Wyschogrod has commented, that Barth displayed an eminently Jewish sense of textual responsibility, for, like the Protestant Reformers, he adopted a policy of rooting theology unashamedly in the biblical text. "Reading a page of Barth," writes Wyschogrod, "is something like shock therapy because it introduces the reader or listener to a frame of reference that attempts only to be true to itself and its sources and not to external demands

1. Karl Barth, *Protestant Theology in the Nineteenth Century* (Valley Forge, Pa.: Judson, 1973), p. 266.

2. Karl Barth, *Church Dogmatics* III/4 (Edinburgh: T. & T. Clark, 1961), p. 514.

3. Karl Barth, *Church Dogmatics* IV/4 (Edinburgh: T. & T. Clark, 1969), p. xii; hereafter cited as IV/4.

4. David Ford in *Karl Barth: Studies of His Theological Method*, ed. Stephen Sykes (Oxford: Clarendon, 1979), p. 198.

that can be satisfied only by fitting the church's message into their mold, a mold foreign to it and therefore necessarily distorting."[5] Wanting to assimilate theology into the foreign mold of the surrounding culture, Wyschogrod suggests, is an essentially Gentile aspiration.[6] Barth's single-minded, almost talmudic devotion to the idea that Christian theology is substantial in its own right — that it does not need buttressing by external disciplines, whether philosophical, sociological, psychological, or whatever, in order to be meaningful — at once sets him apart as old-fashioned and yet also makes him alluring to an increasing number of younger theologians in the present day.

It was Barth's distinguished Roman Catholic interlocutor, Hans Urs von Balthasar, however, who seemed to grasp Barth's ecumenical and historic significance in a way that is still unsurpassed. "We have in Barth," wrote von Balthasar, ". . . two crucial features: the most thorough and penetrating display of the Protestant view and the closest rapprochement with the Catholic."[7] Barth is seen as an intriguing dialogue partner for Roman Catholicism, first, because "in him Protestantism has found *for the first time* its most consistent representative" (*ThofKB,* p. 22). He represents a Protestantism that at once purifies and radicalizes the Reformation's deepest sources as found in Luther and Calvin. At the same time, however, Barth transcends the tight limits of the Reformation insofar as it was preoccupied with soteriological and ecclesiological problems. "In Barth's *Dogmatics,*" von Balthasar observes, "theology attains a breadth of subject matter and historical range that is coextensive with the Catholic understanding" (*ThofKB,* p. 23). By broadening the range of Protestant concerns even as he purified its sources and norms, Barth impressively returned theology to its first principles. He "has never forgotten for a moment," wrote von Balthasar, "that creaturely being has no other meaning but to give glory to God alone: *sola Dei gloria!* All his efforts were harnessed to see this glory, to worship it, to love it above all else, to show how it alone is worthy of our love. Rarely has Christendom heard God's love sung with such infinite, melodious beauty as in this life work" (*ThofKB,* p. 169).

No one has done more than von Balthasar to give Barth an appreciative hearing within the bounds of Roman Catholic theology, even though Barth's own pronouncements on Roman Catholicism are notoriously complex, being at once explosive and yet also irenic by turns. In trying to say something worthwhile about the unwieldy topic of "Barth and the future of Roman Catholic

---

5. Michael Wyschogrod, *The Body of Faith* (New York: Seabury Press, 1983), p. 79.

6. Wyschogrod, p. 75.

7. Hans Urs von Balthasar, *The Theology of Karl Barth* (San Francisco: Ignatius, 1992), p. 23; hereafter cited as *ThofKB.*

theology," I will obviously need to delimit my focus. I propose to proceed as follows. First, I will set forth "the *koinonia* relation" as an idea that not only captures the very heart of Barthian theology, but that also affords a two-edged assessment of Barth's relationship to Catholicism, one in which the affirmations and the criticisms cut both ways. Second, I will apply my analysis of the *koinonia* relation to the debate between von Balthasar and Rahner about the saving significance of Christ's death. Third, despite the clear convergences between Barth and von Balthasar on the death of Christ, their divergences will be explored by thinking about baptism, since Barth would suggest that the idea of our being baptized into Christ's death forces us drastically to modify the traditional Roman Catholic teaching that "grace does not destroy but perfects nature." Fourth, I will briefly comment on how the *koinonia* relation as Barth expounded it can serve to unmask the inadequacies in his own understanding of the sacraments of baptism and the Eucharist, thus opening the way for a broader potential convergence between Barthian and Roman Catholic theology on this stickiest of all ecumenical wickets. Finally, since Barth sees the divine implementation of the *koinonia* relation in our midst as in some sense approximating a model of disruptive revolutionary nonviolence, it would be a shame to pass up the opportunity at least to note the parables of grace that can be discerned from a Barthian perspective in the lonely but persistent strain of peace activism and civil disobedience in the Roman Catholic Church that ranges at least from well-known activists like Dorothy Day and Daniel Berrigan to less famous, more isolated, but perhaps no less significant figures like Roy Bourgeois and Helen Woodson. Not only does Protestantism, for all its would-be doctrinal correctness, have little to match this impressive witness, but those who attach themselves to Karl Barth, whether from the Protestant or the Catholic side, often lack all antennae for this aspect of his thought.

1. The *Koinonia* Relation:
An Exercise in Theological Anatomy

"Fellowship" is the word commonly used in *Church Dogmatics* to translate Barth's word *Gemeinschaft* in *Kirchliche Dogmatik*. Already the losses are evident. Even if this usage of "fellowship" were not slightly off, conjuring up, as it does for us today, the casual mood of the church social hall, at best it would still denote little more than a loose bond of association between comrades or equals. The richer implications of *Gemeinschaft* go by the board, especially as they unfold from the straightforward meaning of "community" out into the deeper level of "communion." Even the word *Gemeinschaft*, however, is not really adequate for Barth's purposes. For the New Testament word that underlies "fellowship" (or "communion") and *Gemeinschaft* is *koinonia*. What makes the word *koinonia* untranslatable, and therefore a good candidate for direct appropriation into English (or any language where it may be needed), is the profound and singular connotation of "mutual indwelling." *Koinonia* in Barth's sense, as in the New Testament, means that we are not related to God or to one another like ball bearings in a bucket, through a system of external relations. We are, rather, something like relational fields that interpenetrate, form, and participate in each other in countless real though often elusive ways. *Koinonia,* both as a term and as a reality, is remarkable for its range and flexibility and inexhaustible depth. In Barth's theology I think it may fairly be said that *koinonia* is the ground of all being. *Koinonia* stands for the final reconciliation and interconnection of all things through a living, luminous system of internal yet diverse relations.

The diversity that is posited within what I am calling "the *koinonia* relation" needs to be emphasized, for this diversity cannot be transcended. Not all existing *koinonia* relations, or types of relation, are interchangeable. From instance to instance, or type to type, certain defining differences are irreducible within the category. The *koinonia* in which God is God, the *perichoresis* of the Holy Trinity, is unique to itself and not substantively replicated by any other *koinonia* relation, even though it is itself the ground, the source, and the goal of all other such relations, and even though such relations are all that there finally is. The *koinonia* of the two natures of Jesus Christ in their hypostatic union is again unique to itself and not replicated substantively elsewhere.[8] The *koinonia* of Christ with his people, in their mystical union, which for Barth includes Israel as well as the church, is yet again something singular with no exact parallel elsewhere. The *koinonia* among believers themselves, as established through Word and sacrament, making them members one of another in a way that recognizes but also surmounts the unsurmountable barrier of death, is another instance of substantive uniqueness. The solidarity of believers with unbelievers in both sin and grace, and the status of believers as the vicarious forerunners before God of those who do not yet or no longer believe, is, though on a somewhat different level, still, for Barth at least, a kind of *koinonia* relation. Although the diversity of examples could be extended, my point here is not to be exhaustive but merely suggestive.

---

8. Barth would especially want to stress that in the *unio hypostatica* (as also in the *unio mystica*), no synthesis or blending between diverse realities (the divine and the human) is posited, and therefore that no common essence, status, or function emerges. *Koinonia* means intimate union between diverse realities without their being confused or changed.

A whole skein of such interlocking but differentiated unities runs throughout Barth's theology. One illustrative remark will have to suffice. "God," Barth writes, "is he who in his Son Jesus Christ loves all his children [i.e., Israel and the church], in his children all human beings, and in human beings his whole creation."[9] The operative word in this far-reaching remark — that little word which so often signals the presence of the *koinonia* relation — is simply the preposition "in." Barth became a theological master in the usage of this preposition just by following the pattern of its usage in the New Testament. Nowhere in the New Testament is the relevant pattern more prominent than in the seventeenth chapter of the Gospel according to John. It will facilitate my attempt to analyze the *koinonia* relation if we keep a portion of this rich and resonant chapter before us, namely, its concluding verses, from 17:20-26 (NRSV). We are breaking into the last part of Jesus' great prayer to his heavenly Father, sometimes called the high priestly prayer for his disciples. Note how often the prayer's discourse hinges on the preposition "in."

> I ask not only on behalf of these, but also on behalf of those who will believe in me through their word, that they may all be one. As you, Father, are in me and I am in you, may they also be in us, so that the world may believe that you have sent me. The glory that you have given me I have given them, so that they may be one, as we are one. I in them and you in me, that they may become completely one, so that the world may know that you have sent me and have loved them even as you have loved me. Father, I desire that those also, whom you have given me, may be with me where I am, to see my glory, which you have given me because you loved me before the foundation of the world.
>
> Righteous Father, the world does not know you, but I know you; and these know that you have sent me. I made your name known to them, and I will make it known, so that the love with which you have loved me may be in them, and I in them.

If we read this sublime material for insight into the nature of the *koinonia* relation, then at least five points will stand out, and these are points pervasive of Barth's theology.

First, the *koinonia* relation involves, as already suggested, a complex skein of mutual indwelling. The *koinonia* relation is always one of unity-in-distinction and distinction-in-unity. It is always a matter of two terms (or at least two terms) and a relationship, in which the relationship is one of mutual

---

9. Karl Barth, *Church Dogmatics* II/1 (Edinburgh: T. & T. Clark, 1957), p. 351, rev.; hereafter cited as II/1.

coinherence so that each term in the relation is somehow contained by the other. As the Father is in the Son, so also is the Son in the Father. The prayer asks that those who believe in the Son will also be in them, the Father and the Son. Consequently, through the Son the Father will also be in those who believe. For the Father will be in the Son, and the Son in those who believe.

Second, the emphasis falls on the oneness of the terms united in *koinonia*. Each term in the relation contains the other as a whole. The total participation of each one in the other establishes a bond of inseparable unity. The *koinonia* relation is a relation that is indivisible, and the indivisibility of the relation allows for the perfection of mutual intimacy. Each term is somehow totally internal to the other. A oneness ensues that cannot be abolished or surpassed. Those who believe are to be completely one, even as the Father and the Son are one. Mutual indwelling leads to a connection of mutual intimacy so complete that the very glory which the Son receives from the Father, given in love before the foundation of the world, is to be shared with those who dwell in them by faith. The Father's love is indivisibly one, embracing these others in his love for the Son.

Third, the oneness of the *koinonia* relation, however unsurpassable it may be, never occurs at the expense of a real distinction between the terms. Each term in the relationship retains its own particular and irreducible identity. The mutual containment of each one by the other, their complete participation in one another through love, is not a kind of mutual engulfment in which the otherness of the other is effaced. Rather it is a mutual enhancement in which the otherness of the other is somehow intensified and sustained. This ongoing integrity of particulars suggests that it is not just the relationship but also the very terms themselves that are indivisible. Just as the Father remains indivisibly and irreducibly the Father and does not become the Son, so the same kind of persistence in self-identity extends to the Son as well as to believers when examined as terms in themselves. It is worth noting in advance that much in the ensuing discussion will hinge on an aspect of this point, namely, that within the differentiated unity of the *koinonia* relation, the integrity of certain particular terms will mean that in themselves they are irreducible and indivisible.

Fourth, the terms within a particular *koinonia* relation are typically (though not without an occasional exception) ordered to one another in an asymmetrical way. One term in the relation may be original or originative while the other is somehow generated or processional. One may be the creative and unconditioned ground while the other is the created and conditioned consequence. One may have and retain the initiative while the other remains essentially responsive. One may propose while the other concurs in a bond of mutual love. While both may be engaged in an act of self-giving to the other, the self-giving of the one may be the condition for the possibility of the self-giving of the other in a way that cannot be reversed. The one may be eternally and inexhaustibly rich while the other may have nothing that it has not received. Obviously the asymmetrical ordering principle is easier to grasp when the one term in the relation is divine while the other is merely human. Yet even within the intradivine *koinonia* of the Holy Trinity as well as within the intrahuman *koinonia* of the church, traces of functional — though not of ontological — asymmetrical relations have traditionally been held to exist. Note that in our passage it is the Father who gives glory to the Son, and the Son who receives glory from the Father. It is the Son who gives to believers the glory he has received from the Father, so that believers may be one as he and the Father are one. It is the Father who gives believers to the Son, and the Son who prays for them to the Father. It is the world that depends on the oneness of believers to know that it is the Father who has sent the Son, and who in the Son has loved those who receive him. Differences within the complete unity of a *koinonia* relation, as Barth often takes pains to stress, are not only differences in the ongoing self-identity of the mutually indwelling terms, but can also involve differences of status or function as seen in the asymmetrical ordering principle that relates them.

Finally, regardless of what special form it may take, or regardless of its associated terms, and regardless of its internal asymmetries, no relation is a *koinonia* relation if it is not ineffable. The *perichoresis* of the Holy Trinity, the *communicatio idiomatum* of our Lord's incarnation, the *unio mystica* between Christ and his people, the *communio sanctorum* or *koinonia* of the saints, the solidarity of believers with unbelievers in election and rejection, in sin and grace — what do such relations all signify, each in its own distinctive way, if not a fixed measure of ineffability? Although these relations may stand in analogy to one another in simple and complex ways, they are otherwise without analogy in the world — or so Barth, at least, is courageous or foolhardy to suggest. The ineffability of the *koinonia* relation always somehow expresses, grounds, or attests the ineffability of the divine love as embodied, enacted, and revealed in our Lord Jesus Christ. The abiding christocentrism of all *koinonia* relations is itself a matter of ineffability. Like Calvin before him, Barth held that God cannot possibly be known without being loved and revered, for no true knowledge of God can exist without *koinonia* with God, without worship and prayer. In the ineffability of God's ways with us fallen, unseeing, and miserable creatures, God is either known and loved through our mutual indwelling with Christ or not at all. In short, as this exercise in theological anatomy has been meant to suggest, the *koinonia* relation is ineffable because it exemplifies the Chalcedonian pattern, and it exemplifies that formal pattern because all of its actual instances somehow converge, though in various ways, on our Lord Jesus Christ. That is to say, the *koinonia* relation is always an ineffable union of mutual indwelling in which the terms participate in one another for the sake of love "without separation or division" (inseparable unity), "without confusion or change" (irreducible identity), and with one term taking precedence over the other (asymmetry). Outside these patterns of mutual indwelling or ineffable communion, nothing is possible, Barth seems to suggest, because outside the skein of *koinonia* in which these patterns are embedded, there is nothing at all.

2. Christ in Our Place:
Reaffirming the Heart of the Gospel

The dispute between von Balthasar and Rahner about the saving significance of Christ's death can be read as a dispute about the *koinonia* relation — or more precisely, as a dispute about a particular *koinonia* relation in some central soteriological aspects. Since the bearing of the *koinonia* relation on this dispute is not obvious, I will first present the dispute in its own terms before going on to interpret it in light of its implications for our mutual indwelling with Christ.

It is not always easy to ascertain just what von Balthasar wished to criticize in Rahner's understanding of the cross of Christ.[10] It is therefore doubly hard to determine whether or to what extent his criticisms are based on an accurate reading of Rahner's position.[11] Things do not get any less complicated when we turn to Rahner's writings themselves. Not only is it sometimes easier to grasp what Rahner wishes to reject — such as a particular version of the so-called satisfaction theory. (Never mind whether that version was ever really taught by Saint Anselm — a hermeneutical quagmire in itself!) It is also almost impossible to understand his view of Christ's saving significance without appreciating the complex, and perhaps fragmentary, but still vast mosaic of his

10. On what is at stake in the dispute between von Balthasar and Rahner, Rowan Williams mentions the problem of "anonymous Christianity," the problem of the "autonomous" subject or consciousness, and the "decisive" problem of Christology. But he does not zero in, as I do here, on the problem of the saving significance of Christ's death as representing the real heart of the matter. See Williams, "Balthasar and Rahner," in *The Analogy of Beauty*, ed. John Riches (Edinburgh: T. & T. Clark, 1986), pp. 11-34, on pp. 30-31.

11. Von Balthasar presents his dispute with Rahner on the saving significance of Christ's death most importantly in the following texts: *Mysterium Paschale* (Edinburgh: T. & T. Clark, 1990) (hereafter cited as *MP*); *The Moment of Christian Witness* (San Francisco: Ignatius, 1994) (hereafter, *MCW*); and "Excursus: The Soteriology of Karl Rahner," in *Theo-Drama*, vol. IV (San Francisco: Ignatius, 1994), pp. 273-84 (hereafter, *TD* IV).

entire transcendental soteriology. Especially important would be the ongoing and mutual ontological openness that Rahner seems to posit of God and humankind for each other, an openness that he seems to establish with no need for direct reference to Christ. A nonexpert like myself, if foolish enough to enter where angels fear to tread, would do well to proceed here with caution. My observations will have to be tentative, amounting to no more than a hypothesis.

Von Balthasar's understanding of the atonement would seem a good place to begin. "The idea that in his suffering Jesus bore the sins of the world," observes von Balthasar, "is a motif that has been almost completely abandoned in the modern world."[12] It is precisely this abandonment of the atonement by modernity,[13] especially when inside the church, that von Balthasar finds so disturbing, and that he sets out if possible to redress.[14] For, like Karl Barth and (modernism notwithstanding) virtually the entire ecumenical and eucharistic tradition, he believes that the world's salvation "was embodied in a unique event" in which Jesus Christ took on himself our hopeless death as sinners before God that we might be delivered and raised to new life (*TD* IV, p. 346; quoting Barth). Von Balthasar remains unswayed by modernists like Immanuel Kant, who dismiss traditional belief that Christ died in our place as a "moral outrage."[15]

Von Balthasar finds five main features of atonement in the New Testament (*TD* IV, pp. 240-44 and 317-19). They are closely related, though the emphasis may differ from one text to the next. The first feature concerns *self-giving:* the self-giving of the Son through the Father for the sake of the world. The cross of Christ took place, from the standpoint of faith, not primarily because human actions sent Jesus to his death, but because the Father and the

---

12. Von Balthasar, "Die neue Theorie von Jesus als dem 'Sündenbock,'" *Internationale katholische Zeitschrift "Communio"* 9 (1980): 184-85, on p. 185.

13. In an unpublished paper, "Criticisms of Penal Substitution," Richard Bauckham helpfully summarizes four standard criticisms of the idea that Christ died in our place in order to bear away the penalty of our sin. As put forward in the sixteenth century by Socinus, and then repeatedly echoed and reechoed by modern figures like Kant, they are: (1) that "satisfaction" (understood as compensation paid by a third party) and forgiveness are incompatible, (2) that any "substitution" of the innocent for the guilty would be unjust, (3) that Christ's sufferings cannot be seen as "equivalent" to the punishment that sinners deserve, and (4) that substitution fosters "antinomianism." (Cited by R. L. Floyd, "Problems Facing the Idea of a Substitutionary Atonement" [unpublished paper]. I am indebted to Floyd for several references and an insightful discussion.)

14. Von Balthasar explicitly associates Rahner with certain Socinian objections to a high view of the atonement (*TD* IV, p. 274).

15. Immanuel Kant, *Religion within the Limits of Reason Alone* (New York: Harper & Row, 1960), p. 134.

Son, in an act of mutual love, freely elected to establish the world's salvation in this way. The second feature involves *exchange:* the wondrous exchange that takes place between the one who is innocent and the many who are guilty before God. In his death Christ takes our sins and gives us his righteousness; he takes our death and gives us his life. Third comes our being saved *from* something: from the consequences of our sin and guilt, from bondage to the ultimacy of death, to which we would otherwise be abandoned by God. Fourth comes that *for* which we are saved: for participation in the eternal life of the Holy Trinity, for participation which begins here and now, for our communion in love and freedom with God. Finally, there is the question of *initiative.* The event of reconciliation is grounded in the initiative of God. In effecting reconciliation God remains true to his perfect righteousness as God while also remaining true to his human creature, despite its shameful lapse into sin.

A noteworthy point of emphasis in von Balthasar's discussion is that there can be no separation between the cross and the Trinity. Von Balthasar writes: "Scripture clearly says that the event of the Cross can only be interpreted against the background of the Trinity and through faith; this is the thrust of the first and fifth motifs, namely, that God (the Father) gave up his Son out of love for the world and that all the Son's suffering, up to and including his being forsaken by God, is to be attributed to this same love. All Soteriology must therefore start from this point" (*TD* IV, p. 319). Neither can there be any separation of the cross from the incarnation. Using an argument that can be traced back in embryonic form at least to Irenaeus in the second century, and which has been regularly reiterated ever since, von Balthasar states that only someone who was at once both truly God and yet also truly human could save us by dying for our sins. "The hypostatic union," he says, "constitutes the condition for the possibility of a real assumption of universal guilt" (*MP*, p. 101, rev.). "For," the argument continues, "the redeeming act consists in a wholly unique bearing of the total sin of the world by the Father's wholly unique Son, whose Godmanhood (which is more than the 'highest case' of a transcendental anthropology) is alone capable of such an office" (*MP*, pp. 137-38). Note that here, however obliquely, the objection to Rahner starts to surface. Only God incarnate, says von Balthasar, was capable of this office. No mere human being, regardless of how admirable or exemplary, could fulfill it; for the human creature, "in his entirety," von Balthasar asserts, "is a sinner before God, there being no distinction possible here between a fallible empirical 'I' and an infallible or transcendental counterpart" (*MP*, p. 121). Again the word "transcendental" signals an unfavorable allusion to Rahner.

Let me sharpen the emerging contrast here by making a distinction between "middle" and "high" Christologies. The kind of Christology that von

Balthasar urges combines a high view of Christ's person with an equally high view of Christ's work. The *work* of Christ is regarded as *materially decisive*, because it brings about our *reconciliation* with the God toward whom we as sinners are *hostile* and by whom we stand otherwise *condemned*. A high view of Christ's *person* is *logically indispensable* to this work, because it is inconceivable that *a mere human being*, no matter how fully actualized in no matter what transcendental a way, could accomplish this work.[16] We might resort to a logical formula: "If *w*, then *p*." Only *a particular person* who was at once truly God and yet also truly human could do a work of this kind. Both the person and the work are *exclusively unique*. Christ dies in our place. He enacts both the mercy and the righteousness of God through *vicarious expiatory suffering*. This *enactment* is as *ineffable* as it is *real*. It views our sin as *radical evil*, and yet saves us from its *penalty* by bearing it and bearing it away.[17]

What I will call "middle Christology" offers a very different picture. In its truly consistent versions, however, the same formula will apply: "If *w*, then *p*." A change in the value of *w* will entail a corresponding change in the value of *p*. The work of Christ is again regarded as materially decisive for our salvation, but the definition of that work has changed. Sin is now more nearly a matter of *bondage* than of guilt, so that what we are saved from is more nearly sin's *power* than its penalty. Consequently, the work of Christ is significant for us, because what it effects is more nearly our *re-empowerment* than our complete re-creation. Because our plight is one of *estrangement* from God more nearly than of enmity and condemnation, the solution is more nearly one of our being re-united with God *through an inner experience* of spiritual re-empowerment. The cross of Christ is significant, not because of vicarious expiatory suffering, but because it shows that Jesus fully took part in the *brokenness* of the human condition *without* forsaking his spiritual union with God. We are saved *not* so much by something fundamentally unique and *unrepeatable* that took place apart from us on our behalf as by a certain communion with Christ which allows *some measure* of his perfected spirituality and destiny to be *repeated or re-*

16. Cf. Bruce D. Marshall, *Christology in Conflict: The Identity of a Saviour in Rahner and Barth* (Oxford: Blackwell, 1987). I am indebted to Marshall for use of the terms "materially decisive" and "logically indispensable" in this context.

17. For arguments that some such view of the saving significance of Christ's death had a decisive influence on the earliest shape of the church's proclamation, and that this view may well reflect Jesus' own understanding of his death, see Martin Hengel, *The Atonement: A Study of the Origins of the Doctrine in the New Testament* (Philadelphia: Fortress, 1981); Nils A. Dahl, *Jesus the Christ: The Historical Origins of Christological Doctrine* (Minneapolis: Fortress, 1991); N. T. Wright, "The Reasons for Jesus' Crucifixion," in *Jesus and the Victory of God* (Minneapolis: Fortress, 1996), pp. 540-611.

enacted in our lives. We are saved by the effect *in us* for which the work apart from us functions as little more than the precondition for its possibility. Consequently, the person who goes with this work, the *p* that is entailed by this *w*, would not be Jesus Christ the incarnate Savior (fully God, fully human) so much as *Jesus Christ the Redeemed Redeemer* (the divinely empowered human being). This person would be materially decisive, because the work he actually accomplished is efficacious for us. But he is not logically indispensable, because it would seem at least *in principle* that any other human being, if sufficiently empowered, might have accomplished or might yet accomplish much the same thing. The person of Christ required by a middle Christology is *unique but not unique in kind.*

Whether Rahner proposes some version of a middle Christology as here outlined is a nice conceptual question that need not detain us here. It will be sufficient to suggest only that such a view of Rahner's proposal is not entirely implausible, and that von Balthasar has made at least a *prima facie* case for reading Rahner, or at least large chunks of Rahner, in this light. It cannot be denied, however, that Rahner wants to press for as high a view of the incarnation, and thus of Christ's person, as he can. Whether he really needs such a high view of Christ's person given his view of Christ's work, or as he (perhaps tellingly) prefers to say, Christ's "saving significance," is another matter, as is the question of whether his anthropologically based Christology can ever finally launch itself as far up into the azure heights as he sometimes seems to want. (Remember his revealing dictum that would regard "christology as self-transcending anthropology and anthropology as deficient christology.")[18] In any case, high views of Christ's person combined with middle views of Christ's work are not unknown in the tradition.

Rahner's rejection of all high views of Christ's work under the label of "the satisfaction theory" or of "extrinsicism" and so on would seem to land him squarely in the middle camp, as would also many of his corresponding affirmations. If what was "really actualized in the life of Jesus," for example, was "his free acceptance of his death" by an act of "free obedience" which surrendered his life "completely to God," and if that same existential possibility is what becomes "historically present to us" through Christ here and now,[19] then we would again seem to be well within the bounds of middle soteriology. For the very essence of middle soteriology is the idea of salvation by spiritual *repetition:* what took place spiritually in Christ is what now takes place spiritually in us,

---

18. Karl Rahner, "Current Problems in Christology," in *Theological Investigations*, vol. 1 (New York: Crossroad, 1982), p. 164 n.

19. Karl Rahner, *Foundations of Christian Faith* (New York: Crossroad, 1982), p. 284.

i.e., the same *sort* of thing is to be repeated, regardless of all differences in degree. Although the Savior is the source of our salvation (or spiritual empowerment), the difference between the Savior and the saved would seem to be both relative and provisional. Consequently, at the consummation of all things it would seem that the Savior will be little more than the first among equals. As Cyril of Alexandria saw very well, this outcome, which loses the true distinction between Christ and the church, was the regular outcome of Antiochian Christology. Von Balthasar may not be entirely fair when he associates Rahner's "dynamic and transcendental anthropology" with "Nestorian christology," but neither may he be entirely off the mark (*MP*, p. 25). Nestorius, after all, was merely a flat-footed representative of a possibility that can be very powerfully elaborated without, it seems, eliminating some inherent weaknesses.[20]

What is at stake between Rahner and von Balthasar can be usefully described as two different views of *koinonia* with Christ. One benefit of reframing the question in this way is that it frees us from a sterile either/or. The question is not whether salvation is "extrinsic" or "intrinsic." For middle conceptions of how Christ and salvation are related, no less than for high conceptions, there are always extrinsic and intrinsic factors to be taken into account. The real question is how these factors are related, and how they are defined in the first place. *Koinonia* with Christ for the middle conception is essentially our participation in and appropriation of Christ's "spirituality," no matter whether it is called his God-consciousness, or the kingdom of God, or the new being, or authentic being-towards-death, or experiential religion, or the hermeneutical privilege of the poor, or womanspirit rising, or the rejection of violence, or the original blessing, or perhaps simply faith, or even faith formed by love. The list goes on and on, but the structure is always the same. What took place *extra nos* is no more than the condition for the possibility of what takes place *in nobis*. The *decisive locus of salvation* is not fixed in what took place in the cross of Christ there and then, but in what takes place in us or among us here and now. Salvation essentially encounters us as a *possibility* that is not actual for us *until* it is somehow actualized in our spiritual and social existence, and the *process* of actualization proceeds by degrees. Though primarily a divine gift, salvation is always *also* a human task.

20. Von Balthasar would seem to be on firmer ground when he states that Rahner's "constant attacks on a one-sided, crypto-Monophysite view of the God-man . . . lead us to suspect that what Rahner is proposing, by contrast, is an extreme Antiochene emphasis" (*TD* IV, p. 281). Oddly, on the other hand, Rahner's decision to present Christ's deity as a transcendental extension of his humanity, and his humanity as transcendentally predisposed toward deity, might suggest a larger framework of evolutionary monism, and therefore a Christology that would itself tend toward "monophysitism."

Koinonia with Christ for the high conception is not so easily described. It is a question that drives us at once into murky environs as well as essentially contested terrain. How to maintain what is valid in the middle view of salvation within the framework of a consistently high conception of Christ's person and work is really the question around which the entire Reformation pivoted, and which perhaps it never fully appreciated or successfully resolved. It is a question that not only separates von Balthasar from Rahner, but also von Balthasar from Barth. What high views, like those of von Balthasar and Barth, share over against middle views, like those of Rahner (or, if not Rahner, say, perhaps, Schleiermacher or Tillich), is the conviction that the decisive locus of salvation is what took place there and then on Golgotha, that our communion with Christ is our communion with the risen Savior who died *in our place,* that salvation encounters us as *a finished and perfect work* so that here and now it can only be received and attested *for what it is,* that neither its *actuality* nor its *efficacy* depends on our acceptance of it, that our accepting it depends rather on its *prior* actuality and efficacy *precisely* for us, and indeed for the whole world. In sum, in a high soteriology it is not Christ who points us to spirituality but spirituality that points us to Christ, who as God with us is the *exclusively unique* object of our worship and our faith. No one else will ever be God incarnate, and no one else will ever die for the sins of the world. High views agree that this conviction is the heart of the gospel,[21] and that it is compatible with much in the middle view though not with the middle framework as a whole. When it comes to understanding the *mode* by which *this* salvation is received, however, we arrive at a momentous division in the ranks and a tragic parting of the ways — as some differences between von Balthasar and Barth may serve to illustrate.

3. Baptized into Christ's Death: Grace as the *Aufhebung* of Nature

Roman Catholic theology typically speaks of salvation as a "process." When salvation is essentially conceived as a process, then either the crucial differences between a high and a middle soteriology are being left in a greater or lesser degree of obscurity, or else, if the stance is fully consistent, some version of a middle soteriology is in view. On the relation between the "extrinsic" and "intrinsic" aspects of soteriology, on what takes place *extra nos* and what takes place *in*

---

21. For some thoughtful reflections on how terms like "substitution" and "expiation" can be distorted and misused, see Gerald O'Collins, *The Calvary Christ* (Philadelphia: Westminster, 1977), pp. 108-9.

nobis and on how they are related, Catholic theology often seems ambiguous at best. The recent statement on "God the Redeemer," published by the papal International Theological Commission, would seem to be a case in point.[22] The statement seems to combine a high view of Christ's person with an unsteady or indeterminate view of Christ's work. Although vacillating between high and middle soteriological elements, the statement seems clearest when asserting the middle elements. The "process of redemption," we read, is something that "continues to the end of time" (ITC, p. 195). Redemption is not so much a completed work (although that note is not entirely missing) as it is a work in the process of completion. It "completes itself in the risen life of the Savior" as that risen life communicates itself to the life of faith over the course of time (ITC, p. 195). Sinners are not redeemed, it seems, until they "open themselves" to grace and, with the "help" of grace, live new lives of obedience and hope (ITC, pp. 195-96). Jesus' "dispositions," we read, must be carried on and completed "in ourselves"; we ask him to "perfect" them in us even as we strive also to actualize them (ITC, p. 197). Redemption is not, apparently, the work of God in Christ alone. Since Christ cannot be separated from his community, he draws the community itself "into the work of bringing about the redemption" (ITC, p. 198).

When von Balthasar writes of these matters, the objective dimension of our salvation achieves a sharper profile. Although he wants to maintain what he calls "the entire existential seriousness" of salvation, he does not essentially conceive of it as a "process." That is, he places all elements of gradualism decidedly in the background. The concept of "process" is fundamentally inadequate to the mystery of this event. It puts the accent inevitably in the wrong place, concentrating our attention on what is happening *in nobis* here and now. Salvation comes to us as the finished work of Christ in which we are already wholly included. In the *pro nobis* of Christ's self-surrender on the cross, says von Balthasar, we find ourselves already taken over by his love and yielded up into communion with the Holy Trinity, into "the opening up of the Triune love for sinners" (*MP*, p. 139). Faith is therefore not our own work, but "the ratification of what God has done in finished form" (*MP*, p. 139). By what God has done for us in Christ, we are already transferred into "the sphere of the triune Love" (*MP*, pp. 139-40). Thus in a simple but profound statement about *koinonia*, von Balthasar can write: "The Christ who lives in me is so deeply within me (and closer than I am to myself) because he died for me, because he took me to himself on the Cross and constantly takes me to him again in the Eucharist" (*MCW*, p. 112).

---

22. See "Select Questions on the Theology of God the Redeemer," *Communio* 24 (1997): 160-214; hereafter cited as ITC.

From a Protestant standpoint, von Balthasar represents an extremely hopeful development in Catholic theology. Rarely has a Catholic theologian incorporated the concerns of Reformation soteriology so sympathetically into the heart of his life's work. One cannot help but feel that with von Balthasar the true face of the Reformation has finally been seen and that its deepest word has really been heard. It is only with a kind of troubled perplexity, therefore, that Protestant theology will still find even von Balthasar clearing a place to speak of how redeemed sinners can somehow "merit" their salvation (*ThofKB*, p. 10), and of how they can themselves "cooperate" in achieving it, "thereby sharing in the work of redemption" (*ThofKB*, p. 375). If a Protestant theology which remains true to the Reformation does not and cannot consent to such ideas, feeling that regardless of whether they may still represent church-dividing differences they are nonetheless matters on which the church truly stands or falls, then it will need to state its case with renewed clarity and conviction.

Karl Barth expressed the typical Protestant worry that Catholic theology takes neither sin seriously enough as sin, nor grace seriously enough as grace. When salvation is seen as a process, he noted, then "sin and grace are understood as quantities."[23] Seeing them as "quantities," as matters of degree, as susceptible of increase or decrease, and therefore as complementary or correlative, is the fatal move. "On this assumption," he observed, "they are compared and pragmatized and tamed and rendered quite innocuous. . . . The practical consequence of all this is that the misery of humankind is not regarded as in any way serious or dangerous . . ." (IV/2, p. 498, rev.). For sin and grace to be seen as the dangerous matters they really are, he continued, they must be seen "as totalities which do not complement but mutually exclude one another" (IV/2, p. 498, rev.). They must be seen, in other words, as categorical. Just as one cannot be a little bit pregnant or a little bit dead, so one cannot be a little bit sinful or a little bit righteous. Sin and righteousness are predicates that either apply to us as whole persons before God, as intensively and extensively as possible, or not at all. The proper metaphor for the victory of grace over sin is not reform but revolution.

The statement that "grace does not destroy but perfects nature" is at best a half-truth.[24] From a Reformation theological standpoint, at least, grace

---

23. Karl Barth, *Church Dogmatics* IV/2 (Edinburgh: T. & T. Clark, 1958), p. 498; hereafter cited as IV/2.

24. For a place where Barth accepts this formulation, see II/1, p. 411. Note that Barth's acceptance is carefully qualified. Grace can be said to "presuppose" and "perfect" nature, because grace involves more than just the negative moment of radical judgment upon sin. (It also involves divine patience as well as radical transformation and ultimate renewal.) Although the formulation is (and remains) "dangerous" (because of the way in which it glosses over the negative moment), says Barth, it is not wrong in what it positively wants to assert. Cf. also II/1, pp. 197-98.

perfects nature precisely by destroying it.[25] "The real God," writes Barth, "where he is known, kills the natural man with all his possibilities in order to make him alive again" (II/1, p. 90).[26] "What the Bible calls death," Barth urges, is not merely "sickness." "What it calls darkness" is not merely "twilight." "What it calls incapability" is not merely "weakness." "What it calls ignorance" is not merely "confusion" (II/1, p. 105). Where the grace of God really comes to lost sinners, they are judged, abolished, and raised again to new life. Created nature is not so much continued in this drastic event as it is superseded and reconstituted (II/1, p. 274). The pattern of grace in the radical overthrow of sin is the pattern of *Aufhebung*. Fallen human creatures are affirmed insofar as they are creatures, negated insofar as they are fallen, and raised again to new life. They are affirmed, negated, and then reconstituted on a higher plane, not partially but completely, not gradually through an existential process but once-for-all through a disruptive, eschatological event that is at once centered in the cross of Christ and yet inclusive of the entire world. The moment in the life of believers corresponding to this cataclysmic revolutionary occurrence is baptism.

"Do you not know," wrote Saint Paul in his Letter to the Romans, "that all of us who have been baptized into Christ Jesus were baptized into his death?" (6:3 NRSV). What this affirmation means, Barth comments, is that Christ's death includes our death in itself, even as his resurrection includes ours in itself

---

25. The connotation of the word "nature" would seem to change from "created" to "fallen" or "corrupted" human nature as we move here from the first statement to the second. My point could thus be reformulated by saying: "Grace perfects human nature as created only as grace destroys human nature as fallen." In other words, those who would accept the second or "Protestant" part of the statement need not disagree that "created nature" is somehow "perfected" and "exceeded" in the *status redemptionis*. What they would actually find missing in the typical "Catholic" statement, however, is an adequate indication of just how entirely (and not partially) "created nature" is deformed by sin in the *status corruptionis,* and consequently of just how drastically it meets with doom in the cross of Christ (Rom. 8:3). While of course it is one and the same baptized human being who is subjected to death and resurrection in and with Christ (Gal. 2:20; Col. 3:1), the condition for the possibility of that human being's continuity (or self-identity) through the abyss of this unheard-of transition (from death as a sinner to resurrection as a new creature) is, from a Reformation standpoint, not at all to be found in some potentiality of "created nature" but solely in the freedom of God's grace (cf. Rom. 11:6). No potentiality of human nature would seem to be either necessary or possible to account for a person's continuity of self-identity through this disruptive transition. If grace is really the necessary and sufficient condition, then any appeal to some presumed natural potentiality would only serve to detract from the actual miracle and mystery of grace.

26. Cf. Karl Barth, *Church Dogmatics* IV/1 (Edinburgh: T. & T. Clark, 1956), pp. 253-54, 296.

as well.[27] It means that Christians are made to be contemporaneous with Christ in his death and that Christ in his death becomes contemporaneous with them. Barth writes:

> Christians are people to whom the irrevocable and irreversible thing has happened, namely, that the crucifixion of Jesus Christ has become a present event for them, not as they are taught about it and persuaded of its significance, . . . but by the Holy Spirit in the power of his living Word. It is present as that which took place at Golgotha: the decisive moment of his history has become the decisive moment of their own history. The old man they were has been crucified with him and totally and definitively robbed of his power (Rom. 6:6, Gal. 2:19, 5:24). As those they were they are dead with him (Rom. 6:8, Col. 3:3). By their participation in his death, old things have perished to return no more; they have been destroyed and terminated (II Cor. 5:17). This death is theirs, the death of their old being, as they have themselves been baptized. . . . The confirmation of the death of the old man . . . is expressed in their baptism with water. (IV/4, p. 145)

The old sinful human being has been put to death with Christ once for all. Our own death as sinners has been effected by him who died in our place. With him we are crucified and done away with, that we might be raised with him to new life. In baptism "our own complete displacement as people of sin" is set before us as that which has already taken place in Christ (IV/4, p. 91).[28]

The relationship between the Christ who died in our place and those who receive him by faith is a *koinonia* relation. It is a relationship of mutual indwelling, of unity-in-distinction and distinction-in-unity. Christ and believers are related by a pattern of mutual coinherence such that each of them is somehow contained by the other in an inseparable bond of unity. Each is contained by the other precisely as a whole, for believers are completely baptized into Christ's death even as Christ now lives completely in them as the one who died for them, clothing them with his perfect righteousness and granting them resurrection life. Nevertheless, each of them retains his own particular and irreducible identity, even as each of them exists in and for the other as an indivisible whole.

Here is one of the deepest moments in the high soteriology of the Refor-

---

27. Karl Barth, *The Christian Life* (Grand Rapids: Eerdmans, 1981), p. 21.

28. Cf. Gregory of Nazianzus: "We needed an incarnate God, a God put to death, that we might live. We were put to death together with him, that we might be cleansed; we rose again with him because we were put to death with him; we were glorified with him, because we rose again with him" (*Oration* 45.28).

mation. It is not only that sin and righteousness are categorical terms in themselves. They are categorical for a particular reason. Sin and righteousness are categorical as predicates of indivisible persons. The person is always completely in the predicate, so to speak, even as the predicate is always completely in the person before God. It is thus Christ himself, the Reformation affirms, who is our righteousness and our life (cf. I Cor. 1:30). Righteousness and life are not abstract, divisible quantities. When we receive Christ as he receives us, we receive his predicates categorically through our *koinonia* with him, which allows for the wondrous exchange. We participate in them as we participate in him, and as he participates in us. There is no place here, at the primary eschatological level, for a process that proceeds gradually by increments or degrees. In the turning point of the ages that took place in the cross of Christ, grace as a whole abolished sin as a whole, so to speak, so that we have already been made completely righteous and alive before God. "You have died," we read in Colossians, "and your life is hid with Christ in God" (3:3). The indivisibility thesis that is everywhere in evidence throughout the skein of *koinonia* relations has, according to Reformation belief, a strong soteriological bearing.

The asymmetrical ordering principle, furthermore, also has a soteriological bearing. It blocks all possibility of our cooperation in the work of redemption.[29] The righteousness and life that we sinners receive categorically

---

29. Interestingly, Barth does allow for our human "cooperation" at the *in nobis* or "existential" level. He does so when writing about sanctification in its aspect as "the awakening to conversion." Barth does not see this awakening, however, as our redemption itself. Rather he sees it as our personal reception of redemption (through our "awakening" to it), and thus as the onset of our active participation in it by faith. Barth stresses repeatedly that in the strict and proper sense our salvation has already been accomplished *extra nos* by Jesus Christ perfectly and once for all. It has thus been accomplished in a way that is all-sufficient and all-inclusive so that it cannot be supplemented, restricted, augmented, or increased. We do not, need not, and cannot "cooperate" in the work of accomplishing it. As accomplished exclusively by Jesus Christ in our place and on our behalf, salvation is fully and finally identical with our living Lord himself in the unity of his person and work. However, we do "cooperate" in our reception of it, or better, of him, in our awakening to conversion. Thus Barth writes that "this awakening is both wholly creaturely and wholly divine. Yet the initial shock comes from God. Thus there can be no question of co-ordination between two comparable elements, but only of the absolute primacy of the divine over the creaturely. The creaturely is made serviceable to the divine and does actually serve it. It is used by God as his organ or instrument. Its creatureliness is not impaired, but it is given by God a special function or character. Being qualified or claimed by God for co-operation, it co-operates in such a way that the whole is still an action which is specifically divine" (IV/2, p. 557). Note that the "asymmetrical ordering principle" may thus be said to obtain here in two distinct senses: not only in the mode by which our salvation has been accomplished by Christ there and then *extra nos*, but also and in another way in the mode by which it is imparted to us and received by us at the "existential" level here and now.

through our mutual indwelling with Christ are his alone to confer. We contribute nothing to Christ in his work of salvation but our unworthiness and shame, which that work by definition removes from us that we might live and be free for communion despite what we have been (and are) in ourselves. The entire gospel, as understood by the Reformation, depends on the affirmation that Christ's righteousness and life become ours as a gift that is received not by works but by faith alone. Because salvation is not properly a process but a once-for-all event that comes to us whole and entire, as a sheer gift, which is Christ himself, salvation is the stable basis and not the uncertain goal of the Christian life.

The asymmetrical ordering principle means that there can be no question of any kind of mutual conditioning between Christ and believers in this event. It is Christ who gives and we who receive, actively participating in his righteousness by grace through faith. The relationship is irreversible. Even the faith by which Christ is received is and remains his gift. How can there be any mutual conditioning between Christ and faith, asks Barth, when faith "lives entirely by him, and derives its whole reality from him" (II/1, p. 133)? What do we have, Augustine asked in constant echo of Saint Paul, that we have not received? The receptive moment is radicalized by the Reformation to exclude any suggestion of symmetry, and therefore of mutual dependency, in the relationship between Christ and faith. Cooperation in Christ's work of salvation is thereby excluded as something neither possible nor necessary. That salvation comes to us as a perfect gift is the very essence of the gospel's good news.

A soteriological bearing, finally, can also be seen in the ineffability postulate of the *koinonia* relation. For how are the extrinsic and intrinsic aspects of our salvation related if not by the ineffable Chalcedonian pattern? What took place *extra nos* is related to what takes place *in nobis* without separation or division, without confusion or change, and with the precedence falling to the *extra nos*. Our mutual indwelling with Christ includes, so to speak, this trans-historical vector of relations. Christ is inseparable from his work, as his work is inseparable from himself. His being is in his act, Barth famously asserts, even as his act is in his being. To enter into communion with Christ means to enter into communion with him as the one who embodies his history. We participate in his history, in his life, death, and resurrection as the history of our salvation, by participating in him by faith. The pattern of this participation can be described in formal, Chalcedonian terms, but the participation, the communion, the *koinonia*, when so described, is ineffable.

Nevertheless, von Balthasar rightly challenges Barth, it seems to me, for rejecting all talk of growth or progress in the Christian life (*ThofKB*, p. 371).

More precisely, Barth, though certainly not ruling out growth or progress, has very little to say about them. Since, when seen from the standpoint of a high soteriology, they have been vastly overemphasized by Protestant and Catholic theology alike, Barth, following Luther, at least functions as a massive corrective. Yet if we wish to think through the full meaning of a high soteriology, von Balthasar points us in the right direction. "Within the absolute predicates," he intriguingly remarks, "and always as expression of the real event, there is room for differing degrees, means, circumstances, for more and less, for drawing closer and moving farther away, for growth and diminution" (*ThofKB*, p. 366). How to conceive and coordinate properly the various soteriological complexities at this point is, it seems to me, one of the great unsettled questions in ecumenical theology today.[30]

My own hunch, for what it's worth, is that baptism may again provide a key. Insofar as baptism is both a gift and a vocation, it combines both the idea of a once-for-all saving event, which baptism attests by being administered to each believer (or in the case of infants, each "proleptic" believer) only once, with the idea that dying and rising with Christ is also our daily vocation. Barth knew how to highlight the "once-for-all" and the "again and again" aspects of our dying and rising with Christ,[31] but unfortunately failed to do justice to the

---

30. My concession to von Balthasar at this point implies that the metaphors of "reform" and "revolution" need not be mutually exclusive in any comprehensive understanding of salvation. "Reform," however, would need to be understood as determined by the context of "revolution." For being baptized into Christ's death means that the central narrative of our salvation is (and remains) revolutionary. The narrative of our salvation is essentially "revolutionary," because it is the narrative of Christ's death and resurrection *extra nos* (in which sin and death are overthrown even as there is established a radically new order of grace). His narrative *is* our narrative — not in the "existentialist" or allegorizing sense, of course, but by virtue of *koinonia*, i.e., of our real participation in what actually took place there and then once for all (a participation by grace through faith, by our contemporaneity with Christ, and of Christ with us, through Word and Spirit). At the *in nobis* level, the one event that always corresponds to this revolutionary narrative is baptism. Beyond that, as I go on to suggest, the *in nobis* level will include various "once-for-all," "again and again," and "more and more" aspects (i.e., aspects that are both "revolutionary" and "reformist") in particular combinations unique to each believer.

31. The "again and again" aspect is what Barth means when he writes, as he often does, of God's grace being "new each morning," and of our constantly "beginning again at the beginning." When we pray the Lord's Prayer, for example, we acknowledge our complete dependence on God's daily providence, forgiveness, protection, and deliverance. From this perspective salvation is not so much a gradual process as something that encounters us ever anew *in continuo actu*. For a subtle but important indication of how Barth would incorporate the "more and more" motif of progressive or gradual growth within an existential context determined and dominated by the "again and again" motif of repetition and continual renewal *in nobis*, see IV/2, p. 631.

"more and more" aspect as well. Perhaps the future of Roman Catholic theology will depend on the degree to which it can follow von Balthasar's lead by eliminating the misplaced concreteness that it has traditionally set on salvation as an existential or ecclesial "process" in favor of a richer, more complex, and more truly christocentric soteriology.[32]

4. The Bread That We Break: Rediscovering the *Koinonia* Relation

Two brief comments will bring these reflections to a close. Roman Catholic believers will undoubtedly shake their heads in dismay at a Reformed theology and a low-church Protestantism that slights a theology of baptism and the Lord's Supper, and especially that slights eucharistic worship. The future of ecumenical theology will also depend, I suspect, on the extent to which these Protestant deficits can be overcome. Here Karl Barth would seem to be more a part of the problem than the solution. Nevertheless, in spite of himself, he may have given us some openings. Barth famously rejected applying the term "sacrament" to baptism and the Eucharist on the grounds that Jesus Christ himself is the only true sacrament. (He preferred to see them as "means of gratitude" rather than as "means of grace.") Yet Barth's logic here seems strangely inconsistent with other positions that he takes. For although Jesus Christ is also the one Word of God, that does not prevent Barth from presenting Holy Scripture and biblical preaching as secondary forms of God's Word. One can only ponder somewhat wistfully about the ecumenical impact if Barth had seen his way clear to match the section on the threefold Word of God in the first volume of

---

32. The idea of "process" would thus be controlled by the idea of "participation." Any process by which it might be said that a person "is being saved" (cf. II Cor. 2:15), for example, or by which salvation is being "worked out" (cf. Phil. 2:12), would be determined by that person's prior participation in "salvation" as the finished work of Christ (through *koinonia* with Christ, who just *is* our salvation) (cf. IV/2, p. 377). Strictly speaking, what would be seen as existing in a process of becoming would not be one's "salvation" as a goal yet to be attained by degrees, but one's "existential appropriation" of the salvation that has already been given and received by faith. "Become what you are!" (by grace through faith) would be the watchword, not "Become what you are not, but might be!" (if you fulfill certain conditions, by grace through faith). "Become what you are!" would put the believer in the mode of pure, if active, reception; "Become what you are not, but might be!" would put the believer in the mode of "cooperating" in the work of salvation. Seeing salvation as a process of divine/human "cooperation," in which human efforts help bring salvation into being, is something which Reformation-oriented Protestants will feel must be completely avoided as contrary to the gospel.

the *Church Dogmatics* with a corresponding section on the threefold sacrament. I can see no reason why he could not have coordinated baptism and the Lord's Supper with preaching, and the idea of the church as sacrament with Scripture as the written Word. Jesus Christ would have remained the one true sacrament in the strict and proper sense even as he remained the one true Word of God.

Moreover, what Barth has taught us about how to understand the *koinonia* relation may be surprisingly applicable to the sacramental question. Here I will have to remain cryptic, but I think it cannot be without interest that I Corinthians 10:16 reads: "The cup of blessing which we bless, is it not a *koinonia* in the blood of Christ? The bread which we break, is it not a *koinonia* in the body of Christ?" If we were to apply the Barthian logic of the *koinonia* relation as I have developed it in this essay to this statement about how the *signum* and the *res* are related, perhaps large segments of the church might converge around the results. "Sign" and "reality" would thus be seen as related by complete mutual coinherence, so that the sign was in the reality even as the reality was also in the sign, without separation and division, without confusion or change, and with the reality taking precedence over the sign.[33] While the bread would remain bread, for example, it would properly be designated "the body of Christ" by virtue of its "sacramental union" (a term accepted by both Luther and Calvin in this context) or "mutual indwelling" with the body of the risen Christ. The kind of *koinonia* relation suggested here might at least help to integrate Lutheran and Calvinist concerns, and might even do so in a way that Roman Catholics would also find promising.

5. An Order That Did Not Previously Exist:
Parables of Grace in the Disruption and the Renewal of All Things

Francine du Plessix Gray may have shown greater insight than she knew when years ago she described the antiwar activities of the Berrigan brothers as "the theology of crisis" in action.[34] What activists like the Berrigans, Dorothy Day, Roy Bourgeois, and Helen Woodson can all be said to represent is a break with

---

33. Support for this way of reading I Cor. 10:16 may be found in Ernst Käsemann, "The Pauline Doctrine of the Lord's Supper," in *Essays on New Testament Themes* (London: SCM, 1964), pp. 108-35, on pp. 109 and 128.

34. Francine du Plessix Gray, *Divine Disobedience: Profiles in Catholic Radicalism* (New York: Doubleday, 1977), p. 137.

utilitarian Christianity.[35] Middle soteriologies of existential empowerment lend themselves all too easily to the kind of instrumentalism in which Christology degenerates into a mere function of soteriology. The radical peace witness within the Catholic Church might be understood better than it sometimes understands itself as the embodiment of a disruptive nonviolent praxis which stands as a living parable of divine grace,[36] at least as that grace was defined by Karl Barth. Barth wrote:

> Grace is the majesty, the freedom, the undeservedness, the unexpectedness, the newness, the arbitrariness, in which the relationship to God [i.e., *koinonia*] and therefore the possibility of knowing him is opened up to man by God himself. Grace is really the orientation in which God sets up an order which did not previously exist, to the power and benefit of which man has no claim, which he has no competence even subsequently to justify, which in its singularity — which corresponds exactly to the singularity of the nature and being of God — he can only recognize and acknowledge as it is actually set up, as it is powerful and effective as a benefit that comes to him. (II/1, p. 74)

Barth himself believed, I suspect, that a church which had a better grasp of grace as a disruptive revolutionary event would be a church better prepared to resist accommodations with the troubling excesses of the modern world, nowhere more evident than in indiscriminate weapons of mass destruction and the conduct of modern warfare. When asked in 1959 to indicate the most vital issue confronting the church, Barth replied: "Atomic warfare," and then added: "How do you explain the fact that the large Christian bodies cannot produce a definite yes or no on the matter of atomic warfare? What significance has this fact, first, in regard to the Church's own message; second, in regard to the world around her?"[37] Perhaps if Roman Catholic theology can somehow find its way

---

35. See H. Richard Niebuhr, "Utilitarian Christianity," *Christianity and Crisis* 6 (July 8, 1946): 3-5; George Hunsinger, "Where the Battle Rages: Confessing Christ in America Today," chapter 4 in this volume; Hunsinger, "The Note in the Bottle," in *Barth, Barmen, and the Confessing Church Today*, ed. James Holloway (Lewiston, N.Y.: Edwin Mellen Press, 1995), pp. 227-93, esp. pp. 259-68.

36. The emergence of exemplary Christian lives was, Barth felt, one of the "basic forms" of the Christian community's ministry. "The community always needs and may point to the existence of specific individuals who . . . stand out as models or examples in their special calling and endowment — [the community's] witness being more clear and comprehensible and impressive in their persons and activity than in those of others" (*Church Dogmatics* IV/3 [Edinburgh: T. & T. Clark, 1962], p. 888).

37. *Christianity Today* 4 (October 2, 1959): 29.

to a higher soteriology of grace, it will at the same time have discovered a theology better able to match and encourage its own most courageous and inspiring praxis.[38]

38. I do not mean to suggest that radical pacifist activism is the only way to be a Christian in contemporary society, but I do mean to suggest that such activism as exemplified by the Christians whose names I have mentioned serves as an important prophetic sign of witness to the gospel. As Robert McAfee Brown wrote years ago, the actions of such Christians may be more nearly "signs" than "models." But the question remains:

> Signs or models? The Berrigans are a legitimate prophetic sign to us so long as we do not let their actions go bail for our inactions, and they will remain an ongoing prophetic sign by continually keeping us off balance, as their very absence from our immediate midst forces us continually to re-evaluate the kind of society that brands them criminals. But if they *free* us to make our own protests in our own ways, they also *bind* us to make those protests more sharply tomorrow than we did yesterday, and to face the uncomfortable possibility that what we may be called upon to do next week is of a magnitude we would not even have considered last month. (Brown, "The Berrigans: Signs or Models?" in *The Berrigans*, ed. William Van Etten Casey and Philip Noble [New York: Praeger, 1971], pp. 60-70, on p. 70)

CHAPTER 12

What Karl Barth Learned from Martin Luther

(1998)

TO WAYNE STUMME, WITH GRATITUDE

The word of Luther is and will be heard afresh. . . . Luther's single-minded, noncalculating investigation of the Scriptures would allow his voice to break through the cultural accretions to the gospel, even when modern findings differ from his.

Heiko A. Oberman[1]

No theologian receives a longer entry in the index volume to Karl Barth's *Church Dogmatics* than Martin Luther. Although John Calvin runs a close second, the entry for Luther exceeds that for Schleiermacher and Aquinas combined, and is far longer than those for any other major figure, including Athanasius, Augustine, or Anselm. Of course, an observation like this reveals very little except that Barth's engagement with Luther was extensive. It tells us nothing about whether the various references are favorable or critical, or whether they are passing or significant. Nor does it disclose any notable allusions to Luther or, more importantly, any lines of his influence that may remain tacit or implicit. Yet it does suggest that Luther was a towering figure in Barth's mind.[2]

1. Heiko A. Oberman, "The Impact of the Reformation: Problems and Perspectives," in *The Impact of the Reformation* (Grand Rapids: Eerdmans, 1994), pp. 173-200, on p. 199.

2. As Gerhard Ebeling has observed, in the early volumes of Barth's *Church Dogmatics*, Luther is cited heavily, but with diminishing frequency as the volumes go on. Although correct in itself, this observation leads Ebeling to draw the conclusion, erroneously, that in Barth's dog-

However, a widespread impression currently exists, mistaken in my opinion, that Barth's assessment of Luther was mostly negative. For example, in *Martin Luther: An Introduction to His Life and Work* (Philadelphia: Fortress, 1986), Bernhard Lohse devotes as much attention to Barth as to any other modern interpreter, yet Lohse finds nothing favorable to report. He presents Barth on Luther as little more than a compendium of complaints. Yet if Barth's debt to Luther is as enormous as I think it is, this all-too-common perception gives one pause. How could Barth's massive accord with Luther come to be so roundly overlooked?

Karl Barth, as everyone knows, was a sharp and vigorous critic. Who else could have written that now famous essay against Brunner that was simply entitled "No!"? Luther is not the only figure for whom Barth's No has seemed louder than his Yes. Yet it is an axiom of Barth's theology not only that the No is always spoken for the sake of the Yes, no matter how one-sidedly the No may be uttered in any particular situation, but also that the No itself is always finally contained by a larger Yes, even when that Yes remains unspoken. This axiom is exemplified in Barth's practice of theological criticism more often than might be supposed. Kant, Schleiermacher, Hegel, and Feuerbach, for example, are well-known targets of Barth's polemical displeasure. Yet as he himself was well aware, his theology would have been unthinkable without them. Something of great value was to be appropriated from each. How much more of great value was waiting to be garnered from the preeminent Reformer! Almost every objection that Barth ever made against Luther was ventured on "Lutheran" grounds. If he sometimes criticized Luther, it was for the sake of Luther — with questions that would never have become possible without all that Luther had bequeathed to him.

Vigorous polemic, of course, is not something that can be said to have distinguished the one theologian widely from the other. Luther, too, knew how to discharge polemical broadsides. Even allowing for the uninhibited conventions of the day, he was infamous even in his own lifetime for dashing off pamphlets with insults for titles like *Against the Papal Ass in Rome, Against the Incendiary Sophists of Louvain University,* or even *Against Jack Sausage,* to say nothing of the offensive content present in certain passages and notorious treatises. Aware that his polemical excess worried even his friends, Luther did not try to conceal his real or possible flaws. He once contrasted himself as a polemicist with Melanchthon: "I was born to take the

---

matics Luther is of diminishing importance. What Barth learned from Luther cannot be appreciated through statistical calculations. See Ebeling, *Lutherstudien,* vol. 3 (Tübingen: J. C. B. Mohr [Paul Siebeck], 1985), pp. 531-32.

field and fight with the hordes and the devil, and therefore my books are very stormy and warlike. I have to dig out the roots and trunks, cut down the thorns and hedges, and fill up the pools; I am the crude lumberjack who has to blaze a trail and prepare the way. But Master Philip goes about quietly, building and planting, joyfully sowing and watering as God has richly given him his gifts to do."[3]

Yet, animating Luther's polemical vehemence was always a profound concern for the truth. Commenting on the story of Paul's bold controversy with Peter at Antioch (Gal. 2:11-14), Luther argued that when it comes to defending the gospel, "we have to be stubborn and unbending," because "what is involved here is not the cause of Peter or our parents or the emperor or the world or of any other creature; it is the cause of God himself."[4] This acute sense that faithfulness to the gospel is a matter of life and death may well have been a disposition that Luther helped inspire in Barth. Certainly the dangers of dogmatism seemed less urgent to both theologians than the need for boldness in the midst of crisis. The Reformation, wrote Barth, in language that echoed Luther, "could not surrender truth to unity."[5] The church's unity was supremely important for both theologians, but not at the expense of the gospel.

Barth, at least, was not oblivious to the risks such boldness might run. He had no use, as he said, for "the intolerance of a man who regards his own way as right and all others as pernicious, or the excited resistance of one who is not sure of his own ground and is thus driven to lash out all the more fiercely."[6] He knew that intolerance was the root of persecution (IV/3, p. 199). Yet he also knew that charges of intolerance can be cheap, and more importantly that they are virtually inevitable. "The Christian who is in some measure alive," he remarked, "even though he be sincerely open and patient, must always give the impression of unfitting and culpable intolerance" (IV/3, p. 496). Living constantly under the threat of death for his beliefs, Luther also understood that boldness must be tempered by openness, forbearance, and charity. He rejected the use of compulsion in matters of faith and conscience. "In no circumstances," as his biographer Martin Brecht points out, "could he approve imposing the death penalty on false teachers. The danger of misuse was too great, as

---

3. Quoted by Martin Brecht, *Martin Luther: Shaping and Defining the Reformation, 1521-1532* (Minneapolis: Fortress, 1990), p. 243.

4. *Luther's Works,* American ed., 55 vols. (St. Louis: Concordia; Philadelphia: Fortress, 1955-86) 26:107; hereafter cited as *LW.*

5. Karl Barth, *Church Dogmatics* IV/1 (Edinburgh: T. & T. Clark, 1956), p. 626; hereafter cited as IV/1.

6. Karl Barth, *Church Dogmatics* IV/3 (Edinburgh: T. & T. Clark, 1961, 1962), p. 199; hereafter cited as IV/3.

could be seen in the executions of innocent people in Catholic territories."[7] Yet, however difficult it might be to strike the right balance in practice between a proper passion for the truth and compassion for one's opponents, Barth and Luther were both agreed that charity at the expense of truth is not charity, and that faithfulness to the gospel must be prepared to run the risk that boldness will be mistaken for intolerance.[8]

Agreement, however, is an easier matter to establish than influence. Barth and Luther might well agree on any number of subjects without Barth's having been taught or influenced by Luther. How can we go about determining what, if anything, Barth may have learned from Luther in particular? How can we know at any given point whether Luther actually influenced Barth? There are, I suggest, at least two ways of figuring this out. First, if an idea can be found in both theologians that has no real precedent before Luther, we may say that Luther has instructed Barth. It will not matter whether Luther's teaching has been mediated to Barth through a host of different sources, or even if (however unlikely) Barth never encountered it in Luther himself. If Barth holds it and Luther originated it, Barth has learned from and is indebted to Luther. Barth will, of course, have encountered many of Luther's ideas not only from Luther, but also from other sources, not least from John Calvin and, more immediately, from his own revered teacher William Herrmann. Secondly, moreover, if Barth has followed Luther at junctures where he faced a real choice between Luther and Calvin, we may feel certain that Luther has influenced him strongly at those points. Although as a Reformed theologian, Barth will often follow Calvin at such junctures, that is not always the case. Indeed, at certain vital points Barth follows Luther not only, broadly speaking, against Calvin and the Reformed tradition, but also against the main lines of the Lutheran tradition. There are points, in other words, where Barth has actually retrieved Luther in order to stand with him not only against modernity, but also against the rest of the Reformation.

---

7. Brecht, *Shaping and Defining*, p. 337.

8. The substantive question of Barth's indebtedness to Luther's theology is independent of his assessment of Luther's character and his attitude toward Luther as a person. In private correspondence Barth confessed to a lifelong aversion toward what he regarded as Luther's arrogance. See Barth, *Letters, 1961-1968* (Grand Rapids: Eerdmans, 1981), pp. 224-25 and 255. During his later years, Barth even kept Luther's works hidden behind a tapestry over his bookshelf. His doubts about Luther's character are reflected in a little-known work by one of his students: Ekkehard Börsch, *Geber, Gabe, Aufgabe: Luther's Prophetie in den Entscheidungsjahren seiner Reformation, 1520-1525* (Munich: Chr. Kaiser, 1958). I would like to thank my colleague Dr. Karlfried Froehlich for these references. Note that Barth's assessment of Luther's character does not differ greatly from Oberman's. See Oberman, *Luther: Man between God and the Devil* (New Haven: Yale University Press, 1989), pp. 298-304.

Not least among the many powerful themes that Barth would absorb from Luther is that of "christocentrism," perhaps the most basic point in all of Barth's theology. Indeed, Barth not only owed this point to Luther but went on to radicalize it. In this respect he would remain truer in some ways to the spirit than to the letter of Luther's thought. But the original impulse had come from Luther and can be traced back to him alone. It remains true, of course, as Hans Frei never tired of reminding us, that modern liberal theology, the theology of Schleiermacher, of Herrmann, and of Barth's youth, was already basically christocentric. A thoroughgoing christocentrism is one of the interesting features that distinguished modern theology from, say, Protestant scholastic theology in the seventeenth century. Unlike many of his generation and even today, however, Barth was no cultured despiser of seventeenth-century theologians. Indeed, it might be said that his theological achievement arose largely through his enormous genius in forging an unheard-of, creative synthesis between the nineteenth and the seventeenth centuries, between the christocentrism of the one and the doctrinal rigor of the other, between the newer personalism and the older biblicism, between the thoroughly modern and the solidly traditional, in a word between Schleiermacher and Polanus. Yet the real christocentrism that Barth absorbed was not finally Schleiermacher's but Luther's.

Schleiermacher's christocentrism can be distinguished from Luther's primarily by its strongly formal tendency. Schleiermacher's theology, we might say, was formally but not substantively christocentric. The saving significance of the Redeemer, as Schleiermacher understood him, was no more than a matter of his "God-consciousness." This was a modern, somewhat secularized way of saying that the important thing about Jesus, the thing that made him savingly significant, was the Holy Spirit. As with all Spirit-oriented Christologies through the centuries, whose prototype has always been Theodore of Mopsuestia, the salient point was not so much that the Holy Spirit points us to Jesus as that Jesus points us to the Holy Spirit. Between the ancient and the modern versions of this Christology, by the way, the main difference has been that the ancients like Theodore upheld the Nicene doctrine of the Trinity, no matter how unstably, whereas the modernists like Schleiermacher did not, thus achieving stability at the expense of orthodoxy. In any case, in all such Christologies, regardless of any specialized terminology, although Jesus is formally central, the substantive center is the Holy Spirit.

Any given Christology, of course, involves a corresponding soteriology. In Spirit-oriented Christologies our salvation is not seen as being uniquely identical with Jesus himself, except perhaps in a manner of speaking, but rather with his spiritual predicates. Our salvation depends primarily on a repeatable, not an unrepeatable, event.[9] It is not finally a once-for-all event apart from us, but a continuing event within us or among us. It does not center on a saving death that could have been suffered for our sakes only by God incarnate, but rather on a mode of spirituality whose originating moment does not generically differ from its dependent moments, that is, from Jesus to us. The originating spirituality in Jesus might differ from its dependent reduplications, as experienced by others, in potency or degree, but not in kind. The spirituality Jesus originated is thus the source and substance of our salvation. He is historically decisive (though not logically indispensable) for imparting this salvation to the church. According to modernist christocentrism, Jesus was so fully human that he might be called "divine," but strictly speaking he was not truly God, could not possibly have been truly God if indeed he was truly human, and does not need to have been truly God in order to originate and impart this spirituality, and thus to function as the Redeemer.[10]

Luther's christocentrism is obviously very different. It is not merely formal but also and eminently substantive. Jesus Christ is not seen as the source of a salvation other than himself. He is uniquely and irreplaceably our salvation. His saving significance is not located abstractly in his predicates or in his spirituality, but in the concrete events of his incarnation, death, and resurrection for our sakes. He is inseparable from his saving predicates, because he is finally

9. There is an important sense, it should be noted, in which Schleiermacher understands the person and work of Christ to be unrepeatable. He posits Christ as the *Urbild* (archetype) and not merely as the *Vorbild* (exemplar) of the church's redemption. By virtue of his supernatural conception, sinless perfection, and absolutely potent God-consciousness, Christ is unique. Nonetheless, the saving significance of Christ is located in his spirituality. Although he remains the unique source of this spirituality for others, and although he instantiates it perfectly, it is by definition repeatable in others — in kind, if not in degree. (For a different view, see Martin Redeker, *Schleiermacher: Life and Thought* [Philadelphia: Fortress, 1973], p. 134.) The repeatability and communicability of Christ's spirituality is, for Schleiermacher, precisely what makes it savingly significant. Whether the inner logic of this soteriological paradigm requires the kind of absolute uniqueness that Schleiermacher ascribed to Christ is another question. Working within the same basic paradigm, Paul Tillich, for example, posited that Christ's spirituality (as the "bearer of the New Being") was "unique" (unsurpassable) but not "exclusively unique" (not unattainable by others). "This uniqueness is not exclusive" (Tillich, *Systematic Theology,* vol. 2 [Chicago: University of Chicago Press, 1957], p. 110).

10. A "rebiblicized" version of Schleiermacher can be found in Hendrikus Berkhof, *The Doctrine of the Holy Spirit* (Richmond: John Knox, 1964). Berkhof, who is curiously sometimes regarded as a "Barthian," locates Jesus' saving significance in his being the "bearer" and "sender" of the Holy Spirit. Like Schleiermacher, the "adoptionist" tendency in his Christology is matched, not surprisingly, by a "modalist" tendency in his view of the Trinity. These tendencies and themes also dominate Berkhof's dogmatics, which is not insignificantly entitled *Christian Faith* (Grand Rapids: Eerdmans, 1979).

identical with them. He himself and he alone, as Luther insisted again and again, is our righteousness and our life. No one else will ever be God incarnate, nor will anyone else ever die for the sins of the world. Only Jesus Christ is such a person, only he could do such a work, and he in fact has done it. He does not give us his righteousness and life except by giving us himself, as he does when we receive him through faith alone. We are not saved by reduplicating his spirituality, which Luther would have denounced as a new form of the law, but by the miraculous exchange whereby he has died in our place as sinners so that we might be clothed in his righteousness by grace and live through his body and blood in eternal fellowship with God. Our salvation is thus permanently anchored not in a repeatable, but in an unrepeatable, event, not in an event that takes place *in nobis,* but in one that has taken place *extra nos.* Since we are given a share in this event by grace through faith, having been baptized into Christ's very death (Rom. 6:3), the substance of our salvation, and not just the source, is Christ himself and Christ alone.

This relentless focus on Christ himself as the entire substance of our salvation constitutes nothing less, we may say, than the breakthrough that caused the Reformation. This point needs to be emphasized over against the growing tendency in scholarly circles to dissolve the Reformation into the late Middle Ages. Of course, it can only be salutary to see that the Reformation had significant antecedents. Nor do we need to overlook that the Reformation had a variety of causes operating on a number of different levels. But it will not do to say, as many are tempted to say today, that while the Reformation breakthrough in soteriology may well have been new for Luther, it was not new in and of itself. One is reminded at this point of a certain law relating historians to revolutions. The law states in part that, given enough time and enough historians, any revolution can be made to disappear. Something like this seems to be happening to the Reformation. As Heiko Oberman has shown, however, the disappearance will not bear scrutiny.[11]

What Luther discovered, notes Oberman, was not that grace is prevenient, for that would have been nothing new. Nor was the novelty of Luther's discovery located in the idea that the sinner is justified by grace through an existential process of sanctification. That idea was as common in the Middle Ages as it was alien to the Reformation. Rather what Luther attacked, states Oberman, was "the whole medieval tradition as it was later confirmed at the Council of Trent" (p. 119). All known scholastic doctrines of justification,

---

11. Heiko A. Oberman, "'*Iustitia Christi*' and '*Iustitia Dei*': Luther and the Scholastic Doctrines of Justification," in *The Dawn of the Reformation* (Grand Rapids: Eerdmans, 1986), pp. 104-25. Page references in the text are to this work.

whether nominalist, Scotist, or Thomistic, finally saw justification as a goal to be obtained at the end of a purifying process *in nobis*. By contrast, Luther saw justification as "the stable *basis* and not the uncertain *goal* of the life of sanctification" (p. 124). Justification by faith alone meant that our righteousness in God's sight is already our real spiritual possession. Although it has yet to become an inherent predicate *in nobis,* nonetheless we now possess it, whole and entire, *extra nos* in Christ by faith. "Christian righteousness," wrote Luther, "is . . . that righteousness by which Christ lives in us, not the righteousness that is in our person" (*LW* 26:166). Not some spirituality being formed within us, but "Christ himself is our Reconciliation, Righteousness, Peace, Life, and Salvation" (*LW* 26:151).

The centrality of Jesus Christ in this strong soteriological sense is something that Barth most certainly learned from Luther. That Christ alone is our salvation, that he is not an incomplete but a perfect Savior, that he is our righteousness on account of his obedience, that he is not the source of our righteousness without also being its reality and ground, that the righteousness we receive from him by faith does not come by portions and pieces but is already ours whole and entire, that it is participatory before it is intrinsic — these are as much themes in Barth as in Luther, but they can be traced back to Luther alone. The christocentrism for which Barth is so famous would scarcely have been thinkable without Luther's Reformation breakthrough.[12]

---

12. Ebeling has Barth in conflict with Luther here (pp. 539-46). Whereas Barth's christocentrism is supposedly "logical-analogical," Luther's is supposedly "forensic-antithetical." Although space does not permit a full discussion, these analytical categories are not felicitous. A "forensic" element is present, I would say, in the christocentrism of both theologians, but dominant in neither case. For Luther in particular, the forensic metaphor is arguably subordinate in justification to the motifs of creation and resurrection, which, as Luther read Rom. 4, finally provided the only precise analogies for God's imputation of righteousness to the godless. "It is the nature of God . . . to justify sinners, to give life to the dead, and to save those who are desperate and damned. For he is the almighty Creator, who makes everything out of nothing" (*LW* 26:314). Thus when God acts to justify the godless, he performs "his natural and proper work" (*LW* 26:314). A careful study would show that Luther used the idea of "imputation" in *two* contexts at the same time: not only in a narrower forensic context, but also in a larger context determined by the ideas of creation and resurrection. The same is true of Barth.

A telling detail of how Luther's christocentrism impacted Barth's can be seen in the way they both spotlight certain New Testament passages. Of great importance to both was I Cor. 1:30, which states that Christ is "our wisdom, our righteousness and sanctification and redemption." In his three-volume account of Luther's life, Martin Brecht returns to this verse repeatedly, singling it out more than even Rom. 1:17 as underlying the breakthrough that sparked the Reformation. See, for example, Brecht, *Martin Luther: His Road to Reformation, 1483-1521* (Minneapolis: Fortress, 1985), p. 228. Like Luther (and, one might add, *unlike*

Another powerful theme that Barth absorbed from Luther involves the theology of the cross. In the last four or five decades, theologians have shown an increasing interest in the suffering of God. Despite a long and venerable tradition concerning divine impassability and the heretical danger of patripassianism, a God who cannot suffer has rightly come to be seen as a God who cannot love. The God of the New Testament has been belatedly rediscovered as a God of suffering love. This striking rediscovery has arisen, it would seem, largely from the impulse of Karl Barth, and the most important source for Barth in the history of theology was undoubtedly Martin Luther.[13]

Here is a juncture where Barth faced a real choice between Luther and Calvin. Although Barth adopted a dialectical strategy that would attempt to do justice to the interests of both Reformers,[14] and although the contrast here between Luther and Calvin can be overstated, the suffering of God was not a theme that Calvin was eager to embrace. Luther and Calvin both saw Jesus Christ as one person in two natures whose true deity and true humanity were joined by a relationship of unity-in-distinction. However, where Luther would focus on the unity, Calvin would in turn press the distinction. Nowhere were these differences manifest more significantly than at the point of the cross. Re-

---

Ebeling), Barth reads this verse to mean that all soteriological predicates are identical with Christ himself.

Another such passage was Col. 3:3. "In Christian doctrine," Barth stated, ". . . we have to take in blind seriousness the basic Pauline perception of Colossians 3:3, which is that of all Scripture — that our life is hid with Christ in God" (*Church Dogmatics* II/1 [Edinburgh: T. & T. Clark, 1957], p. 149; hereafter cited as II/1). The first theologian, it seems, whose christocentrism had assigned such comprehensive hermeneutical significance to this particular verse was Luther. (See, for example, *LW* 26:5-9 and 12:104-7.) The precedence of the Word over reason and experience meant for both theologians — in their common christocentrism — that our being completely righteous "in Christ" was utterly real *coram Deo* despite its hiddenness apart from faith between the times.

In good modernist fashion, Ebeling consistently underplays what these and other verses signify, namely, the *extra nos* aspect that Luther ascribed to Christ's finished and saving work. Because Barth and Luther agree on this decisive point, they have far more in common with each other, despite their differences, than either of them would have with Ebeling. What Ebeling's unfortunate analytical categories (as cited above) seem to be groping toward is the recognition that Barth differs from Luther by, in effect, extending his analysis of the bondage of the will to include also the bondage of the mind. (Barth's rejection of Brunner on natural theology parallels the reasoning in Luther's rejection of Erasmus on free will.) In this way Barth expanded Luther's christocentrism beyond anything in Luther himself.

13. Barth will of course have encountered this idea from others as well, especially Hegel, not to mention various patristic theologians such as Cyril of Alexandria.

14. For a general discussion of this strategy, see my essay "Karl Barth's Christology: Its Basic Chalcedonian Character," chap. 6 in this volume.

membering the abiding distinction of Christ's deity from his humanity, Calvin insisted on the impassibility of the divine nature. Remembering the real unity of Christ's person, Luther by contrast affirmed the suffering of God. Although Barth respected Calvin's distinction, he moved far closer to Luther. For Barth the theology of the cross disclosed the suffering love of God.

Certainly if Barth had followed Calvin, he would not obviously have been led in such a direction. "We know that in Christ," Calvin once stated, "the two natures were united into one person in such a way that each retained its own properties." To him this suggested that sometimes "it was necessary in discharging the office of Mediator that the human nature should act separately according to its peculiar character" *(Comm. on Matt. 24:36)*. It is thus not surprising that Calvin could suppose: "Certainly when he says that the Lord of glory was crucified (I Cor. 2:8), Paul does not mean that he suffered anything in his divinity, but that Christ, who suffered in the flesh as an abject and despised man, was also, as God, the Lord of glory" (*Institutes* 4.17.30). Far from discerning in the cross the suffering of divine love, Calvin was rather inclined to safeguard the divine impassibility: "God has no blood, nor does he suffer, nor can he be touched with hands" (2.14.2). Although these statements are perhaps technically correct, they suggest a basic orientation to the cross in which God seems more detached than involved.[15]

Luther was prepared to run very different risks. As early as the Heidelberg Disputation (1518), we find him asserting: "Now it is not sufficient for anyone, and it does him no good to recognize God in his glory and majesty, unless he recognizes him in the humility and shame of the cross" (*LW* 31:52-53). "He who does not know Christ does not know God hidden in suffering. . . . God can be found only in suffering and the cross" (*LW* 31:53). Although apparently not continuously prominent,[16] ten years later in the midst of eucharistic controversies, the same theme would strongly reappear. Confronted by the objection that the deity cannot suffer and die, Luther retorted: "That is true, but since the divinity and humanity are one person in Christ, the Scriptures ascribe to the divinity, because of this personal union, all that happens to [the] humanity" (*LW* 37:210). Luther's inclination runs opposite to Calvin's: "Therefore it is correct to say: the Son of God suffers. Although, so to speak, the one part (namely the divinity) does

15. These passages are cited by Paul van Buren, *Christ in Our Place: The Substitutionary Character of Calvin's Doctrine of Reconciliation* (Edinburgh: Oliver & Boyd, 1957), pp. 38-39; see also pp. 49-50. I have followed van Buren's translations. The book was originally written as a doctoral dissertation under Barth.

16. Ian D. Kingston Siggins suggests that this theme comes and goes in Luther's writings over the years. See Siggins, *Martin Luther's Doctrine of Christ* (New Haven: Yale University Press, 1970), p. 36.

not suffer, nevertheless the person, who is God, suffers in the other part (namely, in the humanity)" (*LW* 37:210). Or more boldly: "What Christ does and suffers, essentially God does and suffers."[17] Faith affirms, said Luther, what reason cannot possibly grasp, namely, "that a man who dies is God" (*LW* 28:269).[18]

God is never more fully God, urged Barth in echo of Luther, than in the powerlessness and humiliation of the cross. Far from contradicting the divine omnipotence, the cross supremely reveals it. Nothing demonstrates more fully than the cross how great is the omnipotence of God's love — "so great that God can be weak and indeed powerless, as a human being can be weak and powerless." "This is how he is God," continued Barth, "this is his freedom, this is his distinctness from and superiority to all other reality. . . . This One, the One who loves in this way, is the true God" (IV/1, p. 129, rev.). The glory of God is revealed in the face of the Christ who hung from the cross (II Cor. 4:6). "False gods," by contrast, "are all reflections of a false and all too human self-exaltation. They are all lords who cannot and will not be servants, who are therefore no true lords, whose being is not truly a divine being" (IV/1, p. 130).

Divine impassibility must not prevent us from seeing the cross as "the passion of God himself" (IV/1, p. 245). The "mystery of this passion" — the passion of the impassible God — cannot possibly be expressed, as again Barth agreed with Luther, without paradox. Thus Barth could write that "in this humiliation God is supremely God, . . . in this death he is supremely alive, in the passion of this man as his eternal Son he has maintained and revealed his deity" (IV/1, pp. 246-47, rev.). Of course, unlike Luther, Barth recoiled from any suggestion that the cross entailed a contradiction or conflict in God's being itself, an idea he regarded as supremely blasphemous (IV/1, p. 185).[19] The cross,

17. *Werke: Kritische Gesammtausgabe*, 68 vols. (Weimar: Hermann Böhle, 1883-), 20:265; hereafter cited as WA. Cited by Siggins, p. 237.

18. The differences here between Calvin and Luther should not be overplayed. Compare the following two statements. *First:* "In the cross of Christ, as in a splendid theater, the incomparable goodness of God is set before the whole world. The glory of God shines, indeed, in all creatures on high and below, but never more brightly than in the cross." *Second:* In the abandonment of Christ on the cross, "the deity withdrew and hid . . . the humanity was left alone, the devil had free access to Christ, and the deity withdrew its power and let the humanity fight alone." The first statement comes from Calvin, *Comm. on John 13:31*; the second from Luther (*LW* 12:126-27), cited by Paul Althaus, *The Theology of Martin Luther* (Philadelphia: Fortress, 1966), p. 198.

19. Although Luther surely did not go as far as have some recent theologians who appeal to him, he did at times seem to project a conflict between God's righteousness and God's mercy, God's curse and God's blessing, God's wrath and God's love back into God's being itself. With reference to Christ's cross, for example, he once wrote: "There God enters into conflict with God" [da streitet Gott mit Gott] (WA, 45, 370, 35). A careful discussion of this tendency in Luther may be

Barth constantly stressed, was the deepest revelation of God's being, not its contradiction. Moreover, the cross bore its saving significance not in the placating of divine wrath, but in the divine judgment which in mercy assumed the whole burden of the world's sin and removed it through suffering love. With that proviso, however, Barth concurred with Luther on the unavoidability of paradox. Like Cyril of Alexandria before them, who once stated that in Christ God "suffered impassibly" and "died immortally,"[20] they both agreed that the transcendent necessities of faith outweighed any possible offense to reason. Otherwise, God would only appear in a false light as "a remote and aloof spectator or a non-participating supervisor of this event," rather than as what he really is — the merciful God who suffered with us and for us on the cross so that our deepest distress might be removed (IV/3, pp. 414-15, rev.).

As the point about paradox would suggest, a third theme that Barth incorporated from Luther involves the primacy of the Word of God. As for Luther so also for Barth, the Word of God took unrivaled precedence over not only experience but also reason. No theology of the cross, our two theologians agreed, could avoid the scandal and the promise of hiddenness. The content of the Word of God was hidden from both experience and reason as taken in themselves. Although each could be enlisted in the service of God's Word, neither could provide it with a foundation. The Word was too much a *novum,* too high, and too full of hope to be normed and judged by the uncertainties of the human heart or the powers of the human mind. The Word authenticated itself from faith to faith, and in no other way. Although Barth would expand the scope of this theme into areas not admitted or anticipated by Luther, and although it would of course have been

---

found in Theodosius Harnack, *Luthers Theologie,* vol. 2 (Munich: Chr. Kaiser, 1927), pp. 241-55, esp. pp. 242-43 and 253. Others are less careful. Appealing to Luther's commentary on Gal. 3:13, which speaks of an "eternal curse" as well as an "eternal blessing" (*LW* 26:281-83), Gustav Aulen suggests that Luther effectively locates the conflict "within the Divine Being itself." Also appealing to Luther, Jürgen Moltmann posits a "dichotomy in God." Nor does Helmut Gollwitzer refrain from such ideas; in the cross he sees a "cleavage" that goes through God himself: "God himself is forsaken by God, God himself rejects himself." See Aulen, *Christus Victor* (New York: Macmillan, 1969), pp. 106, 114; Moltmann, *The Future of Creation* (Philadelphia: Fortress, 1979), pp. 64-67; Gollwitzer, *Krummes Holz, Aufrechter Gang* (Munich: Chr. Kaiser, 1970), p. 245 (cited by Moltmann, *The Future of Creation,* pp. 64-67); cf. Moltmann, *The Crucified God* (New York: Harper & Row, 1974), pp. 207-49. Barth, who does not push Luther in this direction (cf. II/1, pp. 378-80), rejected every suggestion of a rupture within the divine being.

20. Cyril of Alexandria, "Letter 4" (Second Letter to Nestorius), sec. 5, in *Letters 1-50* (Washington, D.C.: Catholic University of America Press, 1987), p. 40; "Letter 17" (Third Letter to Nestorius), anath. 12, in *Letters 1-50,* p. 92. In a way that remained definitive for theologians like Luther and Barth, Cyril stated: "The manner of the union is entirely beyond human understanding." Quoted by G. L. Prestige, *Fathers and Heretics* (London: SPCK, 1940), p. 169.

mediated to him also by Calvin and Reformed theology in general, little room for doubt can exist that the ultimate source again was Luther.[21]

"Christ cannot be set forth," urged Luther, "any other way than through the Word, and cannot be grasped any other way than through faith" (*LW* 26:356). Nothing but the Word can make us certain in our faith. "It is impossible ever to decide what God wills and what is pleasing to him except in his Word. This Word makes us certain that God cast away all his wrath and hatred toward us when he gave his only Son for our sins" (*LW* 26:388). Therefore we must avert our gaze from everything but the promise of the gospel. "Now it is time to turn your eyes away from the Law, from works, and from your own feelings and conscience, to lay hold of the Gospel, and to depend solely on the promise of God" (*LW* 26:389).

"God has portrayed himself definitely and clearly enough," Luther affirmed, "in his Word" (*LW* 24:23). If we do not wish to go astray, we must therefore begin with God where he wishes to be found. We cannot rely on what we perceive or feel. "We must close our eyes to what we perceive and feel, and cling to the Word of Christ with our heart" (*LW* 24:31). We must not look to the sin that still clings to us so closely, for that will only lead us to despair. "We must not judge according to the feeling of our heart; we must judge according to the Word of God, which teaches that the Holy Spirit is granted to the afflicted, the terrified and the despairing in such a way that he encourages and comforts them" (*LW* 26:383).

21. The Word of God, as Luther understood it, took precedence over far more, of course, than reason and experience. The Word took precedence, for example, over the church. "The church comes into being," stated Luther, "because God's Word is spoken. The church does not constitute the Word, but is constituted by the Word" (*LW* 36:145). It also took precedence over the sacrament. "The Word can exist without the sacrament, but the sacrament cannot exist without the Word" (*LW* 38:189, rev.). "The Word sanctifies everything and is above the sacrament" (*LW* 36:244-45). It also took precedence in our reception of the Holy Spirit. "For God will not give you his Spirit without the external Word" (*LW* 34:286). "The external Word must come first" (*LW* 26:73). At this general or programmatic level, Barth's orientation is no different. "The church is constituted as the church by . . . the Word of God" (*Church Dogmatics* I/2 [Edinburgh: T. & T. Clark, 1956], p. 588; hereafter cited as I/2). "The church is not Christ. The church does not possess his incomparable authority, that of the eternal Word itself. Neither has it authority to do his deeds" (I/2, p. 226). "What does not cease is the extension of the church's work on the basis of its witness to Christ: the proclamation of Christ by the preaching of Christ, the institution of baptism, and the festival of the Lord's Supper; and the gathering of the people out of all nations by this proclamation. . . . But as such they must submit to continual measurement by the original sign-giving . . . of the twelve apostles, and they must be justified at that tribunal" (I/2, p. 227). "The Holy Spirit certainly comes to us, not by an independent road which bypasses the Word and its testimonies, but by the Word and its testimonies" (I/2, p. 236). "The Holy Spirit is . . . the Spirit of the Word" (I/2, p. 236). Like Luther, and in his footsteps, Barth is preeminently a Word of God theologian.

"You are not to be conscious of having righteousness," exhorted Luther. "You are to believe it" (*LW* 27:26). Neither reason nor our hearts can tell us this, especially in the mist of *Anfechtung* or despair. The Word is sufficient for us, "but if we lose sight of the Word, we have no aid or counsel left" (*LW* 27:78-79).

Reason, contended Luther, is no more reliable than our hearts in matters of faith. It does not understand that we cannot live to God without dying to the law (*LW* 26:156). It will always view the content of the gospel as "simply impossible and absurd" (*LW* 26:227). It is therefore "the greatest and most invincible enemy of God" (*LW* 26:229). Reason "neither comprehends nor is able to believe" the doctrines of faith, but instead takes offense at them (*LW* 33:158). Although it is "blind, deaf, stupid, impious, and sacrilegious," reason presumes nonetheless to judge "all the words and works of God" (*LW* 33:173). But these are beyond ordinary comprehension (*LW* 33:175). The gospel is filled with "mysteries and unsearchable judgments" (*LW* 33:188). Neither reason nor any other human capacity can know or understand them without the gift of the Holy Spirit, which is faith (*LW* 13:75).

The upshot is that, apart from the Word of God, ultimate reality remains hidden from us.[22] We do not feel that we are righteous, yet the Word proclaims and promises that it is so. Nor do we comprehend how the mysteries of the gospel can be true, yet the Word confirms them to faith by the Holy Spirit. "Faith in Christ," as one commentator has summarized Luther, "is thus a form of the theology of the cross *(theologia crucis):* we are to believe that we are righteous, innocent, and blessed even though we feel as though we are sinful, guilty, and damned."[23] Likewise, we are to affirm such evangelical truths as that God is one

---

22. On how Luther saw the relationship between "worldly reason and faith in Christ," see Oberman, *The Reformation: Roots and Ramifications* (Grand Rapids: Eerdmans, 1994), pp. 12-18. "Luther, the alleged fideist, formulates the independent force of worldly reason more radically than anyone had ever dared to do before him" (p. 16). Reason is fully competent within its own sphere. It "has not been destroyed by the Fall — it has not even been impaired" (p. 16). Nevertheless, its competence is not unlimited. "In the sphere of faith (unlike in the worldly sphere), it can be assigned no constitutive function" (p. 17). In short, just as reason alone "cannot invade the sphere of revelation" without going astray, so in its own worldly sphere "reason is that original source of life which, undiminished by the fall and disbelief, belongs even to the godless" (p. 16).

23. Randall C. Zachman, *The Assurance of Faith: Conscience in the Theology of Martin Luther and John Calvin* (Minneapolis: Augsburg Fortress, 1993), p. 56. What Zachman says about experience and faith in Luther would apply also to Barth: "The experience of the truth of the Word does not lead us to seek to confirm that truth by what we see and feel; rather, the Word itself discloses its truth and power to us in triumphing over [all contrary appearances as we may see or feel them]. Thus the experience of the truth of the Word leads us to cling more and more to the Word" (p. 68). For Barth as for Luther, evangelical truths are "revealed only in the testimony of Christ through the Holy Spirit" (p. 68).

and undivided in three persons, that the impassible God suffers on the cross, and that God's righteousness comes only to sinners, even though our reason complains that these are impossible, offensive, and absurd. "I believe," wrote Luther in *The Small Catechism*, "that by my own reason or strength I cannot believe in Jesus Christ, my Lord, or come to him. But the Holy Spirit has called me through the Gospel, enlightened me with his gifts, and sanctified and preserved me in true faith."[24]

Perhaps one way to appreciate the powerful impact on Barth of the primacy Luther assigned to God's Word would be to say that it led Barth, almost alone among modern theologians, to grant uncompromising precedence to the Reformation over modernity itself. Barth took Luther extremely seriously that, apart from God's Word, ultimate reality cannot possibly be known, and that it can be apprehended by faith alone. Barth by no means rejected modernity, but he accepted it only on Luther's own grounds. He refused to allow secular epistemologies to set the terms for the validity of the gospel. Instead he took up "an exposed position minimally supported by the prevailing culture and maximally in agreement with mainstream Christianity."[25] The confident skepticism of modernity — of Kant, Feuerbach, Strauss, Marx, Nietzsche, Darwin, Freud, and all the rest — could finally be transcended and left behind, Barth believed, even as modernity's untold contributions were also welcomed and preserved, on the basis of Luther's theological critique of reason and experience.

The strategy by which Barth could trump modernity with the Reformation depended in part on distinguishing between frameworks and particular truths. A comprehensive framework, or what Barth liked to call a "worldview," was one thing, the material within the framework was something else. At the level of frameworks, there could only be conflict between the gospel and its competitors, including other religions, because comprehensive organizing frameworks are mutually exclusive. Any framework that is not determined by the centrality of Jesus Christ, and especially by his saving death, would be unacceptable to the Christian faith. This would apply to Marxism as much as to Hinduism, to modernism as much as to traditionalism, to feminism as much as to patriarchalism, to historicism as much as to essentialism, to tribalism as much as to cosmopolitanism, and so on. At one level, in other words, what all these "isms" have in common is simply that they are "isms." They not only offer comprehensive frames that propose to set the terms for what is or is not real,

---

24. *The Book of Concord*, ed. Theodore G. Tappert (Philadelphia: Fortress, 1959), p. 345. Barth loved these lines and often cited them.

25. David Ford in *Karl Barth: Studies of His Theological Method*, ed. Stephen Sykes (Oxford: Clarendon, 1979), p. 198.

what is or is not possible, and what is or is not significant, but they also do so without reference to the Word of God.

Nevertheless, Barth observed, there may be much material within such frameworks that is not only compatible with the gospel, but useful, in certain circumstances even necessary, for the Christian community to adopt. The gospel sets the standard for determining what can or cannot be eclectically appropriated from elsewhere, but it does not stipulate that Christians will have nothing to learn in practice from other sources. Secular movements such as Marxism, for example, might sometimes arise because the church has failed in its own mission, in this case, by failing to show compassion and concrete concern for the exploited, the marginalized, and the dispossessed. Truth, as Calvin emphasized perhaps more than Luther, is where one finds it, and it would be, he said, an insult to the Holy Spirit not to recognize it, no matter where it happens to come from (*Institutes* 2.2.15). Frameworks were thus distinguishable from any particular truths within them, Barth concluded, even as immediate or proximate sources could be distinguished from theological norms. While the source could actually be anything, even a framework hostile to the gospel, the norm for assessing the truth of particular claims was the gospel itself *(sola Scriptura)*.[26]

In this connection Barth found Luther's critique of reason and experience relevant to modernity, because it allowed him to develop a fundamental distinction between the phenomenal and the real, the manifest and the hidden, the hypothetical and the certain. Only the phenomenal, the manifest, and the hypothetical were the proper domain of reason and experience. Ultimate reality was not. No access to that level of reality, the theological level, was available to them. Whenever reason or experience exceeded its competency by attempting to establish the final limits of the possible, the significant, and the real, the result could only be a worldview or framework in conflict with the gospel.

---

26. For Barth's idea of "secular parables of the truth," see George Hunsinger, *How to Read Karl Barth: The Shape of His Theology* (New York: Oxford University Press, 1991), pp. 234-80. For a parallel account of Aquinas, see Bruce D. Marshall, "Aquinas as Postliberal Theologian," *Thomist* 53 (1989): 353-402. For a philosophical account of "extended principles of consistency," whereby religious communities can assimilate "alien claims" compatible with their own essential doctrines, see William A. Christian, *Doctrines of Religious Communities: A Philosophical Study* (New Haven: Yale University Press, 1987), pp. 212-15 (with explicit reference to Barth). For a philosophical account of "tradition-based rationality" that seems broadly compatible with Barth's approach, see Alasdair MacIntyre, *Whose Justice? Which Rationality?* (Notre Dame, Ind.: University of Notre Dame Press, 1988). Barth, by the way, would be better described as "nonfoundationalist" in his epistemology than as "fideist." Sweeping charges of "fideism" usually seem not only to presuppose some sort of foundationalism, but also to overlook the peculiar logical status of any large-scale frameworks that determine, implicitly or explicitly, what is or is not real, possible, and significant.

Worldviews of this sort, of course, were the common currency of modernity. For modernity typically tried to establish the final limits of the possible, the significant, and the real merely on the basis of what was available to reason and experience, namely, the phenomenal and the manifest. Yet modernity, Barth argued, could just as well have left its observations at the level of hypothesis.[27] Nothing substantive required it to inflate them to the status of a worldview. Even when that occurred, however, worldviews might still embody many elements and degrees of truth, as Barth showed most impressively in his long theological critique of various secular and religious anthropologies (III/2, pp. 71-132).

The truth about eternity, however, and about the eschatological future — and therefore the truth about the final limits of the possible, the significant, and the real — was unavailable to modernity for the very reasons established by Luther. Modernity had unwisely presupposed that reason and experience were sufficient for just about everything in life and in death (and in this respect, it need hardly be said, the current fad of postmodernism is no different). It had therefore systematically sealed itself off from what could be properly known and received only when primacy was accorded to the Word of God as attested by faith. As Luther anticipated and Barth discerned, it had sealed itself off from the central truth of the human condition, from its highest promise and deepest peril, as disclosed by the cross of Christ.

A fourth theme Barth appropriated from Luther involves the way in which that promise and peril are seen as shaping the life of faith. Few theologians have ever aligned themselves more meticulously with Luther than did Barth in adopting the great doctrine of *simul iustus et peccator*. Indeed, this is another place where it can be argued, remarkably, that Barth stands with Luther against Calvin, or at least against Calvin's ambiguities. It might even be said that here Barth stands with Luther against much of the Lutheran theological tradition as well. Barth adopted and championed as have few others the distinctive eschatology with which Luther described the Christian life.

Salvation, as Luther understood it, was not essentially a process but a person, not an existential goal but an accomplished fact, not something to be actualized but something to be received — in short, not a work but a gift. In a move whose significance can hardly be overestimated, Luther broke with every form of soteriological gradualism, that is, with every viewpoint which sees salvation primarily as a matter of gradual acquisition. Righteousness, he argued, was not essentially something that we acquire by degrees, but something that comes to

27. Karl Barth, *Church Dogmatics* III/2 (Edinburgh: T. & T. Clark, 1960), pp. 3-54; hereafter cited as III/2.

us as a whole, just because Christ and his righteousness were perfect in the finished work he accomplished on our behalf.

Justification, as Luther understood it, was an eschatological event that centered on the person of Christ. As such it was an event that had three tenses. In one sense it had already occurred, in another sense it had not yet occurred, while in still a third sense it occurred continuously in the life of faith here and now. Justification, from the first perspective, had already occurred *extra nos*. For "Christ has achieved it on the cross" (*LW* 40:213), stated Luther, and "he has made us righteous by his death" (*LW* 34:163-64). Here justification is spoken of in the perfect tense as a fact accomplished apart from us by Christ (cf. *LW* 26:183 and 40:215). From a second perspective, however, justification in all its fullness had yet to take place. For "we are not yet perfectly righteous. Our being justified perfectly still remains to be seen, and this is what we hope for. Thus our righteousness does not yet exist in fact, but it still exists in hope" (*LW* 27:21). Here justification is spoken of as the object of future hope.

Finally, from still a third, more existential perspective, justification occurred not in the past or the future but here and now. For when God's Word is once heard and believed, Christ becomes present to us, and justifies and saves us (*LW* 26:240). It was in this sense that justification occurred by faith. "For while the act [Christ's saving death] has taken place," noted Luther, "as long as I have not appropriated it, it is as if it had not taken place for me" (*LW* 40:215). Christ "has won [forgiveness] once for all on the cross. But the distribution takes place continuously" (*LW* 40:214). Having once received forgiveness by faith, we continue to receive it again and again each day. "Forgiveness of sins," wrote Luther, "is not a matter of a passing work or action, but of perpetual duration. For the forgiveness of sins begins in baptism and remains with us all the way to death, until we arise from the dead, and leads us to life eternal. So we live continually under the remission of sins" (*LW* 34:164). Here justification is spoken of as an ongoing existential occurrence. As an eschatological event, justification was at once completed on the cross, yet to be fulfilled at the Last Day, and received continuously by faith here and now.

The point in Luther that would become especially important for Barth involved the idea of perfection. The intrinsic perfection of what Christ had accomplished[28] meant that it could not be acquired by degrees, but became instead a gift of perpetual divine operation in our lives. Before taking up this theme in Barth, let us examine it more closely in Luther.

---

28. In a move greatly significant for his view of salvation and its eschatology, Barth, like Luther, understood the work of Christ to be "intrinsically perfect" (IV/3, p. 7; cf. pp. 327, 357-61).

In Christ, wrote Luther, "we find a righteousness that is complete and perfect" (*LW* 27:86). Therefore, we can speak of ourselves in the present tense as those who "are made perfect" through Christ (*LW* 27:32). "In him is everything," wrote Luther; "in him we have everything and he supplies everything in us" (*LW* 26:232). Because in him we find a "perfect and complete" righteousness (*LW* 27:86), we also find in him "our whole righteousness before God" (*LW* 51:287). "Though I am a sinner in myself, I am not a sinner in Christ, who has been made righteousness for us (I Cor. 1:30). I am righteous and justified through Christ, the Righteous and the Justifier, who is called the Justifier because he belongs to sinners and was sent for sinners" (*LW* 12:311). "Faith justifies because it takes hold of and possesses this treasure, the present Christ" (*LW* 26:130). It is the *Christus praesens,* "the Christ who is grasped by faith and who lives in the heart," who is "the true Christian righteousness on account of which God counts us righteous and grants eternal life" (*LW* 26:130). Although Luther did not define justification as a merely incremental process by which we became righteous gradually, he did think of it in some sense as a continuing event. It was an event that occurred in our lives once and for all through faith, and then on that basis continued to occur throughout our lives again and again.

Our being wholly righteous in Christ was thus the continuing ground of our lifelong existence in faith. "The grace of God," wrote Luther, "is never present in such a way that it is inactive, but it is a living, active, and operative Spirit" (*LW* 31:13). Grace is God's ongoing action upon us — "the continuous and perpetual operation or action through which we are grasped and moved by the Spirit of God" (*LW* 12:377-78). Grace is not a "momentary operation," but "the continuation of a work that has been begun" (*LW* 12:377). More specifically, grace is a divine work of "perpetual duration" throughout our life on earth, whereby "we live continually under the remission of sins" (*LW* 34:164). Therefore, although we are and remain sinners in and of ourselves, not just partially but completely, and although nothing less avails before God than perfect righteousness (*LW* 27:86; 34:127), grace is effective within us. Despite the sin which clings to us so closely, wrote Luther, "yet grace is sufficient to enable us to be counted entirely and completely righteous in God's sight because his grace does not come in portions and pieces, separately, like so many gifts; rather it takes us up completely into its embrace for the sake of Christ our mediator and intercessor, and in order that the gifts may take root in us" (*LW* 35:370, rev.).

Barth's break with soteriological gradualism, which he undoubtedly owed more to Luther than to anyone else, can be introduced by recalling a theological argument he had once gotten into with his brothers, Peter and Heinrich, early in 1928. Peter apparently defended the traditional Protestant view of salvation as it had developed after Luther. Although details would take us too far afield, this view was variously represented not only in Reformed but also in Lutheran theologies. A basic distinction between what happened *in nobis* once for all and what then went on to happen gradually was the hallmark of this traditional view. What happened once for all we may conveniently designate as "justification," and what then happened gradually as "sanctification." Under the category of sanctification (or its equivalent), the idea of soteriological gradualism, a process of salvation happening in us by degrees, had been restored to prominence in traditional Protestantism.[29]

Over against the traditional view of his brother Peter, Karl took the radical position that there is no such thing as progress in sanctification.[30] He was unimpressed by the counterargument that to deny such progress would have a crippling effect on ethics. It would be a sad day, he retorted, when Protestantism could find no better motivation for Christian ethics than self-improvement in the Christian life. Barth took his stand staunchly with Luther that all our actions, not only the worst but also the best, exist before God as filthy rags. They all stand in need of justification by faith alone. In and of ourselves we remain sinners throughout our whole lives, not just partially but completely. Although relative distinctions of better and worse, of more and less, are indeed indispensable in practicing the Christian life, Barth stated, they arise only as God is gracious to us as sinners, as those who will never go beyond being sinners in this life. Progress in sanctification, Barth argued against his brother, is something like "different levels on the surface of the earth when seen from the standpoint of the sun."[31] Viewed from 93 million miles away, which suggests what sanctification would really mean, any differences in attainment are negligible.

By the time he wrote on progress in the Christian life nearly thirty years later in *Church Dogmatics* IV/2, Barth's view of sanctification had changed only slightly. Sanctification still meant that grace sets sinners apart for free obedience to God without their ceasing to be sinners. The only real conversion to God had occurred perfectly for our sakes in the life history of Jesus Christ. He

---

29. For a recent survey of post-Reformation developments in the doctrine of justification, see Gerhard Sauter, "God Creating Faith: The Doctrine of Justification from the Reformation to the Present," *Lutheran Quarterly* 11 (1997): 17-102. Sauter shows how, beginning embryonically with almost imperceptible tendencies in Melanchthon and Calvin, later Protestant theology typically came to see sanctification as the "completion" of justification, and eventually as its virtual "replacement." Soteriological gradualism thus reasserted itself in a way that made it difficult to distinguish "the article by which the church stands or falls" from the tendencies of traditional Catholicism.

30. See Barth, *Ethics* (New York: Seabury Press, 1981), p. 410 n.

31. Barth, *Ethics*, p. 414.

himself in his finished work was the one true alteration — and therefore the sanctification — of the human condition. The saving significance of his work was not located in its initiating a gradual process of improvement in our lives. The freedom granted to faith was not a freedom to return to the law. Because our relationship to the work of Christ was mediated through faith alone, the freedom which grace bestowed was always the freedom of pure reception, of bearing witness, and of active participation in that which had taken place *extra nos*. It was the freedom to live a life of gratitude, despite our remaining sinners, by grace alone.

Barth defined the Christian life by Luther's doctrine of *simul iustus et peccator*. Believers were totally righteous in Christ while yet remaining totally sinners in and of themselves *(totus/totus)*. For Luther this doctrine had meant that grace came to faith in three basic modes: once for all, again and again, and more and more — in that order of significance.[32] Calvin followed Luther mainly by highlighting the once-for-all and more-and-more aspects of grace in the life of faith. The again-and-again aspect, however, receded greatly from view, because Calvin did not retain the sharpness of Luther's *simul iustus et peccator*. Instead, though not without ambiguities, he tended to revert back to an Augustinian gradualism which depicted sanctification (or "regeneration") as an existential process.[33] Finally, by retrieving the sharpness of Luther's doc-

---

32. Luther, of course, distinguished between "alien righteousness" *(iustitia aliena)* and "actual righteousness" *(iustitia propria)* (*LW* 31:297-306). Alien righteousness is received on two levels *(in Christo/in nobis)* or in two ways: once for all by faith (as "an infinite righteousness . . . that swallows up all sins in a moment"), and then also gradually ("infused in us without our works by grace alone"). Actual righteousness, by contrast, is received in only one way (gradually), and is *not* instilled in us without our work. Although of course it is not something that we alone work, it is indeed something that we can and do "work with" on the basis of "that first and alien righteousness" (*LW* 31:298-99, rev.). Actual righteousness is thus the "fruit and consequence" of alien righteousness (*LW* 31:300). While actual righteousness is manifest through works of love, alien righteousness is never received except through faith alone. Note that alien righteousness, which as the righteousness of Christ is always complete and perfect in itself, is no less "real" and determinative for us than actual righteousness, because "reality" is not defined for Luther merely by what is taking place *in nobis*, but primarily by what is true of us, though hidden, *in Christo* (Col. 3:3). Christ's perfect righteousness, fully ours by faith, is always "the basis, the cause, the source" of all righteousness instilled in us gradually (*LW* 31:298). Note also that although righteousness is being instilled gradually, it also comes to us whole and entire by grace, again and again, bringing daily forgiveness, daily assurance, and above all, daily participation in Christ, so that through faith we are always completely "one with him, having the same righteousness as he" (*LW* 31:298).

33. My point about Calvin here involves certain subtleties. Although aspects of the doctrine of *simul iustus et peccator* were not completely absent from his thought, they were not always clearly in the ascendancy. The formula per se does not seem to appear in the *Institutes* (see

trine, Barth conspicuously reinstated the again-and-again motif that had been so decisive in Luther's understanding of the Christian life. Nothing is more characteristic of Barth's soteriology than the thesis that grace is new to us as sinners each morning, that it is a continuous and perpetual operation in the life of faith, and that it does not arrive by portions and pieces, but comes to us again and again in the perfection of the finished work of Christ.[34]

Richard F. Wevers, *A Concordance to Calvin's Institutio 1559* [Grand Rapids: Digamma, 1992]), nor did the idea it expresses exercise the kind of control in his soteriology that it did in Luther and Barth. Barth observes a shift in Calvin's *Institutes* from 1539 to 1559. In the earlier edition Calvin divided the soul of the believer into two *parts* which contended with each other like two wrestlers, the sinful part and the regenerate part. Later he shifted to the position that for the regenerate person, sin and grace confront each other as two incompatible *wholes*, namely, as the old human being and the new. Barth cites *Institutes* 3.3.9-10 as indicative of Calvin's shift (*Church Dogmatics* IV/2 [Edinburgh: T. & T. Clark, 1958], pp. 571-72; hereafter cited as IV/2).

It seems fair to say, however, that Calvin never fully secured the implications of *simul iustus et peccator*. Although he could say that all our works, even the best, need to be justified by faith alone (3.17.9; 18.5), and although he could also say that our love, being always imperfect, merits no reward "of itself" (3.11.17; cf. 4.3, 11.14), he could nonetheless at other places surprisingly approach a classically Augustinian-Thomistic conception of something like "condign merit" (e.g., 3.17.4, 5, where we read of a "double acceptance" [*duplicem hominis apud Deum acceptionem*], one of whose grounds seems to be sanctification *in nobis*). He could even endorse the idea that by grace human works functioned as "inferior causes" *(causas inferiores)* of salvation (3.14.21) — a thesis that does not seem compatible with the belief, which Calvin of course strongly endorses, that "Christ alone" is our righteousness (e.g., 3.11.11-14, 17-19). The instability of Calvin's position is precisely what suggests that *simul iustus et peccator* is not securely in place for him. What is most prominent in Calvin is the combining of the once-for-all motif of justification with the more-and-more motif of progress in sanctification (or regeneration). "The Lord freely justifies his own in order that he may at the same time [*simul!*] restore them to true righteousness by sanctification of his Spirit" (3.3.19). "This restoration does not take place in one moment or one day or one year," but rather gradually "through continual and sometimes even slow advances" (3.3.9). Cf. Joseph Wawrykow, "John Calvin and Condign Merit," *Archiv für Reformationsgeschichte* 83 (1992): 73-90. Although I find his argument to be overstated and insufficiently complex, Wawrykow clearly has something to go on. See, for example, the interesting definition of "condign merit" in Oberman, *The Reformation*, p. 176. In another connection Oberman writes intriguingly: "For Luther the *locus* of the *gloria dei* is the *iustificatio impii*, while for Calvin it is the *iustificatio iusti*" (*Dawn of the Reformation*, p. 238n).

34. When grace encounters faith "again and again," so that faith continually begins again at the beginning, as Barth and Luther both emphasized, that did not imply for either theologian that no progress occurred in any sense. The continual return to the beginning was by no means a Sisyphian exercise in futility. It was more like T. S. Eliot's vision in "Little Gidding": "And the end of all our exploring / Will be to arrive where we started / And know the place for the first time." Also suggestive is the line from "Burnt Norton": "Or say that the end precedes the beginning, / And the end and the beginning were always there / Before the beginning and after the end."

The difficult idea of "progress in sanctification" deserves careful study in both Luther and Barth. Luther could at times speak of becoming righteous as a process *in nobis*. "Alien righ-

Last but not least, one final theme may be noted that Barth acquired from Luther — namely, the relationship of grace to freedom. Barth followed Luther by teaching urgently that grace is unconditioned by anything other than itself, and that fallen human beings in themselves have no capacity for grace. The Luther of *The Bondage of the Will* and similar writings made a profound impression on Barth's mind. Although the Reformed tradition would stand with Luther against synergism more staunchly than would the ensuing Lutheranism, Barth's debt to Luther at this point should not be overlooked. What separated Barth here from the main tendencies of the Reformed tradition while aligning him squarely with Luther was the deep inner connection Barth discerned between unconditioned grace, human incapacity, and the doctrine of *simul iustus et peccator*.[35] In other words, the grace that was unconditioned by anything other than itself was the very grace by which our ongoing human incapacity as sinners was overcome — not more and more, but again and again — by the gift of faith. What Barth owed especially to Luther were thus the constitutive elements in what is known as Barth's distinctive "actualism."[36]

The death of Christ, stated Luther, shows that our wills are impotent by nature (*LW* 33:142). Without grace no one can will what is good (*LW* 33:112). In the absence of grace, "free choice cannot will anything good, but necessarily serves sin" (*LW* 33:147). This bondage of the will means that "salvation is beyond our powers and devices, and depends on the work of God alone. . . . It is not we, but

---

teousness is not instilled all at once, but it begins, makes progress, and is finally perfected at the end through death" (*LW* 31:299). Barth could speak of spiritual progress. "To live a holy life is to be raised and driven with increasing definiteness from the center of this revealed truth, and therefore to live in conversion with growing sincerity, depth and precision" (IV/2, p. 566). Yet for both theologians the emphasis is characteristically elsewhere.

To sum up: At the existential level Luther sees grace confronting faith in three ways: once for all, again and again, and more and more — in that diminishing order of significance. In Calvin (who also accepts the once-for-all), the again-and-again aspect recedes from prominence in favor of a strong emphasis on the more-and-more. By contrast, in Barth (for whom the once-for-all is also strong), the retrieval of *simul iustus et peccator* entailed a corresponding reemphasis on the again-and-again aspect so characteristic of Luther, while the more-and-more aspect in Barth greatly recedes from view. "Growth," as Barth reads the New Testament, is more nearly a predicate of the community than of the individual believer (IV/2, pp. 641-60).

(By the way, note that for all three theologians, the "once-for-all" encounter by which grace initiates faith, decisive and sufficient for the fulfillment of justification, is not identical with the "once-for-all" event of salvation as it has occurred in the life history of Jesus Christ. Rather, the once-for-all occurrence of salvation in Christ *extra nos* finds its existential counterpart in the once-for-all moment *in nobis* of justification by faith alone.)

35. While all three of these are present in Luther, only the first two are unambiguous in the Reformed tradition.

36. For a discussion of Barth's "actualism," see Hunsinger, *How to Read*, passim.

only God, who works salvation in us" (*LW* 33:64). "All the good in us is to be ascribed to God," for "the mercy of God alone does everything" with respect to our salvation, and "our will does nothing, but rather is passive; otherwise, all is not ascribed to God" (*LW* 33:35). To say that the will is passive means "the will is not a cause, but a means through which grace is accepted" (*LW* 34:196). Just as God creates us "without our help," so that we contribute nothing to our being created, so God also regenerates us by faith "without our help," so that we contribute nothing to our being re-created (*LW* 33:243). We become children of God "by a power divinely bestowed upon us, not by a power of free choice inherent in us" (*LW* 33:157). However, although there is thus no such thing as a "neutral" free will (*LW* 33:237), nevertheless "[God] does not work in us without us," but actually grants to us by grace again and again the freedom we would not otherwise enjoy (*LW* 33:243). Human beings who are by nature at war with grace are thus transformed into its friends (*LW* 33:250).

Divine grace and human freedom, as Barth understood them, can be conceptualized only by means of an unresolved antithesis. They cannot be systematized or captured by a unified thought. Any attempt at resolving the antithesis will only result either in a false determinism (the risk run by Luther and Calvin) or in a false libertarianism (the risk run by Augustine and Aquinas). Barth's alternative to thinking in terms of a system here was to think in terms of the Chalcedonian pattern. Grace and freedom existed in the life of faith "without separation or division," "without confusion or change," and according to an "asymmetrical" ordering principle. "Without separation or division" meant that no human freedom occurred without grace, and no divine grace occurred at the expense of freedom. Grace granted the freedom for God that human beings were completely incapable of by nature, not only before but also continually after awakening to faith. Grace and freedom also existed "without confusion or change." Divine grace always remained completely unconditioned, even as human freedom always remained completely dependent on grace (again: *totus/totus*). Finally, grace and freedom were related according to an asymmetrical ordering principle. Human freedom was a completely subordinate and dependent moment within the event of grace. Barth wrote:

> There can be no question of coordination between two comparable elements, but only of the absolute primacy of the divine over the creaturely. The creaturely is made serviceable to the divine and does actually serve it. It is used by God as his organ or instrument. Its creatureliness is not impaired, but is given by God a special function or character. Being qualified and claimed for God for cooperation, it cooperates in such a way that the whole is still an action which is specifically divine. (IV/2, p. 557)

Use of the Chalcedonian pattern to elucidate the relationship of grace to freedom, so characteristic of Barth,[37] was anticipated by Luther in his treatise *Against Latomus,* where the same pattern of thought is already set forth *in nuce* (*LW* 32:257).[38] Although other theological sources will also have been important to Barth at this point, most notably Calvin, here too his debt to Luther cannot be overlooked.[39]

It remains true that Barth had real disagreements with Luther. He empha-

37. See Hunsinger, *How to Read,* pp. 185-224.

38. At the end of his treatise *Against Latomus,* Luther drew an important formal analogy between the justified sinner and the Chalcedonian Christ. In both cases, he stated, we predicate "both natures, with all their properties, of the whole person" (*LW* 32:257); and yet we also take proper care neither to separate them, nor to confuse them. Just as Christ is at once fully human and yet also fully divine, so also is the believer at once completely a sinner and yet also completely a righteous person. As long as sin remains in me, Luther stated, it in some sense determines my person as a whole; and yet by faith my person and all my works are always also determined by something greater than my sin — both in reality and in hope. In a way that anticipated Barth, Luther thus used the Chalcedonian pattern to coordinate the divine agency of grace *in nobis,* which he repeatedly argued was not a quality infused into the soul (e.g., *LW* 32:227), with the believer's sinful human agency. Although Luther admitted that this line of reflection needed further development, the christological analogy allowed him to suggest how the believer's human actions could be completely unrighteous in themselves while yet being righteous by grace before God. For as long as we are on earth, two things — namely, sin and faith in God — are "simultaneously present in us and in all our works" (*LW* 32:233).

39. Important differences, however, should not be forgotten. For one thing, whereas Luther had used the Chalcedonian pattern primarily to suggest the condition for the possibility of human righteousness (including works), Barth would use it more explicitly to elucidate the condition for the possibility of human freedom. For another, Luther would often unfold the christological analogy with a different emphasis than would Barth. In relating grace to freedom, Barth could depart from Luther explicitly (e.g., IV/2, p. 752) while still operating within the framework of the christological analogy that Luther had suggested. The question is obviously more complicated than can be dealt with here. For a salutary discussion, see John Webster, "'The Grammar of Doing': Luther and Barth on Human Agency," in *Barth's Moral Theology: Human Action in Barth's Thought* (Grand Rapids: Eerdmans, 1998), pp. 151-78. As a rough approximation, Webster proposes the following: "For Luther, even in action one is utterly passive, that upon which another [God] acts; for Barth, even in receiving [from God] one is a spontaneous doer, acting in correspondence to the action of the one [God] whose act is received" (p. 159). Webster also cites Jüngel's formulation: For Luther, "God acts, and we receive (and only then can begin to act). For Barth, where God acts, we are seen to act — precisely in receiving" (p. 177). A fine distinction, and very finely put, but it must not be allowed to obscure the larger pattern of agreement between Luther and Barth, who concur on the complete bondage of the will apart from grace, on the unceasing need for grace as a "perpetual operation" which never becomes a *habitus* in the life of faith, and on the epistemic status of the grace/freedom relation as resistant not only to all experientially based apprehension and verification, but also to all rationalistic systematization, so that it remains inaccessible except through the Word of God as disclosed to faith alone.

sized the universal Lordship of Christ in a way that relativized Luther's dichotomy between the two realms. Moreover, in a way that was foreign to Luther, he integrated the hidden God with the revealed God, making them two different aspects of the one God taken as a whole. Again, in contrast to Luther, he elevated reconciliation to preeminence so that justification became a subordinate concept which described reconciliation as a whole — as also did sanctification, justification's simultaneous counterpart.[40] Other examples could also be cited.[41] Yet such powerful themes as substantive christocentrism, the theology of the cross, the primacy of God's Word, the doctrine of *simul iustus et peccator,* and the use of the Chalcedonian pattern in relating divine grace to human freedom are no small legacy for one great theologian to have bequeathed to another.

40. Note, however, that in its formal structure Barth's doctrine of sanctification parallels Luther's doctrine of justification directly (e.g., IV/2, p. 572; Barth even coins the phrase *simul peccator et sanctus* [p. 575]). For Barth sanctification is not primarily a saving process *in nobis,* but rather is identical with Jesus Christ himself. He *is* our sanctification (I Cor. 1:30). Our sanctification *in nobis* is a matter of receiving, participating in, and bearing witness to the One who is our sanctification in himself. Barth thus goes beyond Luther only by building on him. He preserves in sanctification precisely the *solus Christus, sola gratia,* and *sola fide* that had structured Luther's doctrine of justification. Barth does not contradict Luther here so much as he develops and cultivates the quintessence of Luther's Reformation breakthrough.

41. Often regarded as separating Barth from Luther, the law/gospel versus gospel/law contrast may actually have more to do with what separated Barth from Lutheranism. See the wonderfully illuminating and nuanced discussion of Luther in Zachman, pp. 40-53.

CHAPTER 13

Truth as Self-Involving: Barth and Lindbeck

(1993)

It is an axiom of Karl Barth's theology that the truth of the Christian gospel is self-involving.[1] This axiom informed some of Barth's most remarkable judgments. Much of the polemical thunder he unleashed against natural, apologetic, and philosophical forms of theology derived, for example, from this axiom. Theology ought never to be pursued or presented by the Christian community, he believed, as though the reality of the living God could be the object of neutral or detached consideration. The polemic was but the negative consequence of a more positive conception. The truth of the gospel, as Barth understood it, was not only entirely self-involving from the human side, but also and primarily from the divine side. From the divine side this truth was the event whereby God had so fully entered into the depths of human distress that the very heart of God was present in the death of Jesus for the sake of the world. From the human side, in turn, this truth was the event whereby the Word of the cross, as mediated by Scripture and proclaimed by the church, was so actualized in the present that those who received it were themselves transformed from the heart. The existential reception of this truth was to be entirely as self-involving as was God's own prior, active, and continuing self-involvement with each and every human being by virtue of that truth.[2]

To say that this truth is self-involving, however, can be taken to imply — and here is the point to be clarified — that the truth of the gospel depends, at

---

1. Portions of this essay's beginning section have appeared in slightly modified form in George Hunsinger, *How to Read Karl Barth: The Shape of His Theology* (New York: Oxford University Press, 1991), pp. 165-73.

2. Hunsinger, pp. 152-84.

least in some minimal sense, on the quality of a person's self-involvement. Consider, for example, the following proposal as recently advanced by George Lindbeck. When the crusader in the pitch of battle cries *"Christus est Dominus,"* and when this cry is used by the crusader to authorize his cleaving the skull of an infidel, then in such circumstances, Lindbeck argues, the utterance *"Christus est Dominus"* is false. The usage of the utterance would so contradict its correlative form of life as to falsify the utterance itself. The cognitive truth of a religious utterance, according to this proposal, depends on how the utterance is used. Religious utterances acquire cognitive truth only insofar as they are rightly used within a correlative form of life molded by such religious activities as prayer, worship, proclamation, and service. Right use — or to pick up the terms of the opening discussion, the proper kind of self-involvement — is thus proposed as a condition for the possibility that the sentence *"Christus est Dominus"* be true. Such sentences correspond to reality and are therefore cognitively true only insofar as the use of such a sentence corresponds to the correlative form of life. Conversely, insofar as the use of such a sentence stands in contradiction to a correlative form of life, the sentence is false. Valid performance (the proper kind of self-involvement) is thus a condition for the possibility of cognitive truth. Cognitive truth in the sense of correspondence with reality is not an attribute religious utterances can have when considered in and of themselves.[3]

Three preliminary points may be made about this proposal. First, it has been associated with a larger theological formation. "As his frequent references to Barth and his colleagues at Yale . . . make clear, Lindbeck's substantive position is a methodologically sophisticated version of Barthian confessionalism. The hands may be the hands of Wittgenstein and Geertz but the voice is the voice of Karl Barth."[4] Surely no question could stand closer to the core of any theological position than that of how truth is conceived. And surely no such conception would be complete without stating how the cognitive and performative aspects of truth are related. Can it fairly be said, however, that Lindbeck and Barth are so closely in agreement on this matter that the words of the one convey the voice of the other?

Second, this latter question can be answered, it would seem, without delving deeply into Lindbeck's own technical vocabulary. The issue at stake has to do with the semantic features of a sentence such as *"Christus est Dominus."* To

---

3. George Lindbeck, *The Nature of Doctrine: Religion and Theology in a Postliberal Age* (Philadelphia: Westminster, 1984), pp. 63-69.

4. David Tracy, "Lindbeck's New Program for Theology: A Reflection," *Thomist* 49 (1985): 460-72, on p. 465.

what extent, if any, do the semantic features of such a sentence vary with the context in which it is used? Is truth in any sense a property of such sentences, or is it purely a relation between such sentences and their contexts of usage? And if truth is in some sense a relation between sentences and contexts, what would be the total relevant context to be taken into account for an utterance such as *"Christus est Dominus"?* The Lindbeck proposal would seem to involve the idea that truth is not a property that pertains to sentences so much as to the forms of life in which sentences are used. It is not sentences in themselves but religious forms of life as a whole which may properly be said to correspond (or fail to correspond) to reality (i.e., ultimate reality). Insofar as this kind of correspondence actually obtained, the religious form of life would be true. Religious sentences would therefore be true only insofar as they were used in conformity with the truth of a religious form of life. Even if truth were defined as the conformance of the mind with reality *(adequatio mentis ad rem),* the same basic relations would hold. The mind would not be conformed to reality apart from the mediation of the form of life. Because truth describes that relationship whereby the form of life corresponds to reality, neither the mind nor the sentence can correspond to reality in some independent or nonmediated way. If the mind and the sentence do correspond to reality, it can only be as they partake of that prior correspondence to reality that is an attribute of the form of life. The truth of the form of life thus mediates any possible correspondence of the mind or the sentence to reality. A mind not shaped by the form of life and a sentence not used in accord with it would lack a necessary condition for the possibility of truth. Namely, it would lack that correspondence to reality which by definition can only be an attribute of a religious form of life that possesses categories adequate to enable such correspondence to occur in practice.[5]

Third, the issues at stake in this proposal can perhaps be elucidated by introducing a distinction between validity claims and reality domains. Four types of validity claim can be distinguished, and each type may be held to represent a different domain of reality. (1) Claims of *intelligibility,* it might be said, relate to the domain of language; they would thus pertain to formal matters of logic, internal consistency, and sense. (2) Claims of *truth* relate to the domain of external reality; they would pertain to matters of cognitive content, predication, and reference. (3) Claims of *rightness* relate to the domain of social reality; they would pertain to performative content, patterns of behavior, and communal

---

5. For a very full discussion of these themes, see Bruce D. Marshall, "Aquinas as Postliberal Theologian," *Thomist* 53 (1989): 357-70. Marshall's account of Lindbeck's work has been strongly endorsed by Lindbeck himself. See Lindbeck, "Response to Bruce Marshall," *Thomist* 53 (1989): 403-6.

norms and values. (4) Claims of *truthfulness* relate to the domain of internal reality; they would pertain to matters of intention, sincerity, and aptness of emotive expression. Intelligibility, truth, rightness, and truthfulness may thus be regarded as distinct validity claims that pertain to the domains of linguistic, external, social, and internal reality respectively.[6]

If these distinctions are adopted, the Lindbeck proposal might be interpreted as follows. In religious matters, at least, claims of *rightness* (and perhaps also of truthfulness) are logically prior to claims of *truth* (and perhaps also of intelligibility), because the domain of *social reality* (and perhaps also of internal reality) necessarily mediates all relations of correspondence to the domain of *external reality* (and perhaps also all construals of the formal domain of language). More precisely, *rightness* becomes a necessary condition for the possibility of *truth,* just because what corresponds to ultimate reality is the religious form of life as such, not minds or sentences independent of that form of life or in conflict with it. A kind of social coherentism seems to be the result. The coherence of linguistic usage with behavior in accord with communal norms *(rightness)* is a condition for the possibility of using a sentence to refer accurately to the external domain of ultimate reality *(truth).* No religious utterance can be true that is not rightly socially embodied, and any religious utterance is false that arises from within the community and yet is so used that it contradicts that rightness by which the community in its form of life corresponds to reality. The sentence *"Christus est Dominus"* as uttered by the crusader when cleaving the head of the infidel is thus false, because the sentence is being used to authorize behavior that contradicts communal norms and values. Its falseness is its contradiction from within the community of what the community's form of life as a whole affirms about ultimate reality.

The question now to be considered is not the possible adequacy or inadequacy of the Lindbeck proposal, but rather the extent to which it may or may not converge with what Barth says about truth as personally self-involving. In what ways might Barth's personalist conception of the truth in Christian theology be thought to concur with Lindbeck's proposal, and in what ways to conflict with it? Points of convergence are not entirely lacking in Barth's theology. The idea that the truth of the gospel is necessarily self-involving entails for Barth the idea that "the existential determination of the Christian" has a significant impact on the validity of the Christian's witness.[7] Anyone who is called to

---

6. Francis Fiorenza, *Foundational Theology: Jesus and the Church* (New York: Crossroad, 1984), p. 294.

7. Karl Barth, *Church Dogmatics* IV/3, second half (Edinburgh: T. & T. Clark, 1962), p. 655; hereafter cited as IV/3.

attest the living God has necessarily been touched and apprehended by God's love. The person's "whole being" has been engaged. The love of God must therefore be reflected in that person's life. Without this reflection of divine love in the person's life and testimony, even the purest orthodoxy "becomes an idle pursuit." "Even the trinitarian God of Nicene dogma, or the Christ of the Chalcedonian definition, if seen and proclaimed in exclusive objectivity" — that is, with no regard for the love that must accompany all such seeing and proclaiming — "necessarily becomes an idol like all others, with whom one cannot live and whom one cannot therefore attest. And there is something menacing and dangerous in an orthodoxy of this kind" (IV/3, p. 655). Here, it would seem, is the idea that the attitude and behavior of the Christian can falsify the most orthodox teachings of the church. Even the venerable dogmas of the Trinity and the incarnation can be turned into their very opposites — idols that render both life and testimony impossible.

Even stronger, if possible, are certain statements Barth makes about "the act of love" as a necessary accompaniment to "the act of witness." As it takes place between one person and another within the Christian community, the act of witness can be fulfilled "only as we love one another."[8] The act of witness pertains to the love of God as attested in Scripture and confirmed in the community. It thus involves imparting information "which would otherwise be inaccessible" and confirming claims "which have no other means of confirmation." One human being witnesses to another when the truth of the gospel is imparted and confirmed in this personal way. "The truth and reality" of the divine love "stand or fall" with the love of the person who attests it. The more important and indispensable the testimony to God's love, "the more important and indispensable is the existence and activity of the one who gives it, the witness" (IV/2, p. 812). Here, it would seem, is a convergence with the more grammatical remark that right performance is a condition for the possibility of using a sentence in a way that is cognitively true. The form of the human action — the extent to which it is grounded in love — is said to answer for the truth and reality of God's love, just as the truth and reality of God's love are said to stand or fall with the form of the human action. The backing for these statements is found in the nature of God's love itself. For God's love is real, says Barth, "not as a general truth about God," but only "in God's constant activity." God's love is such as to actualize itself continually in and through loving human action (IV/2, p. 812). The motifs of actualism and personalism, when taken in combination, would seem to point toward ac-

8. Karl Barth, *Church Dogmatics* IV/2 (Edinburgh: T. & T. Clark, 1958), p. 812; hereafter cited as IV/2.

cepting the proposition that proper self-involvement is a necessary condition for uttering true theological statements.

On closer inspection, however, there are also signs of divergence. Even in the examples just cited, the convergence is not complete. On careful examination, even they seem to have more to do with rightness and truthfulness than with truth and intelligibility per se. The possibility that an otherwise true theological claim can seriously be abused never seems to imply for Barth as unequivocally as for Lindbeck that in some particular instance the abused claim could be falsified without remainder. The basic reason for this difference is that truth and intelligibility never seem to depend as fully for Barth as for Lindbeck on the rightness and truthfulness with which a theological claim is made. Thus in the same passage where Barth speaks of neutralizing orthodox teachings to the point of falsification, he also speaks of "the objective superiority" of the teachings over their human reception (IV/3, p. 655). Presumably, this superiority would imply that even in an abusive situation the truth of the claim could not be completely nullified by the abuse. Or again, in the same passage where he speaks of human love as necessary for attesting divine love, Barth also speaks of the truth and reality of God's love as occurring "primarily and intrinsically" on another and different plane (IV/2, p. 813). Presumably, the difference between these two planes of love implies that the validity of utterances about the divine plane can neither be totally established nor totally undermined by the human plane on which they are uttered. In both passages, it would seem, certain theological circumstances are perceived that mitigate against a more complete convergence with Lindbeck. Barth seems clearly to presuppose that the truth and intelligibility of theological claims are in some sense logically independent of the rightness and truthfulness with which they may either be advanced or contradicted on the human plane. This line of interpretation is borne out by what Barth says elsewhere about questions of intelligibility and truth.

Intelligibility is viewed as independent of social and personal conditions, for example, when Barth states that the content of the gospel is "intrinsically clear" (IV/3, p. 848). The gospel may not be generally knowable, "[b]ut it is generally intelligible and explicable." In principle no special assistance is needed to understand what the gospel is claiming, for its content is marked by "inner clarity, rationality and perspicuity" (IV/3, p. 848). Similarly, the truth of the gospel seems to be viewed as something significantly independent of social and personal conditions when Barth writes that the content of the gospel is "intrinsically true" (IV/3, p. 656). "The love of God does not await my response to love to be eternal and omnipotently saving love. Nor is it the case that the truth is conditioned by the fact or manner of its expression in your or my existence." Its being the truth cannot be conceived as resting on anthropological considerations. "It would be the truth even if it had no witnesses." It also remains the truth despite how its witnesses may perform. "It is the truth even though its human witnesses fail. It does not live by Christians, but Christians by it" (IV/3, p. 656).

Of the skull-cleaving crusader's cry that *"Christus est Dominus,"* therefore, Barth would certainly be able to say that it is meaningless. A situation of absurdity is created by the contradiction between the utterance in its normative usage and the deed it is being used to authorize. Barth would also be able to say that what the crusader means by *Dominus* is manifestly false. For, according to the communally normative definition of Scripture, Christ's Lordship is exercised as suffering servanthood. Up to this point Barth would be in convergence with Lindbeck. He would agree that in these ways the word is falsified by the deed. Yet he would diverge from Lindbeck on the extent of this falsification and on its grounds. For he would also insist that the deed is falsified by the word. Why, he might ask, should the meaning of what the crusader says (and thus its possible truth) be determined simply by the use to which the crusader puts it? Why should meaning and truth be treated so atomistically? Are there not standard and paradigmatic uses that create a background against which any particular use operates?[9] And why should meaning and truth be treated so anthropocentrically? What exactly establishes the total relevant context? Is it not finally determined by God in such a way that cultural-linguistic considerations (or any other anthropological considerations), however valid they may be on their own plane, cannot be either decisive or exhaustive?

Jesus Christ is viewed by Barth as the truth of the gospel. This truth takes secondary form in the written testimony of Scripture, and tertiary form, so to speak, in the verbal testimony of the church. Neither form of testimony occurs in such a way that the truth of Jesus Christ is simply a semantic feature of those sentences by which this testimony is expressed. Yet the verbal form of this testimony is thought to be so indirectly identical with Jesus Christ that he continually discloses himself through it.[10] Neither this indirect identity in itself (realism) nor the event by which Jesus Christ discloses himself through it (actualism) is thought to depend in any logically tight or predetermined way on the rightness or truthfulness of the witnessing community. Rightness and truthfulness in themselves cannot guarantee that even the community's most orthodox statements about Jesus Christ will be divinely attested. Yet neither can

9. For the suggestion of these formulations, I am indebted to personal correspondence from my friend Michael Root. See Root, "Truth, Relativism, and Postliberal Theology," *Dialog* 25 (1986): 179.

10. Karl Barth, *Church Dogmatics* I/1, 2nd ed. (Edinburgh: T. & T. Clark, 1975), pp. 88-120; hereafter cited as I/1.

the community's wrongness or bad faith in using such statements simply undermine the verbal form by which they are indirectly identical with Christ (even though they can create serious and humanly insurmountable obstacles for divine attestation). Even in a situation of abuse as illustrated by the skull-cleaving crusader, the total relevant context would be so established by the pattern of divine activity as mediated by Scripture and proclaimed by the church that *"Christus est Dominus"* would retain a margin of superiority over the abuse to which it was put, standing in real though implicit condemnation over the act of abuse itself (I/1, pp. 110-11, 154).

What is finally decisive for Barth in any consideration of the performative aspect of theological truth is not the human but the divine mode of involvement. Does not God's use of the community's theological utterances, Barth might ask, so overrule its use of them that even its most right, truthful, and orthodox usage does not guarantee that an utterance will actually be divinely attested and thus made to correspond to reality in any given situation, whether for the one who utters it or for the one to whom it may be addressed? Conversely, does not God's normative though indirect self-attestation in the written form of Scripture mean that even the community's most flagrant abuse of scriptural assertions cannot in itself serve totally to nullify the objective superiority of the assertion over the abuse? The first question pertains to Barth's actualism; the second to his realism. The first points to the freedom and sovereignty of God's grace and to the incapacity of either the witness or the addressee to make the utterance (or the mind) correspond to reality apart from the miracle of grace that attests it. In this sense it is the miracle of grace, not use in accordance with a correlative form of life, that is decisive for the correspondence of a theological utterance with reality. What is decisive for the event of correspondence is the divine, not the human, activity.

The second question, in turn, points to the scriptural mediation of God's Word. As God's Word assumes secondary form in the written word of Scripture, Scripture is made into a normative and verbally stabilized witness to the events of divine self-revelation and therefore to the living God. In this normative and verbally stabilized form, Scripture becomes the semantic vehicle by which human utterances are brought into correspondence with the reality of God. Although this vehicle remains inert apart from the miracle of grace, its semantic features were established to play an integral part in the ongoing history of God's self-revelation. The truth of these features needs to be actualized for the addressee in a self-involving way by the miracle of grace in an encounter with the living God, but it is just these features whose truth is actualized. These semantic features, as established by God, retain their objective superiority even in situations where they may be falsified as much as is humanly possible by an act of abuse. In this sense it is Scripture itself, not the correlative form of life it shapes, that serves as the vehicle of correspondence between theological utterances and the reality of God. What is decisive for establishing the cognitive truth of such utterances are the semantic features of Scripture, whose validity rests, once again, Barth believes, on divine, not human, action.

What would finally seem to characterize Barth's overall position on the relationship between self-involvement and truth, therefore, is not the dependence of truth on self-involvement, but the dependence of self-involvement on truth. The cognitive truth of a theological assertion does not finally depend on the rightness of the community's (or the individual's) performance in a correlative form of life. Rightness and truthfulness are by no means irrelevant to the valid assertion of the truth, but neither are they the final and overriding conditions for its possibility. They always have an important and powerful role to play, but never so important that they can condition and determine the truth of assertions embedded in the gospel itself. Even in situations where such assertions are badly abused by adherents, their truth retains objective superiority over the abuse.

To sum up: with respect to how the cognitive and the performative aspects of truth in theological discourse are related, the divergences between Barth and Lindbeck would seem to be more significant than the convergences. Indeed, these divergences may actually reflect certain classical disagreements in the Christian tradition about how to view the relationship between nature and grace. Lindbeck, who quotes from Aquinas far more extensively than from Barth, can perhaps be read as offering a methodologically sophisticated version of the idea that grace perfects but does not destroy nature. This reading must remain tentative, for Lindbeck has not (to my knowledge) addressed this question explicitly. Can it be irrelevant, however, that Lindbeck finds it possible to define the necessary and sufficient conditions for the truth of a theological assertion without once referring to the role of divine agency?

This silence does not imply that no account of God's role could be given, but it does imply something about the limits within which such an account would proceed. Such an account might propose, for example, that what can be described phenomenologically with respect to human agency could also be described from another vantage point with respect to divine agency in such a way that the two accounts would simply be complementary. The account of divine agency would offer another perspective on the question of the conditions for cognitive truth, but would not substantively alter what can be said through phenomenological description. The roles of divine and human agency, it seems, would thereby be conceived as systematically coordinated. That is to say, just as the divine agency would precede, facilitate, and perfect the human, so also the human agency would follow, cooperate with, and contribute to the divine. Insofar as the human agency were independent of the divine, the divine agency would be dependent on the human. Insofar as the divine agency were contradicted by the human (through misuse), the human agency would preclude the divine. These limitations on divine agency might be thought of as the price God was willing to pay for establishing what Lonergan has called "a universe of finalistic spontaneity."[11]

Regardless of whether Lindbeck would subscribe to this hypothetical extension of his argument, it does not seem incompatible with his position. It seems to allow a place for divine agency while still respecting the strong role Lindbeck ascribes to human agency in causing theological utterance to be either true or false. When a theological utterance was used by a member of the community in accord with the correlative form of life, the use would be preceded, facilitated, and perfected by divine agency, just as divine agency would be followed, reciprocated, and supplemented by the use. Quite significantly, making such a role for divine agency explicit adds nothing essential to the analysis of the conditions under which a theological utterance can be true. It complicates the account of use but not the account of conditions for truth. A parallel situation would obtain with respect to the conditions for falsification. Any possible role for divine agency would be so supplanted by the human act of abuse that the utterance would effectively be rendered false. No role is ascribed to divine agency with respect to the conditions for truth or falsity which cannot be sufficiently accounted for by the conception of human use in accord with a religious form of life. Even in the case of an assertion normatively embedded in the gospel, such as *"Christus est Dominus,"* human agency not only plays an indispensable role in making it be true, but also has the decisive power of rendering it cognitively false.

When the Lindbeck proposal is redescribed in terms of its possible location within a hypothetically "Thomistic" scheme of nature and grace, its divergence from Barth's theology is thrown into sharp relief. (The logic of this redescription seems plausible enough to pursue for the sake of the contrast with Barth, regardless of whether Lindbeck would actually subscribe to it, and regardless of whether it would be the best way to understand a "Thomistic" scheme. The redescription and the scheme as sketched need only be plausible enough to advance a discussion which seems likely to continue.) Three points of divergence especially stand out. First, Barth would not allow the possibility of relating phenomenological and theological description through a strategy of

---

11. Bernard Lonergan, *Grace and Freedom: Operative Grace in the Thought of St. Thomas Aquinas* (New York: Herder & Herder, 1971), p. 112 n.

systematic coordination.[12] He would consider it illegitimate to begin with phenomenological description and then afterward to coordinate theological description with it systematically, as though the two modes of description could be unified as relatively independent parts of a larger conceptual whole. The theological losses incurred by such a procedure struck him as being intolerable. The subject matter of Christian theology, he believed, was so singular, heterogeneous, and primordial that it could not be assimilated by any other descriptive mode, but could only be elucidated in terms of its own inner logic. And only as so elucidated could this subject matter then be placed in relationship to relevant instances of phenomenological description. At best this relationship could never be more than one of ad hoc correlation. Although the results of phenomenological description need not be incompatible with the subject matter of Christian theology, those results could never even partially subsume that subject matter in its essential singularity, heterogeneity, and primordiality. No strategy of systematic coordination between these two modes of description could be conceived that did not finally forfeit the definitive uniqueness of the theological subject matter. Systematic coordination was therefore incompatible with theology in a way that ad hoc correlation was not.[13]

Second, this methodological point has a more substantive counterpart. Just as systematic coordination was impermissible between theological and phenomenological description, so also was it impermissible between divine and human agency. It was precisely this impermissibility which Barth characteristically urged against "Thomistic" schemes of nature and grace.[14] Here, too, the project of systematic coordination was thought to result in intolerable theological losses. Although the backing for this judgment was a complex skein of exegetical and doctrinal considerations which cannot be unraveled here, it can at least be indicated that two points especially were thought to be undermined by such "Thomistic" schemes: that the divine freedom is never conditioned by anything other than itself, and that the freedom of the human creature is never actual in relation to God except as elicited and sustained from beyond itself by God alone (and therefore not as based even partially on any infused virtues, dispositions, or habits). Because these two points were regarded as indispensable within the web of Chris-

---

12. For Barth's rejection of any "systematic coordination" between nature and grace, see the more detailed account above on pp. 163-67.

13. See, for example, Karl Barth, *Church Dogmatics* III/2 (Edinburgh: T. & T. Clark, 1960), pp. 1-19, 71-132.

14. Karl Barth, "No! Answer to Emil Brunner," in *Natural Theology* (London: Geoffrey Bles, 1946), pp. 85-105; Barth, *Church Dogmatics* I/2 (Edinburgh: T. & T. Clark, 1956), pp. 375, 790-91; Barth, *Church Dogmatics* II/1 (Edinburgh: T. & T. Clark, 1957), pp. 567-86.

tian belief, and because they could not both be maintained at the same time without paradox, paradoxical modes of thought were embraced as a sign that there theology had reached a point where "the truths of faith have the apex of their intelligibility hidden in the transcendence of God."[15] The logic of paradox and the attendant, more nearly theological categories of miracle and mystery were Barth's alternatives to the logic of systematic coordination with respect to the relation between divine and human agency.[16]

This logic underlies Barth's divergence from Lindbeck, as previously and hypothetically described, on the question of truth in theological discourse. The basic pattern of Barth's reflection might be described as follows. Although the freedom of divine agency is independent of and external to that of human agency, the freedom of human agency is dependent on and internal to that of divine agency. Because the divine agency is essentially external to and unconditioned by the human, no systematic coordination is possible between the divine freedom and even the most correct human use of orthodox theological utterances. Nor is systematic coordination possible between the possibilities of divine freedom and even the most serious human abuse of orthodox theological utterances. Insofar as any correct human use of such utterances is divinely attested and thus actually made to correspond to the living reality of God, it can only be conceived as a miracle of grace and described paradoxically as an instance of double agency such that the freedom and validity of the human use is real only as determined entirely from without by the unconditioned freedom of God. Yet, insofar as any orthodox theological utterance is subjected to serious human abuse, whether by a member of the Christian community or not, there is nothing to prevent that abuse from being positively overruled by the sovereignty of grace in such a way that the event of correspondence occurs in spite of everything, whether with respect to the addressee or the addressor or both (depending on the circumstances). The event of correspondence between the cognitive truth of a theological utterance and the reality of God is thus conceived as being logically independent of right or wrong human use, just because the only logically indispensable condition for this correspondence is the miracle of divine grace. Insofar as the miracle of this correspondence occurs, the divine freedom has actualized itself in, with, beyond, and against the freedom of the human creature, the reality of whose freedom has been elicited and sustained by the miracle of grace alone and included within the mystery of the unconditioned freedom of God.

Third and finally, the divergence between Barth and Lindbeck on the question of falsification pertains to what might he called the vehicle of corre-

15. Lonergan, p. 8.
16. Hunsinger, pp. 185-224.

spondence in matters of theological truth. For Lindbeck this vehicle is the form of life correlative to the use of normative theological utterances. In this conception the relationship between the form of life and Scripture, although described in dialectical terms, is made logically to depend in some strong sense on human use. Just as the use of Scripture shapes the form of life, so also does the form of life shape the use of Scripture, yet it is finally the form of life as a whole rather than Scripture as such which is thought to mediate the correspondence between a normative theological utterance as rightly used and the ultimate or divine reality.[17] Truth is conceived primarily as a predicate of the form of life as it corresponds to the reality of God. Should the question be raised about just how truth as a predicate of the form of life is related to truth as a predicate of God, the answer would presumably proceed along Thomistic lines that the *modus significandi* as such cannot be stated because it cannot be known.[18] In any case, the cognitive truth of normative theological utterances — even those found directly in Scripture itself — is made logically to depend on right human use within the correlative form of life.[19] No scriptural utterance can be true, it would seem, apart from its performative mediation through the correlative form of life. The form of life is conceived as the semantic vehicle through which scriptural utterances must pass, so to speak, in order to correspond to divine reality (or in order to conform the mind to that reality). No account of the truth of scriptural utterances would seem to be possible, within the logic of the Lindbeck proposal, in which the cognitive truth of such statements did not logically depend on performative mediation through the form of life conceived as the indispensable vehicle of correspondence with the reality of God.

In Barth's theology Jesus Christ is indirectly identical with Scripture in a way that can never be maintained of Jesus Christ's relationship with the church. It is therefore Scripture, not the church — not even the church considered in its formal aspect as a correlative form of life — to which the semantic role is assigned of mediating the cognitive truth of theological utterances so that they are brought into correspondence with the divine reality. Regardless of the senses in which that mediation may occur in a context of active relations proceeding from God to humanity and from humanity to God, it is Scripture and not the church which serves as the earthly historical vehicle of semantic correspondence. The semantic features of Scripture (as established by divine agency in and through the primitive, apostolic community) are conceived as a secondary and indirect extension of

17. Lindbeck, *The Nature of Doctrine*, pp. 32-41, 64-65, 116-20.

18. Lindbeck, *The Nature of Doctrine*, p. 67.

19. See Lindbeck, "The Story-Shaped Church: Critical Exegesis and Theological Interpretation," in *Scriptural Authority and Narrative Interpretation*, ed. Garrett Green (Philadelphia: Fortress, 1987), pp. 170, 174.

the mediatorial role exercised by Jesus Christ himself. Although those semantic features in themselves remain inert until actualized by the miracle of grace (i.e., by divine agency), it is precisely those features which are actualized as the normative human witness to the divine self-disclosure. The authority of Scripture depends formally on its embodiment of certain christocentric semantic features even as it depends materially on the event of their divine actualization in the present. These formal and material aspects of scriptural authority are what make Scripture the Word of God, as Barth understands it, in a way that the church can never be, not even when considered as a form of life correlative to right performance. Neither the formal nor the material aspects of scriptural authority are conceived in such a way that they can be made logically to depend on right performance. Nor is it logically possible for scriptural authority so conceived to be coordinated systematically with the authority of the church, as though the two were finally somehow dialectically identical (see I/1, pp. 256-65). The divergence between Barth and Lindbeck on what constitutes the vehicle of semantic correspondence would thus seem to reflect traditional Protestant-Catholic disputes about the relationship between Scripture and tradition (regardless of Lindbeck's standing, of course, as a prominent Lutheran theologian). Barth affirms the unequivocal authority of Scripture over tradition (and therefore over right performance in accord with a correlative form of life) in a way that Lindbeck does not.

When the Lindbeck proposal is redescribed within a "Thomistic" scheme of nature and grace, therefore, the divergences from Barth, despite initial appearances to the contrary, emerge all the more dramatically. Their differences on the relationship between cognitive and performative aspects of the truth in theological discourse would seem to be embedded in certain classical disagreements about the relationship between nature and grace. These classical disagreements have been excavated as underlying some significant divergences regarding the relationships between phenomenological and theological modes of description, between divine and human agency, and between Scripture and tradition. If this hypothetical redescription is not too far amiss, then Lindbeck's position ought not be confused with positions from which it departs. When it comes to stipulating the conditions for cognitive truth, the words are the words of Lindbeck, but the voice is much more nearly that of Aquinas than of Barth.[20]

---

20. "My utilization of contemporary developments has been heavily influenced by the reading and teaching of St. Thomas that I have done since my undergraduate days four decades ago. Aquinas was a constant, even if background, presence while I wrote *The Nature of Doctrine*" (Lindbeck, "Response to Bruce Marshall," p. 405).

CHAPTER 14

The Harnack/Barth Correspondence:
A Paraphrase with Comments

(1986)

In 1923 Adolf von Harnack published an open letter to the despisers of scientific theology — by which he meant the emerging new group of "dialectical theologians" — and this letter was to initiate the climactic phase of his history with Karl Barth. That history had begun years earlier in the winter semester of 1906-7, when the young Karl Barth had moved as a student to Berlin. To his surprise Barth soon came to think more highly of Harnack than of any other professor. Attaching himself to the great theologian as a pupil, he became the youngest regular member of Harnack's seminar in church history, in which he worked with great diligence. Harnack regarded Barth as a promising student.[1]

The second phase of their history was one of which Harnack knew nothing, but which for Barth was that now-famous moment of theological disillusionment shortly after the outbreak of the First World War. Finding the names of his most revered teachers attached to a manifesto acclaiming Germany's war policy of aggression, Barth was so shaken that he felt a need to break decisively with their liberal theological presuppositions. Prominent among the signatories was none other than Adolf von Harnack, whom Barth always mentioned explicitly, among others, when recalling the impact of the manifesto upon him.[2]

1. Eberhard Busch, *Karl Barth* (Philadelphia: Fortress, 1976), pp. 38-39.

2. In a recent article Wilfred Härle has attempted to cast doubt on the significance of the 1914 manifesto for Barth's break with liberalism. Härle documents that there was not one such manifesto but two, and that they did not appear in August, as Barth years later would recall, but in October. These facts by themselves would be of marginal interest. Härle goes on to argue that

The third phase of their relationship, a kind of prelude to the 1923 correspondence, occurred when both men spoke at a student conference in 1920. Barth lectured on the topic "Biblical Questions, Insights and Vistas."[3] He declared God to be "wholly other," dismissed historical method as a means to theological knowledge, and denounced all organic connections between human culture and divine revelation as contrary to the cross of Christ. The effect of Barth's lecture on Harnack was, according to Harnack's biographer, staggering. "There was not one sentence, not one thought, with which he could agree." Harnack could acknowledge Barth's deep seriousness, but Barth's theology "made him shudder."[4] Horrified that the new theology continued to gain ground, Harnack at last threw down the gauntlet in 1923.

The debate, which took place in the pages of *Die Christliche Welt,* occurred in several exchanges. Harnack opened with "fifteen questions," and Barth countered with "fifteen answers." Harnack returned with an "open letter" addressed directly to Barth, and Barth retorted with a very long "answer."

---

no evidence can be found in contemporary documents that the capitulation of Barth's teachers in general and the manifesto in particular played as significant a role for Barth as Barth later attributed to them. Although this question deserves further investigation, a document not available to Härle has since been cited by Busch (*Karl Barth,* p. 81 n. 104) which is contemporary and which pertains to the fundamental point of the impact on Barth of the capitulation of Barth's teachers. Härle goes on to make two further points which in my opinion make his argument dubious. First, although he correctly observes that Barth's break with liberalism was starting to become visible prior to 1914, he mistakenly assumes that these prior developments must rule out a decisive shock of recognition in 1914. He also mistakenly reads Barth's assimilation of religious-socialist motifs as evidence of Barth's break with liberalism. Theologically, however, the assimilation of these motifs was more nearly a supplement to than a break with Barth's early liberalism. The second questionable move occurs when Härle engages in psychological speculations pertaining to Barth's relationship to his father. Even if such speculations were not precarious, they would not necessarily rule out the shock of recognition in 1914 nor would they explain the theological motives for Barth's break with liberalism. See Wilfred Härle, "Der Aufruf der 93 Intellektuellen und Karl Barths Bruch mit der liberalen Theologie," *Zeitschrift für Theologie und Kirche* 72 (1975): 206-24. For an excellent account of Barth's break with liberalism, see Bruce McCormack, *Karl Barth's Critically Realistic Dialectical Theology* (Oxford: Clarendon, 1995).

3. The lecture may be found in Karl Barth, *The Word of God and the Word of Man* (New York: Harper & Row, 1957), pp. 51-96.

4. Agnes von Zahn-Harnack, *Adolf von Harnack* (Berlin: Hans Bott Verlag, 1936, 1951), p. 532. I am borrowing the translation made of this passage by G. Wayne Glick, *The Reality of Christianity: A Study of Adolf von Harnack as Historian and Theologian* (New York: Harper & Row, 1967), p. 223. For a study of the Harnack/Barth correspondence which pays special attention to its prelude in 1920, see Peter Henke, "Erwählung und Entwicklung, Zur Auseinandersetzung zwischen Adolf von Harnack und Karl Barth," *Neue Zeitschrift für Systematische Theologie und Religionsphilosophie* 18 (1976): 194-208.

Finally, Harnack drafted a "postscript," which drew the debate to a close.[5] Although personal relations between the two men remained cordial, the theological rift between them was too fundamental to be overcome.[6]

The Harnack/Barth correspondence continues to be of interest, not only because it was a historic encounter between the leading liberal and the leading dialectical theologian of the day, but also because of the light it casts on Barth's theology in particular. The questions posed by Harnack have recurred again and again in the reception and assessment of Barth's theology. The answers proposed by Barth, though not final in terms of his development, nonetheless indicated the basic intentions which would undergird his massive lifelong theological project. The correspondence thus affords an excellent opportunity not only to observe Barth's theology in process of definition, but also to understand it in relation to the past from which it broke so dramatically. At the same time, the correspondence serves as a concise and accessible introduction to continuing themes in Barth's work.

The exercise which follows is intended to be entirely modest. The correspondence as a whole will simply be paraphrased according to Harnack's original format of fifteen topics. Harnack's questions will be reversed into assertions in order to bring out the constructive standpoint lurking behind his critique. Barth's answers will be summarized on the basis of the entire correspondence. Having set forth the course of debate on its own terms, I will conclude with some critical observations.[7]

1. On revelation and reason, especially as they relate to Scripture.

   Harnack. The Bible's religious content is not unequivocal but quite diverse. If we are to determine it for faith, worship, and life, we need a better basis than merely subjective and individual experience. We need to draw upon historical knowledge and critical reflection. How is theology to deal with the diversity of biblical content, if not rationally, by means of historical analysis? Historical knowledge and critical reflection are indispensable if we are to avoid naive biblicism.

---

5. An English translation may be found in *The Beginnings of Dialectic Theology*, ed. James M. Robinson (Richmond: John Knox, 1968), pp. 165-87. Complete reference to the German original may be found in H. Martin Rumscheidt, *Revelation and Theology: An Analysis of the Barth-Harnack Correspondence of 1925* (Cambridge: Cambridge University Press, 1972), p. 201 n. 2. The German text may be found most conveniently in Karl Barth, *Theologische Fragen und Antworten* (Zürich: Evangelischer Verlag Zollikon, 1967), pp. 7-31.

6. See Busch, p. 147; Zahn-Harnack, p. 534.

7. A detailed analysis of the correspondence may be found in Rumscheidt, *Revelation and Theology*. See also Glick, pp. 222-28.

Barth. God's revelation is unitary, not incoherent. The content of this revelation is autonomous, suprarational, and self-communicating. Knowledge cannot be "historical," properly speaking, if it fails to recognize precisely this living and transcendent quality of God's revelation. No
knowledge which denies or reinterprets this quality can properly be
called "historical." The concept of history is, in effect, to be critically
subordinated to the concepts of theology. This understanding of God's
revelation — as unitary; as autonomous, suprarational, and self-
communicating; as living and transcendent — is grounded in the relationship of God to humanity as disclosed by God's revelation ("the essence of the subject matter"). God's revelation, in other words, is all
these things by definition — and by event. "Critical reflection" would
recognize this event as such and respect it — at least within the context
of theology and faith. Theology depends on the remembrance that the
object of its reflection — God — had previously been for it the living
and sovereign subject. God must become this subject for theology again
and again. The event of God's self-disclosure as indissolubly subject has
nothing at all to do with an anthropocentric and subjectivist concept of
religious experience. Theological method is "scientific" — i.e., appropriate to and governed by its subject matter — to the extent that it recognizes its object as indissolubly subject. In short, revelation affirms, transcends, delimits, and relativizes reason, including critical historical
reason. Is the method to determine the subject matter (Harnack), or is
the subject matter to determine the method (Barth)?

2. On the conditions for the possibility of understanding the content of Scripture.

Harnack. Historical knowledge and critical reflection need to be used if we
are to understand the Bible's diverse content, which is not self-evident
and clear in itself. The Bible's content is not so inconceivable and inde-
scribable — so unhistorical — that we must wait upon inner illumination in order to grasp it. Inner openness or empathy may be necessary,
but that is no substitute for historical knowledge and critical reflection.
In short, biblical content is not self-evident, but neither is it inconceivable. It is accessible to critical historical analysis. An unhistorical transcendentalism goes hand in hand with arbitrary subjectivism.

Barth. The Bible can be understood in the proper (theological) sense of the
term only by the power of the Spirit — who is the same as its content.
The content of the Bible, in other words, is the person of the living God.
This content is acknowledged, and in that sense "understood," only by
faith. This content (the living God), its mode of impartation (the power

of the Spirit), and its mode of apprehension (faith) are all *sui generis*. They are all, by definition, in a class by themselves. They are not, in other words, merely particular instances of something more general, nor are they generally (rationally) accessible. They are equidistant from both religious experience and historical reason, and have no essential connection to either, although a contingent connection to either or both may and does arise. But revelation and faith stand on their own. They do not need either religious experience or critical historical reason to be what they are. They are what they are without them. God's revelation is imparted to us by God, by the power of the Spirit; and it is received by the miracle and mystery of faith (not by this or that mental faculty). Those who on critical historical grounds develop an a priori rejection of miracle and mystery, of revelation and faith, of that which passes all understanding, cut themselves off to that extent from the gospel.

3. On faith, religious experience, and preaching, especially whether faith is subject to phenomenological description and preaching to rational control.

 Harnack. Awakening to faith cannot be had without religious experience, for the two are not different but identical. Faith, being essentially experiential, is subject to phenomenological description. If the two were different, faith would be indistinguishable from uncontrollable fanaticism. Faith can be so distinguished, however, because it can only come about through the preaching of the gospel, and because such preaching is not possible without historical knowledge and critical reflection. Preaching disciplined by historical reason is therefore necessary for awakening a responsible faith. Faith divorced from historically disciplined experience would be irrational and therefore arbitrary.

 Barth. Faith and religious experience are two entirely different things, as different as the earth (the phenomenal) is from heaven (the transcendental, the eschatological, the real). As a matter of fact, however, faith cannot always be phenomenologically distinguished from "uncontrollable fanaticism" or, for that matter, from "religious experience." No human experience as such is identical with the awakening to faith, but religious experience can serve as a symptom or sign of the presence of faith. At best, religious experience has the status of a witness to faith. But experiences, whatever they might be, are not to be confused with or mistaken for faith. The preaching of the gospel, which properly awakens faith as the response, depends not on historical research or critical reflection, but on the word of Christ. In other words, the condition for the possibility of effective preaching is not human reason but divine revelation. Divine revelation is the object and content of both theology and preaching. Each in its own way is concerned with taking up and passing on God's revelation (the word of Christ). To that extent theology and preaching have the same task. There is no reason why they cannot be assisted in this task in an occasional and auxiliary way by "historical knowledge" and "critical reflection."

4. On how one's view of faith pertains to one's view of being in the world.

Harnack. Religious experience is not in a class by itself. It is not contrary to or disparate from all other experience. If it were, the logical result would be either a radical flight from the world or else a lapse into sophistry. The sophistry would arise because even a decision to flee the world would require an act of volition and would still therefore be something worldly. Religious experience *qua* experience is something worldly, just like all other experience. So far from being exceptional, religious experience is an instance of the general class called historical experience. An ahistorical (religious) experience would in practice necessitate a flight from the world, which is not only impossible but self-contradictory.

Barth. Faith involves not a flight from the world, but a more or less radical protest against this world. Faith protests against the world we see on the basis of the world's coming transformation, which we do not see, but for which we hope by the promises of God. The fundamental distance of faith from this world is grounded not only in eschatological hope, but also in creation faith — in our acknowledgment of God as Creator. Either way, the cross of Christ signifies the absolute contrast between God and world. It stands as a negative parable for the original and final unity (not identity) between Creator and creation. Not even our (merely human) protest against the world can justify us in God's sight. Only God's protest — the cross of Christ — can do that. All this has nothing to do with sophistry. But sophistry has everything to do with using a trite concept of creation to bypass the cross — trite, because it so readily glosses over everything against which faith must currently protest for the sake of the cross and in the name of hope.

5. On whether the relation between God and the world is essentially mysterious.

Harnack. God and the world do not stand in absolute contrast. Neither do our life in God and our life in the world. If they really were absolute contrasts, we could make no sense of the heart of the gospel. For at its heart the gospel closely connects and even equates love for God with neighbor-love. A logically necessary presupposition for this equation is a high regard for morality in general. The relation between God and the world (as between life in God and worldly life) is therefore morally and rationally intelligible. An absolute contrast between God and the world would be mysterious, unintelligible, and contrary to the heart of the gospel.

Barth. The heart of the gospel shows us precisely how strange and incomprehensible is the relation between God and the world. It shows us that they are indeed absolute contrasts. One must not confuse, as happens with Harnack, the heart of the gospel with the moral law. Yet even the law, in its own way, bears witness to the absolute contrast between our life in God and our life in the world. The law (including "high regard for morality") enjoins us to love our neighbor. But if we do not do this and indeed cannot do this — as is of course actually the case — then what does that say about the state of our love for God? Our life in the world is the very life in which we love neither God nor neighbor. This point, as disclosed by the law, is the first sign of absolute contrast. The second is like unto it — namely, the miraculous event by which the eternal God intervenes on our behalf in order to overcome the absolute contrast established by our lovelessness and sin. This matter, too, is strange and incomprehensible. Indeed, a greater mystery than our failure to return God's love in creating us is the persistence of God's love in the face of our refusal. Therefore, not only does our lovelessness stand in absolute contrast to God's original love (contrast one), but even more does God's persisting love stand in contrast to our hopeless refusal (contrast two). These strange and utter contrasts, especially the miracle of God's persisting love, can be known only by God's revelation, not by mere human reason, regardless of how critical and historical it may be. The God who overcomes our radical lovelessness is the God who reveals these contrasts to us. But this divine overcoming of our sin is not only something strange and mysterious. It is also dreadful. The God who overcomes is not to be trifled with. For we are not made alive unless we are first slain.

6. On the condition for the possibility of leading people to God.

Harnack. Leading people to God is not different from leading them to what is good. This equation also indicates that we are not faced with absolute contrasts, neither between God and the world nor between life in God and worldly life. No genuine spiritual development can occur without historical knowledge and a high regard for morality. Critical reason is therefore the condition for the possibility of leading people to God, for it is critical reason by which we know of history and morality. What we know in general by reason — here the essence of the good — provides the necessary precondition for what we receive in particular by faith.

Barth. The condition for the possibility of leading people to God is not reason but revelation. Leading people to God is not something we do, but something God does. It is not a matter of what we think we know about history and morality in relation to God, but of God's history and God's "morality" in relation to us. "No one can come to me unless the Father who sent me draws him; and I will raise him up at the last day" (John 6:44). Note the themes in this passage: divine sovereignty, Christocentrism, eschatology, coming to God as resurrection from the dead. These themes do not confirm and build upon but negate and reconstitute what we know in general by reason.

7. On the relation between religion and culture.

Harnack. Between religion and culture there is an intimate connection. Culture — its development, its knowledge, its morality — reveres God. This reverence for God is necessary if we are to protect our culture from atheism. More especially, religion is necessary for a culture's health, vitality, and soundness. The relation between religion and culture is one of mutual immanence. Culture is the bearer of religion; religion is the critic of culture.

Barth. Religion and culture are indeed intimately connected. Religion serves an important cultural function — sanctifying war, mystifying oppression, and euphemizing every collective form of crime. Culture reveres God precisely to the extent that God is useful for such purposes. Is there not therefore something rather suspect about implicitly contrasting the "higher values" or "religious experiences" of our culture to those of "primitive" peoples who have not yet attained to our level? The preaching of the gospel (see #3 above) has nothing to do with the sacralizing of culture, but rather with its desacralization. Whether cultural invocations of God, derived as they are from polytheism, serve to protect us from atheism or actually to implant it among us remains an open question. When culture is the bearer of religion, religion is domesticated by culture. Religion as borne by culture will never be a serious critic, or at least not sufficiently serious, when seriousness is measured by the gospel.

8. On whether religion is continuous with culture, and faith with reason.

Harnack. High cultural achievements, such as Goethe's pantheism or Kant's concept of God, do not stand in simple contrast to true statements about God. If they did, we could not logically distinguish between the value of these statements and barbarism. True theological statements are akin to those of sophisticated cultural refinement, but incongruous with those of barbarism. Faith's knowledge of God completes and purifies the knowledge of God derived from reason (e.g., romantic pantheism, moral theism). To place faith and reason in stark contrast would make it impossible to distinguish the significance of the barbaric from that of the refined, for both would be equally distant from faith.

Barth. True theological statements have nothing to do with high cultural achievements. Faith does not complete and purify knowledge of God derived from reason. All human statements about God stand under the crisis of God's judgment. No way exists from humanity to God, whether that humanity be barbaric or as cultured as Goethe and Kant. The gospel is discontinuous with humanly or independently derived statements about God. Divine revelation and human culture are separated by a great divide. True theological statements are based on revelation, not on reason. They are received and acknowledged only by faith. No way exists from us to God, but a way does exist — the way of God's revelation — from God to us.

9. On the standpoint from which these relations are perceived: critical history versus divine revelation.

Harnack. From the standpoint of critical history, a general rule may be inferred about all physical and intellectual development: contrasts are at the same time steps, and steps are contrasts. Secular conceptions of God (e.g., Goethe and Kant) stand in such a relation to true (that is, Christian) conceptions. The relationship is relative — not qualitative but merely quantitative. It is a matter of degree, not of kind. Historical knowledge and critical reflection make this insight possible.

Barth. From a standpoint based on divine revelation, the difference between faith and reason, or between God's truth and our truth, is exactly the reverse of what Harnack says. It is not a matter of degree, but a matter of kind. Revelation is a transcendent reality such that God's truth always stands in contradiction to our truth. We cannot build from strictly human statements about God, among which there are certainly differences of degree, to the content of the gospel. We can only move from the content of the gospel to an assessment of human statements about God. The condition for the possibility of uttering true statements about God is not to be found in themselves. When true theological statements are uttered, it is always a matter of grace. It always depends on God's free decision from moment to moment, and hence it is always an event. Over this event we have no disposal. The Spirit blows where it will. Our part in it begins and ends in humility, longing, and prayer. By our own efforts, by quantitative stages, we cannot pass from the old world to the new. Only by God's action, whereby we are slain and born anew, do we make the truly qualitative transition.

10. On the relation between experience and eschatology.

Harnack. The highest and final knowledge of God is the insight that "God is love." The sphere of God is one of love, joy, and peace. Transitional moments of terror are not unknown to Christian experience. But one ought not to remain suspended in them throughout the course of this life. These moments are not independent of God's love, and in view of God's love they ought not to be prolonged. The transition is to be completed by entering here and now into the love, joy, and peace God has prepared for us. The terror of crisis and judgment is momentary and transitional, not a prolonged and repeated Christian experience. God is primarily a God of love, not a God of wrath. Christian experience is primarily of love, joy, and peace, not of crisis and dread. The law's terrifying accusations are but the portal through which we pass on the way to receiving the gospel's consolation.

Barth. The insight that "God is love" only goes to reveal that between God and us there yawns an infinite qualitative difference. As our highest and final knowledge of God, the insight is really eschatological. It represents the promised future. It points not primarily to our present experience but to that which is yet to come. It points to the future of God's love as something already disclosed to us but not yet possessed. For now we live between already and not yet, memory and hope; we live between the times. Until the promised future arrives, we will always be in transition. Until then our existence will always be paradoxical. Our belief, for example, will always also be disbelief. We do not believe in the conditions of present reality, not even in our present experience of faith. Faith is faith precisely when it points away from itself toward its object — toward the God who is love, and therefore toward the promised future. Faith lives by the promises of God, and we are saved in no other way than by hope.

11. On experience, reason, and revelation.

Harnack. According to the biblical injunction, we are to think on those things which are true, honorable, just, gracious, excellent, and worthy of praise. To meditate on these things is liberating. Our experience of God can thus not be divorced from our experience of all that is good, beautiful, and true. How are we to devote ourselves to uniting these things with our experience of God if not by historical knowledge and critical reflection? How do we know of the good, the beautiful, and the true if not through critical historical reason? We need this reason in order to have these things upon which to meditate and thus to nurture our experience of God. Once again it would seem that reason is indispensable to faith and to fostering Christian maturity.

Barth. We are not to move from experience and reason to revelation, but from revelation to experience and reason. The former is untroubled and organic; the latter is laden with dialectic and crisis. This crisis is itself the condition for the possibility of the biblical injunction to think on those things which are true, honorable, just, and so on. Revelation is the crisis of all that we call good, beautiful, and true. It is the negation out of which they are to be reconstituted on a higher, critical plane. What their final reconstitution is to be is beyond our capacity to say. What we can say is that all our experiences and judgments of the good, the beautiful, and the true are continually to be assessed in light of their crisis. In other words, such experiences and judgments themselves cannot be normative; but when critically tested in light of revelation, they can at best have the provisional status of parables and therefore witnesses. Their relation to the content of revelation will never be more than likeness in the midst of great unlikeness. It will be a relation of limited correlation, never a relation of organic synthesis.

12. On sin in relation to the form and content of preaching.

Harnack. Sin may be defined as a lack of respect and love. Our lack of respect and love can be brought to an end only through the preaching of God's holy majesty and love. In this preaching there is no place for mixing in every sort of paradox and arbitrary expression. The integrity of preaching — the very means by which our sin is to be overcome — is threatened severely by the use of paradox and arbitrariness. The content of preaching is neither irrational nor antirational. Paradox and arbitrariness therefore have no place in it. Preaching otherwise will be ineffective, and we will be left alone in our sin.

Barth. Sin is rather more serious than mere lack of respect and love. It is enmity with God and estrangement from God. It is our being lost in an alienated and superficial likeness to God. It is a condition which can only end in our annihilation. Given the radical negativity in which we exist, the affirmations of preaching cannot be made without taking unexpected turns and without resorting to paradoxical modes of expression. To suppose otherwise is to be a spectator rather than a participant. A simpler solution would be wonderful, but in this life is not to be our lot. If anything is to be learned from historical knowledge, it would be that none of the great theologians of the church — not, at any rate, Paul or Luther — were able to offer a simpler solution to the problem. Can we say that their preaching was "ineffective"?

13. On the danger of irrationalism in theology.

Harnack. The raw material of religious life — everything subconscious, everything nonrational, fascinating, numinous, etc. — remains less than human so long as it is not disciplined by reason, so long as it is not rationally apprehended, understood, and purified. Only in that way is it protected in its own proper character. Therefore, we ought not to wish to belittle or even reject reason, for reason is a humanizing force in our existence. If the rash work of destroying reason is brought to completion, we can only expect the worst. For reason, again, is a bulwark against dehumanization. On the smoldering ruins of this onslaught against reason, a Gnostic occultism is already arising. In short, reason humanizes everything religious, and to attack reason is to move toward the occult.

Barth. Which theology is it that stands in danger of irrationalism and of succumbing to dark psychic impulses — the one that merely brings reason to the crisis of its limit, or the one that divinizes "feeling"? Which theology is it that thinks critical reason can finally be circumvented by the discovery of a source of religious knowledge within the depths of human self-consciousness? And if we are to worry about occultism, which theology is it that may lose its most gifted adherents to anthroposophy at any moment?

14. On the condition for the possibility of knowing Jesus Christ.

Harnack. The person of Jesus Christ stands at the center of the gospel. Our basis for attaining reliable and common knowledge of this person is critical historical investigation. Without this basis of knowledge we are in danger of exchanging the real Christ for an imaginary one. The real Christ can be retrieved only by historical criticism, and therefore only scientific theology deals with the real Christ.

Barth. The real Jesus Christ can be known only by faith, not by critical historical reason. Critical reason by itself leads only to skepticism. Historical skepticism merely confirms the biblical teaching that we no longer know Christ according to the flesh. Since we need to become aware of this again and again, the more radical and terrifying the criticism, the better for revelation as the real and exclusive basis of our knowledge of Jesus Christ. Revelation is self-authenticating and occurs without external support. Historical criticism, by inspiring fear and trembling, reaches its categorical limit. Precisely this is its service to theology.

15. On scientific method in theology.

> *Harnack.* We are frail creatures subject to sloth, myopia, and numerous other ills. Isn't this all the more reason to maintain an intimate connection between theology and science (historical criticism)? Without a firm connection to historical science, we would have no theology at all. Without the discipline of scientific method, theology would no power to convince and would be of no value for us today. Theology divorced from scientific method threatens to dissolve into illusion. It will lose its ability to be convincing in the modern world.

> *Barth.* Theology is scientific and objective not when it imposes a method on its subject matter, but when it allows its subject matter to determine its method. For what does it mean to be scientific if not to be relevant to the subject matter? Only when theological method reflects the fact that its subject matter is the living God, is it "scientific" in any meaningful sense of the term. In view of this subject matter, the appropriate method is for theology to become a witness to the Word of God — to God's revelation of judgment and love. Theology as witness lets its norms be determined by its object and not by methods derived from elsewhere. Our theological work will find its value and its power to convince, even in the modern world, not by relying on alien methods but by being faithful to the word of God. By dealing with God's word as attested in Scripture, theology deals with the real Christ.

Conclusion

Although a full analysis of the Harnack/Barth correspondence would be beyond the scope of this essay, the foregoing paraphrase allows its main themes to come into focus. Harnack's criticism may be summarized as contending that Barth was subjectivist in method, obscure in conceptuality, and sectarian in ethical implication. By contrast Barth's countercharge seems to have been that Harnack was scientistic in method, reductionist in conceptuality, and acculturationist in ethical implication. I will briefly explore these distinctions.

Harnack believed Barth to be subjectivist in method. Again and again in describing Barth's theological procedure, Harnack argued that Barth leaves everything to "subjective experience," that he verges on "uncontrollable fanaticism," that his arbitrariness gives carte blanche to "every conceivable fantasy."[8] All of these dire consequences followed, as far as Harnack could see, from Barth's refusal to grant historical-critical method a normative status and indis-

8. See *Beginnings of Dialectic Theology,* pp. 165, 166, 174.

pensable role in Christian theological reflection. Historical-critical method was for Harnack the touchstone of scientific objectivity.

Barth, in turn, believed Harnack's method to be scientistic. "Scientism" occurs by conflating scientific method as a fruitful way of thinking with an ideology which presumes this method to have established the conditions for the possibility of all that is meaningful or real. It is a worldview which takes the procedures and structures of science to be monolithic so that they become canonical for all inquiry and knowledge.[9] Support for Barth's critique emerged when Harnack insisted that science presented "the only possible way of mastering an object through knowledge," that the task of theology was "the same as the tasks of science in general," that "each age possesses only one science," and that "as there is only one scientific method, so there is only one scientific task."[10] By contrast, Barth proposed that scientific method was not monolithic but discrete from case to case, more nearly regional than global, never more than a heuristic device to be determined by the peculiarities of its object of investigation (its "subject matter"). Why should it be so surprising, he wondered, if the mysterious subject matter of theology turned out to require a procedure materially (though not formally) different from those of other disciplines — even a procedure which by comparison seemed logically odd? Conformance to the revelation of the living God was for Barth the touchstone of objectivity. Since this revelation was not "historical" (or merely historical) in any ordinary sense of the term, it could not be directly apprehended by historical-critical method as Harnack conceived it, even though historical criticism had a subordinate and propaedeutic role to play in carrying out the theological task.

That Barth was right about the scientism of Harnack's method there can be, it seems, little doubt. Not only did Harnack openly assume scientific method to be monolithic, but as G. Wayne Glick has shown, Harnack also unconsciously incorporated into his understanding of "science" a great many "axiological principles" or value judgments beyond the scope of scientific method itself.[11] But was Harnack right about Barth? Was he right that "revelation is not a scientific concept"?[12] Was he right that Barth's concept of revelation in itself merely opens the door to every kind of arbitrariness and subjectivism? From Harnack to Pannenberg such charges about Barth's theology have

9. I have followed the definition of "scientism" provided by Alasdair MacIntyre, "Philosophy, the 'Other' Disciplines and Their Histories: A Rejoinder to Richard Rorty," *Soundings* 65 (1982): 144. See also the exceptionally lucid discussion by Thomas F. Tracy, "Enacting History: Ogden and Kaufman on God's Mighty Acts," *Journal of Religion* 64 (1984): 29-33.

10. *Beginnings of Dialectic Theology,* pp. 171, 174, 186.

11. See Glick, pp. 7, 80, 89-93, 101-4, 225-27, 332-34, 337-38, 340, 345-49.

12. *Beginnings of Dialectic Theology,* p. 186.

repeatedly been made. Although the issue remains unsettled and cannot be decided here, recent work by Ronald F. Thiemann has shown that at least some versions of the charge can be dismissed.[13]

It is ironic that Harnack should accuse Barth of "subjectivism," for subjectivism was of course one of Barth's deepest worries about the liberal theological tradition as represented by Harnack. It is worth noting that Barth had not answered Harnack here to his own satisfaction. At the time of their correspondence, Barth based his claim to theological objectivity on an appeal to divine revelation as attested in Scripture and on a dialectical method designed to break free of liberalism's own special brand of "subjectivism." Dialectic was the instrument of Barth's assault against a fundamental premise of liberalism — namely, its insistence on finding the possibility for talking about God in the subjective conditions of religious experience (regardless of how disciplined by "science") or in some related anthropological phenomenon. Not until his breakthrough in studying Anselm, however, would Barth feel that he had adequately come to display the objectivist logic alien to liberalism but internal to the Christian faith.[14]

Harnack's perception of Barth's method as subjectivist was compounded by his perception of Barth's dialectic. For although Barth intended his dialectic to work in favor of objectivism, the dialectical conceptuality struck Harnack as totally obscure.[15] Harnack's difficulty is not surprising, for an implicit contradiction seemed to exist between Barth's concept of "crisis" and his concept of "parable." "Crisis" designated the absolute contrast between God and the world. It meant divine judgment against sinful humanity, against every identification

13. See Ronald F. Thiemann, *Revelation and Theology: The Gospel as Narrated Promise* (Notre Dame, Ind.: University of Notre Dame Press, 1985). See also Thiemann, "Revelation and Imaginative Construction," *Journal of Religion* 61 (1981): 242-63. Briefly, Thiemann shows that when charges of "subjectivism" or "fideism" are made against someone like Barth, "foundationalist" assumptions are usually driving the critique. Barth's view of revelation is arguably "nonfoundationalist" without being subjectivist or fideist. Among the philosophical works that I find most helpful for understanding Barth in this regard (though none of them applies without further ado) are: Ludwig Wittgenstein, *On Certainty,* ed. G. E. M. Anscombe and G. H. von Wright (New York: Harper, 1969); Alasdair MacIntyre, *Whose Justice? Which Rationality?* (Notre Dame, Ind.: University of Notre Dame Press, 1988); and more recently Robert B. Brandom, *Making It Explicit: Reasoning, Representing, and Discursive Commitment* (Cambridge, Mass.: Harvard University Press, 1994).

14. See Karl Barth, *Anselm: Fides Quaerens Intellectum* (London: SCM, 1960). "Among all my books I regard this as the one written with the greatest satisfaction" (Barth, *How I Changed My Mind* [Richmond: John Knox, 1966], p. 43). About the significance of the Anselm book for Barth's theological development, McCormack has recently raised doubts. Whether they are entirely correct remains to be seen. (See McCormack, pp. 421-41.)

15. *Beginnings of Dialectic Theology,* pp. 165-66, 171-73.

of the human with the divine. It meant flat contradiction between God's truth and every human attempt at truth, high or low, cultured or uncultured.[16] "Parable," on the other hand, stood for relative correspondence. It meant likeness in the midst of great unlikeness between our words and God's Word, our deeds and God's deed, our protests and God's protest.[17] Clearly, the concepts of absolute contrast and of relative likeness cannot be logically reconciled. How can there be a "parable" in the midst of such a "crisis," or if there can be, how can the "crisis" be so severe?

No wonder, to Barth's express dismay, Harnack focused exclusively on the rhetoric of absolute contrast (which stung him most deeply) and ignored the rhetoric of relative likeness. Barth seemed to be tearing apart every unity Harnack held dear and to offer nothing but chaos to replace it. Barth for his part did not deny the inconceivability of "parable" in the midst of "crisis." Instead, he argued for inconceivability mediated by "miracle." Once "crisis" had destroyed all possibility of human conditions for speaking of God, divine "miracle" dialectically called forth "parables" and "witnesses" without in any way slackening the "crisis." The condition for the possibility of such likenesses was humanly incomprehensible and lay solely in the hands of God.[18]

A further reason for Harnack's professed puzzlement may be found in Barth's failure adequately to distinguish at this time between the normative and the valid. Harnack understandably perceived Barth to be saying that any theological statement was completely invalid which claimed a basis other than God's revelation as attested by Scripture. Barth's position was more complicated, though it has commonly been interpreted that way. Interpreted in light of his later development,[19] however, what Barth wanted to say was something like this: All theological statements derived and grounded independently of God's revelation must be subjected to a process of *Aufhebung*. In and of themselves such statements can never be normative, and therefore theology can never build upon them or enter into synthesis with them, not even critically. At the level of norms and criteria we meet with an absolute contrast.

However, whatever elements of truth we might find in such statements — and we should expect to find some to a greater or lesser degree — will always be

16. *Beginnings of Dialectic Theology*, pp. 168, 169, 180, 184.

17. See especially *Beginnings of Dialectic Theology*, p. 183.

18. *Beginnings of Dialectic Theology*, pp. 180, 183, 184.

19. See especially the discussion of "secular parables" in *Church Dogmatics* IV/3, first half (Edinburgh: T. & T. Clark, 1961), pp. 87-135. See also Barth's procedure in dealing with Christian and non-Christian anthropologies he considers inadequate in *Church Dogmatics* III/2. Barth characteristically subjects these anthropologies, which he regards as "abstractions," to a kind of *Aufhebung*.

embedded in a larger abstraction (because independent of revelation), and the abstraction as a whole will falsify these elements of truth insofar as they participate in it. The elements of truth can be seen for what they are only from the standpoint of revelation, and they can be liberated only by a process which subjects the abstraction to a kind of death and resurrection, or complete cancellation and then reconstitution on a higher or different plane. At the level of truth, therefore, we meet with both absolute contrast and the possibility of relative likeness. The dialectic of *Aufhebung* allowed Barth to say a complete No or a partial Yes (or both), depending on the needs of the situation.[20] In short, theological statements independent of revelation can never be normative and never be valid in themselves. But they can contain elements of truth which, once liberated, can function as likenesses (but no more) to the truth of God's revelation. The rudiments of this dialectical conceptuality were all present in Barth's correspondence with Harnack, but not with sufficient clarity for Harnack to make them out.

Barth for his part was convinced that the scientism of Harnack's method resulted inevitably in a reductionist conceptuality. You rob faith and revelation of content, he wrote to Harnack quite pointedly.[21] Harnack's "simple gospel" was all that was left over once "scientific method" had purged theology of its theme. The reconciliation between the gospel and science was purchased at the expense of the gospel. The simple gospel was a domesticated gospel, causing no offense because it could no longer speak of cross, resurrection, faith, and so on as anything other than the realizations of human possibilities.[22] The scientific method had in effect reduced the gospel to a faith without God.

The reductionism enforced by Harnack's method would become a standard item of critique, articulated against Harnack by critics as diverse as Alfred Loisy, H. Richard Niebuhr, and James Orr.[23] Such reductionism seems to be endemic to liberal theology as a whole, and if Alasdair MacIntyre is correct, it has had exactly the opposite effect from what Harnack had expected and hoped. "The abandonment of theistic content in favor of secular intelligibility," comments MacIntyre, "leads away from even the remnants of theistic practice."[24]

At the time of their correspondence, Harnack was seventy-one years old

20. Cf. Edgar Thaidigsmann, "Aufhebung, Eine theologische Kategorie des frühe Barth," *Evangelische Theologie* 43 (1983): 328-49.

21. *Beginnings of Dialectic Theology,* p. 183.

22. *Beginnings of Dialectic Theology,* p. 179; cf. pp. 177, 183, 185.

23. See the summary in Glick, pp. 280-90.

24. Alasdair MacIntyre, "The Fate of Theism," in *The Religious Significance of Atheism* (New York: Columbia University Press, 1969), p. 29.

and Barth was thirty-six. The old liberal thought Barth was in danger of "sectarianism"; the young radical thought Harnack had capitulated to "acculturation."[25] The old liberal compared Barth to Herostrates, destroyer of the temple by fire, for the pyrotechnics of Barth's dialectic threatened to topple the twin pillars of "science" and "religion" by which the old liberal's great cultural synthesis was upheld and in which his highest aspirations were enshrined.[26] The young radical was convinced that Harnack's failure to appreciate the desacralizing significance of the cross was at the root of his readiness to become a "war theologian" who had made a "religious experience" out of experiences during the war.[27] The old liberal represented H. Richard Niebuhr's "Christ of culture" with all its strengths of relevance and sophistication and its weaknesses of capitulation and confusion. The young radical represented not Niebuhr's sectarian "Christ against culture," but his "Christ transforming culture" — although he knew, as did Niebuhr, that the latter cannot really be had without an incorporation of the former.[28] Unlike both Harnack and Niebuhr, however, the young radical regarded the direct locus of cultural transformation to be not primarily the society at large, but rather a particular community called the church.[29]

In conclusion, it seems fair to suggest that Harnack was incapable of recognizing Barth's theological proposals as legitimate, ultimately because what Barth was proposing vis-à-vis Harnack was a revolutionary theological paradigm. As in the case of the paradigm shifts described by Thomas S. Kuhn,[30] Barth's arose as an attempt to explain certain anomalies and to avoid them. The anomalies were basically two: theologians who defended a war of aggression; a

25. Harnack's worry about "sectarianism" is implicit throughout the correspondence, for example, in his remarks about flight from the world. For an explicit use of the term outside the correspondence, see Glick, p. 225. Barth's corresponding worry appears in nos. 4 and 7 of his "Fifteen Answers." See *Beginnings of Dialectic Theology*, pp. 165, 168.

26. The reference to Herostrates is suppressed in our English translation (*Beginnings of Dialectic Theology*, p. 166). See Rumscheidt, p. 31.

27. *Beginnings of Dialectic Theology*, p. 168. That more was at stake when Harnack signed the two 1914 manifestos mentioned by Härle than the mere *"Dummheit"* to which Härle would like to reduce it (see n. 2 above), may be gauged from Agnes von Zahn-Harnack's defense of her father, fraught as it was with disturbing implications for Germany's future. The dialectical theologians, she states, had a viewpoint from which the war "had shown only its terribleness, its sinfulness, its destructive rage, but nothing of the exaltation which thrills a people ready to give its life as a sacrifice for its brothers" (Zahn-Harnack, p. 530).

28. H. Richard Niebuhr, *Christ and Culture* (New York: Harper & Row, 1961).

29. See, for example, Karl Barth, "Church and Culture," in *Theology and Church* (London: SCM, 1962), pp. 334-64.

30. See Thomas S. Kuhn, *The Structure of Scientific Revolutions*, 2nd ed. (Chicago: University of Chicago Press, 1979).

theological method which eviscerated the content of the gospel. The radical explanation was that both depended at bottom on making anthropological phenomena the condition for the possibility of talking about God. The revolutionary solution was a new paradigm with content inspired by the Reformation, thought-form inspired by Hegel,[31] and countercultural ethic inspired by religious socialism.[32] These would eventually be supplemented by a procedure and logic inspired by Anselm. Together they were to provide a safeguard against liberal capitulations to scientism, reductionism, and acculturation.

---

31. See Michael Welker, "Barth und Hegel," *Evangelische Theologie* 43 (1983): 307-28.

32. For Barth's relationship to "religious socialism," see McCormack, pp. 117-24. See also Friedrich-Wilhelm Marquardt, *Theologie und Sozialismus: Das Beispiel Karl Barths* (Munich: Chr. Kaiser, 1972), pp. 70-83, 114-26, 200-207; Busch, pp. 68-124; George Hunsinger, "Toward a Radical Barth," in *Karl Barth and Radical Politics*, ed. George Hunsinger (Philadelphia: Westminster, 1976), pp. 209-11.

CHAPTER 15

What Can Evangelicals and
Postliberals Learn from Each Other?
The Carl Henry/Hans Frei Exchange Reconsidered

(1995)

"All human truth," writes Hans Küng, "stands in the shadow of error. All error contains at least a grain of truth. What a true statement says is true; what it fails to say may also be true. What a false statement says is false; what it means but does not say may be true."[1] This reminder that claims to truth — especially in the midst of controversy — are always fraught with complexities, pitfalls, and ambiguities seems salutary for the enterprise I am about to undertake. For what I hope to do — even if only in the form of a thought experiment — is to suggest that evangelicals and postliberals might actually have something to learn from each other. No enterprise such as mine can hope to succeed, however, if it does not at least try to remain sensitive not only to matters of straightforward truth and falsity, but also to those gray areas that include grains of truth, omissions of truth, and inadequate formulations of truth, assuming of course, as I think we must, that truth in theology, however fragmentarily, can be approximated even at all. Hans Küng continues:

> It is a simplified view of the truth to suppose that every sentence in its verbal formulation must be either true or false. On the contrary, any sentence can be true *and* false, according to its purpose, its context, its underlying meaning. It is much harder to discover what is meant by it than what it says. A sincere, fearless and critical ecumenical theology, the only kind which

1. Hans Küng, *The Church* (New York: Sheed & Ward, 1967), p. 442.

338

can be constructive, must give up throwing dogmas at the other side. Theology today must be actively concerned to try and see the truth in what it supposes to be the errors of the other side, and to see the possibility of error in what it itself believes. In this way we would reach the situation which it is essential that we reach: the abandonment of supposed error and a meeting in common Christian truth.[2]

My hope is that the following discussion will reflect something of what Küng means by "sincere, fearless and critical ecumenical theology," and that it will thereby contribute to the possibility of "a meeting in common Christian truth" between evangelicals and postliberals today.

I. A Preview of Coming Attractions

The centerpiece of my discussion will be an exchange that took place between two figures whose credentials seem impeccable: Carl F. H. Henry for the evangelicals and Hans W. Frei for the postliberals. In November 1985 Carl Henry gave a series of three lectures at Yale. One of them offered his critique of what he called "narrative theology," with particular reference, among others, to Hans Frei. Frei himself responded to that lecture, and both contributions later appeared in the *Trinity Journal*. In *Types of Christian Theology* Frei returned to Henry's views, placing them in the unlikely company of David Tracy and other modern theologians. Theologians of this type, Frei argued, approach specifically Christian doctrines and beliefs in a way that seems overly determined by general philosophical considerations.

Among the issues that emerge from the Henry/Frei exchange, the most stubborn seem to involve the place of Holy Scripture within the Christian knowledge of God. Henry not only asks Frei very pointedly about the unity, authority, and inspiration of Scripture in their own right, but also about the extent to which these three need to be grounded in a logically prior doctrine of scriptural inerrancy. Above all, Henry seems concerned throughout about the overly disjunctive relationship, as he sees it, between biblical narrative and historical factuality in Frei's theological proposal.

Frei, on the other hand, frames the issues between him and Henry rather differently. He thinks that they disagree primarily about the "sufficiency" of Scripture as opposed to matters of unity, authority, or inspiration. This disagreement seems connected to a further difference about just exactly what the

2. Küng, p. 442.

subject matter or the "factual" referent of Scripture really is. Finally, Frei responds to Henry's question about factuality by posing a counterquestion about differing habits of mind and frameworks of understanding. Whereas Henry presents himself as an exponent of historic Christian orthodoxy, Frei wonders whether some of Henry's central contentions do not actually reflect modes of thought that are heavily conditioned by modernity in significant and unfortunate ways. One of Frei's deepest worries is that evangelicals and liberals, however much they may see themselves as archenemies, have more in common in thinking about Scripture than anything that sets them apart, so that they end up being "siblings under the skin."[3]

In trying to discern what evangelicals and postliberals might learn from each other about Holy Scripture, I will try to uncover various points where concessions might be made from each side. I will look especially for concessions that can be made without compromising the basic convictions that seem definitive of either position. I will therefore be looking for areas of possible convergence rather than for areas of complete or outright agreement. In this thought experiment, I will grant Frei's point that Henry seems bound by an excessive commitment to modernity. I will go on to argue, however, that other and very different formulations of Henry's concerns have standing within the evangelical community, formulations that uphold a strong doctrine of "inerrancy" without Henry's modernist excesses. In particular I will suggest that the views of Abraham Kuyper and Herman Bavinck offer a greater possibility for fruitful evangelical dialogue with postliberalism than the tendency represented by Carl Henry. (And in order not to make things too easy for myself, I will follow not the interpretation of Kuyper and Bavinck advanced by Jack Rogers and Donald McKim,[4] but instead that by Richard B. Gaffin, Jr., of Westminster Theological Seminary, who subjects the Rogers-McKim interpretation to a full-fledged revision and critique.)[5] Once the encumbrances of excessive modernity are shed and left behind, the real theological issues can emerge with greater clarity, and the differences between evangelicalism and postliberalism — though still strong — begin to look more like a matter of degree than a matter of kind.

In the other prong of my thought experiment, I will grant Henry's point that in general the account of scriptural unity, authority, and inspiration

3. Hans W. Frei, *Types of Christian Theology* (New Haven: Yale University Press, 1992), p. 84.

4. Jack Rogers and Donald McKim, *The Authority and Interpretation of the Bible: A Historical Approach* (San Francisco: Harper & Row, 1979).

5. Richard B. Gaffin, Jr., "Old Amsterdam and Inerrancy?" *Westminster Theological Journal* 44 (1982): 250-89 and 45 (1983): 219-72; hereafter cited as *WTJ* 44 and *WTJ* 45, respectively.

among the postliberals is, to say the least, fairly thin and unsatisfying so far. This thinness symptomizes the heavily "formal" character of postliberal theology, at least in the versions of it emanating from Yale. Evangelicalism, after all, is a historic stream of theological reflection that has claims of reaching back to as far as the Reformation or post-Reformation period.[6] By contrast, postliberalism, however promising it may be, is little more than a current of recent provenance. Postliberals would do well, I will argue, to pay careful attention to the historic doctrinal concerns of the evangelicals, however much it may be felt that reformulations are in order. Focusing above all on the historic evangelical plea for an adequately biblical understanding of the saving death of Christ, I will nominate the work of John R. W. Stott and Alister McGrath as representing the kind of proposals from which postliberals would have much to learn.

II. Henry's Appraisal of Narrative Theology

In the course of his critical survey, Henry acknowledges several points of agreement with narrative theology. Although they are not strongly emphasized, they should not be overlooked. The appreciative comments that Henry makes all seem to focus on what might be called the integrity of Scripture. He observes that narrative theologians tend to work with the received scriptural text, taken as it stands. Theologians like Frei, he writes, emphasize "that the entire book is important to the meaning, and not just preferred sections as in nonEvangelical criticism."[7] This acceptance of the received text carries a number of implications. As Henry rightly notes, it means that he and Frei hold significant affirmations in common: namely, that Scripture is a harmonious unity, that historical criticism has not invalidated the relevance of Scripture, that the biblical world is the real world which illuminates all else, and that Jesus is the indispensable Savior (p. 15). It also means that Scripture can function as Scripture "apart from the question whether we can demonstrate the historical factuality of events to which it refers. The authority of the biblical text is independent of confirmation or disconfirmation by historical critics" (p. 4).

Despite this impressive range of common affirmation, Henry proceeds to subject the work of various narrative theologians to severe and vigorous criticism. In what follows I will summarize the concerns he sets forth under several

---

6. As a movement within Anglo-Saxon Christianity, however, evangelicalism is best understood as arising in the early eighteenth century. See David W. Bebbington, *Evangelicalism in Modern Britain: A History from the 1730s to the 1980s* (Grand Rapids: Baker, 1989).

7. Carl F. H. Henry, "Narrative Theology: An Evangelical Appraisal," *Trinity Journal,* n.s., 8 (1987): 3-19, on p. 5. References which follow in the text are to this work.

headings that are similar to but not identical with those that he uses himself, and I will concentrate only on those points that seem to pertain directly to Frei. Henry sees himself as differing from Frei on four main questions: the unity of Scripture, the authority of Scripture, the factuality of Scripture, and the truth of Scripture.

Although discussed only briefly, the unity of Scripture seems to me to be a point on which Frei is questioned to good effect. Is the category of narrative, Henry asks, really sufficient to account for the unity of the Bible, whether in terms of form or of content (p. 9)? "Not all of Scripture," he continues, "falls into the narrative genre" (p. 10). Because so much of the Bible is not narrative, the narrative category cannot account for the Bible's unity. The point is as telling as it is obvious, for the thinness of the narrative account of scriptural unity seems to suggest a larger problem in postliberal theology as a whole. As Gabriel Fackre has pointed out, "most proponents of narrative theology are more concerned with method than with theological content" (quoted on p. 15).[8] Not much is said about doctrinal substance, and doctrine itself is in danger of dwindling into a set of rules with no more than a regulatory function. On the basis of such considerations, Henry concludes rather severely that "Frei diverts attention from revelation" (p. 15). I will return to this criticism at the end of my remarks.

A second question that Henry has for Frei pertains to the authority of Scripture. Among the many and diverse points that arise here, I will mention only one, though it seems to be at the heart of Henry's concerns, namely, a perceived drift toward subjectivism in matters of biblical authority. Henry repeatedly accuses narrative theologians of failing to arrive at a consensus among themselves in their interpretation of Scripture (pp. 8, 9, 19). The lack of hermeneutical consensus in narrative theology indicates that it has "no objective criterion for distinguishing truth from error and fact from fiction." This is "the unresolved dilemma facing narrative theology." Its method cannot eliminate "divergent and contradictory theological claims" (p. 19). Although I suspect that when they are together *en famille*, evangelicals may not be wholly innocent of divergent and contradictory theological claims — if I am not mistaken, it has been difficult even to find a definition of the term "evangelical" around which a consensus can be built[9] — what seems to disturb Henry is a certain absence of objective criteria.

If I do not misinterpret him, Henry seems to hold that if Scripture is really authoritative, then we should be able to arrive at consensus in biblical in-

8. Although I do not mean to equate narrative theology with postliberal theology, they are closely enough related that what Fackre says of the one applies equally well to the other.

9. See, however, Robert Letham, "Is Evangelicalism Christian?" *Evangelical Quarterly* 67 (1995): 3-16. Letham not only offers an illuminating account of distinctive "evangelical" characteristics, but also uses it to explain why evangelicalism has become increasingly fragmented and diffuse.

terpretation by means of objective criteria. Beyond a certain point this seems an odd thing to say. If we take the Nicene-Constantinopolitan Creed and the Chalcedonian Definition as established criteria for the church's interpretation of Holy Scripture — as I think postliberal theologians like Hans Frei and George Lindbeck are prepared to do — then I don't see how these standards *qua* standards can be said to conform to Henry's canons of "objectivity" in the nonperspectival or value-neutral sense that seems so important to him.[10] There are two points here. First, as is notorious, even these standards will not eliminate all significant theological diversity and contradiction; and second, the standards themselves are articles of faith. Could it be that Henry's concerns about an arbitrary subjectivism, while not entirely without merit, are somehow driven by canons of objectivism so stringent that in this life, fallen and finite as we poor creatures are, none of us can ever really meet them? Note that Henry does not shrink from asking in criticism of Fackre as a narrative theologian: "But is his epistemology immune to critical miscarriage and to perversion of tradition?" (p. 18). This is an interesting question. Is Henry's epistemology immune to critical miscarriage and to perversion of tradition? Is anyone's? Here we confront for the first time the counterquestion about a certain peculiar cast of mind that Frei will pose to good effect in his published response.[11]

---

10. It is not clear that all who call themselves "evangelicals" would be willing to subscribe to these ecumenical standards, and in general I would regard this as a serious problem. On the other hand, most such dissenting evangelicals would probably be willing to rule out the kinds of theological positions that these ecumenical standards are designed to rule out. Even among those who might somehow want to endorse a position that is ruled out, however, it would not always be easy (though sometimes it would) from a postliberal point of view to reject the endorsed position out of hand. For an incisive discussion of this and related matters, see Letham, "Is Evangelicalism Christian?"

11. Perhaps as another indication of his worry about "subjectivism," Henry strangely misreads Frei's narrative analysis of the Gospels as proposing a merely "linguistic" or "literary" presence of God. "Narrative hermeneutics removes from the interpretative process any text-transcendent referent and clouds the narrative's relationship to a divine reality not exhausted by literary presence" ("Narrative Theology," p. 13). Does God really speak to us through his Word as Calvin taught, Henry asks, or not? "Narrative exegesis is misguided if it leaves problematical the divine authority of its message and its revelatory identity and fails over and above literary affirmation to indicate an adequate test for truth" (p. 13). It is not enough to stay at the level of literary analysis. Frei (along with Brevard Childs) is said to correlate the biblical text with "God's linguistic presence" — a category that has no conceivable bearing on any fair reading of Frei (or for that matter of Childs) (p. 7; see also p. 9). Henry seems to think, oddly, that if "historical events are not per se a medium of revelation," then God's only mode of presence must be "literary" (p. 7). Frei speaks of God's "presence" in relation to Scripture as "mysterious" but never as "literary." See Frei, *The Identity of Jesus Christ* (Philadelphia: Fortress, 1975). There seems to be no good reason to think that Frei viewed the relationship between Word and Spirit fundamentally differently from Calvin.

A third question has to do with factuality in the biblical narratives. This is undoubtedly the issue in Frei's work that worries Henry the most deeply. Although revelation "is conveyed in and through Scripture," according to Frei, he also holds that realistic narrative "has a loose and unsure connection with historical actuality" (p. 12). This establishes an unhappy "disjunction" between the literary witness of scriptural narrative and the redemptive events it depicts. Positing such a disjunction, laments Henry, has "distortive consequences" in theology as well as being epistemologically "destructive" of the "orthodox heritage" (p. 12). By contrast, writes Henry, "Evangelical orthodoxy routinely affirms" the full "historical factuality" of the biblical narratives along with their "objective inspiration and inerrancy" (p. 9).

Henry rightly sees that for Frei the central question is a question of genre. The Gospels are allegedly misconstrued if they are taken as reliable historical reports whose meaning is to be found in historical events. He also rightly sees that for Frei "the narrative content is not necessarily historical" (p. 6). As Henry does not tire of insisting, however, the relevant question still remains as to whether the events of the history-like narratives — whether miraculous in their depiction or not — "are in fact historical" (p. 6). Again, Henry rightly sees that for Frei the scriptural narration is "realistic" whether or not the depicted action is factual, and that the depicted action functions to render a character in a story. In this sense the narrative form constitutes, not just illustrates, the meaning of the narrative. The meaning is thus located inside, not outside, the text (p. 6).

Beyond a certain point, however, Henry unfortunately fails to grasp what Frei is claiming. Henry asks: Wouldn't Frei have to say that faith retained its full validity and saving power "even if historical investigation were to discredit the empty tomb and Jesus' bodily resurrection" (p. 13)? "It is difficult," the critique continues, "to find a categorical statement that if Christ's body disintegrated in the tomb Christian faith would be impaired. . . . Narrative hermeneutics embraces uncertainty over historicity." Frei's approach is so open to fictional elements in the narratives that it "clouds the foundations of a stable faith. . . . It is incumbent on those who claim that narrative story and history are not compatible to clarify which historical specifics are nonnegotiable" (p. 13). Despite referring to Frei's book *The Identity of Jesus Christ*, Henry does not seem to have read it carefully enough to discover just how Frei has answered these very questions.

Since an account of those answers is better postponed until a later section of this essay, it will be fruitful here to pursue an important theme in Henry's own constructive proposal. This theme concerns how faith in the biblical testimony is related to the question of verifying or disconfirming the events depicted by biblical narratives. This theme is not so much a question of "faith and history" as of "faith and historiography" or of "faith and modern historical investigation." At first glance what Henry has to say on this theme seems fairly straightforward. He states repeatedly that faith is independent of historiography. "The Evangelical belief in the divine redemptive acts does not depend on verification by historical criticism but rests on scriptural attestation" (p. 8). Or again he states: "The biblical redemptive acts are not established as historical only if historical method confirms them, nor discredited if it does not do so, for empirical investigation is always incomplete and its verdicts subject to revision" (p. 12). Henry even acknowledges that "questions about the supernatural fall outside the method's competence" (p. 12). Were there no more to Henry's position than this, he and Frei, as it turns out, would not widely disagree.

On the other hand, elsewhere in the same essay Henry seems to become strangely equivocal. What are we to make, for example, of the following assertion? "Unless the historical data are assimilated not only to faith but also to the very history historians probe, the narrative exerts no claim to historical factuality" (p. 11). This seems to be a claim, again quoting Henry, that "the factual implications of the text" cannot be upheld "independently of historical criticism" (p. 11). Factual implications must apparently be validated by historical criticism. Faith, says Henry in the same vein, cannot focus merely on the narratives "independently of all historical concerns." If "faith" is split off from "reason" and "history," "that would in principle encourage skepticism and cloud historical referents in obscurity" (p. 11). Most surprising of all, despite what we heard about supernatural matters falling outside the competence of historical-critical method, we are told almost in the same breath that a skillful use of this method "would uncover an objective transcendent revelation, even if confined to historical events or acts" (p. 12).

The principle of charity dictates that one should try to construct a plausible account that would reconcile these apparently contradictory statements. Since my knowledge of Carl Henry's writings is not extensive, the best I can do is to offer the following hypothesis. I suspect that Henry's overall position might plausibly be described as one of "systematic consubstantiation." If so, this position will not only separate him from postliberals like Frei, but (as I hope to show) also from evangelicals like Kuyper and Bavinck. "Systematic consubstantiation" between faith and historiography would mean something like the following. Although faith is independent of historiography, it makes systematic use of it in two ways. First, it makes a negative case that events depicted by biblical narratives (for example, Christ's resurrection) have not in fact been disconfirmed by historical-critical method; and second, so far as possible, it makes a positive case (by means of that method) for the historical factuality of those events.[12] Some such position seems to be what Henry means when he writes that evangelicals "lean on inspired Scripture *more than* on historical research for assurance of past salvific events" (p. 5, italics added). Faith, according to this statement, seems to substantiate itself and to find assurance not only through Word and Spirit, but also through historical research. It seems to require a reliance on historical-critical method as well as on Scripture itself, though not in the same way or to the same degree. However, if faith were to forgo a systematic reliance on historical-critical method as a secondary means of verification and certainty, then the consequences as Henry understands them would be dire indeed. For in that case skepticism would not only be encouraged, but the foundations of a stable faith would remain clouded in obscurity. Here is another point to which we will return.

Henry's questions to Frei about the unity, authority, and factuality of Scripture are finally sealed by a question about the truth of Scripture. Once again we confront a very large topic that can be treated only very briefly. In any case, Henry is clearly concerned about what he calls "objective truth," which seems to be defined as truth that can be known in a value-neutral way apart from any self-involving perspectives or presuppositions (p. 8). This kind of truth — namely, disinterested cognitive truth about objective realities — is what Henry seems to have in mind when he suggests that Scripture has two primary functions: first, it conveys "propositional truths about God and his purposes"; and second, it gives us "the meaning of divine redemptive acts" (p. 3). If I understand Henry correctly, it seems that the propositional truths conveyed by Scripture demand our intellectual assent, whereas the meaning of the divine redemptive acts as mediated exclusively by Scripture demands not only our assent but also our personal commitment. More succinctly, whereas the truth demands our assent, the meaning demands our commitment.

When Henry reads Frei, what he finds missing is a concern for this kind of objective truth. What he finds instead is simply a set of ungrounded assertions, however commendable some of them may be. "It takes more than strenuous assertion," he states pointedly, "to establish historical factuality and objective truth. . . . Really to turn the flank of destructive criticism requires an articulate view of revelation and reason and of revelation and history, and a public test of truth" (pp. 13, 14). The significance of Henry's drive to defeat

12. This positive move may, in turn, take one of several forms. It may simply argue that the case for historical factuality is *one* plausible position among others. Or it may take the stronger form that historical factuality is *more* plausible than any other position. Or it may take the still stronger form that historical factuality is the *only* plausible position and that all other possibilities are implausible. If I am not mistaken, Henry seems to gravitate toward the latter position.

modern skepticism on its own terrain — really to turn the flank, as he says, of destructive criticism — can scarcely, it seems, be overestimated. Modern skepticism will not be defeated merely by strenuous assertion. A whole array of conceptual weaponry and armor will be required, none of which can be found in Frei's depleted arsenal. To defend the factuality of biblical narrative against the onslaught of modernity, one needs to wield a public test of truth. To fortify the meaning of the facts attested, one throws up a towering theory of revelation. And to safeguard the truth of biblical assertions, one rolls out the ultimate weapon: a doctrine of inerrancy.

Theologians such as Frei are wrong, Henry urges, to "reduce biblical historicity and inerrancy to second-order questions" (p. 14). It is to Henry's insistence on the centrality of inerrancy that we must turn, however briefly. Although I wish to make only a small observation, it will prove to be important when we come to Kuyper and Bavinck. "Evangelical theology," writes Henry, "roots the authority of Scripture in its divine inspiration and holds that the Bible is inerrant because it is divinely inspired" (p. 14). Only the doctrine of inerrancy, he continues, can finally "protect the identity and centrality of Christ" as well as "the authority and inspiration of the Bible" (p. 19). Note the logical order and relation of these ideas. The authority of Scripture is seen as grounded in its divine inspiration, and this inspiration is then seen as the source of inerrancy in all matters of factuality and truth. Whereas inspiration is the source of inerrancy, inerrancy is the ultimate ground of truth. The doctrine of inerrancy thus emerges from Henry's account with a peculiar logical status and conceptual force. Logically, it is the final ground (though not the source) of biblical truth; and functionally, it serves to make that truth objective, certain, and secure.

III. Frei's Response to Henry's Appraisal

In responding to Henry's critique, Hans Frei opens with his famous plea for a "generous orthodoxy." He states: "My own vision of what might be propitious for our day, split as we are, not so much into denominations as into schools of thought, is that we need a kind of generous orthodoxy which would have in it an element of liberalism — a voice like the *Christian Century* — and an element of Evangelicalism — the voice of *Christianity Today*."[13] With characteris-

---

13. Hans W. Frei, "Response to 'Narrative Theology: An Evangelical Proposal,'" in Frei, *Theology and Narrative* (New York: Oxford University Press, 1993), pp. 207-12, on pp. 207-8. Reprinted from *Trinity Journal*, n.s., 8 (1987): 21-24.

tic modesty, he continues: "I don't know if there is a voice between those two, as a matter of fact. If there is, I would like to pursue it."[14] Frei's opening remark signals that he wants to reframe the entire discussion. Although he approaches both liberalism and evangelicalism with critical sympathy, he will accept neither on its own terms. Only a new framework of understanding, he suggests — one that overlaps both liberalism and evangelicalism, while transcending the limits of each — will show the way forward. Henry's critique gives Frei the opportunity to say something about the possibilities and limitations of evangelical theology, at least as Henry represents it.

Henry's concern about the unity of Scripture elicits no more from Frei than a small concession: "Not all of Scripture is narrative, obviously," he admits.[15] In an early and programmatic essay, Frei had indicated how Scripture's unity might be set forth: "For a beginning," he wrote, "let's start with the synoptic gospels, or at least one of them, because their peculiar structure as narratives, or at least as partial narratives, makes some hermeneutical moves possible which we don't have available elsewhere in the New Testament. And having started there, I would propose to go on to say, let's see how much more of the New Testament can be coordinated by means of this series of hermeneutical moves."[16] Although Frei clearly believed that more was necessary than narrative analysis, he unfortunately never got around to making those larger hermeneutical moves. As I have already suggested, this kind of deficit seems to typify the Yale variants of postliberal theology to this day.

Frei goes on to make a remark in passing that, for all its simplicity, seems to cut to the heart of his disagreements with Henry. Frei states:

> The Bible has a very *particular* story to tell. That doesn't mean all the elements in the Bible are narrative. It only means, so far as I can see, that something like John 1:14 — "And the word was made flesh and dwelt among us, full of grace and truth" — is something that we don't understand except as a sequence enacted in the life, death and resurrection of Jesus. The Christian tradition by and large took verses like that to be the center of its story.[17]

This statement implies that Frei departs from Henry's conception of meaning and truth. He does not share the view that cognitive truth is necessarily propo-

14. Frei, "Response," p. 208.
15. Frei, "Response," p. 208.
16. Frei, "Remarks in Connection with a Theological Proposal," in *Theology and Narrative,* pp. 26-44, on p. 32.
17. Frei, "Response," p. 208.

sitional in form. Remember that for Henry propositions demanding our assent are the only way (or only proper way) that truth is conveyed. As he insists in an essay called "Is the Bible Literally True?" both the metaphors and the stories of Scripture need to be restated in propositional form; otherwise, Henry argues, they cannot really be understood.[18] For Frei, however, the stories are not secondary in significance to doctrines. Although Frei thinks doctrines are indeed conceptual redescriptions of the biblical narratives, it is the narratives themselves that have the priority in conveying meaning and truth. Whereas Henry seems to think the narratives are finally about the doctrines, for Frei it is just the reverse. Although doctrines indeed arise from the narratives and point back to them, it is the narratives that properly convey biblical truth. We don't understand doctrinal statements, Frei argues, except by understanding the stories. A doctrinal statement like "the Word became flesh" is something that we don't understand except through the biblical accounts of Jesus' life, death, and resurrection. A statement like "the Word became flesh" is not a logically prior or independent proposition; it is the center of the gospel *story.*

There are clearly several issues here. Unlike Henry, Frei does not think that cognitive truth is *necessarily* propositional in form, or more precisely, that propositions are the only *proper* form of cognitive truth. Nor does he think cognitive truth is the only *kind* of truth, or even the primary kind of truth, that the Bible conveys to us — though he certainly agrees with Henry that biblical truth is not noncognitive. Rather Frei thinks that biblical truth is primarily narrative in form and that this form of truth demands more than just our cognition. In particular, though the doctrines and the stories are inseparable, Frei thinks that in the end the doctrines are understood through the stories rather than holding, with Henry, that the stories are finally understood through doctrinal propositions. On such matters as these, I will argue, Kuyper and Bavinck represent a form of evangelicalism that seems closer to Frei than is possible for someone like Henry, just because Henry has committed himself more heavily than they have to certain rationalist forms of modernism.

Along with arguing for the primacy of biblical narrative, Frei also argues for the sufficiency of Scripture. Remember that Henry took a position on this matter that was ambiguous or at least complex. Although in principle he did not wish to challenge the idea that Scripture functions independently of modern historical criticism, in practice he insisted that the two must be systematically correlated. What Frei denies is precisely the necessity of systematic correlation. Whereas

---

18. Henry, "Is the Bible Literally True?" in *God, Revelation, and Authority,* vol. 4 (Waco, Tex.: Word, 1979), pp. 103-28. See especially the remarks about metaphor on pp. 109, 113, and 120, and about stories on pp. 105-8.

Henry stands for something like "systematic consubstantiation," Frei pleads by contrast for something like "ad hoc minimalism." That is, for Frei faith and historiography are related in a way that is not systematic but ad hoc; and the ad hoc use that faith makes of historiography is not maximal, as Henry proposes, but minimal. Faith needs no more from modern historical criticism, Frei urges, than two very minimal assurances: first, that Christ's resurrection has not been historically disconfirmed;[19] and second, "that a man, Jesus of Nazareth, who proclaimed the Kingdom of God's nearness, did exist and was finally executed."[20] This much and more, Henry could have learned about Frei's position from a careful reading of *The Identity of Jesus Christ.*

Frei presents a complex set of reasons for this stance of "ad hoc minimalism."[21] Although they cannot all be pursued here, some of them form the background to what he says in response to Henry about the sufficiency of Scripture. Three points in particular are worthy of note. The first has to do with the actual state of the evidence. Frei thinks the existing historical evidence is so sparse and so indeterminate that it can be given a plausible shape by any number of mutually conflicting positions, ranging all the way from extreme skepticism at one end to measured credence at the other.[22] The indeterminate state of the evidence alone would be enough to rule out any such strong reliance on it as Henry requires. In any case, what little relevant evidence that exists is not enough to disconfirm faith in Christ's resurrection, yet it is enough to confirm a certain historical minimum about his life, teaching, and death, and that is basically all that faith needs to know.[23]

Second, whereas the possibility of disconfirmation raises one set of issues, that of confirmation raises quite another, so that the two ought not to be run together and confused. Whereas in principle the resurrection of Jesus could be disconfirmed by historical evidence (though in fact it is not), in the nature of the case his resurrection could not possibly be confirmed by that means. "Actual belief in the resurrection is a matter of faith," writes Frei, "and not of arguments from possibility or evidence."[24] Confronted by the claim that Jesus Christ rose from the dead, historical-critical method simply reaches its categorical limit. In the nature of the case, Jesus Christ can be known for who he is only through our response of faith to his own self-witness as the risen Savior, by

19. Frei, *Identity of Jesus Christ,* p. 151; cf. p. 103.

20. Frei, *Identity of Jesus Christ,* p. 51.

21. For a further account see George Hunsinger, "Afterword: Hans Frei as Theologian," in Frei, *Theology and Narrative,* pp. 235-70, esp. pp. 265-68.

22. Frei, *Identity of Jesus Christ,* pp. 48, 132, 141.

23. Frei, *Identity of Jesus Christ,* p. 151; cf. p. 103.

24. Frei, *Identity of Jesus Christ,* p. 152.

means of Word and Spirit. "Concerning Jesus Christ and him alone," argues Frei, "factual affirmation is completely one with faith and trust of the heart, with love of him, and love of the neighbors for whom he gave himself completely."[25] Note that the response as Frei describes it is not simply one of assent, but one that involves trust and love. Since the truth of the gospel is fundamentally a person rather than a proposition, our proper grasp of this truth always involves us somehow as whole persons.

Unlike Henry, Frei thinks that we properly grasp the truth of the gospel not just with our heads, but also with our hearts and our hands. Although the term "God" as used by the language of faith is "in some sense referential," Frei writes, "it is also true in some sense other than a referential one."[26] In other words, the truth of the gospel requires more than just cognitive confirmation, because the category of truth has performative as well as cognitive and referential aspects. The truth is not just something to be known but also something to be done. Furthermore, these two aspects of truth — the cognitive and the performative — are so deeply interrelated in practice that this interrelation defies all attempts at strict or systematic conceptualization. Hence the word "God" as used by faith, says Frei, "is true by being true to the way it works in one's life, and by holding the world, including the political, economic and social world, to account by the gauge of its truthfulness."[27] In short, "the word 'God' is used both descriptively and cognitively, but also obediently or trustingly, and it is very difficult to make one a function of the other. . . . You have both uses together."[28] As will become clear in a moment, Frei's conception of truth means that in his low-key epistemology the objective and the subjec-

---

25. Frei, *Identity of Jesus Christ,* p. 157; cf. p. 147.

26. Frei, "Response," p. 210.

27. Frei, "Response," p. 210.

28. Frei, "Response," p. 210. Whereas Henry seems to make the question of performance a function of cognitive truth, George Lindbeck seems to move in the opposite direction. "The *only* way to assert the truth is to do something about it. . . . It is *only* through the performatory use of religious utterances that they acquire propositional force." See Lindbeck, *The Nature of Doctrine: Religion and Theology in a Postliberal Age* (Philadelphia: Westminster, 1984), p. 66, italics added. Although Frei agrees with Lindbeck that the cognitive and performative aspects of truth are interrelated, he does not follow him in making the one a function of the other. In "Epilogue: George Lindbeck and *The Nature of Doctrine,*" Frei differentiates himself from Lindbeck by giving qualified support to those whom he describes as "moderate propositionalists." Moderate propositionalism seems to be the idea that the cognitive and performative aspects of truth are at once deeply interrelated and inseparable, while also being relatively autonomous and distinct, so that in principle neither has precedence over the other (though in practice either one may assume precedence, depending on the situation). See *Theology and Dialogue: Essays in Conversation with George Lindbeck,* ed. Bruce D. Marshall (Notre Dame, Ind.: University of Notre Dame Press, 1990), pp. 278-79.

tive, the factual and the meaningful, the cognitive and the performative cannot be so neatly separated and detached from each other as they are in Henry's discourse.

Third, Frei understands the genre of the Gospel narratives differently from Henry. He sees them not primarily as reports about historical facts, but rather as depictions of a particular person. By means of these stories Jesus is depicted as the unique and indispensable Savior. The stories seem more like a realistic though mysterious portrait than a historical report. The values governing the construction of this portrait are not necessarily the same as those that would govern a work of modern history. Although some aspects of the narratives are surely factual in the modern sense, other aspects may well be depictions of the risen Savior in the lineaments of the earthly Jesus. That is, at certain points and to varying degrees, the narratives may actually depict the earthly Jesus in a way that conflates him with the risen Christ, or that superimposes the risen Christ on the earthly Jesus. And yet they may function quite aptly to portray his identity as the Gospel intends to convey it. The validity of the narrative portrayal does not necessarily depend on factuality as narrowly conceived. For the chief "fact" that the narratives wish to convey is precisely that the earthly Jesus and the risen Christ are one and the same.[29]

This understanding of how faith is related to history provides the background for what Frei says to Henry about the sufficiency of Scripture. We refer to Jesus Christ by means of the Gospel story, writes Frei, and "the text is sufficient for our reference."[30] Beyond the minimal use of historical method, faith does not need the kind of systematic external validation that Henry so zealously demands. "It is enough," writes Frei, "to have the reference to Christ crucified and risen."[31] To suppose otherwise is not so much to set about refuting skepticism on its own terms — which would in any case be an inordinately ambitious project — as it is to verge toward a kind of practical atheism. Systematic human efforts at independent validation, however well intended, can all too easily overshadow our reliance on the promises and faithfulness of God. Frei's minimalism, I would suggest, is really an epistemological adaptation of "justification by faith alone apart from works of the law." Ad hoc minimalism seems to honor the Reformation principle of *sola Scriptura* — of the sufficiency of Scripture — in a way that systematic consubstantiation does not.

The question of validation is a function of the question of reference, and reference in the biblical narratives is a complex matter. "I would say," Frei re-

29. Frei, *Identity of Jesus Christ,* pp. 140-41.
30. Frei, "Response," p. 209.
31. Frei, "Response," p. 209.

marks, "that we refer in a double sense. There is often a historical reference and often there is textual reference; that is, the text is witness to the Word of God, whether it is historical or not."[32] Either way, says Frei, the mode of reference is analogical, not (as Henry would have it) literal or univocal.[33] For Frei the sufficiency of Scripture in matters of reference means being bound to the basic patterns of scriptural usage and depiction, not to the literal details. "We start from the text: that is the language pattern," he writes, "the meaning-and-reference pattern, to which we are bound, and which is sufficient for us."[34] The linguistic patterns of the narratives are what identify Jesus Christ, Frei seems to be saying, and these patterns are sufficient, because they stand in a good enough or analogical relation to what is factually the case. What is factually the case, however, is also complex. For the dual referentiality of the narratives pertains to the twofold factuality of Jesus Christ. In other words, the narratives are so constructed that they refer not only to Jesus in his earthly life (whether we can verify that factuality by modern methods or not), but also and at the same time to the risen Jesus Christ who lives to all eternity, and who attests himself to us through those narratives here and now. Faith in Jesus Christ involves a confidence that the Gospel narratives are sufficient for us in the arresting, complex, and subtle ways that they depict and refer to Jesus Christ in this twofold sense. By contrast, a faith that anxiously seeks to prop itself up by means of systematic and external validation, and to invalidate its opponents by defeating them, seems in danger of ceasing to be faith.

From Frei's point of view, Carl Henry consistently makes a series of category mistakes — mistakes about reference, factuality, genre, and truth — mainly because he is excessively committed to the canons of modernity. "I am looking for a way," writes Frei, "that looks for a relation between Christian theology and philosophy that disagrees with a view of certainty and knowledge which Evangelicals and liberals hold in common."[35] Evangelicals and liberals, each according to their own kind, subscribe to modernist views of how we obtain certainty and knowledge in a way that ends up either distorting or denying the gospel. "Unlike Dr. Henry," writes Frei, "I think 'reference' — to say nothing of 'truth' — in Christian usage is not a simple, single or philosophically univocal category."[36] Nor does he think that the concept of "fact" is theory-neutral. Such terms "are not privileged, theory-neutral, trans-cultural"; they

32. Frei, "Response," p. 209.
33. For Henry's argument against analogical reference, and for univocal reference, see "Is the Bible?" esp. p. 118.
34. Frei, "Response," p. 209.
35. Frei, "Response," p. 211.
36. Frei, "Response," p. 210.

are not "ingredient in the structure of the human mind and of reality always and everywhere."[37] They are modern terms that depend on modern ways of thinking. While they need not be banned from Christian theology, they ought not to be used systematically.

The alternative to using modern epistemological categories systematically is simply to use them "eclectically and provisionally,"[38] always striving to grant primacy to the witness of the gospel itself. Theories that are logically independent of the gospel ought not to be used as frames of mind that end up distorting its intrinsic mysteries and certainties. When modernist versions of formal certainty and clarity are leavened by a more modest view that allows for an ineffaceable degree of subjectivity, commitment, cultural-historical location, and other forms of self-involvement in all our cognitive judgments, then fact and meaning, cognition and performance, mystery and clarity, humility and certainty need no longer be so radically divorced from one another as they are by the epistemological excesses of modernity. It should then be possible to see, with postliberals like George Lindbeck and Hans Frei, that we never have truth — and least of all theological truth — except under a depiction. "The truth to which we refer," writes Frei, "we cannot state apart from the biblical language which we employ to do so. And belief in the divine authority of Scripture is for me simply that we do not need more."[39]

IV. Beyond Excessive Modernity: The Promise of Old Amsterdam

At this point my remarks become much more nearly conjectural than analytical. Although I do not know the writings of Abraham Kuyper (1837-1920) and Herman Bavinck (1854-1921) very well, the impression I receive from reading those who do is that these two theologians have not committed themselves as heavily as Carl Henry has to the canons of modernity. Although they hold a high view of scriptural inerrancy, they do not seem as encumbered as Henry does by excessive epistemological anxieties about skepticism, factuality, reference, certainty, and objectivity, even when they also express concern about such matters. In general, their conceptions of scriptural unity, factuality, and truth seem less distorted by the systematic use of theories that are logically independent of the gospel. Above all, their conceptions of inerrancy seem finally to have

37. Frei, "Response," p. 211.
38. Frei, "Response," p. 210.
39. Frei, "Response," p. 210.

a different logical status, and to play a different conceptual role in their theologies, than what we find in the case of someone like Henry. The likes of Kuyper and Bavinck therefore emerge as more fruitful dialogue partners, it seems to me, than the likes of Henry for any future discussion between evangelicals and postliberals. I can do no more here, however, than hastily sketch some themes that might be of interest in such a discussion.

One such theme is the unity of Scripture. When Kuyper discusses this question, he highlights two matters that seem to differentiate him from evangelicals like Henry, while also placing him at the same time within hailing distance of postliberals like Frei or Lindbeck. The first is that the unity of Scripture is the *presupposition* of a faithful reading of Scripture, not a logical inference independent of faith. Since the contents of Scripture are obviously diverse, faith cannot arrive at Scripture's unity unless it takes that unity as the starting point. Kuyper writes: "He who, in the case of Scripture, thus begins with the multiplicity of the human factor, and tries in this way to reach out after its unity will never find it, simply because he began with its denial in principle."[40] Or again he states: "And however much it is your duty to study that *multiplicity* and *particularity* in the Scripture (both materially and formally), yet from that multiplicity you must ever come back to the view of *the unity of the conception,* if there is, indeed, to be such a thing for you as Holy Scripture."[41] One notes with interest Kuyper's view that Scripture's unity does not efface its real diversity as well as his emphasis on the priority of faith as a necessary condition for perceiving that unity. Kuyper shows no anxiety that he has somehow lapsed into a fatal form of subjectivism.

Nor does he try to present Scripture's unity, as Henry does, as a "logical system of shared beliefs"[42] or as a comprehensive "rational unity."[43] Instead Kuyper stresses that "Christ is the whole of Scripture, and Scripture brings the *esse* of the Christ to our consciousness."[44] He also cautions against restricting the Logos to words, even though the Logos is now embodied for us in Scripture.[45] He almost seems to be following George Lindbeck when the latter recommends reading

---

40. Abraham Kuyper, *Principles of Sacred Theology* (Grand Rapids: Eerdmans, 1954), p. 474. Quoted by Gaffin, *WTJ* 44, pp. 256-57.

41. Kuyper, *Principles of Sacred Theology,* p. 480. Quoted by Gaffin, *WTJ* 44, p. 257n. For a somewhat similar view, see David H. Kelsey, *The Uses of Scripture in Recent Theology* (Philadelphia: Fortress, 1975), p. 103.

42. Henry, "The Lost Unity of the Bible," in *God, Revelation, and Authority,* vol. 4, p. 456.

43. Henry, "The Unity of Divine Revelation," in *God, Revelation, and Authority,* vol. 2 (Waco, Tex.: Word, 1976), p. 74.

44. Kuyper, *Principles of Sacred Theology,* p. 477. Quoted by Gaffin, *WTJ* 44, p. 255.

45. Gaffin, *WTJ* 44, p. 255.

Scripture "as a Christ-centered narrationally and typologically unified whole in conformity to a Trinitarian rule of faith."[46] By contrast, when Henry writes of scriptural unity, he does not (to my surprise) concentrate on a Christ-centered reading,[47] he comes close to postulating a dichotomy between propositional content and personal encounter with Christ (as though they somehow failed to form a unity),[48] and he finally elevates cognitive propositionalism over the person of Christ in his account of Scripture's "logically interconnected content."[49] I suspect that Kuyper would have had little sympathy with such moves.

Even more interesting, however, is the view taken by Kuyper and Bavinck when they come to the question of Scripture's factuality. For both theologians, according to Richard Gaffin, "the biblical records are impressionistic; that is, they are not marked by notarial precision or blue-print, architectural exactness."[50] Nevertheless, neither theologian thought that "this impressionistic quality" in any way detracted from the certainty of biblical truth.[51] The truth of Scripture, they held, is appropriate to its unique divine authorship.[52] As the ultimate author of Scripture, God is more like an artist than a photographer.[53] "It is not even [Scripture's] purpose," wrote Bavinck, "to provide us with an historical account according to the standard of reliability which is demanded in other areas of knowledge."[54] The historical narratives of Scripture, he also stated, "are not history in our sense but prophecy."[55] They do not intend to convey "historical, chronological, geographical data . . . in themselves"; rather, what they intend to attest is "the truth poured out on us in Christ."[56]

The doctrine of inerrancy advanced by Kuyper and Bavinck is in accord with their understanding of Scripture's "impressionistic" quality of factuality and truth. Although, as Gaffin demonstrates, inerrancy for them extended to all matters, including historical data, nonetheless they finally understood inerrancy "in an impressionistic, nontechnical sense."[57] They both felt, writes

---

46. Lindbeck, "Scripture, Consensus, and Community," in *Biblical Interpretation in Crisis,* ed. Richard John Neuhaus (Grand Rapids: Eerdmans, 1989), p. 83.

47. See the belated and underdeveloped reference in Henry, "Lost Unity," pp. 468-69.

48. Henry, "Unity of Divine Revelation," pp. 74-75.

49. Henry, "Unity of Divine Revelation," p. 74. See also "Lost Unity," p. 469.

50. Gaffin, *WTJ* 44, p. 278. Cf. p. 276.

51. Gaffin, *WTJ* 44, p. 278.

52. Gaffin, *WTJ* 44, pp. 288-89.

53. Gaffin, *WTJ* 44, p. 281.

54. Herman Bavinck, *Gereformeerde dogmatiek,* 4 vols. (Kampen: J. H. Kok, 1895-1901; 2nd revised and enlarged ed., 1906-11; 6th ed., 1976), 1:356. Quoted by Gaffin, *WTJ* 45, p. 229.

55. Bavinck, pp. 361ff. Quoted by Gaffin, *WTJ* 45, p. 231.

56. Bavinck, pp. 546f. Quoted by Gaffin, *WTJ* 45, p. 259.

57. Gaffin, *WTJ* 45, p. 269.

Gaffin, that "pushing infallibility into the limelight is intellectualism" of the kind "that began with the rationalists."[58] Kuyper even went so far as to remark that "If Satan has brought us to the point where we are arguing about the infallibility of Scripture, then we are already out from under the authority of Scripture."[59] Infallibility for Kuyper and Bavinck, it seems, is not the kind of intellectualistic doctrine that it is for someone like Henry. It does not function as the linchpin of objectivity, certainty, and truth. It seems more nearly to be a nontechnical term for the reliability and sufficiency of Scripture.

With these views of scriptural unity, factuality, and truth, Kuyper and Bavinck arguably stand midway on a continuum that begins with someone like Calvin at one end and stretches to figures like Frei and Lindbeck at the other. Like any careful reader of the Gospels, Calvin was aware that the Evangelists were not overly concerned about strict factual accuracy. "It is well known," he wrote, "that the Evangelists were not scrupulous in their time sequences, not even keeping to the details of the words and actions [of Jesus]."[60] What the Evangelists were really interested in, Calvin tells us, were not the details so much as the *patterns* by which the identity and significance of Jesus Christ could be disclosed to us. "The Evangelists had no intention of so putting their narrative together as always to keep to an exact order of events," he wrote, "but to bring the whole pattern together to produce a kind of mirror or screen image of those features most useful for the understanding of Christ."[61] Kuyper and Bavinck go at least one step further by devising conceptions of factuality, inerrancy, and truth that would seem to conform to the kind of interests and practices that Calvin noticed in the Evangelists. In this connection postliberal theologians like Frei and Lindbeck could then be seen as going at least one step further still. For although they see a greater discrepancy between biblical narrative and historical fact than did their predecessors, they retain a high sense of biblical authority about what they think really matters, namely, the literary patterns of the texts by which Jesus Christ's identity and significance as the risen Savior are really disclosed to us.

What I wish to suggest, therefore, about what evangelicals might learn from postliberals is simply this. Although on these matters they may not wish

58. Gaffin, *WTJ* 44, p. 272. Cf. p. 284.

59. Kuyper, *Dictaten dogmatiek,* vol. 2 (1.66) (Grand Rapids: J. B. Hulst, n.d.). Quoted by Gaffin, *WTJ* 44, pp. 271-72.

60. John Calvin, *Calvin's Commentaries,* vol. 2, *A Harmony of the Gospels: Matthew, Mark, and Luke* (Grand Rapids: Eerdmans, 1972), p. 55 (on Luke 8:19). Cited by William C. Placher, *Narratives of a Vulnerable God* (Louisville: Westminster/John Knox, 1994), p. 7.

61. Calvin, *Calvin's Commentaries,* vol. 1, *A Harmony of the Gospels: Matthew, Mark, and Luke* (Grand Rapids: Eerdmans, 1972), p. 139 (on Matt. 4:5). Cited by Placher, p. 7.

to go as far as theologians like Frei and Lindbeck, they should at least be prepared to go as far as theologians like Calvin, Kuyper, and Bavinck. Freed from the encumbrances of excessive modernity, the real conversation could then begin.[62]

V. Beyond Postliberalism:
The Promise of Evangelical Theology

Carl Henry, it will be recalled, accused Hans Frei of diverting attention from revelation; and Gabriel Fackre observed (more justly) that theologians like Frei and Lindbeck seem more concerned with method than with theological content. As my thought experiment now moves into its final phase, I am prepared to grant that postliberal theology, at least in the versions from Yale, has run up a considerable deficit in producing works of doctrinal substance. In this light the promise of evangelical theology, at the very least, is that it has never allowed itself to focus on questions of method, so dear to academic theologians, at the expense of the kind of real theological work that the church needs in order to fulfill its task of faithfully proclaiming the gospel.

More importantly, evangelical theology, it seems to me, has always had an admirable sense of priorities. Within the field of Christian doctrine per se, it has consistently been the standard-bearer of the Reformation insofar as it has stood — often in a lonely and exposed position — for "Christ alone," "grace alone," and "faith alone" in all matters pertaining to salvation. Although evangelicalism has not always been so strong in upholding other traditional loci such as the doctrine of the Trinity — although the chapter on this theme in Alister McGrath's new book *Christian Theology: An Introduction* makes my observation obsolete[63] — evangelicalism has historically been of inestimable value right down to the present day for its uncompromising insistence on the saving death of Christ as the very heart of the gospel. The cross of Christ, writes John R. W. Stott, "lies at the center of the historic, biblical faith, and the fact

62. Perhaps it might also be mentioned here for the sake of future discussion that, from a postliberal point of view, American evangelicals have typically been at least as excessive (and with consequences no less unfortunate for the progress of the gospel) in committing themselves to the pathologies of American nationalism and militarism as they have in encumbering themselves with the excesses of modern epistemology. The common thread in both cases, if I may say so, seems to have something to do with a lack of Christian self-confidence; an inordinate, or insufficiently self-critical, desire for external validation; and an aversion (in practice) to the theology of the cross.

63. Alister E. McGrath, *Christian Theology: An Introduction* (Oxford: Blackwell, 1994).

that this is not always everywhere acknowledged is in itself a sufficient justification for preserving a distinctive Evangelical testimony." Stott continues: "Evangelical Christians believe that in and through Christ crucified God substituted himself for us, and bore our sins, dying the death we deserved to die, in order that we might be restored to his favor and adopted into his family."[64] Stott is also commendable for his attempt to set forth not only what we were earlier calling the "cognitive" aspects of this doctrine, but also its "performative" aspects or practical implications as well.[65]

In conclusion, let me suggest not only that postliberals would indeed have much to learn from evangelicals in these matters, but also that evangelicals seem to have run up a deficit directly opposite to that of their postliberal counterparts: they are more concerned about content than about theological method. If I may, let me put it like this. Although evangelicals have consistently produced an impressive number of distinguished biblical scholars over the years, especially in the field of New Testament studies, and although more recently they have also produced a distinguished crop of philosophers and of historians of Christianity in North America, they have not done nearly so well in producing truly distinguished theologians, and this shortfall may have something to do with their failure to attend sufficiently to questions of theological method.[66]

It is not surprising, therefore, that when George Lindbeck proposes to widen the scope of postliberalism beyond what we know from Yale, the theologians, undeniably distinguished, to whom he is drawn are Karl Barth and Hans Urs von Balthasar. Lindbeck observes:

> Here are twentieth century theologians whose use of the Bible is more nearly classical than anything in several centuries and who yet are distinctively modern (e.g., they do not reject historical criticism). Both are wary of translating the Bible into alien conceptualities; both seek, rather, to redescribe the world or worlds in which they live in biblical terms; both treat Scripture as a narrationally (or, for von Balthasar, "dramatically") and typologically unified whole; and in both the reader is referred back to the biblical text itself by exegetical work which is an integral part of the theo-

---

64. John R. W. Stott, *The Cross of Christ* (Downers Grove, Ill.: InterVarsity, 1986), p. 7.

65. See Stott, "Part Four: Living under the Cross."

66. In making this observation, I am using the term "evangelical" in the somewhat peculiar sense it has acquired in the English-speaking world over the last 250 years or so. A more generous (and more descriptively apt) usage would widen its scope to include theologians often neglected, excluded, or castigated by self-described "evangelicals": theologians like Thomas F. Torrance, Eberhard Jüngel, and Gerhard Sauter, each of whose work I would regard as distinguished.

logical program. In short, these two theologians inhabit the same universe of theological discourse as the fathers, medievals, and Reformers to a greater degree than do most modern theologians.[67]

Most interesting is then the conclusion that Lindbeck draws: "Discussions between them are possible — perhaps even decidable — by reference to the text because they approach Scripture in basically similar ways."[68] If I am not wholly mistaken about the continuum that seems to run from the likes of Calvin through the likes of Kuyper and Bavinck to the likes of Frei and Lindbeck,[69] then it would not seem amiss to suggest that a similar possibility exists also for evangelicals and postliberals today.

67. Lindbeck, "Scripture, Consensus, and Community," p. 98.

68. Ibid.

69. It may not be amiss to indicate that I don't think there is necessarily a tight fit between one's views of historical criticism and the continuum I am seeking to establish. The continuum pertains to the relationship between *signum* and *res* in Holy Scripture. What the theologians on my continuum all share is a belief that this relationship is positive though not univocal. The rejection of univocity separates them from someone like Henry, just as the affirmation of adequate and reliable reference separates them from modernist skeptics. Not everyone who accepts historical criticism believes that it undermines adequate reference or signification (although there may be disagreements about just what constitutes the *res*). The issue that determines the continuum is not whether one accepts the relative validity of modern historical criticism (about which Calvin of course knew nothing, and toward which Kuyper and Bavinck were largely negative though not without some ambivalence). The issue is whether one affirms the texts of Holy Scripture as inspired, authoritative, and sufficient vehicles of reference to their relevant subject matter (about which the likes of Frei and Lindbeck agree with the rest).

Meditation on the Blood of Christ

(1998)

The "blood of Christ" has not been a prominent motif in recent dogmatic theology. Perhaps the main reason for this development is that theological interest in the "objective" aspect of Christ's saving death has commonly receded where it has not disappeared. As Hans Urs von Balthasar has noted: "The idea that in his suffering Jesus bore the sins of the world is a motif that has been almost completely abandoned in the modern world." In premodern dogmatics, on the other hand, where this idea had not been abandoned, the motif of "Christ's blood" is correspondingly strong. It is striking, for example, to observe just how much rhetorical power and concision theologians like Luther, Calvin, or Aquinas can gain from their unembarrassed use of this motif. Nevertheless, although it is not possible to refer to Christ's blood without speaking about the saving significance of his death, it is possible to speak about his saving death without referring to his blood. Where modern dogmatics remains interested in such themes, it has usually followed the latter course.

The losses for modern theology may be regrettable. For the motif of Christ's blood, as derived from the New Testament, is unsurpassed in its metaphorical range, complexity, and richness. George Herbert, the seventeenth-century English divine and poet, captured much of this complexity when he wrote: "Love is that liquor sweet and most divine / Which my God feels as blood, and I as wine." From this couplet two points immediately emerge. First, the motif of Christ's blood actually embraces the entire sweep of Christian soteriology. It pertains to salvation in its overall basic structure of *extra nos–pro nobis–in nobis*. It extends, so to speak, all the way from the cross to the Eucharist. It is thus a powerful motif that brings out the unity of soteriology in its various objective and subjective or existential aspects. Second, Christ's blood is a metaphor that stands primarily for the suffering love of God. It suggests that there is no sorrow God has not known, no grief he has not borne, no price he was unwilling to pay, in order to reconcile the world to himself in Christ. It implies that this love is falsified wherever it is thought of in sentimental terms, for it is a love that has endured the bitterest realities of suffering and death in order that its purposes might prevail.

As a metaphor for the suffering of divine love, the motif of Christ's blood at once overlaps and yet also transcends at least three broad contexts of significance: the covenantal, the cultic, and the juridical. Metaphorically, these contexts may be designated by the meal, the altar, and the throne of judgment. In a covenantal context the motif of Christ's blood signifies primarily the depth of the divine commitment to rescue, protect, and sustain those who would otherwise be lost. "This is my blood of the covenant" (Mark 14:24 and par.). Offered as wine in the setting of a sacred meal, Christ's blood here especially depicts the *pro nobis* and *in nobis* aspects of his suffering and death. Christ commits himself to others and offers them his life, even as they are then bound to him and receive their life from him, in the giving and receiving of his blood with the wine.

In a cultic context Christ's blood signifies not only the inestimable value but also the terrible cost of the forgiveness of sins and the eternal life promised by the gospel. "Behold, the Lamb of God, who takes away the sin of the world!" (John 1:29). Sacrificed for our sake on an altar whose historical form, so to speak, was the cross, Christ's blood here especially accentuates the *extra nos* and the *pro nobis* aspects of his saving death. The priestly work of Christ, in which he becomes the priest and victim in one, is both expiatory and purifying in its intercessory effects. The blood of Christ is thus said to remove our sin both completely (Rom. 3:25; Heb. 9:12; Rev. 1:5) and continually (I John 1:7; I Pet. 1:2). Christ has sacrificed himself for others, offering himself in their place, that by the intercession of his blood their sin might be removed and their lives be made pure once and for all.

In a juridical context Christ's blood unites both the magnitude of sin and the even greater magnitude of grace in the judgment of God. The forensic metaphors of Paul are designed to show that the uncompromising judgment of God is revealed in the suffering love of the cross. Seen as a juridical event, Christ's cross is the place of judgment where God has "condemned sin in the flesh," satisfying "the just requirement of the law" (Rom. 8:3, 4), yet in a way that brings unexpected acquittal to the guilty since "we [have been] justified by his blood" (Rom. 5:9). Here the motif of Christ's blood again pertains primarily to the *extra nos* and the *pro nobis* aspects of the cross. "Justified by his blood" stands in dramatic counterpoint to the more familiar phrase "justified by faith," underscoring the prevenience of divine grace. While we were yet sinners (Rom. 5:8), Christ paid with his blood the penalty that would otherwise have been ours, so that we might be spared before the judgment seat of God and made new creatures in and with Christ.

Finally, the blood of Christ not only depicts the suffering love of God in its covenantal commitment, its sacrificial self-giving, and its gracious yet uncompromising judgment. It also depicts the royal exercise of divine power. It signifies that God's power is the power of love, and that this power is perfected in weakness. In the book of Revelation, the Lamb is metaphorically displaced from a priestly to a royal context, standing at the throne of God (Rev. 5:13; 7:9-10; 22:1), and living at its very center (7:17). The blood of the Lamb proves itself to be stronger than all God's enemies and is the means through which they are finally conquered (12:11; 17:14). Here the blood of Christ conveys the basic Christian conviction that in reigning from the cross, the suffering love of God will triumph in its very weakness over all that is hostile to itself (cf. I Cor. 1:25).

Bibliographic Information

Part I: Political Theology

1. "The Politics of the Nonviolent God: Reflections on René Girard and Karl Barth." *Scottish Journal of Theology* 51 (1998): 61-85.
2. "Karl Barth and Liberation Theology." *Journal of Religion* 63 (1983): 247-63.
3. "Barth, Barmen and the Confessing Church Today." *Katallagete* 9 (1985): 14-27.
4. "Where the Battle Rages: Confessing Christ in America Today." *Dialog* 26 (1987): 264-74.
5. "Karl Barth and the Politics of Sectarian Protestantism: A Dialogue with John Howard Yoder" (1980). Previously unpublished.

Part II: Doctrinal Theology

6. "Karl Barth's Christology: Its Basic Chalcedonian Character." A briefer version will appear in *The Cambridge Companion to Barth,* ed. John Webster (Cambridge University Press, forthcoming).
7. "The Mediator of Communion: Karl Barth's Doctrine of the Holy Spirit." A portion of this essay will appear in *The Cambridge Companion to Barth,* ed. John Webster (Cambridge University Press, forthcoming).
8. "*Mysterium Trinitatis:* Karl Barth's Conception of Eternity" (1999). Previously unpublished.

9. "Beyond Literalism and Expressivism: Karl Barth's Hermeneutical Realism." *Modern Theology* 3 (1987): 209-23.

10. "Hellfire and Damnation: Four Ancient and Modern Views." *Scottish Journal of Theology* 51 (1998): 406-34.

Part III: Ecumenical Theology

11. "Baptized into Christ's Death: Karl Barth and the Future of Roman Catholic Theology" (1997). Previously unpublished.

12. "What Karl Barth Learned from Martin Luther." *Lutheran Quarterly* 13 (1999): 125-55.

13. "Truth as Self-Involving: Barth and Lindbeck." *Journal of the American Academy of Religion* 61 (1993): 41-56.

14. "The Harnack/Barth Correspondence: A Paraphrase with Comments." *Thomist* 50 (1986): 599-622.

15. "What Can Evangelicals and Postliberals Learn from Each Other? The Carl Henry/Hans Frei Exchange Reconsidered." In *The Nature of Confession,* ed. Timothy R. Phillips and Dennis L. Okholm (Downers Grove, Ill.: InterVarsity, 1996), pp. 134-50. This essay also appeared in *Pro Ecclesia* 5 (1996): 161-82.

"Eplogue: Meditation on the Blood of Christ." Forthcoming as "Blut Christi," in *Religion in Gegenwart und Geschichte,* 4. Auflage (Tübingen: J. C. B. Mohr). The English version appeared in *Pro Ecclesia* 7 (1998): 133-35.

Index